Bawdy City

A vivid social history of Baltimore's prostitution trade and its evolution throughout the nineteenth century, *Bawdy City* centers women in a story of the relationship between sexuality, capitalism, and law. Beginning in the colonial period, prostitution was little more than a subsistence trade. However, by the 1840s, urban growth and changing patterns of household labor ushered in a booming brothel industry. The women who oversaw and labored within these brothels were economic agents surviving and thriving in an urban world hostile to their presence. With the rise of urban leisure industries and policing practices that spelled the end of sex establishments, the industry survived for only a few decades. Yet, even within this brief period, brothels and their residents altered the geographies, economy, and policies of Baltimore in profound ways. Hemphill's critical narrative of gender and labor shows how sexual commerce and debates over its regulation shaped an American city.

KATIE M. HEMPHILL is Assistant Professor of History at the University of Arizona.

Bawdy City

Commercial Sex and Regulation in Baltimore, 1790–1915

KATIE M. HEMPHILL

University of Arizona

CAMBRIDGE
UNIVERSITY PRESS

CAMBRIDGE
UNIVERSITY PRESS

University Printing House, Cambridge CB2 8BS, United Kingdom

One Liberty Plaza, 20th Floor, New York, NY 10006, USA

477 Williamstown Road, Port Melbourne, VIC 3207, Australia

314-321, 3rd Floor, Plot 3, Splendor Forum, Jasola District Centre, New Delhi - 110025, India

103 Penang Road, #05-06/07, Visioncrest Commercial, Singapore 238467

Cambridge University Press is part of the University of Cambridge.

It furthers the University's mission by disseminating knowledge in the pursuit of education, learning and research at the highest international levels of excellence.

www.cambridge.org
Information on this title: www.cambridge.org/9781108733281
DOI: 10.1017/9781108773669

First published 2020
First paperback edition 2022

A catalogue record for this publication is available from the British Library

Library of Congress Cataloging in Publication data
NAMES: Hemphill, Katie M., author.
TITLE: Bawdy city : commercial sex and regulation in Baltimore, 1790–1915 / Katie M. Hemphill, University of Arizona.
DESCRIPTION: Cambridge, United Kingdom ; New York, NY : Cambridge University Press, 2020. | Includes bibliographical references and index.
IDENTIFIERS: LCCN 2019038708 (print) | LCCN 2019038709 (ebook) | ISBN 9781108489010 (hardback) | ISBN 9781108733281 (paperback) | ISBN 9781108773669 (epub)
SUBJECTS: LCSH: Prostitution–Maryland–Baltimore–History. | Brothels–Maryland–Baltimore–History.
CLASSIFICATION: LCC HQ146.B2 H46 2020 (print) | LCC HQ146.B2 (ebook) | DDC 306.7409752/6–dc23
LC record available at https://lccn.loc.gov/2019038708
LC ebook record available at https://lccn.loc.gov/2019038709

ISBN 978-1-108-48901-0 Hardback
ISBN 978-1-108-73328-1 Paperback

For my parents,
Kim and Susan Hemphill,
who almost certainly wish this book was about something else.

Contents

Figures

Acknowledgments

This book has been in the making for more years than I can count, and it never would have come to fruition without a great deal of help along the way. Johns Hopkins University, the Library Company of Philadelphia, the McNeil Center for Early American Studies, the Maryland Historical Society, and the University of Arizona all provided generous fellowship and research support throughout this project. I give my sincerest thanks to those institutions, which have been my intellectual homes, and to the donors that made their support of scholarship possible.

As any historian knows, research would be impossible without the hard work and knowledge of archivists and librarians. At the Maryland State Archives, Alex Jackson, Edward Papenfuse, Rob Schoeberlein, and so many other archivists and staff members provided invaluable help, advice, and patience as I asked them pull ten-pound docket after ten-pound docket off the shelves. At the Maryland Historical Society, Patricia Dockman Anderson, Eben Dennis, Francis O'Neill, and Damon Talbot provided both assistance with documents and an incredible breadth of local historical knowledge. Saul B. Gibusiwa, Amy James, and Tony Roberts at the Baltimore City Archives were a tremendous help to me, as were the Special Collections librarians at Johns Hopkins University. The staff at the Library Company, particularly Connie King, Krystal Appiah, and Linda August, provided their extensive knowledge of the collections as well as stunningly fast document delivery. Their enthusiasm for and amusement at the sources made research an adventure, and I am privileged to have benefited from their expertise. At the Alan Chesney Medical Archives, Marjorie Kehoe and Natalie Elder helped me gather sources to round out my final chapter. They, along with the staffs of other numerous archives and repositories I visited over the course of my research, have my sincerest thanks.

This project began as a dissertation at Johns Hopkins University, and I am indebted to more people at that institution than I can name here. The members of the Gender History Workshop (Geminar) and the Charm School for Baltimore History together formed two of the most cordial, constructive, and sharp communities of scholars I have ever had the pleasure of joining. I am grateful to all the people in those seminars who shaped my thinking over the years: Norah Andrews Gharala, Adam Bisno, Will Brown, Jess Clark, Sara Damiano, Toby Ditz, Steph Gamble, Jamie Gianoutsos, Paige Glotzer, Katie Hindmarch-Watson, Layne Karafantis, Ren Pepitone, Katherine Smoak Radburn, Amira Rose, Mo Speller, Jessica Valdez, and Judith Walkowitz. Thanks especially David Schley and Robert Gamble, who will always be my academic brothers.

My wonderful advisors, Mary P. Ryan, Michael P. Johnson, and the other members of my dissertation committee, Mary Fissell, Ronald Walters, and Matthew Crenson, provided me with thoughtful feedback that helped me to shape and revise this project. I am grateful to them, and especially to Mary and Mike for guiding me through graduate school, for challenging me, and for supporting me through the tumult of the job market. Mary Ryan and Mary Fissell, two scholars whose brilliance is matched by their intellectual and personal generosity, have continued to be my mentors and friends over the years. They have believed in me, supported me, and displayed a truly uncanny tendency to know where I was going with this project long before I understood it. Still, they trusted me to get there. I owe them more than I can say, and I will always hold them up as my gold standard for teachers, scholars, and mentors.

This book is rooted in my love for the city of city of Baltimore, and my affection for "The Greatest City in America" is inseparable from my affection for all the people I got to share it with as I was writing this book in its dissertation form. I am grateful to Katherine Arner, Joe Clark, Christopher Consolino, Natalie Elder, Claire Gherini, Jonathan Gienapp, Craig Hollander, Ada Link, Emily Mokros, and Nick Radburn for their friendship, good humor, and support. Although Brenna O'Rourke Holland, Danielle Skeehan, and Sarah Chesney have the misfortune of not being Baltimoreans, they remain some of my favorite people, and I am grateful to them for helping me to survive Philadelphia and for continuing to be my friends.

Since I joined the faculty of the University of Arizona in the fall of 2014, I have been fortunate to expand and revise this manuscript in the company of supportive and generous colleagues and friends in Tucson. I am grateful to all of them, and especially to Katherine Morrissey, Tyina Steptoe, Jerome Dotson, Erika Pérez, Lora Key, Susan Crane, Jeremy Vetter, Alison Futrell, Laura Tabili, and Kevin Gosner for their guidance and friendship. Katherine and Kim Lowry have kept me fed and cultured in Tucson, Jeremy has chatted with me and made me a master of dodging emails about early morning hikes, and Tyina, Jerome, and Lora have been the best trivia team I could ask for (go Crab Attack). Lauren Hayes and Ashley Wunder helped me to edit this book. Kari Cadenhead, a talented local artist, drew my maps for me and provided invaluable support during the hectic last days of this project. I am indebted to her for her friendship and patience, to which I owe much of my ability to finish this. Thanks also to our business managers, Debbie Jackson and Jose Garcia, for assisting me with funding for images and production.

I am grateful to my editor at Cambridge University Press, Deborah Gershenowitz, for taking an interest in this project and shepherding it through the revisions process. Thanks also to Rachel Blaifeder and the staff at the press for working with me through production, and to Lisa DeBoer for providing the index. The anonymous readers who completed reports for the press modeled intellectual generosity in a way that I aspire to emulate and improved this manuscript dramatically with their thoughtful feedback and suggestions. I am indebted to them.

Last but certainly not least, I want to thank my family. My parents, Kim and Susan Hemphill, have done more for me than I could ever say. They supported me through a risky career choice, years of schooling, and a decision to specialize in a topic that made it really difficult to brag to relatives about my work. They have my eternal gratitude, respect, and love, and this book is for them. I am also indebted to Gill Mozer, who has been my rock for these past three years and who has loved me, talked me through difficult moments, and made me laugh so hard that my cheeks hurt. *Danke.*

Abbreviations

AMR	Alms-House Medical Records, Maryland Historical Society
BAAB	Baltimore Almshouse Admissions Book, Maryland Historical Society
BCC	Baltimore City Court (Dockets and Minutes), Maryland State Archives
BCCC	Baltimore City Criminal Court (Criminal Dockets), Maryland State Archives
BCCOTGD	Baltimore County Court of Oyer and Terminer and Gaol Delivery (Dockets and Minutes), Maryland State Archives
BCoRW	Baltimore County Register of Wills, Maryland State Archives
BCRW	Baltimore City Register of Wills, Maryland State Archives
MVC	Maryland Vice Commission
MVCR	Maryland Vice Commission Report, Enoch Pratt Library

Introduction

In 1846, Baltimore entrepreneur Johns Hopkins opened a "splendid" set of commercial buildings on the corner of Lombard and Gay Streets, just north of the Patapsco River.[1] Hopkins, who made his fortune first as a country merchant and then as an investor in the railroad, intended the buildings to facilitate the trade that was central to both Baltimore's economy and his personal wealth. The buildings were practical, but they were also a symbol of the city's commercial pretensions. In addition to offices and commodious warehouses where merchants and dry goods dealers could keep the variety of products they imported from the countryside and exported through the port of Baltimore, Hopkins funded the construction of a beautifully designed corner hall. The three-story structure, described as one of the "handsomest buildings in the city," was adorned with numerous ornaments, including a trident of Neptune and a Roman spade that symbolized Baltimore's links to maritime commerce and agriculture.[2]

Local newspapers deemed the building "a fine improvement to the neighborhood, both in commercial and architectural points of view," and it became popular with city dwellers and visitors alike.[3] Its upper floors housed a ballroom and meeting rooms where local political clubs, militia groups, and business organizations convened. The space in front of the building occasionally hosted women from local churches, holding

---

[1] "Local Matters," *Baltimore Sun* (hereafter *Sun*), Feb. 12, 1846.
[2] "Local Matters," *Sun*, Mar. 7, 1846.   [3] "Local Matters," *Sun*, Feb. 12, 1846.

I

Christmas bazaars or other fundraisers.[4] In the Corner Hall's basement was the Parisian Restaurant, which served as a "refectory" where businessmen could network and negotiate and where wealthy visitors and locals could go for fine dining. Within a few years, however, the restaurant also became a refectory for guests of another sort. Under the tutelage of its keepers, Alonzo Welsh and Susan Creamer, the Parisian Restaurant developed a reputation as a "bawdy house" and "supper club" for sex workers, who traveled from nearby brothels to drink, mingle, and solicit with other patrons and each other.[5]

For those unfamiliar with nineteenth-century history, the notion of sex workers inhabiting the same space as some of the city's most affluent businessmen and merchants – the kind of men for whom city streets and institutions are named – is, no doubt, a strange one. Americans are accustomed to thinking of prostitution as a marginal industry, one confined to the metaphorical shadows of urban "skid rows." Many nineteenth-century observers would have liked that to be the case in their own cities. However, for much of the long nineteenth century, prostitution was a visible form of commerce whose presence in urban America was difficult to ignore. By the 1890s, Baltimore had a thriving street prostitution trade and nearly 300 brothels and bawdy houses.[6] Hundreds of women lived and worked in these establishments, and dozens of proprietors from around the city – including Alonzo Welsh and Susan Creamer – profited directly or indirectly from their sexual labor.[7] Baltimore was not unusual in this respect. By some estimates, commercial sex was the second most profitable industry – behind only the garment trade – in cities like New York by the 1850s.[8] All told, thousands of women sold sex to make a living or to make ends meet, and they tended to cluster around hubs of mobility and sites of commerce.

---

[4] "Second Street Church Fair," *Sun*, Dec. 21, 1849; "Sharpshooters' Ball," *Sun*, Nov. 24, 1846.

[5] "Local Matters," *Sun*, Nov. 20, 1852; "Local Matters," *Sun*, Nov. 22, 1852.

[6] Joseph Waddell Clokey, *Dying at the Top: Or, the Moral and Spiritual Condition of the Young Men of America* (Chicago: W. W. Varnarsdale, 1890), 90. The Baltimore City Criminal Court saw 280 indictments for bawdy house charges in 1880 (BCCC 1880, MSA C-1849-45).

[7] BCCC (Docket) (hereafter BCCC), May 1855, Case 770, Alonzo Welsh; BCCC, January Term, 1859, Case 506, Alonzo Welsh; BCCC, Case 444, Susan Creamer, September Term, 1855.

[8] Timothy J. Gilfoyle, *City of Eros: New York City, Prostitution, and the Commercialization of Sex, 1790–1920* (New York: Norton, 1992), 124–25.

The existence of a sex establishment in the actual basement of a center of urban trade and commerce was somewhat unusual, but it was also apropos. Prostitution as it developed in Baltimore in the early years of the nineteenth century was intimately connected to the rise of the market economy. It emerged as a visible trade in maritime neighborhoods during the city's early commercial boom period, and it expanded dramatically as a result of many of the same factors that necessitated the construction of the Commercial Buildings. Chief among these were the increased mobility of people and goods and the expansion of cash markets. In the midst of urban growth and capitalist development, disruptions to older models of household economy and changing notions of women's role in the labor market gave rise to new cultures of urban sexual commerce. The period in which the Commercial Buildings were erected to signal Baltimore's commercial aspirations and maturation as a city was a period that saw the emergence of dozens of brothels and bawdy houses in their vicinity. Highly commercialized, organized in their labor arrangements, and often lucrative, brothels were a visible part of Baltimore's sexual landscapes from their emergence in the 1820s until their decline and eventual closure in the twentieth century. It was women from these houses who patronized the Parisian Restaurant, exposing, as they did so, the connections between the worlds of licit and illicit commerce, of commodified goods and commodified sexual labor.

This book traces the evolution of the sex trade as it developed in Baltimore over the course of the long nineteenth century. In doing so, it contributes to the large body of historical scholarship that argues that sexuality "was not an unchanging biological reality or a universal, natural force, but was, rather, a product of political, social, economic, and cultural processes."[9] In Baltimore, as in other American cities, commercial sex grew out of the early capitalist economy's dislocations and unequal division of resources between men and women. The sex trade's labor practices, spatial arrangements, and even sexual offerings shifted in accordance with broader changes in the nature of commerce, urban development, and policing. Tracing shifts in the sex trade provides a window into the ways in which the worlds of sexuality remained intertwined with economy even as Americans at the mid-century increasingly embraced the notion that sex, family, and the realm of intimacy should be

---

[9] Kathy Peiss and Christina Simmons, "Passion and Power: An Introduction," in *Passion and Power: Sexuality in History*, ed. Kathy Peiss and Christina Simmons with Robert A. Padgug (Philadelphia: Temple University Press, 1989), 3.

separated from the cash nexus.[10] It also allows historians to examine the role of the state – broadly construed to include the networks of local officials, courts, and public charities – in shaping the illicit sexual economy.

While *Bawdy City* gives attention to diverse forms of sexual exchange, much of its narrative is structured around the rise and fall of brothel prostitution. Brothels had a relatively brief heyday as a means of organizing sexual commerce in Baltimore and, indeed, in most American cities. Brothels were uncommon in the colonial and Revolutionary eras, when most sexual commerce remained loosely organized and largely street-based. Historian Clare Lyons found that Philadelphia, one of the most established American colonial ports, developed a boisterous and highly public sex trade that included brothels only in the latter years of the eighteenth century.[11] Historians of New York and Boston found that small sex trades emerged in those cities after the American Revolution but did not extend much outside marginal and segregated sailors' establishments until the 1830s, when organized and highly commercialized sex establishments began to develop.[12] Such was the case in Baltimore. It would take until the 1830s for the city to develop specialized sex establishments that required women to board-in, to work under the supervision of a madam (who in some cases was under the supervision of a landlord), and to sell sex on a somewhat professional basis. By the Civil War period, however, brothels would be both a common model of organizing sex work and the model that drew the most sustained attention from the press and connoisseurs of the urban sex trade. Their prominence, which was reinforced in the middle decades of the nineteenth century by courts that were hostile to public forms of prostitution but largely tolerant of contained ones, began to fade by the turn of the twentieth century. Nevertheless, brothels survived in large numbers until their forcible closure at the hands of the Baltimore police in 1915.

---

[10] Carroll Smith-Rosenberg, *Disorderly Conduct: Visions of Gender in Victorian America* (New York: Alfred A. Knopf, 1985); Jeanne Boydston, *Home and Work: Housework, Wages, and the Ideology of Labor in the Early Republic* (Oxford: Oxford University Press, 1994); Amy Dru Stanley, *From Bondage to Contract: Wage Labor, Marriage, and the Market in the Age of Slave Emancipation* (Cambridge: Cambridge University Press, 1998), chapter 6.

[11] Clare A. Lyons, *Sex among the Rabble: An Intimate History of Gender and Power in the Age of Revolution, Philadelphia, 1730–1830* (Chapel Hill: University of North Carolina Press, 2006), 277–78.

[12] Gilfoyle, *City of Eros*; Barbara Meil Hobson, *Uneasy Virtue: The Politics of Prostitution and the American Reform Tradition* (New York: Basic Books, 1987).

Brothels were not the only models of sexual commerce in Baltimore over the course of the long nineteenth century, but their prominence, their visibility in the historical record, and their very boundedness as a historical form makes them a fruitful topic of study. Tracing their trajectory provides a window into the ways in which the growth of the market economy, the rise of industry, and the emergence of new legal discourses concerning rights created new sexual cultures in the city and affected the lives of marginalized women. In a similar vein, analyzing the ways in which the state and local reformers responded to brothels' presence over time can tell historians much about the politics of urban life during a period marked by sharp transition from a nascent commercial economy to an industrial one. Because brothels were such a visible part of the urban world, they became a site at which Baltimoreans developed their notions of property rights, expressed ideas about gender and women's roles in society, reinforced racial divides, and critiqued everything from urban machine politics to the labor practices of industrial capitalism.

One of the great values of Baltimore as a case study in the history of commercial sex – beyond its status as one of the largest US cities in the nineteenth century – is that it was, as Barbara Fields deemed it, "a middle ground" between the South and the North, the slave states and the free.[13] Both before and after the Civil War, the city had one of the largest free black populations of any urban area in the country as a result of migration from Maryland's tobacco regions and other areas of the South. Black women participated in Baltimore's sex trade in various capacities, especially in the latter decades of the nineteenth century and the early decades of the twentieth. Although scholars like Cynthia Blair, Emily Epstein Landau, Alecia P. Long, and Kevin Mumford have written excellent works that engage with black women's role in the sex trade and with the racial dimensions of sexual commerce, race remains an underdeveloped theme in many histories of prostitution. Historians know especially little about it in urban centers outside "the Great Southern Babylon" of

---

[13] Barbara Jeanne Fields, *Slavery and Freedom on the Middle Ground: Maryland during the Nineteenth Century* (New Haven: Yale University Press, 1985). On free black communities in Baltimore, see Christopher Phillips, *Freedom's Port: The African American Community of Baltimore, 1790–1860* (Urbana: University of Illinois Press, 1997); Ralph Clayton, *Black Baltimore, 1820–1870* (Bowie, MD: Heritage Books, 1987); Jennifer Hull Dorsey, *Hirelings: African American Workers and Free Labor in Early Maryland* (Ithaca, NY: Cornell University Press, 2011).

New Orleans or the historically free cities of New York and Chicago.[14] Baltimore, therefore, provides an opportunity to study the ways that the politics of prostitution and its spatial relations intersected locally with the politics of race, both before and after emancipation. The Civil War, emancipation, and subsequent struggles to redefine black Marylanders' relationship to the state changed contemporary understandings of rights and state power in ways that led to increased state efforts to contain prostitution and prevent its encroachment on middle-class neighborhoods. In turn, the subsequent pushing of brothels into poor neighborhoods that quickly became havens for displaced black urbanites functioned to justify racial segregation and reinforce notions of black criminality in the eyes of white authorities.

Commercial sex's role in legitimizing the segregation and subordination of black Baltimoreans was just one way among many in which the sex trade changed Baltimore's social geographies and regulatory structures over the course of the long nineteenth century. As prostitution boomed in Baltimore, local officials and courts struggled to find ways to handle the trade. Urban prostitution was simultaneously an illicit economy, a breach of public order and prevailing gender hierarchies, and a threat to the city's reputation and property values. The city's various efforts to criminalize, regulate, and control it were rooted in everyday citizens' and local and state authorities' (sometimes competing) visions of urban order.[15] Studying them reveals much about the evolution of city building and the development of the state over the course of crucial decades in American political and legal history and, more significantly, positions women as important historical actors in that process.

---

[14] Cynthia M. Blair, *I've Got to Make My Livin': Black Women's Sex Work in Turn-of-the-Century Chicago* (Chicago: University of Chicago Press, 2010); Emily Epstein Landau, *Spectacular Wickedness: Sex, Race, and Memory in Storyville, New Orleans* (Baton Rouge: Louisiana State University Press, 2013); Alecia P. Long, *The Great Southern Babylon: Sex, Race, and Respectability in New Orleans, 1865–1920* (Baton Rouge: Louisiana State University Press, 2005); Kevin Mumford, *Interzones: Black/White Sex Districts in Chicago and New York in the Early Twentieth Century* (New York: Columbia University Press, 1997).

[15] My thinking on the relationship between sexuality policing and urban geography has been shaped by numerous scholars, especially geographers Philip Howell (Howell, *Geographies of Regulation: Policing Prostitution in Nineteenth-Century Britain and the Empire* [Cambridge: Cambridge University Press, 2009]) and Phil Hubbard (Hubbard, *Sex and the City: Geographies of Prostitution in the Urban West* [Aldershot: Ashgate Publishing, 1999], 60–99).

Bawdy City approaches prostitution from the perspectives of social, labor, and legal history. The first section of the book traces the transformation of the sex trade from the 1790s to the eve of the Civil War. Chapters 1 and 2 analyze prostitution's transition in the first decades of the nineteenth century from a largely informal, subsistence trade to one that was organized and specialized in ways that reflected the broader specialization of urban businesses during that time. In the earliest years of the city's development, the sex trade was centered around East Baltimore's waterways that brought maritime trade and sailors into the city. Women of various ages, races, and marital arrangements used sex work as part of an economy of makeshifts, soliciting in taverns and on the wharves and, in most cases, barely scraping by on their earnings. However, increased urban migration and the intensification of gendered divisions of labor in the 1820s and 1830s created both a supply and a demand for sexual labor outside maritime neighborhoods. The sex trade expanded and developed new commercial forms, including brothels in which women boarded-in and worked more or less professionally at sex work. In West Baltimore, first- and second-class houses clustered around the expanded commercial district and catered to white-collar workers, local elites, and well-off artisans. These houses, which were designed to be spaces of sociability that resembled bourgeois homes in their decor and overall characters, were exclusionary when it came to their boarding practices. Older women, married women, and black women were not allowed to labor in the establishments except as domestics. The young, white women who were employed in brothels sacrificed some of their independence, but their reward for doing so was their ability to earn more money by servicing a more affluent clientele. By the 1840s, many brothel workers had moved beyond mere subsistence and, in some cases, gained upward mobility in a society where women's sexual labor was virtually the only type that was valued in the marketplace.[16]

The rise of brothels led to the increased segregation of a trade that had once been well integrated into the mixed commercial spaces of maritime neighborhoods. At the same time, it also embedded sex work even more deeply into the urban economy because of the investment in property, furnishings, and fantasy-fulfillment required to create a successful parlor house or "genteel" sex establishment. Chapter 3 examines the networks of landlords, liquor dealers, publishers, and "legitimate" business owners

---

[16] On ideologies surrounding women's labor in the nineteenth century, see, among many others, Boydston, *Home and Work*.

who profited either directly from the sex trade or indirectly from the large amounts of cash that flowed through it. In Baltimore, as in New York and other cities, investing in the sex trade became an economic strategy for both wealthy and middling dabblers in real estate. As prostitution expanded into a large urban industry, brothels created demand for labor, goods, and services in their neighborhoods, and madams pumped money into local circulation. Although women were increasingly defined in nineteenth-century America as non-producing dependents, their labor as sex workers and the commercialized fantasies they created around prostitution contributed in important ways to the urban economy.

Part II focuses on how the courts, local authorities, and city residents responded to the growth of the sex trade and the rise of brothels and attempted to regulate commercial sex. Chapter 4 traces the local, legal history of prostitution throughout the antebellum decades. During that period, Baltimore's courts responded to the expansion of the sex trade in ways that were in keeping with long-standing common law traditions that defined prostitution as an offense against the public order.[17] In an attempt to restore the communal peace that sex workers violated with their boisterous solicitations and refusal to conform to the gender and sexual norms of their society, the courts initially attempted to incarcerate both brothel workers and streetwalkers. However, this quickly proved impractical given the limitations of city resources. In response, Baltimore's courts began to develop what amounted to a tacit system of regulation, designed to contain prostitution and minimize its harm to the public as much as possible. Although streetwalkers and brothel sex workers were both vagrants by the standards of the common law, the courts summarily punished the former with incarceration in the city's almshouse or jail while awarding the latter due process rights and issuing them graduated, affordable fines. These fines, which provided local courts and public dispensaries with revenue, were licensing fees by any other name. At a time when few Americans believed that prostitution could be suppressed entirely, brothels that kept illicit sexuality legible enough to be monitored but ultimately contained were preferable to more public forms of sex work. Authorities tolerated brothels accordingly, especially since their

[17] William J. Novak, *The People's Welfare: Law and Regulation in Nineteenth-Century America* (Chapel Hill: University of North Carolina Press, 1996), 149–90; Mark Kann, *Taming Passion for the Public Good: Policing Sex in the Early Republic* (New York: New York University Press, 2013), 129–60.

managers were either propertied themselves or personally connected to people who were.

And yet the court's tacit bargain with property owners would not endure in its antebellum form for long. The central arguments in Chapters 5 and 6 are that the Civil War and Reconstruction represented a pivotal moment in the history of prostitution's regulation, at least locally. War brought new economic pressure on households, influxes of newly emancipated and impoverished women from the countryside, and thousands of Union troops whose job it was to secure the city and defend its rail lines. Under such conditions, Baltimore's sex trade expanded rapidly and far beyond its antebellum boundaries. So-called patriotic young ladies turned their attention to servicing enlisted men in local taverns and low-end brothels and officers in local hotels and parlor houses.[18] As has so often been the case during wartime, concerns about soldiers abandoning their duties to go on "sprees" in brothels and contracting venereal diseases that could take them out of commission for weeks or months drew the attention of both military and civil officials to the sex trade. Although Baltimore's sex workers largely managed to stave off crackdowns on their businesses by cooperating with Union officers and providing them with intelligence gathered from unwary or braggadocious clients, discussions of the threat that prostitution posed to public health and the public order continued long after sex workers' contributions to the war effort ended.

While a growing awareness of prostitution's effects on public health would have long-term consequences for the future of the trade, more immediately relevant were the changes the war brought to understandings of property rights and citizens' relationship to the state. War destabilized the institution of slavery both nationally and in Maryland, leading to the creation of a new state constitution that outlawed the institution in 1864 and (ostensibly, at least) ushered in an era of free labor. In Baltimore, anxieties about black migrants' ability to self-regulate under a free labor regime led to an increasingly strident enforcement of vagrancy laws that targeted, among others, public sex workers. Indoor sex workers were somewhat protected from the worst effects of crackdowns on vagrancy, but they too felt the effects of the state's expanded authority in the aftermath of the war. As the Civil War and Reconstruction recast the

---

[18] James Bollar to Michael Hammons, February 7, 1862. From the Catalog of the Historical Shop, Cary Delery. Quoted in Thomas P. Lowry, *Sex in the Civil War* (Bloomington, IN: Xlibris, 2006), 106.

state as an affirmative protector of its citizens' liberties and rights to profit from their own labor, urban dwellers began to lobby the state to take a more active role in securing their property values by providing them with services and abating nuisances. Brothels became one such nuisance. Baltimoreans who had once conceived of prostitution primarily as a threat to public order and morality increasingly framed it as a material threat to their individual rights to enjoy and profit from their property and demanded that the state act to spare them damages.[19]

In response, local officials and the courts began to use a legal precedent that had been set in 1857 but seldom enforced until the latter years of the Civil War in order to usher in a new period of legal and spatial regulation of commercial sex. Previously, it had been sufficient for illicit sex to be contained within brothels, where it could be monitored and pushed out of sight as much as possible. Beginning in the 1860s, however, Baltimore's courts, police, and citizens increasingly began to demand that commercial sex be removed from particular areas of the city and, by extension, forced into others. Wealthy brothel landlords, who grew increasingly disinvested in commercial sex as downtown industrial development created opportunities for more profitable use of real estate, did not resist. Sex workers themselves largely capitulated in order to maintain their working relationships with the police and protect their businesses. The result was the creation of informally organized but established red-light districts whose existence made it possible for officials to order the city and protect the property rights of homeowners in "respectable" neighborhoods.

Part III focuses on how the sex trade changed with the rise of red-light districts and the growth of an industrial economy that altered urban labor and social practices. Chapters 7 and 8 trace the changing demographics of the local sex trade and the gradual – and related – decline of brothel prostitution. As authorities pushed brothels out of "respectable" neighborhoods, sex establishments relocated to areas of the city with poorer housing stock and residents who were less able to protest their incursions. Red-light districts where brothels predominated rapidly became populated by black Baltimoreans, who faced poverty and housing

---

[19] *Hamilton v. Whitridge, Maryland Reports: Containing Cases Argued and Adjudged in the Court of Appeals of Maryland* 11 (Baltimore, 1858), 128–47. See also Peter C. Hennigan, "Property War: Prostitution, Red-Light Districts, and the Transformation of Public Nuisance Law in the Progressive Era," *Yale Journal of Law & the Humanities* 16, no. 1 (2004): 123–98; Adam Malka, *The Men of Mobtown: Policing Baltimore in the Age of Slavery and Emancipation* (Chapel Hill: University of North Carolina Press, 2018).

discrimination and thus had fewer choices about where they took up residence. As the spatial overlap between brothel districts and black neighborhoods grew, black women, who as a group had previously been excluded from brothel prostitution, entered the indoor sex trade in larger numbers and began to remake it to suit their needs and preferences.

For many black women, some of whom had come to Baltimore with their children as refugees from slavery, selling sex became an important part of personal economies of makeshift. At the same time that sex work provided black Baltimoreans with limited opportunities for commercial advancement, it also reinforced long-standing racial stereotypes about black women's libidinousness and black men's unfitness to act as patriarchs. Although middle-class black Baltimoreans attempted to resist these stereotypes by publicizing their efforts to clean up their neighborhoods, they ultimately failed to sway the city's white politicians, who used the alleged "disorder" of black residential enclaves to argue for their containment. The presence of brothels in black neighborhoods, which was a product of efforts to segregate vice, became a means of justifying another policy intended to rationalize urban space and protect property values: Baltimore's residential segregation ordinance of 1910, which precluded black and white Baltimoreans from occupying the same blocks.

At the same time that black women were beginning to enter the brothel trade, white women were beginning to leave it. In Baltimore, as in other US cities, sex work underwent a process of recasualization in the late nineteenth century. This owed to many of the same factors that Timothy Gilfoyle and Elizabeth Alice Clement observed in New York: changing urban land use patterns and policing practices that marginalized brothels, a growth in paid employments available to women that discouraged professional prostitution, and the rise of urban entertainments that changed cultures of courting and opened new opportunities for sex workers to operate safely and independently outside the confines of brothels.[20] As early as the 1870s, the parlor house model that had proven popular for four decades began to fade from prominence. Sexual exchange became incorporated into the courting and leisure culture of young working people to the detriment of indoor sex establishments that were still organized around a Victorian model of courtship and courting. Brothels did not disappear entirely, but those that survived had to adapt

[20] Gilfoyle, *City of Eros*, 197–250; Elizabeth Alice Clement, *Love for Sale: Courting, Treating, and Prostitution in New York City, 1900–1945* (Chapel Hill: University of North Carolina Press, 2006), 212–39.

to new paradigms or else focus more extensively on providing sexual services that were outside the mainstream.

Not all succeeded. In fact, the brothel trade was already in significant decline by the time anti-vice reformers in the Progressive era began to push local authorities to depart from existing regulatory regimes by criminalizing and suppressing prostitution. The final chapter of the book examines the efforts of these anti-vice crusaders, whose campaigns began as a relatively inconsequential backlash against proposals for medical regulation but gained steam in the late nineteenth century as anxieties about urbanization and women's changing social and economic roles prompted an outpouring of concern about women's independence and sexual behavior. In the hands of a diverse group of evangelicals, women's rights organizations, political reformers, and public health advocates, prostitution became a potent symbol of the dangers that industrialization and urban political corruption posed to women and to what historian Mark Thomas Connelly called "civilized morality."[21]

Although brothel prostitution was just one among many forms of immorality and sexual exchange that concerned social purity crusaders and anti-vice activists, the ailing brothel trade would prove one of the easiest and least controversial targets of a movement wrought with various divisions over gender and politics. Eventually, the white slavery scare and the election of a reformist Republican governor would help anti-vice activists to secure the appointment of a Police Board sympathetic to their aims and the creation of the Maryland Vice Commission (MVC), an investigative body tasked with making recommendations concerning sexual vice in the state. Although the MVC's empirical approach to vice was frustrating to morally minded reformers, its aims ultimately aligned with theirs when it came to the suppression of the brothel trade. By 1915, in part because of the recommendation of the MVC, police had shuttered the last of the city's known red-light districts and bawdy houses. It was not the end of the sex trade, whose participants adapted as they always had to changes in local policy, but it was the end of an era.

In telling the story of how Baltimore's sex trade changed along with the urban economy and through various interactions with local authorities, this book joins a sizable body of scholarship on prostitution. Commercial sex has fascinated historians, not the least of which because it sits at the intersection of so many issues concerning gender, sexuality, economy,

[21] Mark Thomas Connelly, *The Response to Prostitution in the Progressive Era* (Chapel Hill: University of North Carolina Press, 2011), 9.

urbanization, law, and biopolitics. I am indebted to them, as well as to Jeanne Boydston and numerous other women's and gender historians who analyzed the ways that gendered divisions and definitions of labor contributed to women's marginalization within the nineteenth century's non-sexual labor market.[22]

Recent debates among scholars of prostitution have shaped my thinking about issues of agency and negotiation that have long been at the center of the field. Chief among these debates concerns the application of Olwen Hufton's model of the economy of makeshifts to prostitution studies.[23] Numerous historians, especially of British and European sex work, have directly or indirectly evoked Hufton's concepts of makeshifts to acknowledge both the ingenuity of women in the sex trade and the challenges they faced in making a living for themselves in a society that shunned them and devalued their non-sexual labor.[24] Indeed, I employ the concept in a similar way, particularly in the early chapters of the book or in discussions of the experiences of women – black women, especially – who were excluded from more elite levels of the trade.

Still, there are limitations to the makeshift economies model, including its inadvertent tendency to minimize the amount of capital that moved through the sex trade and to overstate the survivalist aspects of the trade. By the 1840s, Baltimore's sex trade generated significant enough profits that even women who shared their earnings with landlords or madams could amass significant wealth and live in greater material comfort than the majority of working people. By the twentieth century, many women working in the sex trade were not merely trying to survive, but rather to gain access to leisure or luxuries like jewelry, hats, and clothing. As Judith Walkowitz has noted, an emphasis on survivalism risks presenting sex workers as "devoid of psychological complexity, not to speak of fantasy, narcissism, and desire." It also has the potential to portray them as cut off from the "world of culture and politics."[25]

Baltimore's sex workers were not cut off from the world of politics. Some of them, particularly in the earlier period when prostitution was still

---

[22] Boydston, *Home and Work*.

[23] Olwen Hufton, *The Poor of Eighteenth-Century France, 1750–1789* (Oxford: Oxford University Press, 1974), 16.

[24] See, for example, Catherine Lee, *Policing Prostitution, 1856–1886: Deviance, Surveillance, and Morality* (London: Routledge, 2013), 26–29. See also Judith R. Walkowitz, "The Politics of Prostitution and Sexual Labour," *History Workshop Journal* 82, no. 1 (2016): 191.

[25] Walkowitz, "The Politics of Prostitution and Sexual Labour," 192.

a subsistence trade, scrapped in the way that many poor women did: they used the almshouse, combined multiple forms of labor, and sometimes resorted to crime to make ends meet. Others, however, scrapped in ways that are not easily incorporated in the makeshift economy model: they hired fancy lawyers, forged social connections and professional relationships with politicians and army officers, petitioned the City Council, and threw their money around. Many women told public officials, medical men, and vice reformers that they entered the sex trade to survive, but others insisted that they participated in sexual exchange because they enjoyed the work, found it exciting, and preferred it to other exploitative labor arrangements that were open to them. I have tried throughout this book to honor the complexity of their lives and motives.[26]

I have also endeavored to pay attention to the motives and desires of men who purchased the services of women. Until recently, historians of prostitution have devoted far more attention to sex workers than they have to the men who bought their services. This is in part a product of prostitution studies' roots in women's history and its practitioners' concern with recovering the lived experiences of women, but it is also a reflection of the biases of historical sources. Save for members of the feminist wing of social-purity reform and people concerned with the health of soldiers and sailors, few Americans in the nineteenth or early twentieth centuries expressed any interest, legal or otherwise, in the men who bought sex. Brothel patrons seldom appear in court dockets or police records, and, to my knowledge, none of the dozens of vice investigators who spent months interviewing women about why they participated in prostitution and dutifully recording their responses ever bothered to ask a male patron the same question. Surely, the answer seemed obvious.

Historians of sexuality, however, have an interest in denaturalizing desire, just as feminist historians have an interest in challenging formulations that take for granted that men are the natural consumers of sex and women its reluctant providers. As Julia Laite noted, we cannot forget in our struggles to explain why women sold sex that the ultimate reason was the same as the reason anyone sells anything: "someone was there to buy it."[27] Recent histories of prostitution, most notably Laite's, have endeavored to understand the identities and desires of men who

---

[26] MVCR, vol. 1, 269–88.

[27] Julia Laite, *Common Prostitutes and Ordinary Citizens: Commercial Sex in London, 1885–1960* (New York: Palgrave Macmillan, 2012), 42.

purchased sex in order to shed light on, what, precisely, they were buying.[28] I have asked similar questions. Contrary to narratives that hold men's sexual desires as static or posit that sex became "industrialized" with the rise of the brothel,[29] I found that nineteenth-century men were seldom purchasing quick sexual release when they patronized sex workers. Instead, patrons of brothels were purchasing a broader experience of domesticity, courting, and sociability. It was only when courting moved outside the home and new policing practices rendered the brothel marginal at the turn of the twentieth century that prostitution became more oriented around quick sexual release and, even then, never completely.

In tracing the role that local authorities and courts played in first propping up brothels and then rendering them more marginal, this book also engages with long-standing historical debates over the nature of the early American state and the explanations behind its behavior when it came to prostitution. The patterns that I observed in Baltimore's legal system – the harsh punishment of streetwalkers in comparison to the relative toleration of brothel workers – have been observed in other cities by a number of scholars of prostitution and law. And yet historians have tended to explain authorities' apparent laxity toward brothels as a product of neglect, laissez-faire governance, deference toward wealthy property owners, bribery, recognition that the state was too weak to eliminate commercial sex, or some combination thereof.[30] There is a grain of truth to some of these explanations, but views of what constitute policing and regulation have also been shaped to an excessive degree by an expectation that state action toward prostitution took the form of either criminalization and crackdown or sanctioned regulation through licensing or medical inspection systems. The former occurred sporadically but seldom with much effect; the latter were rare, deeply controversial, and short-lived in the United States. Nevertheless, the absence of either form need not

---

[28] Laite, *Common Prostitutes and Ordinary Citizens*, 43–53. Cohen's *The Murder of Helen Jewett* provides an earlier example of a monograph that gave significant attention to men's role in the sex trade: Patricia Cline Cohen, *The Murder of Helen Jewett* (New York: Vintage Books, 1999).

[29] Timothy J. Gilfoyle, "Prostitutes in History: From Parables of Pornography to Metaphors of Modernity," *The American Historical Review* 104 (Feb. 1999): 130–31.

[30] On courts' treatment of prostitution, see, for example, Lawrence Friedman, *Guarding Life's Dark Secrets: Legal and Social Controls over Reputation, Propriety, and Privacy* (Stanford, CA: Stanford University Press, 2007), 124–40; Kann, *Taming Passion for the Public Good*, chapter 6; Gilfoyle, *City of Eros*, 138–39; Joshua Rothman, *Notorious in the Neighborhood: Sex and Families across the Color Line in Virginia, 1787–1861* (Chapel Hill: University of North Carolina Press, 2003), 98–101.

suggest state inaction. The impulses behind formalized regulatory systems – to render commercial sex legible to the state, to shape its geographies and practices, and to minimize the perceived harm of a trade that was ultimately regarded as ineradicable – were ubiquitous in Baltimore and in other US cities from the mid-nineteenth century until the twentieth. Baltimore's city government and courts repeatedly acted on these impulses until, over time, they created an ad hoc, de facto system for regulating prostitution that was rooted in harm reduction and segregation rather than criminalization.

Expanding our understandings of state action toward prostitution beyond criminalization (or lack thereof) allows for a reassessment of both the nineteenth-century state's role in shaping the vice trade and the traditional periodization of historical studies of prostitution. Under a metric of criminalization and repression, the local state appears either uninterested or inept at policing prostitution until the Progressive era, the point at which sweeping national and local campaigns succeeded in securing the closures of red-light districts in every major city across the country. However, utilizing a broader category of regulation, the early American state appears less incompetent in its approaches and more as it did in William Novak's classic *The People's Welfare*: namely, as an active force in policing public morality and shaping sexual commerce.[31] The state was sometimes inconsistent in its efforts but seldom laissez-faire; the sex trade – although a product of capitalist development – ultimately adapted its shape over time from a complex and unbalanced negotiation between the state and sex workers. Given the ongoing nature of this negotiation, processes that many historians have argued had their roots in the political and social developments of the late nineteenth century, including the rise of regulatory movements and the creation of red-light districts, come to seem less like anomalies of that period and more like extensions and modifications of earlier regulatory logics. The fact that the bulk of the historiography on prostitution is concentrated in *either* the antebellum period or, more commonly, the Progressive era makes it difficult to see connections and continuities over time.[32]

---

[31] Novak, *The People's Welfare*.

[32] For works on the Progressive Era, see, among others, Mara Keire, *For Business and Pleasure: Red-Light Districts and the Regulation of Vice in America, 1890–1933* (Baltimore: Johns Hopkins University Press, 2010), 3. On Progressive Era anti-vice campaigns, see also Neil Larry Shumsky, "Tacit Acceptance: Respectable Americans and Segregated Prostitution, 1870–1910," *Journal of Social History* 19 (Summer 1986): 665–79; Ruth Rosen, *The Lost Sisterhood: Prostitution in America, 1900–1918* (Baltimore: Johns

In addition to pushing for a more expansive view of what constituted a regulatory system around sex work, this book also calls for a better integration of prostitution into histories of capitalism. Implicitly or explicitly, analysis of capitalism has been at the heart of virtually all classic social histories of prostitution, from Christine Stansell's exploration of prostitution's roots in the New York labor market and its gendered divisions of labor to Timothy Gilfoyle's work on prostitution's relationship to industrial modernity, land use practices, and the broader urban economy.[33] And yet, with the notable exception of works like Seth Rockman's *Scraping By*, many urban studies in the new history of capitalism have not necessarily viewed these works' findings as relevant to their own narratives or inquiries. This is, in part, a result of the field's growing focus on capital rather than labor,[34] but it also speaks to the fact that issues of gender and, indeed, of women's history remain underaddressed within the field. A recent critique of the history of capitalism by Amy Dru Stanley noted that new works on the American economy often "leave unasked how the productive and reproductive work of women – free and unfree – created wealth across the country."[35]

Studies of prostitution are one means of remedying this deficit, as they provide especially stark examples of both the ways in which women's sexual labor generated capital for diverse economic actors in cities and the ways in which investment in prostitution was a tool for promoting urban growth and development. Brothels owned or managed by women shaped neighborhoods, spawned subsidiary businesses, and challenged urban authorities to clarify their visions for the city as both a place of residence and a site of commerce. Women selling sex bolstered a number of legitimate and semi-legitimate commercial and cultural venues in the city and funded the facilities that provided medical care to the working men and women whose labor enabled the city's commercial and industrial growth.

Hopkins University Press, 1982); Brian Donovan, *White Slave Crusades: Race, Gender, and Anti-Vice Activism, 1887–1917* (Champaign: University of Illinois Press, 2006); Connelly, *The Response to Prostitution in the Progressive Era.*

[33] Christine Stansell, *City of Women: Sex and Class in New York, 1789–1860* (New York: Knopf, 1986); Gilfoyle, *City of Eros.*

[34] Jeffrey Sklansky, "Labor, Money, and the Financial Turn in the History of Capitalism," *Labor* 11, no. 1 (2014): 23–46.

[35] Amy Dru Stanley, "Histories of Capitalism and Sex Difference," *Journal of the Early Republic* 36 (Summer 2016): 384. See also Ellen Hartigan-O'Connor, "Gender's Value in the History of Capitalism," *Journal of the Early Republic* 36 (Winter 2016): 613–35; Brenna O'Rourke Holland, "Free Market Family: Stephen Girard and the Culture of Capitalism in Philadelphia," PhD dissertation, Temple University, 2014.

For much of the nineteenth century, businesses based around the sale of sex were institutions at the center – geographically and figuratively – of the transition to the modern, capitalist city. While more work remains to be done on this subject, it is my hope that this book will revive a conversation about women's contributions to economic development.

Finally, this book speaks to issues relevant to the architects of modern policies concerning sex work and sex trafficking. One consistent theme throughout this work is that Baltimore authorities' attempts to regulate and criminalize sex work seldom accomplished what the authors and agents of reform hoped that they would. Particularly in the Progressive era, advocates of suppression and criminalization claimed to be acting on behalf of helpless women in order to spare them shame, exploitation, and abuse. Yet many reformers had a poor and distorted understanding of how the sex trade actually worked, one rooted more in their fantasies and fears about brothels than in the empirical realities they claimed to observe. When sex workers tried to complicate or challenge reformers' narratives about their lives and labors, reformers dismissed them as fallen, "feeble-minded," or otherwise too naive to understand their own victimization. Reformers' insistence that sex workers were not to be trusted, combined with their own ultimate refusal to address the economic factors and the gendered inequalities that drove so many women into sex work, ensured that whatever solutions they came up with to the problems in the sex trade usually only exacerbated those issues. Instead of alleviating the very real miseries that sometimes accompanied brothel prostitution, state and reformist interventions led to more extortion by police, more pimping and procuring, more exploitative labor practices, and worse outcomes for sex workers.[36] In an era that has witnessed a revival of discourses about sex trafficking and "prostituted women,"[37] this book should be read as a cautionary tale.

[36] Numerous historians have made similar observations. See, for example, Clement, *Love for Sale*, 93–94; Luise White, *The Comfort of Home: Prostitution in Colonial Nairobi* (Chicago: University of Chicago Press, 1990), 4–6.

[37] Jo Doezema, *Sex Slaves and Discourse Masters: The Construction of Trafficking* (London: Zed Books, 2010); Jyoti Sanghera, "Unpacking the Trafficking Discourse," in *Trafficking and Prostitution Reconsidered: New Perspectives on Migration, Sex Work, and Human Rights*, ed. Kamala Kempadoo with Jyoti Sanghera and Bandana Pattanaikv (Boulder, CO: Paradigm Publishers, 2005), 4–7.

A NOTE ON TERMINOLOGY

There has been a good deal of discussion in recent years about the terminology that historians of sex work use to describe our subjects. Some historians continue to use "prostitute" – in quotation marks or otherwise – to describe women who sold sex, citing its relevance as a historical term that captures specific meanings and associations about sexual commerce and women's sexual expression.[38] Others have chosen to avoid that usage, which they understand to be both derogatory and inappropriate in that it attaches a static, permanent, and stigmatized label to women who mostly sold sex temporarily, sometimes amid many other types of labor.[39] I mostly fall into the latter category. While I continue to use "prostitute" when describing the ideologies and attitudes of public officials, common citizens, and various reformers and experts, I have opted to use "sex worker" or similar variants when speaking in my own authorial voice. I have done so out of many of the same concerns that other historians have expressed, the most significant of which is that the word "prostitute" has a long and negative history.

The Latin verb from which prostitute is derived, *prōstituere*, carried with it a connotation of public exposure and dishonor.[40] From the late 1700s through the early republic, American newspapers used "prostitute" less frequently to describe sex workers than they did to describe the actions of officials and political figures who betrayed the public interest for the sake of their parties or their own selfish desires.[41] When the term was applied to women who sold sex, it carried with it the suggestion that such women were betraying, dishonoring, and debasing themselves. Although this etymology is admittedly obscure, "prostitute" continues to convey negative meanings and associations. As Lizzie Smith noted, "The term 'prostitute' does not simply mean a person who sells her or his

---

[38] Linda Mahood, *The Magdalenes: Prostitution in the Nineteenth Century* (London: Routledge, 2012); Laite, *Common Prostitutes and Ordinary Citizens*, 27.

[39] Lee, *Policing Prostitution*, 11–12.

[40] Jill McCracken, *Street Sex Workers' Discourse: Realizing Material Change through Agential Choice* (New York: Routledge, 2013), 99–100. See also Melinda Chateauvert, *Sex Workers Unite: A History of the Movement from Stonewall to SlutWalk* (Boston: Beacon Press, 2013).

[41] This statement is based on my own observations after having searched newspapers for keywords related to sex work and prostitution. See, for example, Antilon, "To the Printers of the Maryland Gazette," *Maryland Gazette* (Annapolis, MD), Feb. 18, 1773; "'How Men Differ,'" *Maryland Gazette* (Annapolis, MD), Nov. 30, 1826.

sexual labour ... but brings with it layers of 'knowledge' about her worth, drug status, childhood, integrity, personal hygiene and sexual health."[42]

Notably, historians already avoid uncritical reproduction of historical terms that were used just as frequently as "prostitute" to describe women who engaged in sex work: fallen woman, nymph du pave, frail sister, soiled dove, good-time girl, Cyprian, and whore. It is worth continuing that trend, not the least of which because words have the power to shape our thinking about human worth in profound ways. The dehumanizing effects of the term "prostitute" continue to function in ways that excuse violence against sex workers and tacitly reinforce that they are different from and less valuable than other women. Just as many historians of slavery have started to favor the term "enslaved people" over "slaves" to describe those who suffered under bondage, historians of commercial sex should strive to use language that acknowledges the personhood and humanity of our historical actors.

---

[42] Lizzie Smith, "Dehumanising Sex Workers: What's 'Prostitute' Got to Do with It?," *Conversation*, July 29, 2013. https://theconversation.com/dehumanising-sex-workers-whats-prostitute-got-to-do-with-it-16444.

PART I

THE RISE OF PROSTITUTION IN
THE EARLY REPUBLIC

Selling Sex in the Early Republic

Bawdy-house keeper Ann Wilson was a fixture in Baltimore's early sex trade. Born sometime in the 1790s, Wilson had allegedly started selling sex while in her late teens, when the city itself was barely into adolescence. In the years that followed, she became well known around town, where her stout frame and large build earned her the nickname "Big Ann" among the local sporting set. Wilson lived on a section of Wilk Street (later renamed Eastern Avenue) nicknamed "the Causeway" or "the Crossway" because of its location adjacent to a bridge over a canal that ran north from Baltimore's deep-water harbor at Fells Point (see Figure 1.1). She may have taken up residence in the neighborhood initially as the wife of a sailor, for she often went by "Mrs. Wilson." However, by the time she first started appearing in court dockets on disorderly house charges in the 1820s, there was no husband in her life. Tasked with raising numerous children on her own, Wilson made her living by dabbling in a variety of commercial pursuits: she offered board to seamen in port, ran betting games, sold liquor without a license, and rented rooms to women – black and white – who sold sex. Her house, which was situated just blocks from the wharves amid a smattering of taverns, groceries, and inns, was in a prime location to take advantage of foot traffic from sailors and visitors to the city. It quickly became a center of early Baltimore's raucous, mixed-race, and loosely organized prostitution trade.[1]

[1] "Baltimore: Correspondent of the Whip," *The Whip*, July 2, 1842, in *The Flash Press: Sporting Male Weeklies in 1840s New York*, ed. Patrica Cline Cohen, Timothy Gilfoyle, and Helen Horowitz (Chicago: University of Chicago Press, 2008), 190–91. Wilson

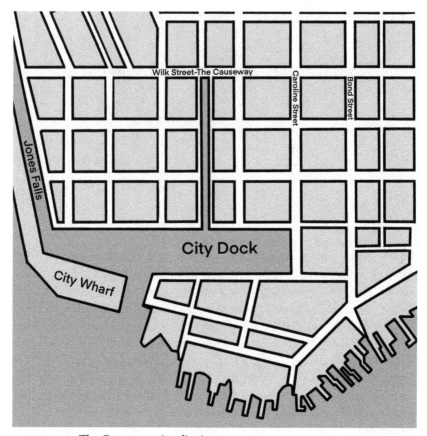

FIGURE 1.1 The Causeway vice district.
Map by Kari Cadenhead based on Thomas H. Poppleton, *This Plan of the City of* Baltimore
(1822), 1:7,300

Even so, life was not easy for Wilson. At the time she lived there, Fells
Point was a rough neighborhood characterized by violence and poverty.
Seasonal labor patterns governed life for much of the local population,
and residents' fortunes ebbed and flowed with the pace of trade and the
availability of waged work.[2] Though Wilson ran her own business, she

appeared in Baltimore City Court at least as early as 1825 on charges of keeping a
disorderly house: Baltimore City Court (Docket and Minutes), June Term, 1825, Case
487, Ann Wilson, C184-2, MSA 16659. *Matchett's Baltimore City Director for
1849–1850* (Baltimore: Richard J. Matchett, 1849), 426, https://archive.org/details/match
ettsbaltimo1849balt, accessed November 4, 2010.
[2] On the seasonal nature of labor in port cities, see, among others, Seth Rockman, *Scraping
By: Wage Labor, Slavery, and Survival in Early Baltimore* (Baltimore: Johns Hopkins

was no more insulated from the turbulent economy of early Baltimore than others whose livelihood depended on maritime commerce. She went through periods of hardship and impoverishment, sometimes having to resort to the almshouse to sustain herself. Nevertheless, she managed over the years to scrape together enough to support herself and her children and to gain a limited degree of upward mobility. By 1840, she had expanded her enterprise to include ten female boarders between the ages of fifteen and forty-nine, an unusually high number for a brothel in a neighborhood where street and tavern prostitution predominated. Try as she might, however, she never earned enough to retire from the trade. Wilson kept her house until her death in the early 1850s.[3]

Wilson's property ownership and long tenure in the sex trade made her somewhat unusual, and yet many aspects of her life – where she lived, how she sustained herself, and how she incorporated sex work into her broader household economy – were typical of women who sold sex in early nineteenth-century Baltimore. Prostitution emerged at the same time the city did and cropped up around waterways, where it ebbed and flowed with the maritime economy, with influxes of sailors into and out of town, and with seasonal expansions and contractions in the labor market. Sexual exchange was embedded in the culture of the neighborhoods that surrounded the wharves, and women of all ages – black and white – sold sex in the streets, in taverns, at home, or in boardinghouses like Ann Wilson's. Sex workers generally operated independently and pocketed most or all of the proceeds of their labor, but most failed to achieve more than subsistence in a trade that was still marginal and occasionally cash-poor in the first decades of the century. Sex work was a means of survival that made a great deal of sense given that early republic women had few options for supporting themselves outside a sexual connection with a man, but it was hardly a glamorous or financially rewarding means of making a living. For many, if not most, women who participated in the trade, sex work was part of an economy of makeshifts rather than a profession in and of itself.

At the time Ann Wilson entered prostitution, commercial sex was just beginning to take root in Baltimore, which was still a young and underdeveloped port city. Baltimore Town had been founded as a port in 1729, but for years after its establishment, it amounted to little more than a

University Press, 2009), 24, 136; Stansell, *City of Women*, 3–18; James Vickers, *Young Men and the Sea: Yankee Seafarers in the Age of Sail* (New Haven, CT: Yale University Press, 2007), 204–13.
[3] 1840 US Census, Baltimore, Maryland, Ward 2, p. 24, Ann Wilson.

sleepy cluster of dwellings and a few boats along Maryland's Patapsco River. Eventually, increased trade and the merger of the town with the nearby settlements of Fells Point and Jonestown positioned Baltimore as a growing hub of commerce. The city became an important locus of ship-building during the Revolutionary era, and its merchants took advantage of shipping disruptions brought about by war to expand their role in the West Indies trade.[4] By the time Ann Wilson was born, the city was on the brink of a boom period. Baltimore's population doubled within the span of a decade in the 1790s.

In the early nineteenth century, infrastructural improvements and the growth of wheat agriculture increased the fortunes of the city and made it an entrepôt in the grain trade. Barrels of wheat flour produced in Maryland, Virginia, and points west passed from the deep-water harbor of Fells Point to Latin America, the Caribbean, and Europe. Tobacco, lumber, manufactured goods, and thousands of enslaved laborers would flow through the city to and from points around the United States and abroad. Although the trade on which the city depended faltered somewhat with the foreign relations crises of the 1790s and Jefferson's embargo, Baltimore continued to attract visitors, residents, and commercial investment. Baltimore's port bustled with activity, and both its fortunes and its population continued to grow, albeit unevenly.[5]

Prostitution, which sprung up in many colonial cities in the eighteenth century, began to be a visible trade in Baltimore around the time of the city's incorporation in 1796. Although Baltimore's sex trade was considerably younger than those that existed in colonial cities like Philadelphia and New York, it resembled those trades in a number of ways.[6] Like prostitution in other urban ports, sex work in early Baltimore first

---

[4] Suzanne Ellerly Chapelle, Jean B. Russo et al., *Maryland: A History* (Baltimore: Johns Hopkins University Press, 2008), chapter 2.

[5] Dorsey, *Hirelings*, 16–17; Robert Brugger, *Maryland: A Middle Temperament, 1634–1980* (Baltimore: Johns Hopkins University Press, 1996), 84–185.

[6] On the connections between sex work and the maritime economy in other cities, see, among others, Gilfoyle, *City of Eros*, 25–26, 49; Linda M. Maloney, "Doxies at Dockside: Prostitution and American Maritime Society, 1800–1900," in *Ships, Seafaring, and Society: Essays in Maritime History*, ed. Timothy J. Runyan (Detroit, MI: Wayne State University Press, 1987), 217–25. Notably, Clare Lyons found that while Philadelphia's waterfront neighborhoods had their share of bawdy houses, sex establishments were not confined to one area of that city. However, Philadelphia appears to be somewhat unique in this respect; other port cities seem not to have developed a significant prostitution trade outside waterfront neighborhoods until the 1820s. Lyons, *Sex among the Rabble*, especially 110.

emerged as a visible trade around the waterways. Court records and pardon papers contain only a few mentions of bawdy-house keeping or streetwalking in the first decade of the city's incorporation, but visitors to the city frequently observed the connections between maritime and sexual commerce.[7] When future Pennsylvania Congressman William Darlington toured Baltimore as a young man in the summer of 1803, he wandered over to the deep-water harbor of Fells Point to admire its ships and the dense clusters of dwellings to the north of its wharves. Darlington noted that the neighborhood was "a fine place for trade" as well as a popular resort for sailors. Local shops and taverns boasted signs that catered to seafarers, including one that read "Come in Jack, here's the place to sit at your case, and splice the main brace" (i.e., get drunk). Darlington also noted commerce of another kind. He remarked with some amusement that a section of the wharves known as Oakum Bay was "a noted place for those carnal lumps of flesh called en francais *Filles de joie.*"[8]

Fifteen years later, a Wilmingtonian calling himself "Rustic" confirmed Darlington's observations about Fells Point, albeit with considerably less amusement and good humor. Rustic wrote in his travel journal, "[Fells Point] is the rendezvous for all the heavy shipping ... There were several fine ships at anchorage: some just arriv'd and others about to embark. But it has the appearance: & I was enform'd was a place of great dissipation, prostitution & wickedness."[9] By the time Rustic came to Baltimore, the Causeway where Ann Wilson lived and worked had become the city's main site of sexual commerce.

Early prostitution's roots in maritime communities were a product of the mobility, precariousness, and unique cultures of labor that characterized life for sailors and their families in the early republic. Although prostitution changed a great deal over the first half of the nineteenth century in terms of its forms and labor arrangements, one point of consistency was that it thrived when there were high rates of population mobility and large numbers of women struggling to earn a living in the paid labor market. Maritime communities had both of these

---

[7] Court records from Baltimore County's Court of Oyer and Terminer and Gaol delivery list scattered bawdy and disorderly house and vagrancy cases in the 1790s.

[8] William Darlington, Journalissimo of a Peregrination to the city of Baltimore: performed in the year domini 1803. William Darlington Papers, New York Historical Society, New York, NY. Thanks to Seth Rockman for sharing information about this citation.

[9] "A Manuscript Account of a Journey from Wilmington to Baltimore and Back," 1818, MS 523, 15. Special Collections, Milton S. Eisenhower Library, Johns Hopkins University, Baltimore, MD.

characteristics – and in exaggerated form – before the rest of the city developed them. The neighborhoods along Baltimore's wharves were always in flux. Labor patterns were seasonal, with commerce and employment opportunities peaking during the warm months when the harbor was easily navigable and trade was steady. During that time, it was not unusual for men who labored at sea to leave for weeks or months at a time on voyages along the coast or around the Atlantic. Their absences left their wives or female family members to manage households and raise children on their own, often without the benefit of their Husbands' wages, which might be delivered only at the end of a voyage or delayed in reaching home. Fells Point, which Darlington and Rustic identified as a center of the early sex trade, had an unusually high number of female-headed households. Because maritime labor was dangerous and often unpredictable, the women who kept those households lived with the uncertainty that they might never see their husbands, fathers, or male relatives again once they boarded their ships.[10] Women had to fend for themselves for long stretches of time.

Sailors' wives, like other women who were forced to labor for wages, struggled to make ends meet in an early republic economy that provided them with limited economic opportunities. As Jeanne Boydston argued in her classic study *Home and Work*, the decades following the Revolution marked a period of labor transition in which it was increasingly assumed that women were – and should be – nonproductive dependents of men rather than workers who made contributions to the household economy.[11] The waged labor market reflected this shift. Work for women was never lacking in Baltimore; indeed, local newspapers in the early years of the city were filled with advertisements from employers seeking housemaids and other domestic workers, and women provided much of the labor in the spinning and needle trades. However, employers justified paying women very little on the assumption that women were merely supplementing a household wage rather than supporting themselves independently. Most of the jobs that were open to women paid wages that were below the level required for subsistence. Domestic work, which was

---

[10] Rockman, *Scraping By*, 165–66. See also: Karen A. Wulf, *Not All Wives: Women of Colonial Philadelphia* (Ithaca, NY: Cornell University Press, 2000), 97–98; Ruth Wallis Herndon, "The Domestic Cost of Seafaring: Town Leaders and Seamen's Families in Eighteenth-Century Rhode Island," in *Iron Men, Wooden Women: Gender and Seafaring in the Atlantic World, 1700–1920*, ed. Margaret Creighton and Lisa Norling (Baltimore: Johns Hopkins University Press, 1996), 55–69.

[11] Boydston, *Home and Work*.

by far the most common occupation, produced scarcely enough income for a worker to support herself, much less a family (the existence of which might prevent her from gaining domestic work in the first place). Many women participated in an economy of makeshifts in which they made ends meet through a variety of seasonal and often cobbled-together economic pursuits. These included opening their houses to boarders, cooking for and selling alcohol to lodgers and sailors, doing housework for wealthier families, scrapping, checking into the almshouse to labor in exchange for food and shelter, and at times participating in sex work.[12]

Sex work for women struggling to get by was part and parcel of an early republic economic structure in which most women had to attach themselves sexually to men in order to survive. Sex workers in maritime neighborhoods found themselves with a ready clientele during the warm months. In the early years of the city, sailors drove much of the demand for sexual services. The nature of maritime labor meant that they were without women for weeks or months at a time, and the uniqueness of their work gave rise to specialized subcultures of leisure, masculinity, and sexuality. As Paul Gilje has argued, sailors often embraced a rough and ribald concept of masculinity that was focused on strength, bravery, and virile conquest of women. At the same time, many also idealized the home and the women they left behind as they embarked on long voyages.[13] Seafarers who came into port often sought out both domestic and sexual modes of interaction with women residing on shore, and many found it most easily through commercial transactions. Cities became sites of potential for sexual and ribald fun and short-term romance for sailors who arrived in port with a month's pay or more in their pockets.[14]

Prostitution became enmeshed in the broader network of dockside businesses that catered to sailors and local workers whose livelihoods depended on trade. Boardinghouses that provided shelter, washing, food, and other domestic services and taverns that provided drink and entertainment were both favorite sites of solicitation for jacks looking for

[12] Hufton, *The Poor of Eighteenth-Century France, 1750–1789*, 16.
    On women's economic strategies in the Early Republic, see Stansell, *City of Women*; Rockman, *Scraping By*, 100–31; Alice Kessler-Harris, *Out to Work: A History of Wage-Earning Women in the United States* (Oxford: Oxford University Press, 1983).
[13] Paul A. Gilje, *Liberty on the Waterfront: American Maritime Culture in the Age of Revolution* (Philadelphia: University of Pennsylvania Press, 2007), 34–65.
[14] On sailor's wages: Gilje, *Liberty on the Waterfront*, 3–32. See also W. Jeffrey Bolster, *Black Jacks: African American Seamen in the Age of Sail* (Cambridge, MA: Harvard University Press, 1997), 186–87.

female companionship. This sale of sex and other services was part of what historian Seth Rockman referred to as the "commodification of household labor," a process that took place in the early nineteenth century as mobile male populations turned to commercial exchange for services that might otherwise be provided by wives.[15] Some sailors sought out women for the purposes of quick, anonymous sexual exchanges or short flings, while others paid women to act as surrogate partners who performed many kinds of labor for them, including cooking, laundry, and general companionship. Arrangements sometimes blurred the boundaries between purely commercial and genuinely affectionate. Notably, women who acted as domestic surrogates relieved sailors of having to perform "feminine" tasks, like sewing and mending, that they would be expected to perform at sea and thus allowed them to experience – however briefly – a more traditionally gendered labor regime.[16]

In Baltimore, as in other cities at the turn of the nineteenth century, selling sex was not an especially lucrative trade for the women who participated in it. Although it generally paid better than other forms of work open to women, the value of sexual labor could and did fluctuate with the economy. Following the specie contractions of the 1790s, Baltimore's economy was so cash-poor that some women who sold sex did so on a virtual barter system, as had been common in the early modern period. When William Darlington observed the *"filles de joie"* in Fells Point in 1802, he noted that they were not paid in cash. The area that they operated out of had been nicknamed Oakum Bay on account of the fact that sex workers who labored there exchanged sexual services for "rope yarn and old cables" from sailors.[17] In addition to not being especially valuable, old rope yarn and cable also required considerable labor in the form of spinning to transform them into a salable product. For the women who were willing to trade sex for such meager compensation, prostitution was less a means of getting ahead economically than a desperate measure to avoid abject poverty.

Even as cash flowed more freely over time, women who sold sex continued to struggle to make ends meet. The embargo of 1807 and the prohibitions on wheat trading during the War of 1812 hit Baltimore's young, maritime-oriented economy hard and caused the shipping trade to

[15] Rockman, *Scraping By*, 23. On the demand for prostitution in establishments that boarded sailors in port, see Bolster, *Black Jacks*, 186–87; Rockman, *Scraping By*, 101–2; Maloney, "Doxies at Dockside."
[16] Gilje, *Liberty on the Waterfront*, 34.   [17] Darlington, Journalissimo.

stagnate. The sex trade declined with it. Just a few years after Baltimore recovered from the economic devastation wrought by these trade prohibitions, the Panic of 1819 heralded a new economic depression. The flow of sailors to the Causeway's brothels and taverns slowed, along with trade as a whole, and high unemployment rates meant that fewer men had money to spend on sex. Circumstances were bad enough that even women who owned their own establishments suffered. In the winter months of 1820–21 and 1821–22, when trade was especially stagnant because of cold weather and freezes, Ann Wilson found herself on the verge of impoverishment. As many women did in the winter months, Wilson begged admission to the almshouse, which provided her warm lodgings, regular food, and treatment for venereal disease during the slow period for commercial sex. She checked herself out in the spring, when business was likely to be better.[18]

It would take years for the growing availability of bank notes and other paper money and the expansion of wage labor to improve compensation for sex work, and even that could not relieve seasonal doldrums entirely. Women in the sex trade had such narrow economic margins that they were often forced to resort to charitable facilities and hospitals when illnesses rendered them unable to work, even temporarily. Records from the Marine Hospital and the almshouse list over a dozen sex workers who entered those institutions' medical wards, most of them pregnant or visibly infected with venereal or tubercular diseases.[19]

Because the early sex trade was part of the makeshift economy, it was deeply integrated into the culture and social life of Baltimore's poor. Relatively few women were professional prostitutes in any sense of that term, and prostitution in East Baltimore's maritime communities would maintain this informality through much of the nineteenth century.

---

[18] Baltimore City and County Poor Relief and Welfare Services, Admissions Record, 1814–1826, 4108, Ann Wilson, MS 1866–1, Maryland Historical Society. On poor Baltimoreans' use of the Almshouse, see Rockman, *Scraping By*, 194–230. See also Ruth Wallis Herndon, "Poor Women and the Boston Almshouse in the Early Republic," *Journal of the Early Republic* 32 (Fall 2012): 349–81; Jacqueline Cahif, "'She Supposes Herself Cured': Almshouse Women and Venereal Disease in Late Eighteenth and Early Nineteenth Century Philadelphia," PhD dissertation, University of Glasgow, 2010.

[19] Baltimore City and County Poor Relief and Welfare Services, Admissions Record, 1814–1826, 7408, Betsey McLillton; 7424 and 8144, Margaret Paine; 7871, Caroline Walton, 8190, Mary Wager; MS 1866–1, Maryland Historical Society. See also Francis Donaldson, Alms-House Medical Record, 1844–1845. Francis Donaldson, Marine Hospital Notes, MS 3000, Box 32, Folder 3, MDHS. Donaldson's notes contain the records of nine sex workers suffering from phthisis or illnesses related to pregnancy.

Sex work was loosely organized and largely conducted on an individual basis, and many women moved in and out of sex work in their youth and throughout their lives as need dictated. This behavior, while not entirely without social repercussions, was more accepted in poor neighborhoods than it was in more genteel ones. Laboring people did not always approve of sex outside marriage (although their conceptions of marriage and what it entailed were often flexible), but they understood better than their elite counterparts that sex was often transactional, be it in the context of prostitution or in a woman marrying a man for his wages. As such, they did not usually attach a permanent stigma to women who worked as prostitutes, nor did they insist on clear boundaries between the illicit world of the sex trade and the more licit world of everyday life and commerce. In neighborhoods like Fells Point, the children of brothel keepers attended Sunday school at the local church alongside the children of more respectable families, and young boys were allowed to play in the streets in front of houses of ill fame. Women who sold sex in their youth married and started families later. The world of sexual commerce was porous, casual, and integrated into the social fabric of many waterfront communities.[20]

The casual nature of sex work meant that it was a survival strategy open to women from a variety of age groups and life circumstances. Many sex workers in East Baltimore, including Ann Wilson, were widowed, separated, or married women with absent husbands who were selling sex as a means to support their families. Mary Bower, who lived not far from Wilson's dwelling in Fells Point, performed sex work to keep her household afloat. At age thirty-eight, Bower lived with her two sons, aged seventeen and nineteen. Although both of her sons worked, Bower had a difficult time maintaining the household. In addition to taking a young ship carpenter and his wife as boarders, Bower gave her occupation to the census taker as "lady of pleasure."[21] Although the bulk of women

[20] Numerous newspaper accounts mention children playing in the neighborhood of the Causeway. Additionally, testimony given in an investigation into election misconduct indicated that at least one brothel keeping family (James and Ann Manley) sent their children to the local Sunday school. Maryland, Governor (1865–1869: Swann), *Record of Proceedings of the Investigation before His Excellency Thomas Swann, Governor of Maryland, in the Case of Samuel Hindes and Nicholas L. Wood, Commissioners of the Board of Police of the City of Baltimore, upon Charges Preferred against Them for Official Misconduct* (Baltimore: W. K. Boyle, printer, 1866).

[21] 1860 US Census, Baltimore, Maryland, Ward 2, Dwelling 982, Family 1511, p. 168, Mary Bower.

involved in prostitution were younger than Bower and more casually involved in the trade, familial situations like hers were common. Up to a quarter of women who participated in sex work in the early republic were married, and economic hardship ensured that some continued to perform sexual labor until they were advanced in age. In 1814, a woman named Ann France accused a farmer named Thomas Potter of raping her after she visited his mother's house in search of liquor. Pardon requests submitted on behalf of Potter described France as "a Notorious drunkard, a dirty, hackneyed prostitute of seventy-one years of age."[22]

Other women were unmarried and barely more than girls when they took up the trade, often in an attempt to escape difficult or restrictive home lives. Just as wives in the early republic were bound to their husbands by law and by unequal labor opportunities, daughters were bound to their parents, specifically to fathers who acted as family patriarchs. They were expected to live at home until marriage, work in support of the household, and be obedient. And yet many young women yearned for a degree of independence from their families, parental control, and the drudgery of menial labor they performed as part of their domestic duties. Some married early, while others turned to sex work to escape the domestic realm in the period between childhood and marriage. As Clare Lyons argued, prostitution was sometimes a "sexual lifestyle" for young women, one that allowed them to engage in sexual license and pleasure while also supporting themselves.[23] Some young women seemed to relish the independence and opportunities to meet men that prostitution provided, and they formed short-term relationships with their clients that were intimate as well as commercial. Other women entered prostitution in a bid to escape the violence that characterized life in their households. Such was the case for Elizabeth Shoemaker, an eighteen-year-old Fells Point resident who had a difficult relationship with her father and his wife. Following the death of Elizabeth's mother, her father had married a woman who resented and abused Elizabeth. In protest, Elizabeth ran away from home and resorted to "one of those sinks of Iniquity," where her stepmother complained that she spent her "night[s] in riot and debauchery."[24] Another young woman, Elizabeth Miller, ran away to a

---

[22] Governor and Council (Pardon Papers), 1814, Thomas Potter, Box 16, Folder 64, S1061–16.

[23] Lyons, *Sex among the Rabble*, 285.

[24] Maryland Governor and Council (Pardon Papers) MSA S1061–15, folder 106, quoted in James D. Rice, "Laying Claim to Elizabeth Shoemaker," in *Over the Threshold: Intimate*

house of ill fame, because her father and mother forced her to scrap during the day and beat her if she did not return with sufficient money. Life in a house of ill fame, she said when summoned before a justice of the peace by her father, was preferable to laboring on the streets and suffering abuse.[25]

In addition to being diverse in terms of the age of its participants, early Baltimore's sex trade was racially mixed. Baltimore was a slave city. In 1790, enslaved people made up approximately 9 percent of its population, a statistic that excluded the large number of men and women who migrated seasonally between Maryland's wheat and tobacco fields and urban work.[26] In the wake of two decades of manumissions that followed the Revolution, the city became home to a sizable free black population, which would grow into the largest in the country by the midcentury. Because the majority of enslaved laborers in the city were domestic workers and because freedwomen were more apt to work in nonagricultural employments in the city than freedmen, Baltimore's black population was disproportionately female. Between 1810 and 1820, the number of free black women residing in Baltimore doubled, and black women came to outnumber black men in the city by a ratio of three to two.[27]

Black women faced many of the same challenges that white women did in early Baltimore's economy, but their difficulties were exacerbated by personal histories of enslavement, uneven sex ratios among the city's black community, and restrictions placed on them as a result of their race. Many of the freedwomen who arrived in Baltimore were accustomed to agricultural labor and may have lacked skills like knitting or needlework that were trained into their white counterparts from the time they were children. Their inexperience, coupled with some householders' preference for white domestic servants, may have stymied them as they attempted to compete for paid employments.[28] Meanwhile, the dearth of

---

Violence in Early America, ed. Christine Daniels and Michael V. Kennedy (New York: Routledge, 1999), 185–201.

[25] "Habeas Corpus," *Sun*, June 2, 1852.

[26] Mariana L. R. Dantas, *Black Townsmen: Urban Slavery and Freedom in the Eighteenth-Century Americas* (New York: Palgrave Macmillan, 2008), 58–59.

[27] Dorsey, *Hirelings*, 55–56; Phillips, *Freedom's Port*, 58; Fields, *Slavery and Freedom on the Middle Ground*. On manumission practices, see also T. Stephen Whitman, *The Price of Freedom: Slavery and Manumission in Baltimore and Early National Maryland* (Lexington: University Press of Kentucky, 1997).

[28] Seth Rockman found that black women who entered Baltimore's almshouse were less likely than white women to tell the admitting officers that they had skills beyond housework. Rockman, *Scraping By*, 124.

black men in the city and legal and social intolerance of interracial unions meant that many black women could not marry or otherwise form households with men who might contribute wages or economic support. Although many black women found alternative means of surviving the early republic's harsh economic climate by forming extended kinship networks, taking washing, and huckstering, some followed a path common among their white counterparts and turned to selling sex to supplement their earnings.[29]

Black and white sex workers, like the black and white populations of the city as a whole, lived and labored alongside one another. Baltimore was similar to most Southern cities in that it was not residentially segregated in the first decades of the nineteenth century. Because black men and women so frequently performed domestic labor for white Baltimoreans, it was common for city neighborhoods to be racially integrated, albeit through residential arrangements that reflected social inequalities. Black laborers and their families often lived in alley houses that abutted white residences, or they even (in the case of domestics) resided with white families in more affluent areas. As historian Seth Rockman has noted, Baltimore's labor market was similarly integrated from the 1790s until the 1830s. Black and white men worked together on public improvement projects around the city as well as in a number of other unskilled or semi-skilled jobs that did not require apprenticeships, and local employers treated white and black women as interchangeable when it came to domestic service. The maritime trade in Fells Point and Old Town drew both black and white workers, who labored together – not always harmoniously – as sailors, ship caulkers, and day workers. In some cases, they were even paid the same wages. It would not be until the 1830s that growing tensions over slavery, fears of slave revolt, and hardening racial ideologies would bring about the privileging of white laborers and the exclusion of black workers from trades.[30]

Just as the general labor market was racially integrated in early waterfront communities, so too was the market and the customer base for sexual labor. Early spaces and zones of sexual commerce were as racially mixed as the rest of city life. Black sex workers mingled with white ones

---

[29] Christopher Phillips found that laundry work was by far the most common type of employment for black women in antebellum Baltimore. He estimated that nine out of ten black female household heads worked as laundresses after 1817 and that about a third of all laundresses lived in Fells Point and headed households because their husbands were away on ships. Phillips, *Freedom's Port*, 110.

[30] Rockman, *Scraping By*.

on the wharves or in taverns, brothels, and bawdy houses that catered to white, free black, and enslaved clientele. Ann Wilson's establishment was notorious for both renting rooms to black sex workers and allowing interracial sex. Similarly, James Dempsey's disorderly house on Fleet Street was known for attracting what newspapers referred to as an "abandoned set of loafers and prostitutes, black and white," as well as a mix of free and enslaved male patrons.[31] When police raided Dempsey's house in 1839, they found among its patrons an enslaved man named Wilkey Owens, who, presumably, was one of the many enslaved men living in Baltimore who was allowed to hire out his own labor and keep a portion of his wages.[32] Most of the brothels on Brandy Alley, which subsequently became Perry Street, attracted similar demographics. An 1839 advertisement for a fugitive slave, Henry Kennard, noted that Kennard was "well known among the negro haunts in Brandy Alley."[33] Despite city officials' paranoia about black gatherings and suspicion of white and black city residents socializing with one another during their leisure time, raucous establishments that catered to neighborhood residents of both races were common. Gambling, dancing, drinking, and prostitution were all popular forms of recreation in East Baltimore's alleys.

In some cases, black men and women even managed to own or supervise their own bawdy houses, though limited economic resources and the restrictions placed on black Baltimoreans made this comparatively rare. For a time in the 1830s, two free black women named Juliana Bosley and Mary Benson kept rival houses located next to one another in Fells Point.[34] More commonly, black women managed houses on less centrally located streets or small alleys in Old Town. Iby Tomlinson, a black woman living in Dutch Alley, owned a "negro brothel" that attracted white clientele, and several similar establishments existed in Salisbury Alley.[35] One of these houses, kept by Margaret Perry, explicitly catered

---

[31] "Nuisances," *Sun*, Nov. 16, 1839.

[32] "Nuisances," *Sun*, Nov. 16, 1839. On black men, wage labor, and hiring out, see Frederick Douglass, *Narrative of the Life of Frederick Douglass, an American Slave. Written by Himself* (Chapel Hill: University of North Carolina, 1999), 102–9; Phillips, *Freedom's Port*, especially 7–29; Jonathan D. Martin, *Divided Mastery: Slave Hiring in the American South* (Cambridge, MA: Harvard University Press, 2004); Whitman, *The Price of Freedom*.

[33] "Twenty Dollars," *Sun*, Jan. 28, 1839; "Watch Returns," *Sun*, Feb. 28, 1839.

[34] "Proceedings of the City Court," *Sun*, Oct. 30, 1837.

[35] Tomlinson was arrested in 1828 for "keeping a disorderly house" in Dutch Alley. While this charge was not specific to brothels, the next charge in the court docket was an

to white men in the hopes of cashing in on what historian Edward Baptist called the "erotic haze" that surrounded black and "mulatto" women in the minds of white Southerners. Although Perry was light-skinned enough that she appeared to be of "Anglo-Saxon" origin, newspapers claimed that she "gloried in laying claim to affinity to the African race." Forgoing the significant legal and social privileges that came with being read as white, Perry specifically described herself as a "yellow" woman in her business dealings. While this may have been a personal decision, it also had an eroticized appeal in a city like Baltimore, where slave trading firms like Franklin and Armfield were well known for purchasing light-skinned enslaved women in order to sell them as sexualized commodities.[36] In 1837, when Perry's neighbor, Caroline Trotter, accused her of keeping a disorderly house, Perry had her lawyer read a statement in open court claiming that Trotter was a fellow sex worker who was bitter that gentlemen's preferences for Perry had reduced Trotter to performing sewing work and fixing up ball gowns for Perry's "lady" visitors.[37]

Sex between black sex workers and white men and vice versa was common in Baltimore's early prostitution trade and, indeed, continued to be common in East Baltimore until the eve of the Civil War. In 1839, police arrested a fifteen-year-old white girl named Mary Jane Long in a house on Brandy Alley that was "frequented by blacks as well as whites" and sent her to the almshouse.[38] An anonymous 1842 chronicler of the Causeway's vice district noted, with no small degree of titillation, that it was possible to enter some brothels and "view the Circassian and sable race beautifully blended together, and their arms intermingled so as to form a lovely contrast between the alabaster whiteness of the one, and the polished blackness of the other."[39]

indictment of a white man, David Grouse, for "fighting in a negro brothel" in the same alley as Tomlinson's house. It is likely that Grouse's melee attracted the attention of local authorities, who also decided to charge Tomlinson with a criminal offense. BCC, January Term, 1828, 90, Iby Tomlinson; BCC (Docket), January Term, 1828, 91, David Grouse.

36 Edward E. Baptist, "'Cuffy,' 'Fancy Maids,' and 'One-Eyed Men': Rape, Commodification, and the Domestic Slave Trade in the United States," *American Historical Review* 106 (Dec. 2001): 1622.

37 "Proceedings of the City Court," *Sun*, Nov. 3, 1837.

38 "Youthful Depravity," *Sun*, Dec. 30, 1839.

39 "Baltimore: Correspondent of the Whip," *The Whip*, July 2, 1842, in *The Flash Press*, 190–91. On black women's participation in prostitution, see Blair, *I've Got to Make My Livin'*; Tera W. Hunter, *To 'Joy My Freedom: Southern Black Women's Lives and Labors after the Civil War* (Cambridge, MA: Harvard University Press, 1998); Mumford, *Interzones*; Landau, *Spectacular Wickedness*.

Brothels, in general, were less common in the late eighteenth and early nineteenth centuries than they were in later decades, and those that did exist differed from the establishments that would exist later in the nineteenth century in terms of their level of commercialization and specialization. In keeping with prostitution's integration into poorer neighborhoods in the early republic, sexual commerce was not yet spatially separated from places of general resort, work, or commerce for laboring people. The establishments where sex workers conducted their transactions – what were called brothels and bawdy houses at the time – were usually not devoted entirely to sexual commerce. Much of the sexual solicitation that took place in early Baltimore happened in the wharves, in the streets, or in taverns that catered to maritime laborers and other workingmen. Women and their clients carried out their sexual transactions in rooms rented from boarding houses, inns, or taverns if they could not do so within the home. The casualness of the trade and its spatial overlap with other forms of commerce would persist in East Baltimore through the Civil War period.

Taverns were particularly popular venues for prostitution. Local drinking spots were important social and political sites in the Revolutionary era and the early republic, and they were usually masculine spaces.[40] However, low-end taverns in waterfront neighborhoods attracted a mix of patrons, black and white, men and women. For the "disreputable" women who composed the majority of taverns' female visitors, solicitation in indoor spaces carried less risk of arrest than more visible, public means of solicitation like streetwalking. The constant stream of male patrons into Causeway taverns provided a ready clientele for sex workers, and taverns also gave women the opportunity to have men buy them drinks or provisions in addition to paying them for sexual services. Tavern keepers, for their part, welcomed the arrangement as a boost for business. *The Viper's Sting and Paul Pry*, a short-lived sporting paper published in Baltimore in the 1840s, noted that mutual arrangements between prostitutes and tavern keepers were common. Its writer commented that the eastern part of the city was dotted with what appeared to be "well-kept taverns, while in reality they are vile brothels, frequented by

---

[40] Christine Sismondo, *America Walks into a Bar: A Spirited History of Taverns and Saloons, Speakeasies and Grog Shops* (Oxford: Oxford University Press, 2011); Vaughn Scribner, *Inn Civility: Urban Taverns and Early American Civil Society* (New York: New York University Press, 2019), 14–15.

the lowest prostitutes."[41] The Causeway alone featured several taverns that regularly rented rooms to sex workers, and Old Town's L Alley and Pitt Street were host to several grog shops that were known to attract rowdy and bawdy clientele. One commenter complained that a groggery in Pitt Street (later, Fayette Street) drew a crowd that caused the neighbors to be "disgusted and abused, day and night, with the obscene language and drunken orgies of a horde of wretches."[42] A German immigrant whose fourteen-year-old daughter had run away from home lamented the presence of such havens of vice in the city. Suspecting that her daughter was selling sex, the woman initially "sought for her in a stew kept by Mary Pearson." Not finding her there, the mother checked a local tavern, where she discovered her seated at the bar, attempting to attract the attention of men.[43]

Boardinghouses and inns, particularly those that catered to sailors, were also common brothel sites. The areas around Fells Point and the harbor were dotted with small lodging establishments whose keepers depended on the traffic of maritime laborers in and out of the harbor for business. Some of these inns and boardinghouses allowed men to bring women back to their rooms, while others boarded sex workers as part of a larger strategy to extract money from their male patrons. Ann Wilson's brothel, which boarded several women, doubled as a sailor's boardinghouse. Similarly, James and Ann Manley, who kept a small travelers' and sailors' hotel on the Causeway in the 1850s, were in the habit of renting some of their rooms to sex workers. The Manley's neighbor, Mary A. Keul, employed the same business model. At the time of the 1860 census, Kuel kept a hotel that had four female boarders between the ages of nineteen and thirty-three, an arrangement that (viewed in light of the Causeway's reputation) suggested that she was running a brothel.[44] Baltimore's Salisbury Street, Brandy Alley, and

---

[41] "Vile Cribs," *Viper's Sting and Paul Pry*, Aug. 11, 1849.
[42] "A Bad Neighborhood," *Sun*, Aug. 1, 1840.   [43] "Depravity," *Sun*, June 13, 1839.
[44] 1860 US Census, Baltimore, Maryland, Ward 2, p. 170, dwelling 1003, family 1537, James and Ann Manley; 1860 US Census, Baltimore, Maryland, Ward 2, p. 358, dwelling 1004, family 1538, Mary A. Keul. On boardinghouses and prostitution, see Gilfoyle, *City of Eros*, 115, 167–68. In his history of prostitution in antebellum Salt Lake City, Jeffrey D. Nichols referred to boardinghouses and taverns as "allied businesses with sex work." Nichols, *Prostitution, Polygamy, and Power: Salt Lake City, 1847–1918* (Champaign: University of Illinois Press, 2008), 91. On anxieties about prostitution in boardinghouses, see Wendy Gamber, *The Boardinghouse in Nineteenth-Century America* (Baltimore: Johns Hopkins University Press, 2007), 102–3.

Guilford Alley also featured boardinghouses that were well known as resorts for "debauchery."[45]

In many cases, sex work in boardinghouses was part of a larger economy rooted in fleecing sailors of their earnings and keeping them in cycles of debt. Many businesses that catered to sailors were owned by "land sharks," who made their livings by exploiting maritime laborers. Sailors were vulnerable to exploitation because their rowdy reputations and unfamiliarity with the cities they visited limited their boarding options, and their tendency to be paid in lump sums in advance or following voyages meant that they often had cash on hand. Many boardinghouse keepers intentionally overcharged sailors for board and drink and kept women on hand in order to encourage them to spend their money and prevent them from straying from the establishments to seek entertainment or sex. In some cases, sea captains even colluded with land sharks to ensure that sailors spent all of their money and advances and were thus driven back to sea to resolve their debts and earn their living. Sexual commerce thus became part of a strategy for ensuring a ready supply of laborers to perform the difficult and often miserable work of securing the passage of goods across the Atlantic.[46]

Sex work was integrated into illicit, informal, and illegal economies outside boardinghouses as well. Disreputable taverns and brothels in the early republic were often sites of theft and of traffic in illicit and stolen goods. Many sex workers in low-end bawdy and assignation houses, particularly those that lined Chestnut (also called Potter) Street in Old Town, supplemented their income from sex work and domestic labor by stealing from their clients. Though there is little evidence that the kind of sophisticated panel houses[47] that existed in cities like New York existed in antebellum Baltimore, court and newspaper records contain a number of examples of East Baltimore sex workers who took advantage of men when they were in flagrante delicto or sleeping. Caroline Davenport, keeper of a brothel on the Causeway, was charged in 1837 with stealing a pocketbook from Captain George Hayden, a visitor to her house. The *Sun*'s wry commentary – "We forbear, at present, to state the circumstances under which the robbery was perpetrated" – left little doubt that

---

[45] "Nuisances," *Sun*, Nov. 16, 1839.

[46] Harold Langley, *Social Reform in the United States Navy, 1798–1862* (Annapolis: Naval Institute Press, 1967), 74–77. On businesses that exploited sailors, see also Bolster, *Black Jacks*, 227.

[47] Panel houses were houses built with false panel walls that allowed a sex worker's accomplice to slip into a room unnoticed and steal her client's money or personal items.

Hayden had been in a compromising position at the time of the theft.[48] In a similar incident, Harriet Price, the long-time African American keeper of a house in Old Town, was charged with stealing a breastpin from one of her male clients, John Roberts.[49] Though both Davenport and Price faced legal penalties for their actions, many crimes like theirs likely went unreported by men who were not in the city long enough to pursue prosecution or who were loath to notify the police – and, by extension, the press – that they patronized brothels. So long as women avoided stealing from local men who composed a regular clientele, they were relatively free to supplement their incomes by stealing from travelers and visiting seamen.

The prevalence of theft in East Baltimore's houses had much to do with the poverty of the neighborhood and the lower profit margins of selling sex to sailors and laboring men. At times, competition for resources grew so intense that casual sex workers abandoned all pretense of artfulness and outright assaulted and robbed visitors to their neighborhoods. In 1846, Mary Brown, Ellen White, Ann White, and Julia Ann Stafford were charged with robbing William Johnson of four or five hundred dollars. Johnson, who was not from Baltimore, had wandered into Wilk Street without knowing its reputation. One of the women threw a stone at Johnson's head, stunning him. The rest surrounded him, hit him over the head with a bottle, and picked his pocket in the scuffle. By the time Johnson realized that he had been the victim of theft, the women had already scattered and stashed the stolen money in one of the local houses. Despite a thorough search of the area, police never recovered it.[50]

The money may have disappeared because some women in East Baltimore's sex trade supplemented their earnings from selling sex by fencing stolen goods, laundering illegitimate or counterfeit money, and acting as semi-licit pawn brokers. While early Baltimore had numerous "legitimate" or semi-legitimate pawnshops that provided loans to poorer members of the community, such shops did not serve all city residents equally. By law, pawnshops could not serve enslaved people without explicit permission from their enslavers, and some explicitly refused to accept goods from black Baltimoreans on the grounds that the property was assumed to be stolen.[51] Proprietors of early sex establishments

---

[48] "Robbery," *Sun*, Nov. 9, 1837. On panel houses, see Gilfoyle, *City of Eros*, 108, 150, 173.
[49] "Local Matters," *Sun*, Sep. 20, 1850.   [50] "Charge of Robbery," *Sun*, Dec. 12, 1846.
[51] Seth Rockman located pawn shop advertisements that specifically noted that no goods would be accepted from black men and women. Rockman, *Scraping By*, 187.

tended to be more willing to serve black patrons and to assume the risks associated with taking goods of questionable provenance, and their businesses became destinations for marginalized city residents who required loans or payments. Many women had frequent contact with local watchmen and courts as a result of their activities. Harriet Price, one of Baltimore's few black sex establishment keepers, appeared in court no fewer than twelve times on various charges, two of which were related to possession of items alleged to have been stolen. In one instance, Price was alleged to be holding a gold watch taken from Henry Rowe of Alexandria, VA. In another incident that did not result in her arrest, police searched her house for stolen merchandise after seventeen-year-old Frank Bowen was arrested for stealing fancy goods from Boury's on Baltimore Street, where he worked as a porter. Bowen told the magistrate that he had taken the goods to Price's house, where authorities eventually recovered them.[52] Price was also partnered for a time with a local thief named Giles Price, who was eventually sold into term slavery in Georgia after he was arrested outside Harriet's brothel with stolen money on his person.[53] Harriet Price was not alone in her attempts to supplement the proceeds of prostitution with the discounted purchase of stolen goods or with theft. When George Cordery stole a lot of spermaceti candles from the docks, he sold part of his loot to Sarah "BlackHawk" Burke, who operated a well-known brothel north of the harbor.[54]

Brothel keepers' and other sex workers' practice of trafficking in stolen goods put them at risk of arrest and incarceration for theft, but that was just one of several legal hazards that accompanied sex work in the late eighteenth and early nineteenth century. Although exchanging sex for money was not technically illegal in early Baltimore, local authorities could, and did, police prostitution as a public nuisance under the common law. They did so often as part of what historian Jen Manion has described as a post-Revolutionary project by elites to reestablish social hierarchies by curtailing rowdiness and sexual misconduct and insisting that men and women conform to their "proper" social roles.[55] Prostitution as it existed in the early nineteenth century not only promoted forms of sexual

---

[52] "Stealing," *Sun*, June 25, 1842. On Price, see BCC, September Term 1837, Cases 398 and 742; BCC, October Term, 1839, Cases 246, 247, and 829; BCC, May Term, 1847, Case 292; BCC, May Term, 1849, Case 863; "Local Matters," *Sun*, May 19, 1841.

[53] "Central Watch Saturday Morning Aug. 19," *Sun*, Aug. 21, 1837.

[54] "Baltimore City Court," *Sun*, July 13, 1843.

[55] Jen Manion, *Liberty's Prisoners: Carceral Culture in Early America* (Philadelphia: University of Pennsylvania Press, 2015), especially 3. See also Mark E. Kann, *Taming Passion*

licentiousness incompatible with good republican citizenship but also violated a gendered order that insisted that women's place was in the home rather than in streets or taverns.[56] Women who labored as street-walkers or sold sex in public places were therefore at constant risk of being hauled into court for disorderly conduct or, more commonly, vagrancy.

Following the Revolution, paranoia about rapid urban growth fueled concerns among elite Baltimoreans that the municipality was being over-run by idle, disorderly, and "unworthy" paupers, which ensured that local ordinances and state laws concerning vagrancy were especially harsh. In 1804, the Maryland legislature passed a law specifying that "every woman who is generally reputed a common prostitute ... shall be adjudged a vagrant, vagabond, prostitute or disorderly person" and allowing accused vagrants to be confined at hard labor in the almshouse for two months.[57] In 1811, Baltimore Mayor Edward Johnson com-plained to state officials that the 1804 law was insufficient to prevent the city from being overrun by dissolute persons and beggars. The state legislature responded by passing an even stricter vagrancy law that stated that persons in Baltimore City deemed vagrants or vagabonds could be sentenced to a year in the newly constructed state penitentiary.[58]

Enforcement of the vagrancy statutes could be vigorous and devastating for sex workers and other poor women.[59] In 1816, during a peak period of paranoia over vagrancy, Baltimore's Court of Oyer and Terminer heard sixty-two separate vagrancy cases. About a fifth of these resulted in the offenders' convictions and remand to the penitentiary for a year. While it is not clear how many of the accused "vagrants" were sex workers, it is the case that over 70 percent of those charged with vagrancy and three-fourths of the 186 people sent to prison for the offense during the period when the 1811 vagrancy law was in force were women, mostly

---

for the Public Good: Policing Sex in the Early Republic (New York: New York University Press, 2013), especially chapter 3.

[56] Manion, *Liberty's Prisoners*, 85–94.

[57] "An Act Relating to Vagrants in Baltimore City," *Maryland Code*, chapter 96, sections 2 and 3 (1804).

[58] "An Act Relating to Vagrants in the City of Baltimore," chapter 212, 1811, Maryland Code; "An Act Relating to Vagrants in the City of Baltimore," chapter 189, 1818, Maryland Code.

[59] On the potentially devastating effects of vagrancy laws on vulnerable populations of streetwalkers and the urban poor, see Rockman, *Scraping By*, 172, 214. For a discussion of the legal and economic roots of vagrancy statutes and prohibitions in the postbellum period, see Stanley, *From Bondage to Contract*, 98–137.

Maryland-born, white, and in their twenties.[60] In prison, they were forced
to labor at "wool picking," sewing, or the arduous, unpleasant task of
washing for the duration of their confinement.[61] After 1819, the state
rescinded the harsh vagrancy law requiring confinement in the
penitentiary and returned to the earlier practice of sending women to
the almshouse for months of labor. Although this was a less severe
punishment – among other things, the almshouse was easy to escape –
women who faced it were given virtually no due process rights or rights to
trial. Under the more lenient law, vagrants were simply called before a
magistrate – often at the complaint of a single witness and without the
benefit of counsel – and remanded to labor at the magistrate's discretion.
The constant threat of being arrested and incarcerated for months at a
time must have weighed heavily on women who barely made their living
soliciting sailors or cruising local taverns for clients.[62]

Women who kept sex establishments had more legal protections on the
basis of their access to property, but they too faced the possibility of
arrest, high fines, or even incarceration. Keeping a disorderly or bawdy
house was a misdemeanor offense that entitled the accused to a jury trial if
she or he so chose, but the fines on conviction were high, especially in the
late eighteenth century. In 1789, Elizabeth Cowell was summoned to
court on the complaints of three witnesses, John and Elizabeth Winchester
and James Clemments, who claimed that she kept a disorderly and bawdy
house. The court fined her the staggering sum of £30 and required her to
post an additional £50 security for her future good conduct.[63] By the first
decades of the nineteenth century, penalties for the offense became less
severe, but prosecutions grew more frequent. In 1813 and 1816 fifty-five

---

[60] BCOTGD, 1816. While courts of oyer and terminer were often reserved for more serious
offenses, Baltimore County's court functioned as its sole criminal court from the 1791 to
1817 and was created "for the trial of all offenses committed in said county" (J. Thomas
Scharf, *History of Maryland from the Earliest Period to the Present Day*, vol. 2 [Balti-
more: John B. Piet, 1879], 774).

[61] Maryland Penitentiary (Prisoner Record), MSA SE65–1: http://msa.maryland.gov/mega
file/msa/stagsere/se1/se65/000000/000001/pdf/se65–000001.pdf.

[62] On the summary judgment of vagrants, see, for example, James D. Schmidt, *Free to
Work: Labor Law, Emancipation, and Reconstruction, 1815–1880* (Athens: University
of Georgia Press, 1998), 76.
    Almshouse admissions records suggest that large numbers of those committed to the
institution left it without being officially discharged by the Trustees of the Poor. Almshouse Admissions Book, 1814–1825. Seth Rockman estimated that elopements
accounted for a quarter of all departures from the Almshouse in 1825. Rockman,
Scraping By, 196, 212.

[63] BCOTGD, Case 114, January Term, 1790, Elizabeth Cowell.

persons were charged in the Baltimore County Court of Oyer and Terminer with keeping a bawdy or disorderly house – the latter an umbrella
charge that encompassed gambling dens, places of resort for loud crowds,
or illegal liquor dens, as well as brothels.[64] Only six of the individuals
charged with the offense were actually convicted, and most of them were
sentenced to much smaller fines than the one that had befallen Elizabeth
Cowell. However, even the more modest $10 fine that was typically issued
in these cases exceeded the financial abilities of some defendants. Some
defendants went to jail for weeks or months. Black defendants, who had
more limited access to financial resources than white ones, tended to
remain in jail the longest. They also faced the threat of a more serious
loss of liberty if they could not raise the revenue to pay the fine and their
jail fees within a sufficient amount of time. In 1813, Betsey Hawlings was
fined $10 for keeping a disorderly house and committed in default of
payment. Although Hawlings was not listed in the court docket as black
(court clerks were often careless about such distinctions in the early
period), a notation on her case read "committed & sold," which suggests
that she was likely a free black woman who was sold into slavery as a
result of her conviction.[65]

Punishment for the keepers of disorderly houses grew more severe after
1817, when the Baltimore County Court of Oyer and Terminer was
renamed the Baltimore City Court and tasked with hearing only those
cases that originated from within municipal boundaries.[66] Chief Justice
Nicholas Brice and his compatriots on the court raised the standard fine
levied on those found guilty of keeping a disorderly house from the
previous amount of $5 to $10 per offense to $20 plus court costs. In some
cases, court costs could exceed $10, and any defendant who failed to pay
the fines and costs promptly was incarcerated in the city jail.[67] Brice and
his fellow justices also issued harsher sentences to certain defendants
whose establishments they deemed particularly offensive to public morals.
Unis Miller, who was found guilty of keeping what was apparently
a particularly raucous disorderly house on Caroline Street, was fined
$50 and costs, sentenced to six months in jail, and ordered to remain in
the institution until she paid her fine.[68] Five other women brought to

[64] BCOTGD, 1813 and 1816.
[65] BCOTGD, Case 303, January Term, 1813, Betsey Hawlings.
[66] "Circuit Courts," Maryland Manual On-Line: A Guide to Maryland & Its Government,"
Maryland.Gov: http://msa.maryland.gov/msa/mdmanual/31cc/html/ccf.html.
[67] BCC, 1825.　　[68] BCC, November Term, 1825, 606, Unis Miller.

court around the same time as Miller were sent to jail for between two and three months.[69] Incarceration was an especially harsh punishment, as it required women and men who kept bawdy houses to spend weeks living under unpleasant conditions and losing out on the money they might earn from their establishments. The measures that Brice and his compatriots used against brothel keepers were intended to be suppressive.

Even as late as the 1820s, sex workers' rewards for shouldering and surviving the risks that accompanied prostitution in East Baltimore's casual trade were usually meager and limited to basic subsistence. Most women left the trade after a few months, married, and settled into other forms of work. Those who remained could expect to cycle in and out of prostitution and often in and out of the city's workhouses and public medical facilities. Even brothel keepers like Ann Wilson, who were more fortunate than most sex workers in that they owned property, rarely earned upward mobility for themselves; their best chance was usually providing it to their children. In Wilson's case, she kept her son at home with her for protection but sent her daughters away to school so that none of the stigma of her trade would attach to them. Her money, divorced from the circumstances of its earning, afforded her daughters a degree of privilege, and – according to some sources – allowed them all to attract respectable husbands. George Konig, another Causeway brothel keeper and member of a Democratic political gang in the 1840s and 1850s, leveraged his political connections, as well as the money he and his wife, Caroline, earned through brothel keeping to launch his son into a political career. George Konig Jr. became a United States congressman.[70] Neither Wilson nor Konig Sr. ever escaped the trade.

In Fells Point and other East Baltimore neighborhoods, the sex trade would remain informally organized, oriented toward sailors and other laboring men, and integrated into the local tavern and boardinghouse economy through the Civil War period. Mobility, seasonal labor patterns, and economic precariousness continued to characterize life in the Causeway, even as the city as a whole matured and developed some of the hallmarks of refinement that had been largely absent in its early days as a port. By the 1820s, however, the sex trade would begin to expand beyond maritime neighborhoods as the transience and anonymity that

[69] BCC, (Docket and Minutes), 1825.
[70] "Baltimore: Correspondent of the Whip," *The Whip*, July 2, 1842, in *The Flash Press*, 190–91; Tracy Matthew Melton, "The Lost Lives of George Konig Sr. & Jr., a Father–Son Tale of Old Fell's Point," *Maryland Historical Magazine* 101, no. 3 (2006): 332–61.

characterized life along the wharves came to characterize urban life as a whole. As the trade gradually took root at the outskirts of commercial and leisure districts, it would follow a path common to many industries and commercial ventures and adapt more centralized, specialized labor arrangements. The world of commercial sex that Ann Wilson had helped to make would be a much different world from the one that evolved in the Western part of the city.

2

The Expansion of Prostitution and the Rise of the Brothel

Eliza Randolph was born less than two decades after Ann Wilson, but she came of age in a different world. When Randolph was a young woman, American cities like Baltimore were experiencing rapid economic and demographic growth. Crops flowed in from the countryside as transportation infrastructures improved, and rural youth flocked to urban areas to seek employment. Randolph, a native of New York, was herself one of the many migrants who made their way to the city in the first decades of the nineteenth century.[1]

The Baltimore in which she arrived little resembled the small port surrounded by agricultural land that had greeted Wilson decades earlier. In the years following the War of 1812, local elites and boosters sought to remake Baltimore into a modern hub of commerce, an entrepôt befitting a young nation whose fortunes were tied to the expansion of cash markets. Employers and entrepreneurs hired laborers to dredge the harbor, grade the streets, and construct buildings and commercial edifices reflective of a city whose urban pretensions and "natural advantages" made it – in the minds of its residents, at least – a rival of New York.[2] By the time Randolph came to Baltimore, turnpikes and the nation's first railroad

---

[1] 1850 US Census, Baltimore, Maryland, Ward 13, p. 358, dwelling 1396, family 1522, Eliza Randolph.

[2] Charles G. Steffen, *The Mechanics of Baltimore: Workers and Politics in the Age of Revolution, 1763–1812* (Urbana: University of Illinois Press, 1984), 3–26; Dorsey, *Hirelings*, 16–17; Brugger, *Maryland: A Middle Temperament*, 84–185; Rockman, *Scraping By*, 16–44; David Schley, "A Natural History of the Early American Railroad," *Early American Studies* 13, no. 2 (2015): 443–66.

connected the city to the western breadbasket region, and the built environment expanded significantly outside the one square mile that had housed most of the urban population in the earliest years of the century. Baltimore had become home to massive and ornate commercial buildings and one of the world's first grand hotels, as well as one of the nation's fastest growing populations of any US city. The neighborhood in which Randolph initially settled – called the Meadow by contemporaries – was still at the northern outskirts of the inhabited city when she arrived, but barely. Development was pushing up from the south, where the streets were rapidly becoming lined with sites of trade and commerce as well as hotels and inns that catered to visitors to the city.

It was in the context of Baltimore's period of rapid urban growth and economic transformation that Eliza Randolph entered the city's sex trade. Although she would go on to distinguish herself as a pioneer of new kinds of sexual entrepreneurship and labor, the start of her career gave few indications that her experience in sex work would be different from that of dozens or hundreds of other women who passed before her. At the time that Randolph moved to the Meadow, which encompassed the area around Davis and North Streets' intersection with Bath Street (see Figure 2.1), the neighborhood was little more than the western half of the city's answer to the Causeway. Although Baltimore's emerging center of commerce and wealth sat just blocks away, the Meadow was characterized by rowdiness and violence, poverty, and a nascent vice trade. Gambling houses and taverns lined its streets and played host to an ungenteel mix of black and white laboring men, sailors, loafers, and poor women and girls who fought with one another, exchanged sex, and drank.[3] Geography itself conspired to rob the area of any pretenses of gentility. The Meadow sat on low ground near a curvature in the path of the Jones Falls where the current was strong. The neighborhood's streets were so saturated with water that the local Adelphia Theater was known popularly as "the old Mud," and visitors described the area as plagued by "fumes" that rose from the muck and pools of stagnant water.[4] When Eliza Randolph first took up residence in a house of prostitution owned

[3] See, for example, "Leg Bail," *Sun*, May 28, 1838; "Middle District – Nov. 2," *Sun*, Nov. 6, 1839.

[4] John Hazlehurst Boneval Latrobe, *Picture of Baltimore: Containing a Description of All Objects of Interest in the City* (Baltimore: Fielding and Lucas, 1832), 59–60; John F. Weishampel, *The Stranger in Baltimore: A New Hand Book* (Baltimore: John F. Weishampel, 1888), 143.

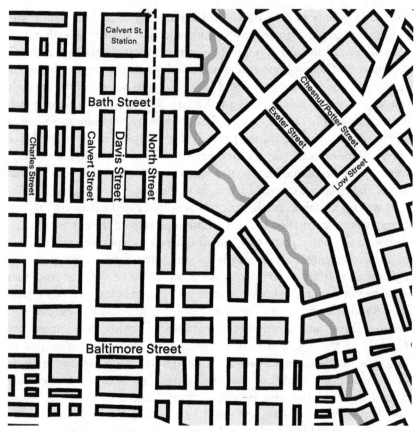

FIGURE 2.1 The Meadow (left) and Old Town (right) vice districts, circa 1856. Map by Kari Cadenhead

by Elizabeth Osborne, there was little to suggest that she would someday own a brothel deemed "fit for a gentleman to enter."[5]

And yet Randolph arrived in Baltimore at the start of a boom period for commercial sex, one that was already beginning to transform sexual commerce and the West Baltimore neighborhoods in which it thrived. Beginning in the late 1820s, prostitution underwent a marked expansion as a result of increased mobility, new structures of waged work, and the rapid population growth. Urbanization and the migrations it entailed disrupted intimate and familial relationships even as capitalism's

[5] "Baltimore: Correspondent of the Whip," *The Whip,* July 2, 1842, in *The Flash Press,* 190–91.

gendered divisions of labor made it difficult for women to subsist outside the household economy.[6] As the emergence of new labor structures threw courtship and marriage practices into flux, an increasingly capitalistic society sought a market-based solution to the social and sexual dislocations of the period. That solution was the widespread commodification of women's sexual labor. Prostitution, which had in earlier decades been a marginal form of commerce confined to maritime communities, became a visible and highly profitable sector of the urban economy. By the 1830s, prostitution would straddle class lines and expand its presence into middle-class neighborhoods to the west of the Jones Falls. The Meadow's brothels, once outposts for local toughs, gradually transformed into destinations for skilled laborers and businessmen.

As sex work became more common and integrated into the fabric of the city's commercial and social life, its spatial arrangements and labor structures changed. In the early years of the nineteenth century, prostitution was a casual trade conducted mostly by independent women who operated out of mixed-economic spaces like taverns and inns. In the latter decades of the antebellum period, prostitution adapted itself to new cultural emphases on women's relationship to the domestic sphere and – in a departure from the economy of makeshifts model – became increasingly professionalized. While older, more casual forms of sex work did not disappear – indeed, they continued to be common, particularly in East Baltimore – the 1820s and 1830s witnessed the rise of brothels where a number of sex workers resided full-time and labored – at least in part – under the direction of a madam who profited from their sexual labor.

Eliza Randolph was at the forefront of the transition to brothel prostitution. Although she started as a sex worker in the 1830s, she quickly advanced to the position of manager in one of Elizabeth Osborne's houses. Randolph's status as a madam positioned her to reap significant financial rewards; growing demands for sexual services among professional men ensured that prostitution, once largely a subsistence strategy among poorer women, became a highly profitable industry in Baltimore. Within a few years, she had amassed enough capital to strike out on her own. In the early 1840s, she purchased a 33' × 50' lot of land at the intersection of Park and Clay Streets, just east of Lexington Market.[7]

[6] Boydston, *Home and Work*; Stansell, *City of Women*.
[7] Baltimore City (Register of Wills), Inventories, 1868–1869, Book 88, Eliza Randolph, pp. 171–74, MSA T603-22; "Baltimore: Correspondent of the Whip," *The Whip*, July 2, 1842, in *The Flash Press*, 190–91.

There, she paid for the construction of a three-story brick dwelling that she opened as a brothel. Her house, which quickly became famed as one of Baltimore's preeminent upscale parlor houses, boarded nearly a dozen white women who worked full-time catering to the demands of lower professionals, artisans, and country merchants.[8] The cleanliness, gentility, and decorum that Randolph demanded from her boarders would make hers a model establishment for the many Baltimore madams who sought to attract the patronage of men who could afford to pay more for sexual services. The expectations that Randolph placed on sex workers and the nature of her interactions with them provide a window into the ways in which the sex trade evolved, professionalized, and grew more exclusive in terms of who was allowed to participate in the more organized sectors of the trade.

In Baltimore and many other major US cities, prostitution expanded dramatically after 1820. Commercial sex had been a part of urban life since the eighteenth century, but the post–War of 1812 transportation revolution and the ensuing growth of cities fueled the development of a sex trade whose size and level of commercialization far exceeded that of the colonial period or early republic. With the construction of turnpikes, roads, and canals and the nationwide embrace of commerce and the expansion of markets, port cities like New York, Philadelphia, Boston, and Baltimore all attracted large numbers of new residents in the middle decades of the nineteenth century. Baltimore, whose early fortunes were boosted significantly by the construction of the National Road linking Cumberland, Maryland, to Wheeling, Virginia, experienced especially rapid growth. Between 1820 and 1860, the city's population increased from roughly 63,000 people to more than 212,000, with much of the expansion resulting from migration.[9] As the city's commercial fortunes expanded with its links to the West, newly emancipated enslaved people flocked to the city from the countryside in search of nonagricultural work; German and Irish immigrants arrived via ships after fleeing civil wars and famine; and young men and women from all around Maryland and the surrounding states came to the city in the hopes of securing employment. The city's growing resident population was augmented by seasonal

[8] 1840 US Census, Baltimore, Maryland, Ward 7, p. 29, Eliza Randolph; 1850 US Census, Baltimore, Maryland, Ward 13, p. 358, dwelling 1396, family 1522, Eliza Randolph.
[9] James D. Dilts, *The Great Road: The Building of the Baltimore and Ohio, the Nation's First Railroad, 1828–1853* (Stanford, CA: Stanford University Press, 1993), 281–83; William R. Sutton, *Journeymen for Jesus: Evangelical Artisans Confront Capitalism in Jacksonian Baltimore* (University Park: Pennsylvania State University Press, 1998), 141.

workers, sailors and other temporary visitors, and merchants and farmers who carted goods and produce to and from the countryside via the city's improved commercial gateways.[10] As the population grew, so too did the sex trade. By the 1830s, Baltimore newspapers were complaining of "open profligacy" about town, and prosecutions for offenses like keeping a bawdy house rose significantly from previous years.[11] The number of bawdy or disorderly house cases prosecuted in 1840 were double what they had been in 1830, with cases that were specifically designated as bawdy cases rising from seven to thirty-three.[12]

Just as prostitution in the early years of the century was a product of the transience and economic disjuncture that characterized life in maritime neighborhoods, prostitution's expansion in the latter decades of the antebellum period was the result of a number of related transformations in economic and family life. The same expansion of markets that drove the growth of American cities also brought profound disruptions to the intimate lives of people of all social classes. As much as Americans in the nineteenth century imagined – indeed, insisted – that the worlds of commerce and the domestic realm were separate, changes in the nature of production and work altered men's and women's relationship to sex, marriage, and family in fundamental ways. With household production declining and a growing number of people moving out of agricultural work, early marriage and large families ceased to be the default, especially for middling men and women. By the mid-nineteenth century, the average age at first marriage was twenty-six for men and just over twenty-two for women, a slight increase from the colonial period.[13]

At the same time that marriage ages crept upward, the relationship between sex and marriage was also changing. Toleration for premarital sexuality declined, with women in particular facing heavy social stigma for engaging in sexual activity outside wedlock.[14] Sex within marriage was also curtailed in some cases. Although many nineteenth-century

---

[10] Rockman, *Scraping By*, 16–44.

[11] Howard, "To the Editors of the Baltimore Sun," *Sun*, May 28, 1838.

[12] BCC, 1830 and 1840.

[13] James Matthew Gallman, "Relative Ages of Colonial Marriages," *Journal of Interdisciplinary History* 14 (Winter, 1984): 609–17; Catherine A. Fitch and Steven Ruggles, "Historical Trends in Marriage Formation: The United States 1850–1990," in *The Ties That Bind: Perspectives on Marriage and Cohabitation*, ed. Linda J. Waite et al. (New York: Aldine de Gruyer, 2000), 63; Gilfoyle, *City of Eros*, 102.

[14] Lyons, *Sex among the Rabble*, Part III; Daniel Scott Smith and Michael S. Hindus, "Premarital Pregnancy in America 1640–1971: An Overview and Interpretation," *Journal of Interdisciplinary History* 5 (Spring, 1975): 537–70.

Americans embraced sexuality as an important part of marital life, others limited sexual activity for reasons of health or reproductive control. The growth of the manufacturing and commercial economy and land short-ages in the countryside encouraged middling couples who aspired to upward mobility for themselves and their offspring to have fewer chil-dren. As Susan Klepp has argued, women in the post-Revolutionary era often sought to divorce themselves from the constant pressure to reproduce and embraced "rationalized marshaling of resources through family planning."[15] While married women sometimes accomplished this feat through the use of emmenagogues, or herbal remedies to induce menstruation, others resorted to abstinence as a means of family plan-ning.[16] As the stigma against nonreproductive sexuality increased among Protestants and evangelicals – some of whom borrowed the language of economics to argue that the body had a sexual economy that required "saving" rather than "spending" bodily fluids – the practice of limiting sex within marriage became a marker of civility and restraint among some Americans.[17]

Later marrying ages, stigma against "respectable" women's participa-tion in extramarital sexuality, and strategic family planning all combined to increase the demand for sex that could be had through commercial transactions. Baltimore was well poised to meet that demand. The con-stant bustle of people into and out of the growing city created a sense of anonymity, one that gave rise to new cultures of sexuality and sexual license. Close family ties and community surveillance characterized life in rural America, but urbanization disrupted these older practices. As an increasing number of people moved to cities in search of work or visited seasonally to transport goods, opportunities for young men and women to exist independent of family control increased. Transient boarding arrangements and the accessibility of wages that were theirs to control enabled men to form their own sexual subcultures. Young working men, including members of the middle class, patronized sex workers frequently. In some cases, they did so as part and parcel of a masculine culture rooted in free sexual expression and domination of women; in other cases, they

[15] Susan E. Klepp, *Revolutionary Conceptions: Women, Fertility, and Family Limitation in America, 1760–1820* (Chapel Hill: University of North Carolina Press, 2009), 8.

[16] Klepp, *Revolutionary Conceptions*, 180–214.

[17] Klepp, *Revolutionary Conceptions*, 180–214. See also Thomas Laqueur, "Sexual Desire and the Market Economy during the Industrial Revolution," in *Discourses of Sexuality: From Aristotle to AIDS*, ed. Domna C. Stanton (Ann Arbor: University of Michigan Press, 1992), 185–215.

sought out companionship and the simulacra of traditional courting behavior. Sometimes, it was a complicated mix of both.[18]

As influxes of transient workers, travelers, and merchants drove the demand for sexual services among men, changes in the nature of manufacturing and exclusion of women from well-paid employment ensured that there was a ready supply of women to provide them. The same disruptions to older economic arrangements that prompted men to seek work in the city also displaced a number of wives, sisters, and daughters from their roles within the household economy. Women who came to cities like Baltimore in the hope of securing employment that would allow them to send money home or to support themselves faced mixed prospects. In the warmer months of the year, female laborers were in demand as middle-class households sought out domestics and as tailors and other artisans sought out semi-skilled workers whose "slop" labor could be had more cheaply than that of male artisans. However, seasonal lulls in production made work scarce in the colder months, and women's wages were low even when work was steady. Domestics could expect to make only $8–$10 per month, while seamstresses taking piecework often made half as much.[19]

Women's difficulties in earning a living were less a product of the actual market value of their labor than of an increasingly influential ideology that relegated them to the role of dependents to their husbands and fathers. As Chapter 1 made clear, such ideologies were not new in the 1820s; indeed, they dated back nearly a century. However, in a fundamental irony, notions of natural female dependency gained the most cultural ground during the very period that the mobile nature of labor was ensuring that more women than ever were not attached to familial households. A post–War of 1812 recasting of the laborer as male and the rise of a religiously influenced concept of separate spheres in the 1820s and 1830s affirmed women's marginalization within the world of waged

---

[18] On masculine cultures of sexual license, see Cohen, *The Murder of Helen Jewett*, 10–11, 238, 403; Patricia Cline Cohen, Timothy J. Gilfoyle, and Helen Lefkowitz Horowitz, *The Flash Press: Sporting Male Weeklies in 1840s New York* (Chicago: University of Chicago Press, 2008); Gilfoyle, *City of Eros*, 102.

[19] Rockman, *Scraping By*, 100–31, 140, 142; Margaret Lynch-Brennan, *The Irish Bridget: Irish Immigrant Women in Domestic Service in America, 1840–1930* (Syracuse: Syracuse University Press, 2009), 90–91. See also William Sanger, *The History of Prostitution: Its Extent, Causes, and Effects throughout the World* (New York: Harper & Brothers, 1859), 526–27.

labor, even as more women than ever took up waged work. The result was that compensation for women's labor remained largely below subsistence level.[20] Employers, citing the notion that women's wages need only be supplemental to those of a male wage earner or a "family wage," justified paying women only a fraction of the actual value of their labor, usually far less than they could live on. At the same time, employers' use of women's labor to drive down the cost of producing ready-made clothing or packaging tobacco also reduced the number of well-paying jobs available to men and exacerbated household dependence on women's wage earning.[21]

The disjuncture between the notion that women should not be workers and the reality that many poor white and black women could not hope to survive without laboring for a wage virtually guaranteed that there would be a steady supply of women who had to sell sex in order to make ends meet. The connections between poor wages and prostitution were apparent even to Americans at the time. In an article asserting the right of seamstresses to better compensation, Philadelphian Mathew Carey argued that the paltry wages paid to women left them to choose between "STARVATION OR POLLUTION."[22] A Baltimore editorialist with the moniker Magdalene claimed that the low wages and poor working conditions of domestic servants were responsible for luring into prostitution "those unprotected girls who are doomed to toil for a mere pittance, and whose residence in a respectable family depends on their submission without repining, to every species of petty tyranny, contempt, and imposition."[23] While the melodramatic registers of claims that low-paid women would become "a disgrace to their sex, and a bane and a curse to society" arguably reinforced female dependency by casting women as objects of charity rather than as independent workers, they nevertheless held a grain of truth.[24] Many women who worked for a wage existed in a state of nearly constant economic vulnerability in which the possibility of having to sell sex to get by was never a distant one.

---

[20] Boydston, *Home and Work*, 54.

[21] Boydston, *Home and Work*; Rockman, *Scraping By*, 100–131.

[22] Mathew Carey, *Miscellaneous Essays* (Philadelphia: Carey and Hart, 1830), 194. Originally quoted in Rockman, *Scraping By*, 143. See also Lori Merish, *Archives of Labor: Working-Class Women and Literary Culture in the Antebellum United States* (Durham, NC: Duke University Press, 2017), chapter 3.

[23] Magdalene, "Letter to the Editor," *Sun*, Apr. 2, 1840.

[24] Carey, *Miscellaneous Essays*, 279–80.

Baltimore women who entered sex work after the 1820s found themselves laboring in a trade whose geographies were much expanded from the small, maritime-based trade that had thrived in the early nineteenth century. As the rise of transportation infrastructures in the western part of the city created new commercial gateways, new sites of sexual exchange cropped up alongside sites of commercial trade and mobility. Chief among these sites was the new business district. In the early days of the city, the blocks to the north of Baltimore's harbor basin had been filled with groggeries and cheap housing. However, as the city's boosters sought to secure its status as a center of commercial transport and trade in the early nineteenth century, they scrambled to replace ramshackle dwellings and undeveloped land with commercial buildings befitting one of America's major ports. In 1816, a group of prominent Baltimore businessmen with an eye to expanding trade formed the Baltimore Exchange Company, whose mission was "to erect, for the purposes of commercial utility, a public building in the city of Baltimore."[25] Four years later, the Baltimore Exchange opened in the area just west of Gay Street and bounded by Second and Lombard Streets. The four-story complex housed offices, counting rooms, a bank, a reading room, a hotel, and a branch of the US Customs Office and was intended not just to facilitate commercial and financial transactions but also to project the power and status of the young city with its size, grandeur, and ornamentation. Three decades later, local merchant Johns Hopkins, who made his fortune in the country trade before investing in railroads, erected his own Commercial Buildings to achieve a similar purpose.

Just three years after the Exchange Building opened for business, the prominent Baltimore novelist John Neal drew a parallel between central Baltimore's commercial pretensions and the rise of a certain kind of gendered falseness in the city. W.H.O., a character in Neal's 1823 novel *Randolph*, wrote that the Exchange was "the best contrived building, and, to my taste, more entirely beautiful, of the kind, than any that I have ever seen, except that at Berlin." And yet, he continued:

Here is the same base, showy spirit, of which I have before complained. It is plastered all over; and this plaster is cunningly managed, by the application of gray paint, to look like stone; nay, even the real stone about it, is *painted*. Upon my word, I should, prefer the sober honesty of Dutch brick; – this is *rouging*, with a vengeance.[26]

W.H.O. went on to draw a relationship between the city's physical development and the emergence of "painted woman," a figure that came to symbolize anxieties about the deception that urban anonymity, mobility, and the increased availability of material markers of gentility could foster: "The publick authorities, and publick edifices, paint and patch, and cheat; and how can they have the face to scold the women for such things?"[27] While "painted women" were not necessarily sex workers in the parlance of the nineteenth century, Neal's statement was prophetic regarding the effects that the expansion of commercial infrastructures had on the development of the sex trade. The neighborhoods around Baltimore's "rouged" commercial buildings would gradually be filled with "rouged" women who feigned fanciness as did the built environment.[28] The Meadow, which sat in the northern part of the city just blocks away from commercial buildings and mercantile exchanges, developed a thriving sex trade by the 1830s.[29] By 1841, the area featured at least seven bawdy houses.[30]

At the same time that the Meadow developed as a site of prostitution at the borders of the business district, sex workers also began to relocate to land-based transportation corridors. Women like Eliza Randolph moved into the area around Park and Garden Streets to take advantage of the proximity to Howard Street, Lexington Market, and the drop-off points for stagecoach lines and turnpikes that flowed into the city from the west. Traffic along those routes was often brisk, with Baltimore chronicler Thomas Scharf writing that during the busiest seasons, the area "westwardly from Howard Street, along Franklin to its junction with Pennsylvania Avenue, and out the avenue to George Street, and often beyond it ... [was] nightly blocked up by the ponderous Conestoga wagons."[31] Merchants, draymen, and rural visitors to the city who came bearing

---

[26] John Neal, *Randolph: A Novel in Two Volumes*, vol. 1 (Philadelphia, 1823), 60, 66–67.

[27] Neal, *Randolph*, 66–67.

[28] On painted women and their connection to prostitution, seduction, and insincerity, see Karen Halttunen, *Confidence Men and Painted Women: A Study of Middle-Class Culture in America, 1830–1870* (New Haven, CT: Yale University Press, 1982), xv, 106.

[29] James H. Miller, "Case Notes for Maria Gassaway," Alms-House Medical Record, 1833–1837, Maryland Historical Society, Baltimore, MD. Gassaway, a sex worker, claimed to have been seduced into the trade by a woman in the North part of the city.

[30] "City Court – October Term," *Sun*, Oct. 28, 1841.

[31] Scharf, *The Chronicles of Baltimore*, 406.

grain, flour, or tobacco were particularly likely customers for prostitution, and sex workers flocked to areas where they congregated in order to drum up business.

As urban boosters in the late 1820s began to construct railroads that they hoped would allow Baltimore to compete with the trade brought to New York by the Erie Canal, sex establishments would cluster around rail stations as well. The opening of the Susquehanna Railroad's Calvert Street Station in the fall of 1850 proved to be a particular boom for the Meadow, which sat in close proximity to its terminus. The station and rail depot opened on the corner of Calvert and Franklin Streets, just to the north and east of where Elizabeth Osborne and Eliza Randolph operated in the 1840s. It was a hub for passenger trains, eight to ten of which passed through or departed from Baltimore every day.[32] The location of the station ensured that many disembarking passengers had to walk through or around the Meadow on their way to hotels or connecting trains, which provided foot traffic to the vice district. By the time of the 1860 Census, enumerators noted that Ward 11, the area that encompassed much of the old Meadow, featured eleven "bawdy houses" and "houses of ill fame." In total, these houses had sixty-two "inmates," all single women, residing in them. The enumeration for Ward 10, which sat at the outskirts of the Meadow, included two additional dwellings. One of these housed fifteen women, including two servants and one woman who had been explicitly identified as a sex worker in other records.[33]

As prostitution expanded its geographies, it also changed its character. In the early nineteenth century, it had been common for commercial sex to take place in taverns, saloons, sailors' boardinghouses, and other spaces of mixed commerce. Although this continued to be the case in the Causeway, West Baltimore's sex trade and – to a more limited extent, the sex trade in Old Town's alleys – grew increasingly specialized as sex work moved into residential spaces. Assignation houses whose keepers made their money by renting rooms on an hourly or daily basis to sex workers and their clients appeared around Lexington Market and in

[32] Scharf, *History of Baltimore City and County*, 344–45; Weishampel, *The Stranger in Baltimore*, 147–48.

[33] All data cited here collected from the 1850 and 1860 US Federal Census Schedules for Baltimore City, Wards 10 and 11; US Federal Census, 1850; Ward 10, Baltimore, Maryland; Roll: M432_284; 59B-113; Ward 11, Baltimore, Maryland, Roll: M432_284, 114–217; US Federal Census, 1860, Ward 10, Baltimore (Independent City), Maryland; Roll: M653_461, 1–108; Ward 11, Baltimore (Independent City), Maryland; Roll: M653_463, 1–258.

Garden Street.[34] By the 1830s, board-in brothels gradually began to supplant more casual forms of prostitution in the Meadow. These houses, which varied in their affluence and characters, nevertheless shared the common traits of being supervised by a madam who managed (and sometimes owned) the establishment and of boarding women who labored as sex workers on a nearly full-time basis rather than casually or sporadically. Sexual exchange was at the core of their business models rather than one among many types of exchange in their establishments.

The rise of specialized sex establishments in the 1820s and 1830s was a product of a variety of factors, one of which was the emergence of brothels as part and parcel of a broader expansion of the city's service and leisure trades. The brothels that emerged in West Baltimore were located at the outskirts of Baltimore's central commercial district and situated alongside a number of other businesses designed to provide entertainment, room, and board to the city's growing body of professionals and visitors. Following the arrival of the B&O railroad, downtown, once home to a number of small, family inns, became a locus of what Baltimore chronicler Thomas Scharf referred to as "the finer buildings made necessary by railroads."[35] Fashionable visitors to the city could find lodging at David Barnum's City Hotel, opened in 1826; Eutaw House, opened in 1835; and Guy's Hotel, a 150-room establishment that opened on Monument Square in 1855.[36] As central Baltimore's quality lodgings attracted travelers and merchants to the area, a variety of eating and leisure venues. By 1860, Ward 9, an area just south of the Meadow, was home to six hotels, sixty restaurants, thirty-one bars, saloons, and taverns, and dozens of "segar" and confection shops.[37] In the face of such a proliferation of hotels, inns, restaurants, and shops, the keepers of sex establishments sought to complement rather than to compete with the offerings of other businesses in the commercial district. Instead of operating out of the hotels – most of which were run by wealthy capitalists who had little interest in allowing sex workers to mingle with their respectable patrons on their properties – sex workers took up residence in establishments where sex and flirtation were the primary draws for visitors.

---

[34] "City Court – June Term," *Sun*, June 14, 1841; "Assignation Houses," *Sun*, Mar. 3, 1840.

[35] Scharf, *History of Baltimore City and County*, 515.

[36] Scharf, *History of Baltimore City and County*, 515–17. See also A. K. Sandoval-Strausz, *Hotel: An American History* (New Haven, CT: Yale University Press, 2007).

[37] Statistics from a survey of the US Federal Census, 1860 Population Schedule, Ward 9, Baltimore City.

Brothels and assignation houses became part of a broader network of entertainment and leisure establishments downtown.

The rise of specialized sex establishments was made possible by sexual commerce's growing integration in the world of the emerging middle class. When selling sex had still been a trade directed primarily toward maritime clientele, both the women who sold sex and the property owners who allowed sex in their establishments had dabbled in a variety of commercial pursuits out of necessity. After all, sex alone did not pay well enough to achieve levels above basic subsistence. As prostitution became more integrated into the culture of the commercial and tourist districts, however, this changed. The growth of business and hotel districts transformed the neighborhoods that brothels inhabited from marginal communities into tony areas where the urban bourgeois felt comfortable gathering and spending their money. Park Street near where Eliza Randolph relocated from the Meadow had "once [been] as notorious for its damnable deeds as ever the 'Five Points' was in its Palmiest days," but by 1850 it was a thriving residential neighborhood that housed professional men and families.[38] Local tourism guides deemed it "the most fashionable part of the City" and urged visitors to Baltimore to stroll through it and admire its "elegant dwellings."[39] As white-collar men were drawn into the vicinity of the Meadow, Park Street, and other informal and loosely organized red-light districts, the market for sexual services expanded into the ranks of comparatively well-paid urban professionals and artisans. Establishments that were capable of attracting their business could command higher prices for the services of their female boarders and thus allow their keepers to support themselves without resorting to participating in other illicit commerce or economies of makeshifts.

The rise of brothels was further reinforced by changing demographic patterns and, more specifically, by the growing demand for housing that came with a mobile population. In the early days of Baltimore's development, casual forms of prostitution were able to thrive, in part, because many sex workers were local to the city. Anecdotes about parents seeking out their wayward daughters in their neighborhoods' brothels and mentions of older women venturing out to support children with their

[38] "Baltimore: Correspondent of the Whip," *The Whip*, July 2, 1842, in *The Flash Press*, 190–91.

[39] *The Stranger's Guide to Baltimore, Showing the Easiest and Best Mode of Seeing All the Public Buildings and Places of Note* (Baltimore: Murphy & Co., 1852), 15.

earnings abounded in the early years of the century.[40] Local women could visit taverns or sailors' boardinghouses to conduct business, stay for a short period, and then return home, an arrangement that rendered board-in sex establishments unnecessary.

By the 1830s, however, young women were coming to the city from the countryside, from other states, and even from across the Atlantic. Many of the newcomers did not have familial connections or places to stay in Baltimore, and some of them arrived with very little money to their names. For women who became sex workers in the 1830s and beyond, brothels often addressed basic housing needs. Provided that she was sufficiently suited for work in prostitution, a woman could enter a brothel at no upfront cost and pay the amount of her board through sexual labor. Census information bears out the idea that brothels held unique appeal to "strangers" to the city. Of the sixty women who lived in Ward 11's Meadow brothels in 1860, almost half were from places other than Maryland. Twenty women were from other US states or the District of Columbia, and seven were foreign-born. It is impossible to tell how many of the remaining thirty-three Maryland-born women were from Balti-more, but it is possible that many of them were new to the city as well.[41] Brothels provided women unfamiliar with Baltimore with shelter and nourishment in the form of daily suppers, as well as a ready supply of clients.

Brothels' ability to attract the patronage of middle-class men in a way that more casual sex establishments could not was rooted in the distinct-ive gender ideologies of the mid-nineteenth century. By the 1830s, middle-class Americans' ideas about the proper roles of men and women had grown more rigid. The ideology of "separate spheres" predominated among the urban bourgeois, who embraced the notion that women were inherently suited to the domestic world of the home and unsuited to the rough and tumble world of public life.[42] In practice, relatively few women outside the more privileged members of the white middle class could afford to avoid entering the "public" world of paid labor, but ability to exempt women from working outside the home nevertheless became an important marker of gentility and class status among more well-heeled

---

[40] For example, see "Depravity," *Sun*, June 13, 1839.
[41] 1860 US Census, Baltimore, Maryland, Ward 11.
[42] For a critical analysis of the concept of separate spheres, see, for example, Linda K. Kerber, "Separate Spheres, Female Worlds, Woman's Place: The Rhetoric of Women's History," *Journal of American History* 75 (June 1988): 9–39.

urbanites. The woman who retained a delicate refinement and remained within the home was a lady, while the woman who traversed the city streets and performed hard physical labor for a wage was "low" and questionable in her virtue. Although sex workers fell short of antebellum standards for genteel womanhood by virtue of their lack of chastity and sexual restraint, brothel denizens missed the mark less dramatically than their streetwalking peers did. One urban flaneur who visited the "Crossway" (Causeway) in the early 1840s commented that the neighborhood was of such low character that "if a girl leaves that path of rectitude and takes up her abode in this abominable place, she is at once sunk below (in the eyes of every respectable person) the brute creation." However, that same observer offered modest praise for Eliza Randolph's Park Street establishment, which he deemed suitably refined in its offerings and thus "fit for a person to enter."[43] The fact that brothels kept women relatively contained within a space that resembled a middle-class home in its décor and domestic pretensions was a nod to middle-class preferences for courting and sociability.[44] Ultimately, it enabled brothels to draw in men who would not deign to patronize streetwalkers or to solicit in taverns or groggeries.

Women who lived in board-in brothels found themselves laboring under different arrangements from those of their predecessors or peers in the more casual sectors of the sex trade. In early Baltimore's sex trade, most sex workers had worked independently, controlling the pace of their own labor and reserving its (often meager) financial benefits for themselves and their families. The rise of brothels, however, signaled a growing tendency toward capitalist labor arrangements within the sex trade. Women who entered indoor prostitution out of a need for housing or a desire for steadier working conditions found themselves laboring under the supervision of madams, most of whom were older women – in the Meadow, the average age of madams was thirty-six – who had once

---

[43] "Baltimore: Correspondent of the Whip," *The Whip*, July 2, 1842, in *The Flash Press*, 190–91.

[44] See Chapter 3 for more information on brothels' décor. Historian Ellen K. Rothman distinguished between "courtship," which was assumed to lead to marriage, and "courting," which might be used to encompass a variety of romantic, sexual, or affectionate activities that need not lead to marriage. Ellen K. Rothman, "Sex and Self-Control: Middle-Class Courtship in America, 1770–1870," *Journal of Social History* 15 (Spring, 1982): 409–25.

participated in prostitution but had since transitioned to managerial positions.[45] In some cases, supervision was loose, as madams conceived of themselves less as taskmasters and more as boardinghouse keepers who allowed their guests sexual freedoms in exchange for inflated rents. Such was the case with Jane Christopher, who described her house as "a boardinghouse for ladies where gentlemen might call occasionally and pay them a visit."[46] In many cases, however, madams played a more active role in enforcing labor discipline. Madams who took cuts of their boarders' earnings on top of what they charged for rent had a distinct interest in ensuring that women maintained a good place of labor, just as those who strove to present their clients with a genteel, cultivated had an interest in governing their tenants' conduct.[47] The rise of brothels effectively resulted in sex workers losing some of their independence and taking on a status similar to that of other waged workers.

The emerging classes of indoor sex establishments also introduced new levels of commercialization into the sex trade. The antebellum decades witnessed the expansion of markets and the development of a more self-consciously consumerist retail culture, and the women who composed the new managerial class within brothels were on the vanguard of applying their logics to sexual commerce. As the encroachment of the commercial district presented opportunities to draw a "better" class of men into brothels, madams seized them by creating experiences in shopping and sociability that they calculated would appeal to well-heeled clients. In order to render their brothels as more enticing sexual marketplaces for urban professionals and merchants, many calibrated every aspect of their houses – from the women housed in them to the practices of flirtation and monetary exchange – to suit the tastes of their patrons. They strove to create a kind of boutique atmosphere in their brothels, wherein male customers could "shop" for the type of woman they desired. It was not unusual for brothel keepers to board between half a dozen and a dozen sex workers in their houses, all carefully chosen to appeal to myriad

---

[45] Statistics derived from an examination of the 1860 US Census, Baltimore, Maryland, Ward 11.

[46] "Local Matters," *Sun*, Nov. 20, 1852.

[47] Data on rents charged to sex workers is lacking for antebellum Baltimore, but both contemporary accounts and historical ones from other cities note that it was common for madams to charge both inflated rents and bed fees. See, for example, Gilfoyle, *City of Eros*, 168–70; Cohen, *The Murder of Helen Jewett*, 111.

tastes. One visitor to Eliza Randolph's house commented that it boasted "about a dozen girls of all sizes, shapes and ages."[48]

While brothelkeepers catered to a variety of tastes, they particularly favored young women who could project an air of innocence and inexperience in matters of sexuality, as demureness often played into male fantasies of prostitution. As numerous historians have noted, virgins were considered especially desirable in the context of the sex trade, not only because they were sometimes believed to cure sexually transmitted infections but also because their deflowering provided men with a special sense of dominance or victory. Visitors to brothels often dwelled on sex workers' apparent youthfulness and innocence. One commenter on Baltimore's vice scene wrote of Eliza Randolph's brothel:

There is one [woman] I particularly noted for her extreme youthful appearance and modest deportment; one profane word uttered by any one, would cause a blush to crimson her spotless cheek for very shame. At first sight of her, I knew the sphere she was then filling was not suited to her nature. Oh! that she could be "plucked as a brand from the burning," she would yet be an honor to her family and society.[49]

Like most brothel descriptions found in sporting papers, the man's description of the sex worker functioned on two levels. Ostensibly, it lamented that a young woman so innocent found her way into a sex establishment; print media – sporting papers in particular – had to be careful to cloak features that might be interpreted as advertisements for brothels in condemnatory, moralistic language. At the same time, the supposed "tragedy" of virtuous young women's fall from grace was also a thrill for the man who might claim her innocence. Some men seemed particularly to enjoy the idea of "ruining" a woman who might otherwise be fit for courtship in their ordinary lives. In either case, brothel clients wished to purchase women who did not look like they should be for sale, and madams did their best to provide.[50]

---

[48] "Baltimore: Correspondent of the Whip," *The Whip*, July 2, 1842, in *The Flash Press*, 190–91.

[49] "Baltimore: Correspondent of the Whip," *The Whip*, July 2, 1842, in *The Flash Press*, 190–91.

[50] On the eroticization of virginity, see Gilfoyle, *City of Eros*, 68–70, 349, n. 33; Mary Spongberg, *Feminizing Venereal Disease: The Body of the Prostitute in Nineteenth-Century Medical Discourse* (New York: New York University Press, 1997), 110–12; Donna Dennis, *Licentious Gotham: Erotic Publishing and Its Prosecution in Nineteenth-Century New York* (Cambridge, MA: Harvard University Press, 2009), 100; Steve

Some madams appeared to tap into niche markets within the trade, ones that commodified particular "types" of women. Ann Thomas, who kept a house in the Meadow, apparently catered to men who favored younger and less experienced sex workers. Save for a boarder who was probably her sister, Thomas boarded no women over the age of twenty – or, at least, none who admitted that she was over the age of twenty. Bell Young, a sex worker who moved brothels during the census enumeration period in 1860, gave her age as twenty to the census taker who recorded her presence in the brothel of Ann Wilson (no relation to the Fells Point brothel keeper) on June 18, 1860. When she moved to Ann Thomas's house ten days later, Young gave her age as eighteen.[51] Still other brothel keepers traded on novelty; Annette Travers's brothel in the Meadow, for instance, housed two twenty-five-year-old women who were most likely a set of twins.[52]

In addition to cultivating a variety of workers for their establishments, madams specifically sought out boarders who were capable of interacting comfortably with middle-class and professional men in ways that satisfied their standards for social decorum (minus the sexual restrictions, of course). One of the most popular types of brothels in antebellum Baltimore was the parlor house, which was an establishment organized around a large parlor where men could chat with one another, drink, and engage in flirtation with women before retiring to the bedrooms upstairs with their chosen sex worker. Parlor houses, to a greater degree than assignation houses or rented room houses, demanded that sex workers entertain guests and socialize in ways that resembled courting behavior. In order to ensure that sex workers could satisfy this requirement, madams sought out women capable of projecting an air of gentility. In reality, such "airs" were just that; most women who sold sex in brothels were from economic backgrounds not dissimilar to those of streetwalkers or casual sex workers. Literacy rates among sex workers in even the most upscale houses were 10 percentage points lower than the national average for women, which suggests that many sex workers had

Marcus, *The Other Victorians: A Study of Sexuality and Pornography in Mid-Nineteenth-Century England* (New York: Basic Books, 2009), 156–57.

[51] 1860 US Census, Baltimore, Maryland, Ward 11, p. 239, dwelling 1399, family 1525, Bell Young; 1860 US Census, Baltimore, Maryland, Ward 11, p. 132, dwelling 840, family 889, Bell Young.

[52] 1860 US Census, Baltimore, Maryland, Ward 11, p. 128, dwelling 815, family 859, Ann Traverse.

grown up poor and without the benefit of education.[53] However, madams took on boarders who could conceal their backgrounds and behave according to the standards of higher classes. Many brothel keepers barred women from engaging in the sort of ungenteel behaviors that were common in the lower tiers of the sex trade, including drinking to excess during working hours, swearing or using overly lewd language, fighting, or supplementing their income through theft.[54]

Madams also enforced strict standards of cleanliness among women in their houses, for practical as well as cultural and class-based reasons. As Kathleen Brown has noted, bodily cleanliness – having good breath, white teeth, clean clothing, and minimal body odor – was an important signifier of gentility from the eighteenth century onward.[55] Sex workers who hoped to attract the attentions of middle-class and professional men had to adapt to genteel hygiene and beauty standards common among the urban bourgeois. Upscale brothels required women to wash their faces, hands, and genitals with soap regularly. Their keepers equipped every bedroom with washstands to assist them in that purpose. Estate inventories from Eliza Randolph's house record a total of twelve washstands (some apparently quite fancy and valued at $10 each), or one for each boarder in her house.[56] Hannah Smithson's smaller assignation and bawdy house featured six washstands made of pine, marble, or curled maple, as well as five wash bowls, several water pitchers, and a "tooth mug" used to hold a toothbrush.[57] Brothels also enforced high standards of dress and grooming. Every bedroom of a brothel typically included dressing mirrors that assisted women in grooming routines and dressers for the storage of clothing.

---

[53] US Census, Population Schedule, Baltimore Ward 10, Baltimore (Independent City), Maryland; Roll: M653_461, 1–108; Baltimore Ward 11, Baltimore (Independent City), Maryland; Roll: M653_463, 1–258; Catherine Hobbs, "Introduction: Cultures and Practices of U.S. Women's Literacy," in *Nineteenth-Century Women Learn to Write*, ed. Catherine Hobbs (Charlottesville: University of Virginia Press, 1995), 12.

[54] On the restrictions placed on sex workers' conduct, see, for instance, Sanger, *The History of Prostitution*, 541, 551.

[55] Kathleen Brown, *Foul Bodies: Cleanliness in Early America* (New Haven, CT: Yale University Press, 2009), especially chapter 5.

[56] Baltimore City (Register of Wills), Inventories, 1868–1869, Book 88, Eliza Randolph, pp. 171–74, MSA T603-22.

[57] Baltimore County Register of Wills (Orphan's Court Proceedings), December Term, 1848, Hannah Smithson, C396-24; BCRW (Inventories), January 4, 1848, Inventory of Hannah Smithson, C340-61.

Because the image of gentility that brothels demanded sex workers to project was accessible only to women who met certain physical and cultural standards, brothel prostitution was far more exclusionary than other types of sex work. Whereas it was not unusual in the informal sectors of the sex trade for women of all ages, racial makeups, and marital statuses to sell sex alongside one another, brothel prostitutes came from a much narrower demographic range. As of 1860, all of the sex workers who resided in brothels in the Meadow were white and between the ages of sixteen and thirty-three, with the average age being twenty-three. None of them was raising children (at least not in the establishments themselves), and all of them appeared to be single. This would be a common pattern in West Baltimore's brothels, which were overwhelmingly populated by young, white women.[58] Older women and black women of any age were seldom present.

Black women's exclusion from parlor houses had much to do with the intersecting and gender stereotypes. Black women were often portrayed by whites as inherently licentious and oversexed, traits that rendered them unsuitable for sex work in houses that catered to male fantasies of deflowering innocence or engaging in mock-courting practices. In a slave city like Baltimore, racial mixing in intimate spaces was itself controversial outside the context of a defined service relationship. Racial boundaries began to harden in the antebellum period as high-profile slave revolts sparked fears among urban residents and the rise of the abolition movement prompted Southern slaveholders to defend their "peculiar institution" in ever more strident terms. In keeping with the practices of both the respectable urban classes and the mobile slaveholding elite to whom they almost assuredly catered, brothel keepers maintained strict divisions between black and white women and employed only the latter as sex workers.[59]

Brothel keepers did, however, employ black women in other roles. In fact, they were particularly eager to have black women – slave or free –

---

[58] This observation is based on data collected from the 1850 and 1860 US Census enumerations from Baltimore Wards 10 and 11. The average age of Baltimore's brothel sex workers was roughly in line with the average age of sex workers in other cities. In his study of 2,000 sex workers in New York, William Sanger found that the bulk were between the ages of eighteen and twenty-three. Sanger, *The History of Prostitution*, 452–53. In Boston and Philadelphia, the average age of sex workers was between twenty-one and twenty-three years of age. Hobson, *Uneasy Virtue*, 86.

[59] Sarah Katz, "Rumors of Rebellion: Fear of a Slave Uprising in Post–Nat Turner Baltimore," *Maryland Historical Magazine* 89 (Fall 1994): 328–33.

serve as domestic servants in their establishments so that their presence might establish the prestige of the household and reinforce the gentility of the white sex workers. Elizabeth Osborne, who owned numerous Meadow houses and boarded eighteen young white women, claimed ownership of two enslaved people who did the work of maintaining her house. One, a boy under the age of ten, probably performed basic errands around Osborne's properties. The other, a woman between twenty-four and thirty-six, likely did all of the cooking and cleaning work. Osborne's command of enslaved labor undoubtedly added to her establishment's air of luxury and refinement, as slave-ownership was a mark of status in border cities like Baltimore.[60] It also made her unusual; most women in the brothel trade did not keep or own slaves.

However, many madams imitated the racial structures of wealthy Southern households by hiring free black or mulatto women as maids and housekeepers. Jane Cunningham employed two black women, Henny Williams and Lucy Little, as live-in domestic servants in her Meadow brothel.[61] Jane Robinson, who kept a brothel with four sex workers in Ward 6 in 1850, employed two live-in "mulatto" domestics, Elizabeth Linstance and Anna Warfield.[62] Not only did the presence of black women working as servants reinforce the affluence of particular houses, it also reinforced the gentility of white sex workers by exempting them from doing the dirty work of cooking, cleaning, and performing intimate labor like washing and dressing other women. As Kathleen Brown argued in her book *Foul Bodies*, notions of cleanliness and of who is "rightfully" allotted "dirty work" have historically functioned to establish and reinforce racial difference.[63] By relegating black women to performing dirty, difficult, and menial tasks around the household, brothel keepers like Osborne, Cunningham, and Robinson used black women's supposed "degradation" as a foil through which to establish white sex worker's femininity, fragility, and refinement.[64] The work that black women

---

[60] 1840 US Census, Baltimore, Maryland, Ward 7, p. 15 (stamped), Elizabeth Osborne.

[61] 1860 US Census, Baltimore, Maryland, Ward 11, p. 132, dwelling 838, family 887, Jane Cunningham. New York's first-class houses had arrangements similar to Baltimore's. According to William Sanger, New York brothels typically employed between three and seven servants, who were "almost invariably colored women." Sanger, *The History of Prostitution*, 554.

[62] 1850 US Census, Baltimore, Maryland, Ward 6, p. 359, dwelling 180, family 214, Jane Robinson.

[63] Brown, *Foul Bodies*, 252–54.

[64] Numerous historians have noted that white women defined themselves racially by highlighting their differences from black women. See Marisa J. Fuentes, *Dispossessed Lives:*

performed in brothels freed white brothel denizens to enjoy significant amounts of free time, during which they could read novels, exchange letters, and otherwise engage in cultural pursuits.

Black women were employed as sex workers in a few black-owned houses, but such establishments were generally few and far between. Although Baltimore had the largest free black population in the nation by the mid-nineteenth century, its rates of black property ownership lagged behind those of other, comparably sized cities.[65] Poverty, housing shortages, and lack of social connections to wealthier landlords made it difficult for black women to gain access to suitable properties for sex establishments, just as legal and structural barriers like curfews hampered the operations of their houses. Harriet Price (alias Carroll or Anderson), one of antebellum Baltimore's few black madams, owned and managed brothels in Old Town's Low Street and Salisbury Alleys for at least fourteen years. Price's establishments were not lavish by any means, and they certainly did not command the kind of prices for sexual services that Meadow establishments did.[66] And yet they were the most prestigious black-owned brothels in the city. Prior to the 1850s, Price was the sole black woman to appear in extant City Court records as a bawdy-house keeper.[67] After 1850, black women gained some ground in the trade: sixteen were charged in the City Court with keeping a bawdy house over the course of three sample years. Not all of these women kept houses that qualified as brothels, however, and black women remained underrepresented among the proprietors of sex establishments. Although black men and women collectively made up 13 percent of Baltimore's total population in the 1850s, they made up only 4 percent of those charged

---

Enslaved Women, Violence, and the Archive (Philadelphia: University of Pennsylvania Press, 2016), 86–87. See also Deborah Gray White, Ar'n't I a Woman? Female Slaves in the Plantation South (New York: W. W. Norton, 1999); Hartigan-O'Connor, "Gender's Value in the History of Capitalism," 631.

[65] Phillips, Freedom's Port, 98.

[66] Harriet Price's frequent name changes appear to have been the result of her taking the last names of her male partners. For a time, Price was "mistress" to a free man of color named Giles Price, who worked as a blacksmith and thief in Baltimore ("Central Watch-Saturday Morning, Aug. 16," Sun, Aug. 29, 1837). After their relationship dissolved, she married a man named Carroll, whose last name she also assumed. "Central Watch-Saturday Morning, Aug. 16," Sun, Aug. 29, 1837. On Price's indictments, see, for example, BCC, October Term, 1839, Case 246, Harriet Price; BCC, June Term, 1841, Case 534, Harriot Price; BCC, May Term, 1846, Case 428, Harriot Price.

[67] Baltimore City Court records exist only for the years 1821, 1825, 1826, 1828, 1830, 1839, 1840, 1841, 1846, 1847, and 1849.

with keeping bawdy houses.[68] Black women who wished to work in the indoor sex trade thus found themselves with severely limited options, and most black sex workers remained streetwalkers.

Though racism undoubtedly played a major role in black women's exclusion from brothel prostitution, it is also possible that black sex workers preferred less formal labor arrangements within sex work. Brothels required women to submit to supervision and regimented sexual labor. For women who had been enslaved or who otherwise had long histories of laboring in white households, such arrangements may have been less desirable than casual forms of prostitution that offered more independence and flexibility. Brothel prostitution was also not open to women who bore child-rearing responsibilities, as many black women did. Despite the fact that streetwalking and other forms of casual sex work provided more modest compensation than brothel prostitution, they were decidedly more accommodating to women who had households to maintain and children to raise. The lack of black-owned brothels may have resulted in part from brothels' unsuitability as a labor arrangement for black women.[69]

Women who did take up residence in brothels found that the expectations placed on them extended beyond a certain standard of bodily hygiene and a willingness to board in-house and work full-time as sex workers. Brothels, especially those that were higher-end parlor houses, often required that women perform not just sexual but also emotional forms of labor. Whereas casual prostitution was often based on a relatively direct exchange of money for intercourse, brothel prostitution tended to feature more prolonged social interactions between sex workers and their male clients. Men who patronized brothels yearned for heterosocial interaction and the trappings of courting, and some even made a habit of making social calls to brothels even when they did not expect – or could not afford – to purchase sex. The design and furnishing of brothels reflected these habits and desires. High-end brothels in particular featured parlors furnished with sofas, spittoons, rocking chairs, pianos, and art on

---

[68] Statistics gathered from surveys of the Baltimore City Court (Criminal Docket) for the years listed in note 67.

[69] Rockman, *Scraping By*, 24, 54. Some historians have suggested that black women's experiences of sexual exploitation under slavery may have made them especially reluctant to embrace prostitution. See, for example, John D'Emilio and Estelle B. Freedman, *Intimate Matters: A History of Sexuality in America*, 3rd edition (Chicago: University of Chicago Press, 2012), 136–37.

the walls, all of which were intended to allow men and women to linger and socialize as a group outside the bedroom. Women who worked in parlor houses were expected to charm and regale gentlemen callers in the parlor by playing the piano, singing, discussing culture or current events, or otherwise engaging in witty conversation.[70]

Sustaining men's interest through flirtation and charm required women to possess good conversational skills and a general adeptness at social interaction. This was especially true given the challenges that came with managing interactions that deliberately blurred the boundaries between explicit commercial exchange and "authentic" intimacy. High-end houses catered to men who simultaneously relished their ability to pay high prices for access to an exclusive sexual space and enjoyed the fantasy that their interactions with sex workers extended beyond the cash nexus. Women who worked in brothels were required to sustain the fiction that their interest in men extended beyond money and that they felt genuine attraction and even affection for their clients. Indeed, this illusion was such a core part of some high-end brothels' appeal that men could become deeply embittered if it was shattered. One brothel guide published in New York in 1859 complained that women in Eliza Randolph's brothel failed to obscure the cash nexus in their dealings with their male visitors. "This lady keeps a first class house," the reviewer wrote, "but we don't like her arrangements[.] It's either treat, trade, or travel. Gentlemen are not over fond of such disgusting language, especially from such pretty young ladies."[71] The unconcealed commercialism of an establishment where women insisted that men purchase drinks for women (treat), buy sex from them (trade), or leave (travel) was off-putting to men who yearned for a more sociable experience.

The reviewer of Eliza Randolph's house finished his commentary on the brothel with a short couplet, "Oh, you little fellows, / Don't us whores see fun." The couplet, which implied that the prostitutes in Randolph's establishments condescended to and took advantage of their clients, was unusual for its use of the term "whores."[72] That vulgar descriptor was

---

[70] Estate inventories of brothels frequently listed sofas, rocking chairs, and pianos. See also the account of Harry Davies published in Norma Cuthbert, *Lincoln and the Baltimore Plot, 1861: From the Pinkerton Records and Related Papers* (San Marino, CA: Huntington Library, 1949), 29–30.

[71] Free Loveyer, *Directory to the Seraglios in New York, Philadelphia, Boston and All the Principal Cities in the Union* (New York, 1859), 37. Thanks to Eric Robinson of the New York Historical Society for his assistance with this source.

[72] Loveyer, *Directory to the Seraglios*, 37.

seldom applied to brothel workers, and it was almost certainly intended to be demeaning. Women who failed to maintain the right emotional posture and to manage their clients' experiences appropriately could easily lose status in the eyes of the men who patronized them, which might in turn lead to outbursts of violence. As a result, the stakes of emotional labor and its satisfactory performance were high for women who labored within brothels.

While brothel prostitution demanded a great deal from women and deprived them of a portion of their earnings, it also offered sex workers a number of benefits. One of these was comparative protection from the policing that so often befell streetwalkers and sex workers in lower-end houses. Another was higher earning potential. When it came to sex, brothel keepers may not have owned the "means of production" in the strictest sense, but they did own the means of increasing the value of sexual labor. By presenting a cultivated, tastefully decorated space designed to cater to all preferences, madams made prostitution into a pastime suitable for men who could afford to pay more for sexual services. Madams' investments in their houses (detailed more in Chapter 3) also allowed sex workers to surround themselves with material signifiers of gentility, which enabled them to "increas[e] the value of the commodity they offered for sale" and live in relative comfort.[73] One commenter in 1840 described Baltimore's brothel workers as experiencing "flattery, pleasure, finery and gold ... friendship, gay delight, licentiousness and extravagance."[74] While this was doubtless an exaggeration – and while evidence on pricing and sexual services is sketchy for antebellum Baltimore – there are indications that the fanciest brothels charged $2–$5 for a single sexual encounter and could earn each sex worker $25–$50 per week or more in income even after madams extracted rent or cuts. Women laboring in smaller or more middling brothels might earn somewhat less, but they nevertheless earned more than casual sex workers, who performed sex as part of an economy of makeshifts and who operated on a virtual barter system at times, or their peers in "legitimate" occupations. Women who performed domestic

---

[73] Rebecca Yamin, "Wealthy, Free, and Female: Prostitution in Nineteenth-Century New York," *Historical Archaeology* 39, no. 1 (2005): 4–18, p. 4; Katherine Hijar, "Sexuality, Print, and Popular Visual Culture in the United States, 1830–1870," PhD dissertation, Johns Hopkins University, 2008, pp. 457–516.

[74] Magdalene, "Letter to the Editor," *Sun*, Apr. 2, 1840.

labor in the 1840s might expect to make less in a month than some brothel workers made in one night.[75]

Although madams sometimes extracted substantial portions of sex workers' earnings via rents or other fees, women who labored in brothels were skilled at negotiating for preferential employment terms. Brothel prostitution was less casual than streetwalking and tavern prostitution, but it was nevertheless a fairly transient profession, and many women took advantage of their mobility to secure the best and most profitable labor arrangements. Sex workers typically changed brothels multiple times over the course of even the shortest of careers in prostitution. Elizabeth Black, who worked as a seamstress and an actress in the Baltimore Museum in between spates of selling sex, worked in half a dozen different brothels and assignation houses over the course of several years in the sex trade. In 1848, Black took up residence in a Holliday Street brothel kept by Mrs. Gray. On Christmas Eve of that year, she met Jane Christopher, who kept a house at 86 North Street in the Meadow. Black soon relocated to Christopher's brothel and resided with her sporadically over the next four years, each time spending two weeks to a month at her establishment. In between extended sojourns at Christopher's place, Black lived at Ann Bartlett's brothel in Potter Street twice, paid occasional visits to Mary Kelly's house in between longer stints of residing there, lived with Margaret Hamilton in Lovely Lane for a short time, and passed evenings in Mell Fry's saloon and bawdy house in Potter Street. When she was not living in a bawdy house, Black took full advantage of other commercial spaces the city had to offer. She visited the third tier of the Holliday Street Theater to solicit men and patronized Susan Creamer's and Alonzo Welsh's Parisian Restaurant. Though some of Black's frequent moves may have been the result of tensions caused by her drinking, she nevertheless exerted considerable agency in choosing

---

[75] Sanger, *The History of Prostitution*, 601. See also Gilfoyle, *City of Eros*, 60, 164. The profitability of brothel prostitution as compared with streetwalking varied over time and place. Kevin Mumford, Timothy Gilfoyle, and Elizabeth Alice Clement have all suggested that sex workers in the late nineteenth century preferred streetwalking to brothel prostitution because they could keep what they earned. Historian Luise White made a similar observation in her study of twentieth-century Nairobi. Other historians, including Cynthia Blair, have suggested that brothels provided better earning potential. Mumford, *Interzones*, 101–5; Clement, *Love for Sale*, especially chapter 3; Blair, *I've Got to Make My Livin'*; Luise White, *The Comforts of Home: Prostitution in Colonial Nairobi* (Chicago: University of Chicago Press, 1990), 13–16. See also Rosen, *The Lost Sisterhood*, 38–50.

where and how she worked within Baltimore's sex trade. By exercising mobility, sex workers forced madams to be competitive with their terms of employment.[76]

While some women moved brothels frequently in the hopes of finding the best labor arrangements, others – particularly those who intended to make a long-term career of prostitution – secured their fortunes by finding madams willing to mentor them. Despite their more hierarchical labor structures, brothels were not always sharply exploitative. Many madams got their starts as prostitutes and shared in the stigma that attached to sex workers within polite society. This shared experience of oppression and participation in a niche trade could create feelings of solidarity capable of bridging the gaps between management and labor.[77] Some madams behaved almost maternally toward women in their houses, and many allowed sex workers under their roofs to learn from them and take on responsibilities in their houses in preparation for eventual elevation into managerial roles. As a result, some brothel workers enjoyed significant upward mobility within the trade. It was not unusual for women who remained in prostitution for significant lengths of time to save enough money to strike out on their own in the business, as Eliza Randolph had done during her time in Elizabeth Osborne's houses. Randolph herself would go on to mentor Emma Morton, a young, Virginia-born woman of French descent who worked in her house in the early 1850s. By 1860, Morton had control of her own brothel in the Meadow and had gained a reputation as one of the area's most refined and prominent madams. Other women advanced into managerial positions when the owners of their houses went into retirement.[78]

The brothel trade attracted labor because it provided women with protection and (sometimes) opportunities for upward mobility, but its ultimate origins lay with the market revolution of the early nineteenth century. The rise of brothel prostitution reflected the growing commercialization of American society, the rise of capitalist labor arrangements, and the disruptions to intimate relationships that came with growing mobility and urbanization. As Baltimore's rapid growth

---

[76] "Criminal Court," *Sun*, Nov. 18, 1852; "Criminal Court," *Sun*, Nov. 20, 1852.

[77] Edith Houghton Hooker, *The Laws of Sex* (Boston: Gorham Press, 1921), 60; MVCR, vol. 1, 13–16.

[78] 1850 US Census, Baltimore, Maryland, Ward 13, p. 358, dwelling 1396, family 1522, Eliza Randolph and Emma Morton; 1860 US Census, Baltimore, Maryland, Ward 11, p. 238, dwelling 330, family 416, Emma Morton; 1850 US Census, Baltimore, Maryland, Ward 9, p. 358, dwelling 291, family 415, Margaret Hamilton.

as a port drew merchants, traders, sailors, and laborers into the city, older courting practices and family structures broke down. Men turned to commercial sex and to brothels modeled on middle-class homes to satisfy their desires for sex and intimacy, and they did so – ironically – during the very period that saw Americans defining the realms of the domestic and intimate as separate from the cash nexus. Meanwhile, the "gendered definition of labor" that cast women as dependents ensured that there was a steady supply of women who were willing to commodify their sexual and emotional labor in order to survive and thrive in a turbulent urban world. The brothel, which reflected in so many ways the racial, class, and gender stratifications of urban life, was emblematic of market capitalism's ability to shape and define even the most intimate realms of human experience.[79] It was also, as Chapter 3 will discuss, a commercial form that was deeply embedded in the broader world of urban capitalism and business.

---

[79] Historian Amy Dru Stanley made a similar argument for the late nineteenth century. Stanley, *From Bondage to Contract*, 219.

3

Brothel Prostitution and Antebellum Urban Commercial Networks

In the early 1840s, bawdy-house keeper Hannah Smithson faced a serious predicament. Smithson, who had entered the prostitution business as a proprietor just as the indoor trade was beginning to boom in the late 1830s, had attracted the attention of local citizens and authorities with her Garden Street house. The house was a lavish establishment in which Smithson rented rooms to sex workers and other couples seeking a place of assignation. Smithson, who wanted to reap the benefits of catering to a more affluent clientele, furnished it with hundreds of dollars' worth of personal property in order to make it attractive to men who could pay a premium for sexual services. Her efforts worked too well. In 1840 and 1841, local citizens complained that they had observed steady traffic of "respectable"-looking women and men into Smithson's house, an allegation that prompted public outcry. As prostitution grew more spatially segregated through the rise of brothels, many members of the public expected there to be a clear boundary between the worlds of "fallen" women and the worlds of respectable people. Smithson's perceived lack of respect for this boundary led to her being indicted for keeping an assignation house.[1]

Smithson, realizing that the charges against her were serious, hired a well-known local temperance speaker named T. Yates Walsh to be her lawyer and to mount a defense on her behalf. In the course of the ensuing trial, Walsh argued that any allegations that Smithson catered to

---

[1] "The City Court – March 7, 1840," *Sun*, Mar. 9, 1840; "Licentiousness," *Sun*, June 19, 1841; BCRW (Orphan's Court Proceedings), December Term, 1848, Hannah Smithson, C396-24; BCRW (Inventories), Jan. 4, 1848, Inventory of Hannah Smithson, C340-61.

respectable people were false. He claimed that Smithson was scrupulous in her letting policies; women of ill-repute could rent rooms for assignation, while genteel women and any men accompanying them were turned away. The odd respectable woman who did manage to enter the establishment was there for reasons that had nothing to do with sex: one was a medical attendant sent to treat Smithson for an unnamed chronic disease, another a deliverer of butter, another a seamstress sent to do sewing work for the house, and yet another a messenger sent to collect Smithson's payment for her children's board at school. A doctor who regularly attended to Smithson supported this account and affirmed that he had never seen anything untoward occurring on the premises.[2]

There was an irony at the heart of Walsh's strategy. By providing alternative explanations for non–sex workers' presence in the house, Walsh sought to assure the court that Hannah Smithson respected the hierarchies and gender conventions of nineteenth-century society. And yet, even as he argued that she maintained a clear separation between respectable and notorious people, he inadvertently highlighted the degree to which commercial exchange brought the two groups into contact with each other within the walls of her house. Admittedly, many of the commercial transactions that Smithson made were everyday exchanges – paying doctors and dairy sellers, clothing makers and school tutors – that were similar to those made in any urban household. However, the unique practices of conspicuous consumption required to create an upscale brothel ensured that madams like Smithson put large amounts of money into the local economy. The costs associated with brothel keeping, combined with the growing profitability of prostitution, ensured that madams in the 1830s and 1840s participated more extensively than ever before in the city's networks of credit and debt.

Women involved in indoor sex work forged complex economic connections or business relationships with property investors, dealers in goods, insurance agents, bankers, lawyers, publishers, and liquor dealers around Baltimore. Proceeds gained from commercialized sexual exchanges flowed out to dozens of other businesses and individuals, many of whom took advantage of the fact that prostitution was socially stigmatized to extort madams and prostitutes and expand their own wealth. Sex, which both dominant religious and cultural ideologies and capitalist labor regimes situated firmly within the (ostensibly)

[2] "The City Court – March 7, 1840," *Sun*, Mar. 9, 1840, 4; "City Court," *Sun*, June 28, 1841.

noncommercialized sphere of the home by the 1830s, became more fundamentally enmeshed into the world of urban commerce and real estate. Meanwhile, a sex trade that had long been part of women's economies of makeshift became a means by which diverse urban entrepreneurs profited.

Brothel prostitution's integration into urban economic networks began as soon as women sought properties for use as bawdy houses. Unlike street prostitution, which required only that women have possession of their own bodies and access to semi-private spaces, brothel prostitution required that madams have access to dwellings that were sizable enough to rent rooms to anywhere from four to eighteen women each. In most cases, madams secured access to the required properties by entering into rental arrangements for land, housing, or both. Wealthier madams like Hannah Smithson and Eliza Randolph built and owned their own houses but paid annual ground rents to the persons who owned the lots on which they were built. Ground rents, a remnant of the colonial era unique to Maryland, Pennsylvania, and Virginia, were used in Baltimore to promote rapid urban development by offering financial incentives to landowners for improving lots while also making home ownership more affordable to working people by exempting them from paying the full purchase price of their land upfront. Usually, the terms of rental were 6 percent of the price of the land, but madams sometimes paid considerably more, perhaps owing to the stigma of their professions. Eliza Randolph paid annual ground rents amounting to almost 10 percent of the $5,500 value of her three leased lots on Park Street, while Smithson paid only $97.50 for hers.[3]

Most madams, however, owned neither their houses nor their lands. The high price of buying or constructing a house precluded almost all sex workers who were not widows or longtime participants in the trade from owning property, especially given that women in the sex trade's lack of social capital made it difficult for them to access loans or mortgages. By the 1850s and 1860s, few madams were listed in the census as possessing any real property. Instead, most rented their houses from landlords who saw the sex trade as a potential source of profit and upward mobility.

[3] On ground rents, see *The Architecture of Baltimore: An Illustrated History*, ed. Mary Ellen Hayward and Frank R. Shrivers Jr. (Baltimore: Johns Hopkins University Press, 2004), 58; Baltimore City (Register of Wills), Inventories, 1868–1869, Book 88, Eliza Randolph, pp. 171–74, MSA T603-22.

In Baltimore as in other cities, brothel landlords emerged as part and parcel of a broader process of the commodification of housing that occurred in US cities. During the same period that the home was ceasing to be a site of production and economic sustenance for craftsmen and their families, new classes of urban landholders and property owners began to transform the home into a source of steady income and profit. In Baltimore, the rapidly expanding urban population created demands for shelter and lodging that were met through the construction of row-houses by real estate speculators working in concert with landholders. These speculators, who ranged from large landholders to small groups of artisans who pooled their resources, improved lots with houses in the hope of renting them to tenants or selling them at a premium and continuing to extract ground rents.[4]

Many investors who preferred to rent their properties found leasing newly constructed houses to sex workers to be an attractive economic strategy. As Timothy Gilfoyle and other historians of prostitution in antebellum cities have noted, the risk of criminal prosecution that came from renting a house as a bawdy house meant that landlords could justify overcharging madams for access to their properties.[5] Property owners could and did lease dwellings on inflated monthly rents or on rent-to-own plans with high interest rates with the knowledge that madams' limited options for housing would encourage them to acquiesce even to exploitative terms and conditions.[6] The profitability of brothels ensured that their keepers could usually afford to meet even the steepest rent demands, which made them reliable and lucrative tenants. By the 1840s and 1850s, brothels were so established as a reliable source of income for property owners that they became deeply embedded in an urban culture of real estate speculation. Landlords with an eye on long-term profits could use sex establishments as a temporary means of making money from the development of otherwise undesirable land. As historian Mara

---

[4] Elizabeth Blackmar, *Manhattan for Rent, 1785–1850* (Ithaca, NY: Cornell University Press, 1989); Robert L. Alexander, "Baltimore Row Houses of the Early Nineteenth Century," *American Studies* 16 (2) (Fall 1975): 65–76.

[5] Gilfoyle, *City of Eros*, especially 166–69. See also Judith Kelleher Schafer, *Brothels, Depravity, and Abandoned Women: Illegal Sex in Antebellum New Orleans* (Baton Rouge: Louisiana State University Press, 2009), 146–57; Joel Best, *Controlling Vice: Regulating Brothel Prostitution in St. Paul, 1865–1883* (Columbus: Ohio State University Press, 1998), 72–77.

[6] This observation is based on 1850 and 1860 US Federal Census records for brothels, especially those in Wards 10 and 11.

Keire had argued, real estate investors could buy up lots at the outskirts of urban development, construct cheap housing, rent the dwellings to sex workers, and enjoy a steady stream of income as they waited for the city's boundaries to expand and encompass their properties. When the land that brothels sat on became valuable for other industrial or business uses, they could simply evict madams in preparation for redeveloping the lots.[7]

For the most part, brothel landlords were "respectable" businesspeople who profited from the sex trade without sullying their reputations by directly involving themselves in its day-to-day operations. However, in the early days of brothel prostitution, it was not unusual for brothel landlords to reside near the properties they rented as bawdy houses. This was particularly true in East Baltimore, where the average brothel landlord tended to be a middling person or small-scale entrepreneur who rented one or two properties to commercial sex proprietors in order to secure financial mobility. Rosanna Calder, an Irish immigrant living in Fells Point, was one example of this phenomenon. Calder was a widow with several children who had inherited a grocery business and fairly substantial real and personal property holdings from her late husband. Her properties sat near the Causeway vice district. Perhaps motivated by a desire to cash in on the area's existing vice trade, Calder rented one of her dwellings to a local madam, who kept it as a brothel.[8] Priscilla Howard, one of the few African American women to be indicted for the offense of renting a house to be used as a brothel, made a similar choice. She leased a dwelling at 153 Caroline Street, just off Causeway, to white brothel keeper Margaret Fay. People with occupations as diverse as hatters, sailors, and teachers were all implicated in renting properties for use as houses of ill fame in the 1840s.[9]

As sex work grew more professionalized, small-scale entrepreneurs did not disappear, but an increasingly large portion of the brothel trade came to be dominated by wealthy men (and a few women) who made their livings as grocers, dry goods importers, and real estate investors. In some cases, these men bought up properties from the women who had previously owned them. In the 1840s, for instance, madam Elizabeth Osborne

---

[7] Keire, *For Business and Pleasure*, 10.

[8] BCCC, May Term, 1855, Case 359, Rosanna Calder, C-1849-4.

[9] BCCC, May Term, 1852, Case 886, Priscilla Howard. Observations about brothel landlords' occupations was obtained from cross-referencing lists of people indicted and convicted for "Renting a House as a Bawdy House" in the Baltimore City Court and Baltimore City Criminal Court with city directory and census records.

owned several houses in the Meadow vice district, but the costs of improving and managing her houses put her into severe debt. Osborne owed money to numerous dry goods firms around the city, and also had open debts totaling thousands of dollars to local upholsterers, paper hangers, and book keepers. Desperate to prevent her creditors from seizing her properties, Osborne fraudulently transferred her deeds to Samuel H. Goldsmith, a friend and budding real estate speculator.[10] When Elizabeth Osborne traveled to New York and died prematurely in the mid-1840s, Samuel and his wife, Sarah H. Goldsmith, gained control of her properties. By 1860, Sarah and Samuel claimed ownership of a combined total of $110,000 of real property, which included at least four highly profitable brothels on the 100 block of North Street in the Meadow. Other brothel keepers built or procured houses on their own and sought out sex workers as tenants. Customs house agent Lewis Goldsmith (no apparent relation) and his wife Martha profited from leasing several of their properties to Mary Kelly, Melvina Frey, Clara Norris, and other madams who ran them as sex establishments.[11] Andrew Fitzpatrick, a grocer, rented at least eleven different properties near his Wilk Street store to various women and men for use as brothels.[12]

Leasing properties to brothel keepers appears to have been an especially important strategy for landlords who came from marginalized or stigmatized groups in early Baltimore, including Irish and Jewish immigrants. Sarah H. Goldsmith was a Dutch Jewish woman who had immigrated to Baltimore in the early nineteenth century. Although Sarah and Samuel Goldsmith had considerable wealth as a result of assets accumulated through Sarah's previous marriage, they may have found themselves with limited options to continue their commercial prosperity in the United States. Anti-Semitism ensured that Jewish entrepreneurs often had trouble securing credit for their businesses. As historian Wendy Woloson noted, companies like Dun and Bradstreet often took Jewishness into account when evaluating creditworthiness and trafficked in

---

[10] John Johnson, *Reports of Cases Decided in the High Court of Chancery of Maryland*, vol. 2 (Annapolis: James Wingate, 1852), 370–92. Elizabeth Osborne was indicted multiple times on bawdy and disorderly house charges in the late 1830s to mid-1840s. See, for instance, BCC, February Term, 1840, Case 218, Elizabeth Osborne.

[11] BCCC, January Term, 1855, Cases 222–27, Lewis and Martha Goldsmith.

[12] BCC, May Term, 1849, Cases 838–45, Andrew Fitzpatrick; *Matchett's Baltimore Directory, 1849–1850* (Baltimore: Richard J. Matchett, 1849), 131.

stereotypes of Jews as dishonest swindlers.[13] The Goldsmiths, who made much of their money in real estate investment and speculation, may have rented properties as brothels to ensure that they had a liberal amount of cash on hand in the event that they were unable to secure credit. Andrew Fitzpatrick, an equally prolific brothel landlord, may have turned to brothel renting for similar reasons. Fitzpatrick was a young Irishman who arrived in the city during an early wave of immigration, and profiting from women's sexual labor enabled him to expand his real estate holdings and get ahead in the city during decades of intense nativism from its Know Nothing government. By 1860, Fitzpatrick had accumulated sufficient wealth through his grocery business and the brothel trade that he managed to move away from Eastern Avenue and open his own hotel in the Centre Market Space.[14]

While real estate owners like Fitzpatrick and the Goldsmiths were some of the most prominent figures to profit directly from women's sexual labor, the rise of brothel prostitution also expanded the networks of shopkeepers and merchants who benefited indirectly from sexual commerce. Brothels required their keepers to participate in a culture of consumption to the degree that earlier forms of sex work had not. In order to attract more affluent clientele, madams not only had to supply good-looking, genteel-seeming sex workers but also to decorate their establishments in a style befitting bourgeois refinement. After all, being a member of the middle class in America was not simply a matter of having a particular amount of money or type of employment; it was a matter of participating in a culture of shared values and tastes that encompassed, among other things, the acquisition of certain types of consumer goods that marked status.[15] This had been true since the mid-eighteenth century, but it became even more the case in the nineteenth as the availability of inexpensive, domestically produced consumer goods increased. The rise of factories in New England and the boom in slave-produced cotton in the South reduced the costs associated with making

---

[13] Wendy A. Woloson, *In Hock: Pawning in America from Independence through the Great Depression* (Chicago: University of Chicago Press, 2009), 71–75.

[14] *Woods' Baltimore City Directory* (Baltimore: John W. Woods, 1860), 129.

[15] On the relationship between taste and social class, see, among others, Linda Young, *Middle Class Culture in the Nineteenth Century: America, Australia and Britain* (New York: Palgrave- Macmillan, 2003), 153–88; Richard Bushman, *The Refinement of America: Persons, Houses, Cities* (New York: Vintage, 1993); Catherine E. Kelly, *Republic of Taste: Art, Politics, and Everyday Life in Early America* (Philadelphia: University of Pennsylvania Press, 2016).

consumer products like textiles even as newly improved transportation infrastructures made it cheaper to bring goods to new markets. The result was a dramatic expansion in the availability of affordable products that could be marketed to broad segments of the population. People of the class who might have found themselves with sparse furnishings and bare floors had they lived in the eighteenth century could afford in the nineteenth to purchase carpeting, mattresses, and home décor accents. With the rise of cheap newspapers in the 1840s, the United States developed a culture of advertising that encouraged consumption of these types of goods and reinforced the relationship between social status and material signifiers.[16] Brothel keepers who wanted to render their establishments suitable for the patronage of men above the seafaring classes had to do so through buying.

In addition to attracting a more affluent class of clients, brothel keepers' and sex workers' conspicuous consumption of material goods and furnishings reinforced the sensuality and sexuality of their houses. Historians of the United States and Europe have traced the ways in which the cultures of consumption that began to emerge in the late 1700s were inherently gendered and, more specifically, feminized. Women were assumed to be the natural market for consumer products, and consumption itself – particularly of clothing, household goods, or luxuries – became associated with femininity as a result of what Mary Louise Roberts described as "the late eighteenth-century linking of commodities with seduction and the creation of desire."[17] Necessary though it was to maintain the growing American economy, conspicuous consumption was tinged with danger, associated during the American Revolution with lack of patriotism and during the nineteenth century with excessive and frivolous luxury.[18] Such stereotypes about feminine consumption often had negative consequences for women, whose association with desire for

[16] Yamin, "Wealthy, Free, and Female," 4–18, p. 4. On the rise of nineteenth-century consumer culture, see Ann Smart Martin, *Buying into the World of Goods: Early Consumers in Backcountry Virginia* (Baltimore: Johns Hopkins University Press, 2008); Halttunen, *Confidence Men and Painted Women*, especially 105.

[17] Mary Louise Roberts, "Gender, Consumption, and Commodity Culture," *The American Historical Review* 103 (June 1998): 817–44.

[18] Benjamin Irvin, "Of 'Manly' and 'Monstrous' Eloquence: The Henpecked Husband in Revolutionary Political Debate, 1774–1775," in *New Men: Manliness in Early America*, ed. Thomas A. Foster (New York: New York University Press, 2011), 195–216; T. H. Breen, *The Marketplace of Revolution: How Consumer Politics Shaped American Independence* (Oxford: Oxford University Press, 2004), 173–75.

commodities was at times used to justify their exclusion from the world of politics and republic governance.[19] For brothel keepers and sex workers, however, stereotypes of consumption as licentious and associated with feminine lust functioned to their advantage, as they could use gaudy furniture and ornate clothing to signal the luxurious sensuality of their establishments. Conspicuous consumption highlighted women's sexuality, desirability, and femininity and reinforced the perception that their establishments, while reminiscent of middle-class homes, were not subjected to the restraints that ordinarily governed the realm of the domestic.

Over time, the women in the Meadow and other areas of West Baltimore began to devote more energy and, by extension, more money to furnishing and design. Perhaps no one captured brothels' dependence on consumer goods to consolidate an impression of gentility and luxury more than Henry Bebie, a Swiss-born artist who lived in Baltimore and painted a number of works depicting brothel scenes between 1850 and 1870.[20] The most ostentatious of his paintings, entitled *Conversation (Group of Baltimore Girls)*, shows a number of well-attired young women socializing and grooming one another in a room adorned with mirrors, an elaborate mantle, a gold clock, and various furnishings and drapes accented with red velvet (see Figure 3.1). The woman at the center of the image is seductively draped on a settee, her feet displayed in an exaggerated manner that historian Katherine Hijar has argued was common in risqué and fetishistic art. In the background, a number of women converse with a man in Marine officer's attire in a room decorated with a variety of paintings and portraits. Hijar noted that the women's gestures and overall deportment set them apart from supposedly rowdier and less refined street prostitutes like those that appeared in literature at the time.[21] While it is undeniable that the women's gestures added to their air of refinement, the sex workers' appearance of gentility depended as much on the backdrop as it did on their behavior. The combination of fine

---

[19] On women's exclusion from politics, see Rosemarie Zagarri, *Revolutionary Backlash: Women and Politics in the Early American Republic* (Philadelphia: University of Pennsylvania Press, 2007), especially chapter 5.

[20] Henry Bebie (1799–1888), *Conversation (Group of Baltimore Girls)*, Painting, Peale Museum, Baltimore, Maryland. Historian Katherine Hijar argued that Bebie's painting was part of a trilogy of brothel scenes, although two of the other paintings have been misidentified as depicting less objectionable subject matter. Katherine Hijar, "Sexuality, Print, and Popular Visual Culture in the United States, 1830–1870," PhD dissertation, Johns Hopkins University, 2008, 457–516.

[21] Hijar, "Sexuality, Print, and Popular Visual Culture," 457–516.

FIGURE 3.1 *Conversation (Group of Baltimore Girls)*, painting by Henry Bebie (1799–1888).
Courtesy of the Maryland Historical Society, Baltimore, Maryland

furnishings with mirrors and dressing stands that had strong associations with feminine vanity created a simultaneous air of refinement and excess. By investing in material trappings of wealth and playing to associations about consumption, brothel keepers enhanced the appeal of their establishments to wealthy patrons, and, in so doing, also elevated the value of sex workers' labor.

It is impossible to know whether Bebie's painting was inspired by or based on an actual establishment in the city, but it undoubtedly captured something of the actual transition that took place in the quality and fashioning of sex establishments in the 1850s. An inventory taken of Eliza Randolph's properties on her death in 1868 provides a concrete example of the kind of investment that keepers of bawdy houses made in ensuring their properties – and, indeed, their very bodies – were well decorated and genteel in appearance. Over the course of nearly three decades in the sex trade, Randolph amassed a sizable amount of real property that was a testament to her efforts to make her three-story house and two-story back building into refined spaces of sociability and sexual exchange. Randolph's parlor, which greeted visitors on their entrance to the house, featured various furnishings intended to allow visitors to lounge and enjoy entertainment: a piano valued at $100, comfortable sofas and chairs, chandeliers for lighting, paintings on the walls, and spittoons placed around the room for tobacco chewers. Randolph's house also featured a second common area in the form of a barroom equipped with many bottles of liquor, stools, and rocking chairs.[22] The private spaces of the house were no less lavish. In addition to the usual (and practical) array of bedsteads and marble-topped washstands, the bedrooms contained a number of decorative flourishes: clocks; wax fruit, flowers, and other small ornaments on the dressers; pictures and mirrors hung on the walls; and venetian blinds covering the windows. Every floor in the main house was covered with rag carpets, an affordable option that was popular among the members of the middling classes in the mid-nineteenth century.[23]

Fine clothing complemented Randolph's choices in furnishings. In her wardrobes were two silk dresses valued at $10, three "mireno" (merino wool) and "other" dresses valued at $2 each, and thirteen assorted calico dresses. In total, Randolph owned $1,309 worth of personal property and $5,600 of real property at the time of her death.[24] Her investments in her house attracted genteel customers who made her business exceedingly profitable and allowed her access to the upper echelons of local society. When Randolph died, the executor to her estate was none other than lawyer and Democratic politician William Pinkney Whyte, who was a sitting US Senator and the future Attorney General of Maryland.[25]

Randolph owned more real and personal property than most madams, but the general style of her house's furnishings was typical of a higher-end establishment. Hannah Smithson's Garden Street assignation house featured a similar array of consumer goods whose quality and style mimicked those found in middle-class homes. Smithson's house was three stories, with servants' quarters and a kitchen in the basement, a sitting

[22] Baltimore City (Register of Wills), Inventories, 1868–1869, Book 88, Eliza Randolph, pp. 171–74, MSA T603-22.
[23] Baltimore City (Register of Wills), Inventories, 1868–1869, Book 88, Eliza Randolph, pp. 171–74.
[24] Baltimore City (Register of Wills), Inventories, 1868–1869, Book 88, Eliza Randolph, pp. 171–74.
[25] Baltimore City (Register of Wills), Inventories, 1868–1869, Book 88, Eliza Randolph, 171–74.

area, and four to six bedrooms on the second and third levels, and she designed her rooms and parlors to have stylish and comfortable touches. She bought artwork for the walls, fashionable Brussels carpeting for the floors, and card tables and Britannia spittoons for her parlor. Each bedroom was carpeted and furnished with a bedstead; at least one feather or straw mattress; a dressing table made of mahogany, marble, or curled maple; a mirror; a washstand; and curtains or blinds for the windows. At the time of Smithson's death in 1848, her personal property was appraised at just over $500, and the total value of her estate was estimated to be just over $3,000.[26] In this sense, her holdings were in line with those of most Meadow brothel owners in the mid-nineteenth century. The majority of Meadow brothel keepers were listed as having $500 in personal property in the 1860 census, though the totals ranged from $100 for the smallest, least affluent brothels to $1,000 for large, well-appointed establishments.[27]

Madams' consumption of furniture and other home accents spread dispersed money throughout Baltimore's local economy. Information about where and how brothel keepers procured their furnishings is lacking in the historical record, but given that most furniture manufacturing was still concentrated in small shops and factories in early America, it is reasonable to assume that they purchased directly from the manufacturer or from neighborhood shopkeepers.[28] In the decades before shops with standardized, fixed pricing became common, madams could be subjected to considerable exploitation in commercial transactions, just as they could be in rent. Considerable evidence from late nineteenth- and early twentieth-century vice commissions suggests that furniture dealers and shopkeepers conspired to inflate prices for madams. In some cases,

---

[26] "City Court," *Sun*, Mar. 9, 1840; "Licentiousness," *Sun*, June 19, 1841; BCRW (Orphan's Court Proceedings), December Term, 1848, Hannah Smithson; BCRW (Inventories), Jan. 4, 1848, Inventory of Hannah Smithson, C340-61, Maryland State Archives (MSA), Annapolis, Maryland.

[27] Data on the relative wealth of brothels is derived from a combination of US Federal Census Schedules and Local Tax and Orphan's Court Estate Inventory records. 1860 US Census, Population Schedule, NARA microfilm publication, Baltimore Ward 10, Baltimore (Independent City), Maryland; Roll: M653_461, 1–108; Baltimore Ward 11, Baltimore (Independent City), Maryland; Roll: M653_463, 1–258.

[28] David A. Hounshell, *From the American System to Mass Production, 1800–1932: The Development of Manufacturing Technology in the United States* (Baltimore: Johns Hopkins University Press, 1984), 12.

they overcharged madams for pianos or other furnishings by as much as four times the usual sale price.[29] The absence of earlier evidence concerning sales terms means that historians can only speculate about whether such exploitative schemes existed in the earlier period. However, it is reasonable to suspect – especially given the social stigma that surrounded prostitution and the personal nature of commercial transactions – that they may have. The fact that Elizabeth Osborne owed considerable debts to paperhangers and dealers in goods – despite owning several apparently affluent brothels – supports this suspicion.[30]

As the presence of brothels in West Baltimore neighborhoods lined the pockets of real estate investors and merchants who could supply furniture, art, and credit, it also created pockets of demand for domestic labor. Because brothels generally had multiple women living in them and a constant supply of soiled sheets, they required a greater than average amount of cooking, cleaning, and washing. Some also employed the services of dressers who came in to assist the women of the house with their daily routine of getting ready to see clients, as many corsets and dresses of the period had ties or stays that required a second set of hands to secure.[31] In keeping with nineteenth-century trends toward "dirty," intimate work being displaced onto women of color, brothels usually depended on black women to perform this labor.[32] Some houses, including Eliza Randolph's, employed black women as live-in cooks or domestic servants who also managed the household inventories and did the shopping. In Randolph's case, she employed a woman named Mary Deloise, with whom she apparently had a tense relationship; in 1844, Randolph accused Deloise of attempting to poison her and her tenants by adding oxalic acid to the tea service.[33] Many other brothels relied on networks of local laborers to keep their houses in good order. Especially in West Baltimore, several brothel clusters were located on blocks where there were high concentrations of black domestic workers, especially washwomen, living nearby. Women who took washing from brothels did not profit from the sex trade to nearly the same degree as landlords,

---

[29] MVCR, vol. 1, 44–66, especially 66.

[30] Johnson, *Reports of Cases Decided in the High Court of Chancery of Maryland*, vol. 2, 370–92.

[31] On black women's employment as maids and domestics in brothels, see, for instance, Jacqueline Jones, *Labor of Love, Labor of Sorrow: Black Women, Work, and the Family, from Slavery to the Present* (New York: Basic Books, 2010), 150–53. On black women's role in dressing sex workers, see Cohen, *The Murder of Helen Jewett*, 111.

[32] Brown, *Foul Bodies*, 120–23.   [33] "Poisoning," *Sun*, May 17, 1844.

liquor dealers, and restaurateurs did, and their work was hard and unglamorous. Nevertheless, brothels likely provided a market for domestic labor among women who resided near the city's informal vice districts, and they could sometimes be counted on to offer better pay than other domestic labor arrangements because of the stigma that attached to their business.[34]

The investment that madams made in furnishing, maintaining, and staffing their brothels was probably exceeded in the long term by the amount they spent on alcohol. Virtually all tiers of the sex trade had close ties to the liquor trade, as alcohol consumption was central to what historian Richard Stott has described as "jolly fellowship" in the early republic.[35] Even as temperance fever swept much of the country in the 1820s and 1830s, large cities like Baltimore remained havens for male subcultures whose conception of leisure revolved around drink, conviviality, and sport. The men who patronized brothels were more often than not members of the sporting subculture who delighted in shirking (at least temporarily) the strictures that governed respectable life. The sale of alcohol in sex establishments helped to create a festive and jocular atmosphere for men while also having the side benefit of loosening both their inhibitions and their purse strings.

Alcohol also functioned as a status symbol that differentiated high-end houses from their lower-class counterparts. In Baltimore as in other cities, the type of drink that was sold at a brothel was one of the primary indicators of a house's standing. Houses that sold lager beer or hard liquor were usually regarded as being of the lowest class, while wine marked the better class of houses. Champagne, if it was stocked, was usually indicative of an elite establishment.[36] The keepers of high-end

---

[34] 1850 US Federal Census; Baltimore Ward 10, Baltimore, Maryland; Baltimore Ward 11, Baltimore, Maryland; 1860 US Census, Population Schedule; NARA microfilm publication, Baltimore Ward 10, Baltimore (Independent City), Maryland; Roll: M653_461, 1–108; Baltimore Ward 11, Baltimore (Independent City), Maryland; Roll: M653_463, 1–258.

[35] Richard Stott, *Jolly Fellows: Male Milieus in Nineteenth-Century America* (Baltimore: Johns Hopkins University Press, 2009), particularly 97–128. On urban masculinity, see also Amy Greenberg, *Cause for Alarm: The Volunteer Fire Department in the Nineteenth-Century City* (Princeton: Princeton University Press, 1998); Greenberg, *Manifest Manhood and the Antebellum American Empire* (Cambridge: Cambridge University Press, 2005); Lorien Foote, *The Gentlemen and the Roughs: Violence, Honor, and Manhood in the Union Army* (New York: New York University Press, 2010); Steven Maynard, "Rough Work and Rugged Men: The Social Construction of Masculinity in Working-Class History," *Journal of Canadian Labour Studies* 23 (Spring 1989): 159–69.

[36] Sanger, *The History of Prostitution,* 558, 572.

brothels prided themselves on the quality of their offerings and touted them in their advertising. An 1859 brothel guide praised Margaret Hamilton's establishment on Frederick Street for having "good wines constantly on hand."[37] The reviewer also recommended Maggy King's house in Watch-House Alley (so named because it was home to the Central District Watch-House), which he noted kept a regular stock of "Good wines &c. of the very best brands."[38] The sale of champagne and "good wines" was crucial to the overall impression of refinement and luxury that parlor-house keepers strove to promote, even as the inflated prices of the spirits lined madam's pocketbooks.[39]

While alcohol sales had long been linked to prostitution, alcohol became a particularly fundamental part of the business model for the new class of brothels. The young professionals, artisans, and elites who patronized West Baltimore's emergent class of parlor houses expected to be able to utilize brothels as social spaces. They relished opportunities to sit in sex establishments' parlors, listen to music played by the ladies of the house, converse with sex workers and male guests, and flirt with the women from whom they might eventually purchase sex. In some cases, men even limited their visits to brothels to social calls. Otis K. Hillard, a patron of Annette Travers's house at 70 Davis Street in the Meadow, made a habit of visiting the brothel with his friend and leaving after spending time in the parlor talking and kissing Anna Hughes, a sex worker with whom he had an ongoing relationship. Hillard, like other patrons, also made a habit of spending the night in brothels after engaging in intercourse.[40] That high-end brothels allowed and fostered this type of sociability and unrushed sexual exchange distinguished them from lower-tier bawdy and assignation houses and enabled them to attract men who could pay more for sexual services. And yet it also meant that the women of the house had the potential to lose out on the income because they spent more of their time engaging in uncompensated forms of intimate and emotional labor than they did engaging in intercourse. Madams and prostitutes who wanted to keep their profits high without alienating their clientele by pressuring them to engage in sex turned to alcohol sales as a solution to their conundrum. The sale of spirits and wine at drastically

---

[37] Loveyer, *Directory to the Seraglios*, 37.   [38] Loveyer, *Directory to the Seraglios*, 37.

[39] Sanger, *The History of Prostitution*, 541, 551.

[40] Cuthbert, *Lincoln and the Baltimore Plot*, 29–30. On men's tendency to pay purely social calls to brothels, see also Cohen, *The Murder of Helen Jewett*, especially 113.

marked-up prices allowed "hostesses" to make money even if "gentlemen callers" wished to limit their visits to the parlors rather than the bedrooms.

High-end brothels' reliance on supplies of good wine and liquor to maximize their profits created economic partnerships between sex workers and liquor dealers. Madams, after all, had to purchase their alcohol somewhere. Women who worked in the highest class of brothels were sometimes able to obtain liquor licenses from the City Court that allowed them to stock and sell their own spirits. Madams in lower-tier houses often did not possess such licenses, and therefore relied on a more varied set of arrangements. Some, like Catherine Peduze, simply ignored local licensing laws. In 1830, Peduze, who worked as a sex worker and madam for at least twenty-two years during the antebellum period, was charged both with keeping a disorderly house and selling liquor illegally. She was fined $24 for the latter offense, a penalty that was likely insufficient to cancel out the profits of illegal liquor sales, but nonetheless steep for the period.[41] Other brothel keepers, perhaps hoping to avoid large fines and the attention of the authorities, refrained from selling liquor directly and instead placed orders with nearby taverns and groggeries. When Ann Power was charged with keeping a house of ill fame in 1840, for instance, one of her clients testified that Power never stocked liquor in her establishment. Rather, she made it clear to her clients that it could be sent for on request.[42] Having a brothel in the neighborhood could thus prove profitable for both liquor suppliers and small-scale sellers, who made their money from brothel orders.

In addition to contributing to liquor dealers' profits, bawdy houses benefited restaurants and cafes in their neighborhoods. Most brothels had their own kitchens and their own cooks, and sex workers probably took the majority of their meals in-house. However, brothels' ability to attract new clients depended on their women making occasional appearances in public spaces, and restaurants proved fashionable sites to see and be seen. The dozens of cafes and eateries in areas nearby the Meadow became sites of solicitation for sex workers and their clients, none more famously so than the Parisian Restaurant. The restaurant sat – aptly enough – in the basement of the Commercial Buildings, on the corner of Lombard and Gay Streets. Its proprietors, Alonzo and Susan Welsh, embraced and actively sought the patronage of sex workers, whose presence attracted

---

[41] BCC (Docket and Minutes), June Term, 1830 Case 331, Catherine Peduze.
[42] "City Court – February 17," *Sun*, Feb. 18, 1840.

male customers and increased drink sales. While there are few indications that the Welshes allowed sex to take place in the saloon building itself, the couple appeared to rent out rooms of their residence on Baltimore Street as assignation spaces for sex workers and their clients.[43] Their restaurant's popularity with sex workers was so well known that local hack drivers began to linger at its bar to pick up business. Several hack drivers who based themselves around Barnum's Hotel testified in court that they made a practice of picking women up from known brothels and bringing them back and forth to the Welches' eatery, as well as taking women from the eatery to the city's theaters.[44]

Theaters, like restaurants, were a popular place of resort for brothel denizens and streetwalkers alike, and sex workers and their clients composed a ready base of patrons for Baltimore's playhouses.[45] Many theaters set aside entire tiers of their establishments for sex workers and their clients, who took advantage of the darkened houses to mingle with male audience members and solicit potential clients. John B. Ray, a private officer at Baltimore's Holliday Street Theater and later a watchman for the Fifth Ward, recalled that the third tier of that establishment was known for being exclusive to sex workers and men interested in buying their services. Admission to the third tier was inexpensive, women who lived in local bawdy houses could easily retire back to them with whatever men they managed to pick up – if they had not already accomplished their purposes in the theater. Independent sex workers could do the same by renting a room in a local assignation house. Elizabeth Black, a sex worker who operated out of a variety of brothels, including Ann Bartlett's house in Chesnut Street, both solicited in the Holliday Street Theater and occasionally acted in shows at the Baltimore Museum.[46]

For their part, most theaters owners in the early nineteenth century were accepting of the prostitution trade if not outright supportive of sex workers monopolizing their third tiers. After all, not only did sex workers themselves pay admission to the shows, they also drew in male patrons

[43] "Proceedings of the Courts," *Sun*, June 9, 1853, 1. The Welshes were charged multiple times for keeping bawdy and disorderly houses throughout the 1850s. Baltimore City Criminal Court (Docket) (hereafter BCCC), 770, Alonzo Welsh, May, 1855; BCCC, 506, Alonzo Welsh, January Term, 1859; BCCC, 444, Susan Creamer, September Term, 1855.

[44] "Local Matters," *Sun*, Nov. 19, 1852; "Local Matters," *Sun*, Nov. 20, 1852.

[45] On Baltimore theaters, see Scharf, *History of Baltimore City and County*, 678–98; Patricia Click, *The Spirit of the Times: Amusements in Nineteenth-Century Baltimore, Norfolk, and Richmond* (Charlottesvillea: University of Virginia Press, 1989).

[46] "Local Matters," *Sun*, Nov. 19, 1852; "Local Matters," *Sun*, Nov. 20, 1852.

who were familiar with theaters' reputations as places of solicitation.[47] Some theaters even embraced their associations with the bawdier aspects of urban nightlife by offering risqué and sexually charged spectacles that drew both public controversy and patrons. In 1848, the Holliday Street Theatre hosted Dr. Collyer's famed "model artistes," a troupe that recreated famous paintings like Lord Leighton Frederic's *The Bath of Psyche* and Tiepolo's *Time Discovering Truth* using live models who were clad only in semi-transparent, flesh-colored silk bodysuits. The troop had previously performed in New York and Philadelphia, but the fact that the models appeared nude under the stage lighting outraged moralistic Baltimoreans.[48] One critic of the production claimed that it was little more than a front for the "hideous purpose of debasing the feminine character of American women to the gross indelicacy which must pervade it, to fit them to become deliberate spectators of fantastic obscenity."[49] The critic believed that European-style model artiste shows were insulting to the morals of American women and likely to lure young people of both sexes into lust and sexual vice. Incidentally, that may well have been what the theaters intended, or at least the idea they were flirting with in order to attract patronage.

By the eve of the Civil War – and influenced in part by the backlash against shows like Collyer's – a growing number of local theaters attempted to distance themselves from their reputation as havens of vice, but change happened slowly and was met with resistance from sex workers. Several establishments attempted to create a more respectable image for themselves by implementing policies that discouraged sex workers and the men who solicited them from attending productions. The Howard Athenaeum, for instance, wrote in its advertisement for the farce "The Queen" that unescorted gentlemen wishing to attend would

---

[47] Claudia D. Johnson, "That Guilty Third Tier: Prostitution in Nineteenth-Century American Theaters," *American Quarterly* 27, no. 5, Special Issue: Victorian Culture in America (December 1975): 575–84.

[48] *Baltimore Clipper*, Jan. 3, 1848; *Baltimore Clipper*, Jan. 22, 1848; "Dr. Collyer's Model Artistes," *Sun*, Jan. 13, 1848; "Model Artistes," *Sun*, Jan. 17, 1848; "Suppression of Obscenity," *Sun*, Feb. 18, 1848; "Dr. Collyer as a 'Model Artist,'" *Sun*, Feb. 26, 1848.

[49] "Model Artistes," *Sun*, Jan. 17, 1848. See also "Communication from the Mayor Relative to the Model Artists," City Council Records, RG 16, Series 1, Box 82, No. 611, Baltimore City Archives (BCA), Baltimore, Maryland; "Report of the Joint Committee on Police on the Mayor's Communication Relative to Model Artists," 1848, City Council Records, RG 16: 1, Box 83, No. 755; "A Further Supplement to the Ordinance for Licensing Theatrical Exhibitions in the City of Baltimore," 1848, City Council Records, RG 16:1, Box 83, No. 973, BCA.

have to pay a 50 percent markup of the general admission price and that unescorted women would not be admitted at all.[50] Officers at the Roman Amphitheatre denied a particularly well-known white "woman of the town" admission to one of the theater's productions on the suspicion that she was soliciting. The woman, however, turned to a creative solution to circumvent her ban; she donned blackface in an attempt to disguise her appearance and sneak into the "colored" section of the venue.[51] Theaters remained important sites of solicitation throughout the antebellum period.

By the 1840s, prostitution had grown and extended to a degree that it spawned print enterprises based around publicizing details of the sex trade's operation. Many American cities, Baltimore included, developed "flash" or "sporting" newspapers that combined bawdy stories and jokes with gossip columns and exposés about local sex establishments and their goings-on. Baltimore's short-lived sporting paper, *The Viper's Sting and Paul Pry* (1849–50), took its name from a famed busybody character in a British play and, in keeping with the moniker, made a habit of publishing blind items about improprieties in the brothel districts, for example:

Wonder who those two young men are, who live in B— street, not far from W—, who start for the Bethel [a black Methodist church] every night, and the first place they find themselves is in Wilk St.? Don't come home, Tom and gas so much about the Bethel; and George had better look out, or the Viper will give him a harder sting.[52]

Although the intent of these blind items was ostensibly to warn men and women away from sexual vice – a common defense employed by flash printers hoping to avoid obscenity prosecutions – this was something of a veneer. Sporting papers made most of their revenue from a combination of surreptitiously advertising for the vice districts and blackmailing their frequenters and proprietors. Such papers traded in their ability to reveal the locations of houses of ill fame so that those desiring to visit could find them easily and other readers could experience the vicarious thrill of touring the urban underworld without ever leaving their homes.[53] At the same time, they brought in additional revenue by threatening to make

[50] Scharf, *History of Baltimore City and County*, 695.
[51] May's Dramatic Encyclopedia of Baltimore, MS 995, Roll 7, R.A. 3 1846; R.A. 5 1846. Originally referenced in Click, *The Spirit of the Times*, 45.
[52] "Wonder If," *The Viper's Sting and Paul Pry*, Feb. 9, 1830. The original read "iwho" rather than who, but I have corrected it here.
[53] Cohen et al., *The Flash Press: Sporting Male Weeklies in 1840s New York*.

certain madams or brothel patrons the targets of the anti-vice rhetoric they used to adapt a moralistic pose for their papers. One correspondent to *The Viper's Sting and Paul Pry* recounted witnessing a man who needed money for liquor walk into Tripolett's Alley and demand it from a sex worker named Sally (possibly Sarah "BlackHawk" Burke, a long-time brothel keeper in the central part of the city). The man claimed that he was writer for the *Viper* and that he would write an exposé about Sally and her clientele if she did not give him money. Sally was forced to throw a small bag of coins down to him. The editors of the *Viper* vehemently denied that the man was on their staff or that they ever accepted bribes in return for coverage or omissions, but their denials should be taken with a grain of salt. Blackmail made up such a significant chunk of the profits for many sporting papers that some subsisted almost entirely on the proceeds of extortion.[54]

As flash papers pioneered the practice of subtly advertising for the expanded brothel trade, publishers also created pocket-sized brothel guidebooks that became popular among male travelers and sporting men seeking to locate houses of ill fame in unfamiliar cities.[55] Brothel guides provided readers with the names and addresses of local brothels, as well as details about what type of accommodation men could expect to receive in each house. One *Directory to the Seraglios* published out of New York devoted multiple pages to Baltimore's houses and praised several for their fine selections of women. Its unnamed author wrote of Kate Murphy's brothel, "This lady keeps a very popular house, where gentleman may enjoy the comforts of connubial feelings, and see some of the prettiest girls Baltimore can boast of."[56] The phrase "connubial feelings," while certainly euphemistic, also conveyed that parlor houses like Murphy's sought to replicate a particular kind of relationship experience for men, namely one in which they enjoyed a rapport with the women of the house. The guide went on, "The hostess sees that her visitors are well entertained, and gents will always meet with great

[54] "Black Mail," *Viper's Sting and Paul Pry*, Aug. 18, 1849; Cohen et al., *The Flash Press*, 51.

[55] Katherine Hijar, "Brothels for Gentlemen: Nineteenth-Century American Brothel Guides, Gentility, and Moral Reform," *Common-Place* 18 (Winter 2018), http://common-place.org/book/vol-18-no-1-hijar/; Pamela D. Arceneaux, "Guidebooks to Sin: The Blue Books of Storyville," *Louisiana History: Journal of the Louisiana Historical Association* 28 (Autumn, 1987): 397–405.

[56] Loveyer, *Directory to the Seraglios*, 38.

attention and courtesy by her charming boarders."[57] Of Maggy King's house, the guide noted, "This amiable lady keeps a first class house, pretty and sociable lady boarders; and strangers may rely on good treatment &c, from the hostess and her agreeable lady boarders."[58]

In touting the gentility and pleasantness of houses like Murphy's and King's, brothel guidebooks played a crucial role in both helping men to navigate the urban sex trade and in furthering its mythos. Brothel guides devoted considerable space to assuring men that they would be "safe" in particular houses, which undoubtedly spoke to strangers' fears that they might end up in a panel house or other, similarly exploitative establishments. At the same time that they made the sex trade "familiar" enough to remove its air of intimidation, brothel guides also touted the sex trade as fantasy spaces that would provide men with exotic offerings and pleasures beyond those that they could ordinarily access. Brothel guides fostered an image of the city as a space of pleasure and male sexual license and, in doing so, played an important role in advertising for brothels. As much as madams created fantasies around prostitution by decorating their establishments in particular ways or hiring particular "types" of women, they ultimately depended on print to foster fantasies of brothels as genteel spaces perfectly calibrated to produce male pleasure.[59] Brothel guides furthered popularity of the sex trade even as they profited from its expansion.[60]

And yet the relationship between publishers and participants in the sex trade was not always a rosy one. Like landlords and dealers in goods, brothel publishers sought to extract money from women in the sex trade. There is some evidence to suggest that publishers of brothel guides demanded payments in exchange for publishing positive reviews or refraining from publishing negative ones. A guide published in New York in 1859 listed fifteen Baltimore brothels and assignation houses and provided descriptions of the nine that the editors deemed "first class,"

---

[57] Loveyer, *Directory to the Seraglios*, 38.　　[58] Loveyer, *Directory to the Seraglios*, 39.

[59] On the role of print in promoting particular fantasies of commercial sex, see especially Gail Hershatter, *Dangerous Pleasures: Prostitution and Modernity in Twentieth-Century Shanghai* (Berkeley: University of California Press, 1997); Hijar, "Brothels for Gentlemen."

[60] Brothel guidebooks frequently remarked on the orderliness or roughness of particular houses so that clients could know in advance whether they needed to be cautious. See, for instance, *The Gentlemen's Companion of New York City in 1870*, reprinted in *New York Times*, www.nytimes.com/interactive/projects/documents/a-vest-pocket-guide-to-brothels-in-19th-century-new-york-for-gentlemen-on-the-go, accessed August 10, 2017.

including Eliza Randolph's. In reality, the guide omitted some of the most well-known brothels in the city – Ann Thomas's and all but two other houses in the Meadow – and elevated some houses that were second-tier at best to high status. It is possible that the New York–based editors were not familiar enough with Baltimore to correctly identify the city's best houses, but it is equally likely that the list reflected establishments whose keepers were willing to compensate the editors to have their brothels reviewed positively.[61]

More legitimate publishers also made money from publicizing information about the sex trade. In the 1830s, the growing availability of steam presses allowed for faster, cheaper printing of newspapers and created a new wave of inexpensive dailies throughout the United States. These so-called penny papers attracted readers by adopting a sensationalized approach to news, fixating on scandalous local happenings and crime to a greater degree than their predecessors had. The Baltimore *Sun*, founded as a penny paper in 1837, regularly sent reporters into the City Court to observe the proceedings. Especially in the early years of its publication run, the paper included irreverent accounts of trials involving women and men arrested in the city's vice districts for keeping bawdy houses, fighting, public drunkenness, and other disorderly behavior. Although the rowdy, often humorous coverage of the city's underbelly ceased in later years as the paper developed an air of respectability, the *Sun* continued to publish lists of women who were brought before the court on bawdy-house charges. This practice functioned as a form of public shaming or advertising, depending on the audience, and more than once, the *Sun* had to address reader accusations that its coverage of brothels was promoting immorality and obscenity. Whether or not the editors of the paper intended to advertise for brothels, they undoubtedly used the luridness and appeal of the sex trade to attract readers to their papers.[62]

By the 1850s, Baltimore's newspaper publishers had been joined in the market by smaller publishers who made their trade in selling obscene and

---

[61] Loveyer, *Directory to the Seraglios*, 38–39.

[62] For an example of allegations that the *Sun* promoted immorality by publicizing news of sexual vice, see "Editorial Immorality," *Baltimore Sun*, June 19, 1841. On the role of cheap print in sensationalizing crime and urban underworlds, see Amy Gilman Srebnick, *The Mysterious Death of Mary Rogers: Sex and Culture in Nineteenth-Century New York* (Oxford: Oxford University Press, 1995); Cohen, *The Murder of Helen Jewett*; Karen Halttunen, *Murder Most Foul: The Killer and the American Gothic Imagination* (Cambridge, MA: Harvard University Press, 1998).

erotic literature in and around the city's vice districts. As historian Donna Dennis has noted, a trade in erotic and "obscene" books and media grew during the antebellum years. Most of the printers who distributed novels and illicit newspapers were located in New York City, but their wares circulated far and wide via the mail and local transportation networks. The rise of Baltimore's downtown vice districts created new markets for risqué print as visitors to the city sought to partake in its more illicit pleasures, and the areas around Baltimore's major hotels developed a trade in the sale of erotic and bawdy books. In 1850, one petitioner wrote to the City Council to complain that boys were hawking obscene books in the streets.[63] Although the books were not named, they were probably the same New York titles that circulated widely in other ante-bellum cities. Brochures of "fancy" materials that circulated at the time boasted more than a hundred "Rich and Rare" novels, including the perennial favorite *Fanny Hill* and more than fifty titles by the ever-popular "Charles Paul DeKock," a tongue-in-cheek nom de plume employed by an American bawdy writer. Most books could be had for twenty-five or fifty cents.[64]

As the printers and hawkers of obscene materials cashed in on the city's image as a site of sexual possibility and adventure, other entrepre-neurs made their livings catering to those who were unlucky enough to experience the downsides of sexual freedom. Chief among these were sufferers of "venereal diseases," or what would now be called sexually transmitted infections. Even before prostitution was a major industry in Baltimore, rates of venereal infection among the urban population were remarkably high. Scattered institutional records suggest that around 5–10 percent of the American population was afflicted with some form of venereal malady, with urban dwellers being more likely than their rural counterparts suffer from disease. Samplings of admissions and medical records from the Baltimore almshouse in the 1820s and 1830s indicate that over 6 percent of all those who came to the institution seeking shelter or medical treatment suffered from syphilis, gonorrhea, or "lues venerea." In some years, particularly when there were no cholera epidemics to swell

---

[63] Petition of J. P. Delacour, Baltimore City Council Records, RG 16, Ser. 1, Box 87, BCA.
[64] P. F. Harris, *Advertisement*, Feb. 19, 1855, reprinted in Helen Horowitz, *Rewriting Sex: Sexual Knowledge in Antebellum America: A Brief History with Documents* (New York: Palgrave Macmillan, 2006), 142–43. On the erotic print industry in the nineteenth century, see Dennis, *Licentious Gotham*; Elizabeth Haven Hawley, "American Publishers of Indecent Books, 1840–1890," PhD dissertation, Georgia Tech, 2005.

the population of the medical wards, venereal sufferers comprised up to 12 percent of patients admitted to the almshouse. On average, around eighty individuals arrived at the institution each year suffering from either gonorrhea or syphilis. Those numbers did not include people who were asymptomatic at the time of their admissions, nor did they include people whose illnesses could be passed off as something else that was less controversial – that is, "sore legs" or uterine problems.[65] Given the likely underestimation of venereal disease cases in institutional records, some historians have speculated that as much as 15 percent of adult Americans in large cities may have been infected with syphilis or gonorrhea by the mid-century.[66]

By many accounts, the rapid expansion of urban sex trades in the 1830s contributed to a sharp rise in the number of cases of syphilis and gonorrhea in the urban population. The most complete statistics on venereal disease infection rates in mid-nineteenth-century America come from William Sanger, a physician who was employed on New York's Blackwell Island. In 1857, Sanger conducted an extensive study of prostitution in its local and international contexts. Among other information he presented were reports of syphilis cases in New York City and Brooklyn in the 1850s. Sanger, who treated a number of penitentiary inmates and city paupers suffering from syphilis, claimed that the rates of venereal infection among New Yorkers were both tremendously high and on the rise in the years leading up to his data collection. Sanger attributed that staggering statistic to the growth of the city's prostitution trade.[67] He was not alone in positing this connection between prostitution and venereal infections. Many nineteenth-century physicians and moralists assumed

---

[65] Statistics based on data gathered from Trustees of the Poor, Baltimore Almshouse Admissions Book (hereafter BAAB), MS 1866.1, Maryland Historical Society (MDHS); Trustees of the Poor, Baltimore Country Trustees of the Poor, Minutes, MS 1866. One estimate from 1827 suggested that 12 percent of Baltimore almshouse inmates were infected with syphilis (*Annual Report of the Executive Committee of the American Society for the Promotion of Temperance*, vol. 1 [1827], 64). On the stigma associated with venereal disease, see, among others, Kevin Siena, *Venereal Disease, Hospitals, and the Urban Poor: London's "Foul Wards," 1600–1800* (Rochester, NY: University of Rochester Press, 2010), 30–61.

[66] In a study of the Philadelphia almshouse, Jacqueline Cahif found that around 20 percent of all medical patients in the institution suffered from venereal disease. Cahif, "'She Supposes Herself Cured': Almshouse Women and Venereal Disease in Late Eighteenth and Early Nineteenth Century Philadelphia," 258. Similarly, Kevin Siena found that venereal disease cases accounted for about 20 percent of all hospital admissions in early modern England. Siena, *Venereal Disease, Hospitals, and the Urban Poor*, 10, 71.

[67] Sanger, *The History of Prostitution*, 586–94.

syphilitic and gonorrheal infection were intimately linked to sexual impropriety and to sexual commerce. They proposed any number of moral explanations for why this was so: they claimed that prostitutes' bodies were dirty, that immorality itself produced disease, and that an excess of semen deposited in a vagina by multiple partners would mutate into a poison – an explanation that conveniently placed the blame for venereal disease on female promiscuity while assuring readers that male promiscuity was perfectly safe.[68] While their explanations varied, their assumptions that sex work and disease were connected were remarkably consistent.

While many of the proposed linkages between prostitution and sexually transmitted infection were rooted in logic that now seems spurious at best, it was probably the case that the sex trade was an efficient vehicle for transmitting bacterial diseases. This was not because of any moral failing on the part of women, but rather because of the nature of venereal infections and their transmission. Many sexually transmitted infections, including syphilis, tend to be most infectious and virulent shortly after they are contracted. Women and men who had sex with multiple partners in a short span of time were among the most likely to transmit the diseases to other people. Because it was not unheard of for sex workers to see ten to twelve clients per night in lower-end brothels, a single infection passed on by a client could rapidly affect both the woman selling sex and dozens of her other clients.

Medical records from the almshouse and other charitable hospitals testify to sex workers' battles with venereal infection, as well as the devastating effects that infection could have on their bodies. In 1834, Theresa Weyman, the sixteen-year-old who labored as a sex worker in a house in the north side of the city, arrived at the almshouse dressed only in rags and stricken with "chancur" and condylomata on her labia and boils on her groin. Weyman had been involved in the sex trade for a matter of months, but what was likely secondary syphilis rendered her unable to continue working.[69] Around the same time that Weyman entered the institution, another young woman named Maria Gassaway came to the almshouse in a similar state. Gassaway, also sixteen, had

---

[68] James Glenn, *The Venereal Disease; Its Primary Cause Explained* (New York, 1857). See also Spongberg, *Feminizing Venereal Disease: The Body of the Prostitute in Nineteenth-Century Medical Discourse.* On the association between venereal disease and prostitution, see also Philippa Levine, *Prostitution, Race and Politics: Policing Venereal Disease in the British Empire* (New York: Routledge, 2003).

[69] AMR (1833–1837), Theresa Weyman, 1833, MS 2474, MDHS.

spent a year "sur a pave." Gassaway told physicians that she had contracted gonorrhea immediately after entering the trade and that she
developed chancre and severe buboes, that is, swollen lymph nodes in
the groin.[70] Both she and Weyman had to submit to incarceration and
labor at the almshouse in order to gain access to treatment and shelter
during a period in which their illnesses prevented them from working.

Young sex workers like Weyman and Gassaway may have suffered the
worst physical manifestation of venereal infection, as syphilis eventually
entered a period of latency that meant that older sex workers did not feel
its effects after the first months or years of their careers. Nevertheless,
even those women who had been in the trade for some time suffered
multiple bouts of active infection with the disease. Louisa Stewart, who
sold sex for six or seven years before coming to the almshouse in 1845,
suffered several, apparently distinct syphilitic infections over her time
in sex work.[71] Ann Wilson entered the almshouse two separate times
in 1820 and 1821, each time apparently suffering from "venereal."[72]
Margaret Paine, an Irish-born sex worker who had lived with her mother
and stepfather in Baltimore for only eight months, was sent to the
almshouse in 1824 for "insanity" that may have been the result of
advanced syphilitic infection. Less than a year after Paine was initially
released from the institution, she returned and was diagnosed with
rheumatism and "venereal," both of which were symptoms of syphilis
that had progressed to its constitutional stage. Paine's illness was so
severe that she spent two and half years in the institution.[73] All told,
355 people were admitted to the almshouse with some form of "venereal"
illness between 1813 and the first months of 1826. Three-quarters of these
were women, and a substantial number of them came from the Second
Ward, which housed the Causeway brothel district and the wharves.
Although most venereal patients were able to use the almshouse to their
own ends, eloping from the institution when it suited them and returning
as they needed, the months-long periods of confinement and painful
treatment regimens administered at the institution were unpleasant side
effects of their sexual labor.[74]

---

[70] AMR (1833–1837), Maria Gassaway, September 12, MS 2474, MDHS.

[71] Francis Donaldson, Alms-House Medical Record, 1844–1845, Case 75, Louisa Steward,
11–17.

[72] BAAB, December 29, 1820, Entry 4108, Ann Wilson; BAAB December 3, 1821, Entry
4837, Ann Wilson.

[73] BAAB, August 28, 1824, 7424, Margaret Paine; BAAB, October 12, 1825, 8144.

[74] Statistics derived from an examination of the BAAB.

Given the proliferation of venereal disease and the painful and pro-longed nature of treatment at the almshouse, it is perhaps unsurprising that the medical marketplace around allegedly painless venereal cures expanded in Baltimore around the same time as prostitution. There had been a small market for such medicines for a long time; before Baltimore was even incorporated, entrepreneurial men had been peddling cures for "secret diseases" that promised to be quicker and less painful that the mercury cures offered by regular physicians. In 1787, for instance, the *Maryland Journal and Baltimore Advertiser* featured ads from Lawrence Storch, a German immigrant who claimed to be able to cure any "foul diseases without resort to Mercury," and M. Jeanin, a French immigrant to Baltimore and a dentist who advertised that he could effect a venereal cure "in the course of two or three weeks, without confinement or danger to the patient."[75] However, with the rise of the penny press, the trend toward democratized medicine, and the growth of the sex trade in the 1830s, the number of medical practitioners and druggists peddling venereal cures and advertising in local papers expanded. Over the first half of the nineteenth century, Baltimoreans would produce or distribute upward of forty different medicinal remedies that were specifically and explicitly advertised as being effective against venereal complaints. Alongside the classic Hunter's Red Drops, local newspapers featured promotions for a diverse array of treatments, including Minerva Pill Anti-Syphilitic; Dr. Poett's Gonorrhea Eradicator; Husselbaugh's Infalliable Anti-Gonorrheal Specific; Old Dr. Cumming's Unfortunate's Friend for "private" complaints; Cross Specific Mixture for gonorrhea, gleets, and analogous problems; and Dr. Magdin's of Paris Le Cordial de Lucine ou L'Elixir de L'Amour for gleet, *fluor albus*, and urinary and reproductive problems (Lucina was the ancient Roman goddess of childbirth).[76] Those remedies and others were stocked by at least sixty-six city merchants, including booksellers, apothecaries and druggists, confectioners, and dealers in dry goods. Forty-three shops that sold venereal remedies were located in or directly around the main commercial thoroughfare on Baltimore Street.

By the 1840s, a number of practitioners created their own, for-profit clinics or "lock hospitals" intended for the treatment of "secret diseases."

---

[75] "Dr. Lawrence Storch," *The Maryland Journal and Baltimore Advertiser*, May 18, 1787; "M. Jeanin, Dentist, from France," *The Maryland Journal and Baltimore Advertiser*, Mar. 6, 1787.

[76] *Baltimore Gazette and Daily Advertiser*, Oct. 9, 1835; *Sun*, Apr. 18, 1838; Dec. 13, 1838; Dec. 17, 1857; May 23, 1838; Dec. 20, 1838.

Between 1838 and 1860, at least fifteen different men calling themselves physicians – some with regular medical education, some with no apparent qualifications save empirical knowledge – regularly touted their services and treatments for venereal complaints in local daily papers. Dr. J. M. Johnson, who claimed to be a "member of the Royal College of Surgeons, Licentiate of the Apothecary's Hall, London, and late Professor of an eminent American Medical College," advertised his lock hospital almost daily in Baltimore newspapers and other papers from as far as Harrisburg and Gettysburg, Pennsylvania.[77] Dr. Hitzelberger, who had actually received regular medical training, claimed that the afflicted could visit his practice or write to him by mail to seek remedy

When the most horrible of all diseases, the secret disease, has fastened itself upon the constitution, causing ulcerated sore throat; ulceration of the wind-pipe, known as consumption of the throat; disease of the bones, of the nose, and palate of the mouth; ulcerous sores, and copper-colored blotches on the head, breast, arms, and legs, eruption and pustules on the skin, strictures and gleet.[78]

Venereal clinics did not owe their existence exclusively to the sex trade; indeed, many of their proprietors also traded in remedies against "the solitary vice" (i.e., masturbation) and against "menstrual blockage" (pregnancy, in many cases), which were problems that extended beyond sex workers. Abortion in particular proved a popular service and was sometimes its own subsidiary industry catering to diverse urban women.[79] However, venereal clinics almost certainly made a portion of their money catering to both sex workers and their clients. The locations of their venereal clinics suggested their connectedness to the world of urban sexual commerce. Many venereal clinics were located in areas near clusters of brothels in the Meadow and Old Town, where they were poised to take advantage of foot traffic to and from the houses.[80]

---

[77] For samples of Johnston's advertisements over time, see "Baltimore Lock Hospital," *Sun*, Sep. 25, 1841, 3; "Dr. Johnston," *Sun*, Sep. 13, 1848; "Dr. Johnston," *Sun*, July 18, 1855, 4. On Pennsylvania advertising, see, for example, "Baltimore Lock Hospital," *The Star and Sentinel* [Gettysburg, PA], Oct. 21, 1870.

[78] "Secret Diseases Cured in Two Days," *Sun*, July 21, 1843.

[79] On abortion and reproductive control methods, see Andrea Tone, *Devices and Desires: A History of Contraceptives in America* (New York: Hill and Wang, 2001); Janet Farrell Brodie, *Contraception and Abortion in Nineteenth-Century America* (Ithaca, NY: Cornell University Press, 2004).

[80] Contemporary sources suggest that many merchants and peddlers took advantage of a proximity to brothels to sell anti-venereal cures and preventatives. William Sanger, for instance, noted that liquor stores in New York neighborhoods where brothels

Venereal proprietors also played up the connections between their businesses and the world of illicit sex. The proprietary remedies and venereal clinics that sprung up in Baltimore in the 1830s and 1840s actively promoted the idea that venereal diseases were linked to immorality and to improper sexual behavior. Eighteenth-century anti-venereal physicians had seen little need to explain venereal disease or its causes. Nineteenth-century physicians, on the other hand, were at the forefront of the trend toward "incitement to discourse" around matters of sex.[81] No longer content with simply proposing to cure those "unfortunate" enough to be afflicted with venereal ailments, advertisers increasingly took it upon themselves to explain venereal disease as being the result of sexual mistakes or moral failings. Ads for Dr. J. B. Mills's practice, for instance, described "secret diseases" – a shame-tinged euphemism that gained popularity in the 1830s – as being among the "diseases of imprudence." Drs. Huet and Harval at the French Medical House claimed that syphilis and gonorrhea were nothing short of the "Evil effects of improper intercourse."[82] While relatively few ads mentioned prostitution specifically, the language in the advertisements was suggestive. Several ads characterized the diseases as resulting from "youthful folly," which might include either masturbation or participation in urban sporting culture. One proprietary medicine producer even went so far as to name his venereal cure "The Cyprian Julap," which was a reference to both the cult of Aphrodite and common slang for a prostitute.[83]

References to prostitutes and sexual improprieties as the source of venereal problems worked to the advantage of anti-venereal practitioners and helped to drive business. Much of what venereal practitioners traded on, besides the promise of non-mercurial cures, was the promise of privacy. They, unlike regular physicians, could offer discreet care that did not require confinement, special diets, or medications with unsubtle side effects. By furthering the idea that venereal diseases were particularly loathsome and embarrassing afflictions, venereal physicians made the promise of secrecy in treatment into an especially valuable commodity. By reinforcing the stigma around venereal disease, they made it more

---

predominated tended to stock "Pine Knot Bitters," a favorite treatment of the lower classes. Sanger, *The History of Prostitution*, 596.

[81] Foucault, *The History of Sexuality*, vol. 1, trans. Robert Hurley (New York: Vintage Books, 1990), 17–35.

[82] "Dr. J. B. Hills," *Sun*, Feb. 17, 1857; "No Cure No Pay," *Sun*, May 21, 1850.

[83] "Dr. Graeffnell's Cyprian Julap," *Sun*, May 7, 1852.

likely that sufferers would pay a premium for "confidential" and "discreet" medicines. When commercially oriented physicians proclaimed, "Privacy must ever be a grand desideratum to those who are so unfortunate [as to be stricken with venereal disease]," they were not simply acknowledging an existing demand for confidentiality.[84] They were also producing it. If they managed to make young men considering a trip to the brothel more fearful that they would face a potentially debilitating illness afterward, so much the better; many proprietary medicine dealers also marketed their medicines as preventatives and prophylactics against infection.[85]

Venereal clinic proprietors' willingness to reinforce the stigmas surrounding prostitution while simultaneously marketing their drugs as preventatives that might enable male sexual license captured something of the contradictions and complexities that surrounded sexual commerce by the mid-nineteenth century. The rise of brothel prostitution spatially segregated the sex trade to a greater degree than ever before and weakened some of the long-standing relationships between sex workers and other commercial spaces. At the same time, the unique demands of maintaining a successful brothel also created a slew of new economic connections between sex workers and real estate investors, dealers in goods, domestic laborers, alcohol dealers, theater and restaurant proprietors, print media workers, and venereal medicine sellers. The money generated by sexual commerce flowed through the urban economy as prostitution became an increasingly visible part of city life. And yet even as various investors and merchants profited from the sale of sex and from the image as of the city as a site of sexual license, they also profited from the stigma that accompanied the sex trade. Because sex workers engaged in a legally dubious business that ensured their social ostracization (at least by respectable people), landlords and other merchants could take advantage of their situations, charging them above-market rates for rent, loans, and consumer goods. Printers and patent medicine dealers made their money by reinforcing the image of the sex trade as secretive, shadowy, and potentially dangerous so that they could profit from exposing its secrets and rendering it safer and more legible to men. Like capitalism itself, which depended on women's labor for the maintenance of the labor pool while systematically devaluing that labor, many of those who

---

[84] "Dr. Hunter's Celebrated Pills," *Patriot & Mercantile Advertiser*, Aug. 8, 1818.
[85] "Dr. Hunter's Celebrated Pills," *Sun*, May 28, 1838.

profited most from sex work did so in ways that were exploitative to sex workers.

Nevertheless, indoor sex workers' connections to the financial elite in Baltimore – particularly freeholders and landlords – carried clear benefits. As Chapter 4 will detail, these included relative protection from an antebellum legal system that was not eager to challenge the rights of wealthy property owners.

PART II

REGULATING AND POLICING THE SEX TRADE

4

Policing the Expanding Sex Trade

On a warm July day in 1855, Margaret Hamilton stalked through the Centre Market, cowhide whip in hand. Hamilton, a Pennsylvanian by birth, had been a sex worker in a brothel on Baltimore's Lovely Lane since at least the late 1840s. On paper, she had little to recommend her in the context of a sex trade that was growing increasingly genteel: she lacked the air of decorum that was usually associated with West Baltimore's more refined sex workers, and she had a terrible temper. During her tenure in the prostitution business, she found herself embroiled in several physical fights with fellow sex workers, and she appeared nearly as frequently in local courts on assault charges as she did for charges of keeping a bawdy house. Like so many other women who managed sex establishments in the latter decades of the early republic, however, Hamilton usually escaped serious criminal penalties. The criminal court in Baltimore did not take assault seriously unless it involved a deadly weapon or gross bodily harm, and by the 1840s, it had largely ceased to punish women involved in the city's thriving brothel trade with anything more than affordable fines for plying their trades.[1]

It had not always been so. Legally speaking, brothel keepers and indoor sex workers had long been privileged in comparison with women who solicited in the streets, but they had not been exempt from crushing punishments in the late eighteenth or early nineteenth century. As Chapter 1 noted, bawdy-house keepers in the decades following the Revolution

---

[1] 1850 US Census, Baltimore, Maryland, Ward 9, p. 358, dwelling 291, family 415, Margaret Hamilton; digital image, Ancestry.com. For examples of Hamilton's assaults, see "Local Matters," *Sun*, Jan. 23, 1849; "Doing Well," *Sun*, June 12, 1855.

often faced steep fines and even jail sentences as Baltimore authorities attempted to reassert their vision of public order by cracking down on "disorderly" houses. In the 1820s, the policing of prostitution only intensified as growing evangelical fervor ushered in a new era of moral reform and religious revivalism. Moral reformers, incensed rioters, citizen complainants, and Baltimore's newly created penny papers all exerted pressure on local courts to police establishments that promoted illicit sexuality, including assignation houses and brothels. Although they were generally more concerned with public forms of commercial sex than private ones and black sexual disorder more than white ones, Baltimore's courts treated all forms of prostitution as criminal offenses that were potentially punishable by incarceration.

And yet the need to reckon with city's rapidly expanding sex trade eventually forced authorities to make choices about how they policed and punished prostitution, choices that said much about their visions for the city and for urban order. Few people in the antebellum period believed that it was possible to eliminate commercial sex entirely, but local authorities did hope to limit the disorder that accompanied prostitution's growth. They did so by ensuring that it took the forms least offensive to their concept of the public peace. In the 1840s and early 1850s, this meant policing prostitution in ways that cracked down on forms of sex work that visibly or aurally disrupted neighborhoods, subverted the city's racial hierarchies, or explicitly undermined men's control over their wives or daughters, all while quietly tolerating the forms of sexual exchange that conformed to authorities' standards of peaceful conduct. As brothels rose to prominence and became embedded in the city's commercial networks, Baltimore authorities treated them as preferable to other sexual labor arrangements or forms of sex work. They created a bifurcated system of punishment in which they continued to penalize streetwalking and casual prostitution harshly but tolerated brothel prostitution and the women who participated in it so long as they did not transgress in other ways against the public peace. It was under this system of toleration that brothel keepers like Margaret Hamilton managed to avoid jail time and grow their businesses despite the illegality of keeping a bawdy or disorderly house. Comparatively protected by the nature of the sex work they performed and by the legal standing that their access to property and wealth provided them, Hamilton and other brothel keepers thrived economically.

Still, even as Margaret Hamilton succeeded amid a system that tolerated brothel prostitution, the ad hoc détente between local authorities and sex workers proved over time to be an unstable one. There were signs by the eve of the Civil War that Baltimoreans' concept of the public peace was shifting in ways that would make the city less legally hospitable to indoor sex workers. Although Hamilton could not have known it as she gripped her whip and surveyed the Centre Market for her target, she herself was on the cusp of ushering in yet another phase of legal wrangling over bawdy houses, one that would generate a legal innovation that would have ramifications for brothel keepers and their businesses for decades to come.

The policing of prostitution had been a concern for Baltimore authorities since the emergence of the sex trade in the years following the Revolution, but the need to regulate public disorder and curb illicit forms of sexual expression intensified in the 1820s. The same period that saw the rapid expansion of Baltimore's sex trade and the rise of the brothel also witnessed intense evangelical revivalism and the emergence of gender ideologies that emphasized that women's "natural" place was within the domestic sphere.[2] The religious fervor that swept the country prompted a growing number of Americans to seek to perfect their society by removing alcohol and temptations toward excessive sexuality from their communities. Reformers like Sylvester Graham and William A. Alcott emphasized the physical and spiritual dangers of unrestrained sexual desire and expression for both men and women, and they urged Americans to adopt more strenuous methods of self-restraint and denial in matters of sexuality.[3] Other reformers, including New York's Reverend John R. McDowall, launched campaigns against urban prostitution as a means of eliminating temptations for urban youth and securing the morals of city residents. In 1830, McDowall and his New York Magdalen Society published a Magdalen Report that purported to reveal the astonishing scope of vice in New York City in the hopes of motivating city residents to lash out against houses of prostitution. While the report was ultimately met with public consternation over the publication of scandalous

---

[2] Since the publication of Barbara Welter's classic article (Welter, "The Cult of True Womanhood: 1820–1860," *American Quarterly* 18, no. 1 [1966]: 151–74), dozens of historians have refined, modified, and expanded on the rise of domestic ideology. For a synthesis of their findings, see Mary P. Ryan, *Mysteries of Sex: Tracing Women and Men through American History* (Chapel Hill: University of North Carolina Press, 2009), especially 88–102.

[3] Cohen, *The Murder of Helen Jewett*, 230–33; April R. Haynes, *Riotous Flesh: Women, Physiology, and the Solitary Vice in Nineteenth-Century America* (Chicago: University of Chicago Press, 2015), especially chapter 1.

allegations and sensational details about the extent of vice in the city, it nevertheless encouraged greater public conversation about the danger of the urban sex trade.[4] Prostitution, with its tendency to highlight the seductive and ribald aspects of women's sexuality and to allow women to exist in public spaces and outside domains of male control, alarmed even those who were not devoutly religious with its undermining of the prevailing gender ideology. During a period when women were ideally supposed to be chaste, demure, and eager to assume roles as wives and mothers, sex workers stood out as anomalous and alternatively pitiable and threatening.

Baltimoreans were slow to translate their growing discontent with the sex trade into formal organizations to combat vice. In 1831, a small group of Baltimore reformers attempted to follow in the footsteps of the New York Magdalen Society and start a ministry for fallen women. They rented a dwelling in which to house and reform repentant sex workers and set about attempting to attract both sex workers and respectable citizens to their ministry. However, the groups' organizers were met with a great deal of public indifference. Few sex workers were interested in their message, and both the landlord and female attendants of the house were wary of being associated with the sex trade. "Such is the opposition of some, and the indifference of others, that as yet we have not been able to move forward," wrote one member of the society.[5] Although moral reformers attributed their failures to public indifference toward the sex trade or disdain for sex workers, the reality was more complicated. For one thing, Baltimore was a heavily Catholic city, and cross-denominational Christian mobilization against vice was challenging during a period when Protestants moralists used allegations of rampant sexual immorality to discredit the Catholic church (Baltimore experienced

---

[4] New York Magdalen Society, "Magdalen Report" (New York: 1831), 10. On antebellum moral and social reform campaigns, see, among many others, D'Emilio and Freedman, *Intimate Matters*, 140–42. Bruce Dorsey, *Reforming Men and Women: Gender in the Antebellum City* (Ithaca, NY: Cornell University Press, 2002); Ronald G. Walters, *American Reformers, 1815–1860*, revised edition (New York: Hill and Wang, 1997); Larry Whiteaker, *Seduction, Prostitution, and Moral Reform in New York, 1830–1860* (New York: Garland Publishing, 1997), 41–66; Hill, *Their Sisters' Keepers*, 16–27.

[5] S.W. to Rev. J. R. McDowall, Baltimore Magdalene Society, Mar. 28, 1831, letter printed in J. R. McDowall, *Magdalen Facts* 1 (January 1832): 54–55. On Magdalen Societies, see Gilfoyle, *City of Eros*, 182–84; Michael Meranze, *Laboratories of Virtue: Punishment, Revolution, and Authority in Philadelphia, 1760–1835* (Chapel Hill: University of North Carolina Press, 1996), 272–79; Lyons, *Sex among the Rabble*, 323–53.

a Carmelite convent riot in 1839 after a woman claiming to be an escaped nun inflamed public suspicions that women were being physically and sexually abused in the building). For another, Baltimore was a slave city, and many moral reform organizations – including the Magdalen Society and the Female Moral Reform Society – had some degree of overlap with the abolition movement. Not only did the moral reform and abolition movement share prominent members, including Arthur Tappan and Sojourner Truth, but they were also united in their critiques of male sexual license. Critics of prostitution decried young women's ruin at the hands of lustful men; abolitionists condemned slavery as a licentious institution that promoted sexual immorality by giving white men unchecked authority over the bodies of black women and thus made the Southern states into "brothels." Demands that men be held accountable and restrain their lust implicitly threatened white male power. They were destabilizing and challenging the racial and sexual hierarchies that structured life – and, indeed, the economy and labor system – in antebellum Baltimore. For this reason, Baltimoreans may have shied away from joining or embracing organizations that focused on attacking the urban sex trade.[6]

Nevertheless, many city residents were disturbed by what they saw as the sudden proliferation of vice in their city, especially as the sex trade boomed in the 1830s. As brothel prostitution rose to prominence and sex work grew more commercialized and professionalized, the sex trade emerged from the shadows, so to speak. No longer confined to the poor areas around the waterways, prostitution spread to the city's bourgeois neighborhoods and tourist districts. Sex workers rubbed shoulders with respectable guests in spaces of entertainment such as theaters and museums and promenaded along main thoroughfares. They shopped the public markets and hovered around commercial areas. They also crowded the pages of local newspapers, at least metaphorically. The 1830s saw the emergence of penny papers that diverged from the practices of older, subscription-based newspapers that focused on commercial and international news. Penny press papers like the Baltimore *Sun*, which were intended to be sold cheaply on the streets, attempted to attract readers by publicizing sensational, local news stories, especially as they pertained to crime and vice. The *Sun* and other papers regularly sent reporters to the

---

[6] On the connection between anti-slavery activism and anti-vice activism, see Haynes, *Riotous Flesh*.

City Court to watch and report on local trials, including those of madams and sex workers. By the late 1830s, the city's literate population could rarely go a day without seeing some news of prostitution to complement what they witnessed each day as they walked the streets of their neighborhoods and commercial districts.

Public consternation over the growing prostitution trade manifested itself in a number of ways, including violence directed against houses of ill fame and their occupants. Between 1830 and the 1860s, US cities ranging from New York to Richmond witnessed brothel riots and other vigilante actions in which men burst into bawdy houses, smashed their contents, and attacked their occupants.[7] Baltimore never saw the same scale of organized brothel rioting as New York did, but numerous women who kept bawdy houses had their houses attacked, stoned, or broken into in the antebellum decades.[8] In 1837, more than half a dozen Baltimore men broke into Eliza Randolph's house in the Meadow and proceeded to fire guns, throw brickbats, and beat the patrons of the house. That same night, Sarah Walters, also of the Western district, charged a man with rioting in her house.[9] Ann Bartlett's brothel on Potter Street in Old Town was the site of numerous incidents of vandalism throughout the 1840s and '50s. In September 1854, Frank Remious destroyed the porch of Bartlett's house; only a month and a half later, Hyde Mitchell was arrested for destroying Bartlett's furniture.[10]

Several local men made hobbies of attacking sex workers. In 1842, Henry Deal assaulted sex workers Elizabeth Donough and Elizabeth Turner by knocking them down and then kicking Turner under the chin. The *Sun* commented of Deal's assault: "Deal seemed to think it was all very good fun ... there appears to be amongst a certain class of young man, an idea that they can knock, and kick and cuff a girl, because she is a prostitute, with impunity – nay, that their zeal in such performances is highly praiseworthy." Though Deal was held in jail in default of bail, his brush with the criminal courts did not dissuade him for long. Three

---

[7] Rothman, *Notorious in the Neighborhood*, 111–13; Hill, *Prostitution in New York City, 1830–1870*, 116–18. On violence toward women involved in prostitution, see especially Cohen, *The Murder of Helen Jewett*, 78–86, 124; Gilfoyle, *City of Eros*, 76–91.

[8] In 1839, for example, the Baltimore City Court (BCC) heard the cases of two men charged with attacking the dwelling of Elizabeth Briggs, a local madam. BCC (Docket), May Term, 1839, Cases 383–84, MSA C-185.

[9] "Disgraceful Riot," *Sun*, Nov. 21, 1837; "City Court," *Sun*, Dec. 22, 1837.

[10] "Destructiveness," *Sun*, Sep. 12, 1854; "Destructiveness," *Sun*, Nov. 1, 1854.

years later, he was arrested again for a gross and unprovoked assault against local sex worker Jane Campbell.[11] Notably, such assaults against sex workers were not necessarily motivated by moral concerns about sex work; they were often assertions of dominance committed by men who resented the exclusive nature of brothels and wished to assert their right to exert control over women and the proceeds of their sexual labor. Nevertheless, the violence was symptomatic of a broader resentment of prostitution and of women who participated in sexual commerce.

Increased attention to prostitution in the latter decades of the antebellum period put significant pressure on Baltimore's City Court. Though many Christian movements at the time emphasized the value of moral suasion as the key to changing hearts and minds, most were not averse to legal means of curbing the city's commercial sex trade.[12] By the 1820s, citizen complaints against disorderly houses were beginning to increase, likely as a combined result of the growth of the sex trade, growing public disdain for prostitution, and the financial incentives that the city offered citizens for making criminal complaints against disorderly establishments. Reporting witnesses were typically granted half of whatever fines were levied against convicted bawdy-house keepers, and city residents came forward in large numbers, sometimes reporting multiple houses at the same time in the hopes of receiving payouts.[13] The court and its grand juries, which by the late 1830s were under pressure from penny papers like the Baltimore *Sun* thanks to scathing editorials about the problems of vice in the city, was tasked with following through on these complaints. Between 1839 and 1840, the number of bawdy-house cases – that is, cases in which the alleged disorder of the house was explicitly sexual in nature – presented by the grand jury rose from ten to thirty-three annually. In almost every

[11] "City Court – Saturday, Mar. 26, 1842," *Sun*, Mar. 28, 1842; "Local Matters," *Sun*, Mar. 19, 1845.

[12] Heather Lee Miller, *From Moral Suasion to Moral Coercion: Persistence and Transformation in Prostitution Reform, Portland, Oregon, 1888–1916* (Portland: University of Oregon, 1996).

[13] *The General Public Statutory Law and Public Local Law of the State of Maryland, from the Year 1692 to 1839 Inclusive: with Annotations Thereto, and a Copious Index*, vol. 2 (Baltimore: John D. Toy, 1840), 1695.

subsequent sample year, the number of presentments continued to increase until by the 1840s, it was not unusual for grand juries to pursue more than a hundred bawdy-house cases each year.[14]

Initially, at least, City Court chief justice Nicholas Brice and his compatriots responded to public pressure by prescribing incarceration as a punishment for keeping a bawdy or disorderly house rather than – or in addition to – the traditional fines. The period from 1825 to 1830 saw a number of bawdy and disorderly house keepers sentenced to jail terms on conviction for the offense. In the 1820s, most of these jail terms were between two to six months in length and accompanied by fines of $20–$50, enormous sums for people who were still scraping by in a sex trade that was only beginning to transition out of a subsistence business.[15] Such penalties were intended to be harsh and suppressive toward the women and men involved in the trade. They represented the court's attempts to satisfy a public that was alarmed by the apparent growth of vice in the city.

However, these attempts proved short-lived. Problems arose almost immediately as the growing number of brothels placed a strain on city resources. As prosecutions for bawdy-house cases increased and the punishments shifted from fines to incarceration, the city's carceral complexes grew strained. Baltimore's city and county jail had been constructed in 1802, when the population of the city had been around 26,500 people. By the time of the 1830 census, Baltimore's population was more than 80,000. Although the jail underwent some improvements in 1817, its size placed constraints on the number of prisoners it could reasonably house. This was especially true given that crime in general was quite high in the city in the 1830s and that the jail facility still housed debtors and other private prisoners in addition to persons arrested for criminal violations.[16] By 1830, the city was already beginning to scramble to cope with overcrowding. That year, the average term of incarceration for bawdy and disorderly house keepers dropped to one week. No doubt hoping to free up space for new prisoners, the state also passed a law capping the amount of time prisoners could be jailed for failing to pay fines or court costs at thirty days.[17]

---

[14] Based on examinations of City Court records from 1839, 1840, 1841, 1846, 1847, and 1849 and of Baltimore City Criminal Court from 1852, 1855, 1859, and 1860.
[15] BCCC, 1821 and 1825.   [16] Scharf, *History of Baltimore City and County*, 200–2.
[17] Laws of Maryland, 1830, chapter 145.

Perhaps for reasons of overcrowding, the incarceration of bawdy-house keepers ceased by the late 1830s. Although no one explicitly admitted as much, expending resources to incarcerate people who owned property, earned a steady (albeit illicit) income, and otherwise avoided being drains on the public coffers was not a priority in the context of a legal system that was increasingly concerned with preserving property rights.[18] By 1839, fines for keeping bawdy houses dropped back down to $10 in most cases, and magistrates eased off on their use of incarceration as a punishment.[19] In ten sample years of City Court records between 1839 and 1860, almost 1,000 people were indicted and tried for keeping bawdy or disorderly houses. Only ten of them were sentenced to any jail time.[20] One, Alberto Mingo, was sentenced to spend a month incarcerated for his role in managing a disorderly establishment; the remaining defendants were sentenced to a week or less.[21] As was usually the case in the justice system, black men and women were more likely than their white counterparts to be given sentences that compromised their freedom and suppressed their businesses.

As the use of imprisonment as a punishment for disorderly house keepers waned, Baltimore authorities looked toward a more pragmatic approach to intervention in the city's prostitution trade, one better suited to their imperatives for maintaining public order using limited resources. Increasingly, the city began to adopt informal policies designed not to suppress the sex trade – a task that, frankly, seemed impossible given its increasing scope and the high demand for commercial sex in the mid-nineteenth century – but rather to control its shape and render its presence less objectionable to respectable urban residents. In practice, this meant embracing and formalizing what the court had already begun to do in the earlier decades of the nineteenth century, namely, to distinguish forms of prostitution that were highly disruptive to the public order from those that were merely distasteful.

---

[18] Numerous historians of Southern carceral culture, most notably Edward Ayers, have noted that urban areas that were integrated into broader commercial capitalist networks tended to punish property crime with incarceration more than any other offense. Property criminals made up the vast majority – often upward of 80 percent – of criminals in penitentiaries. Ayers, *Vengeance and Justice: Crime and Punishment in the 19th Century American South* (Oxford: Oxford University Press, 1984), especially Part 1.

[19] BCC, 1830, C184-5, MSA 16662.

[20] This statistic is based on examinations of City Court records from 1839, 1840, 1841, 1846, 1847, 1849, 1852, 1855, 1859, and 1860. The odd spacing of the sample years reflects the uneven distribution of surviving court dockets.

[21] BCC, November Term 1849, 408, Alberto Mingo, C184-11, MSA 16668.

Under the regulatory system that had developed out of necessity by the 1840s, public forms of prostitution were still dealt with by denying women due process rights and incarcerating them in the almshouse on the basis that they were disruptive to the peace and order of the community. Brothel prostitution, while undoubtedly objectionable from a moral standpoint, began to be treated more judiciously. Local residents and authorities preferred that prostitution take place off the public streets and in fixed locations where it was easier to contain, control, and monitor, and so they adopted a system of punishment that was also a tacit regulatory system for brothels. More specifically, they began to punish the majority of brothel keepers with fines that allowed them to buy their way out of their legal troubles while reserving harsher punishments only for those brothel keepers who transgressed against the public order in egregious ways. In this way, they incentivized brothel prostitution relative to other forms of sex work while still appearing to punish the women and men who managed the trade.[22]

The newly formalized regulatory approach to addressing brothel keeping began even before trial did. Baltimore's City Court convened in three sessions every year, one in January or February, one in May or June, and one in October or November. Prior to the 1840s, disorderly house and bawdy-house cases tended to be spread over each of these terms, probably as a result of the ad hoc civilian complaint process. It was not unusual for at least some of the men and women accused of the offense to be jailed to await trial once the court returned to session. After 1840, however, it became common for the bulk of bawdy-house cases to be concentrated in one term of the court, usually the summer term. In court dockets, the names of those charged with keeping a bawdy house appeared one after the other, in sequentially numbered cases, which suggests that the court routinized its process of dealing with bawdy-house keepers by investigating and summoning them all at the same time. The growing routinization of the presentment process was accompanied by a virtual end to pretrial incarceration. The court rarely ordered the sheriff, who was charged with summoning accused bawdy-house keepers, to arrest or hold madams in jail pending their days in court. Of the forty-three individuals

---

[22] Sociologist Joel Best observed a pattern of regulated brothel prostitution in St. Paul, Minnesota. Best, *Controlling Vice*. On the toleration of brothel prostitution in the nineteenth century, see also Kann, *Taming Passion for the Public Good*, 152.

charged with keeping a bawdy house in 1841, only one, Caroline Cole, was listed as having been jailed. By 1847, not a single one of the sixty-three men and women charged with keeping a bawdy house was incarcerated prior to trial.[23] At most, they were required to post securities for their appearance.

Once they came before the court, bawdy-house keepers followed a fairly established routine. Those who stood accused had the option either to plead guilty or requested a jury or bench trial. Those persons who were convicted or who pled guilty were fined between $1 and $500 each, with $5–$25 being relatively standard.[24] Typically, the amount of the fine was graduated according to the size and perceived level of disorder of the accused's brothel or assignation house. On June 24, 1841, for instance, the City Court heard eight separate bawdy-house cases, those of Ann Bartlett, Mary Cooke, Sarah "BlackHawk" Burke, Cecilia Gray, Elizabeth Osborne, Harriet Rhineman, Leathy Ann Talbot, and Ann Thomas. All eight women were convicted and fined for the offense, but each was assigned an amount "according to the extent of the apparent means which were used severally by these abandoned women, in their disgraceful and pernicious traffic." Elizabeth Osborne and Sarah Burke were fined $200 and $100, respectively, amounts that reflected the fact that both were well-off property owners who kept large brothels. Leathy Talbot, Ann Bartlett, and Mary Cooke, on the other hand, each paid only $10 plus court costs, a standard fine for smaller bawdy houses.[25]

The graduated nature of the fines and the overall profitability of prostitution ensured that the vast majority of men and women who pled or were found guilty of keeping a bawdy house could afford to pay their fines and court fees. Only three of forty bawdy-house defendants whose cases resulted in guilty pleas or verdicts in 1841 were committed to jail in default of payment, and all were released after a month based on an 1830 act that limited jail time to thirty days for individuals who could not afford to pay fines of less than $50. The remainder of the women and men who were convicted either paid their fines outright or otherwise found individuals to post security for their eventual payment.[26]

[23] Baltimore City Court (Docket and Minutes), Case 594, Caroline Cole, June 1841, C184-8, MSA 16665.
[24] Baltimore City Court records from 1839, 1840, 1841, 1846, 1847, and 1849.
[25] "City Court – June Term – 1841," *Sun*, June 24, 1841, 4.
[26] BCC, Case 229, Elizabeth Downs, June 1841; BCC, June Term, 1841, Case 587, Margaret Nightengale; C184-8, MSA 16665.

The court's use of fines rather than incarceration meant in practice that the proprietors of sex establishments could pay for the right to continue their trades. Especially as the sex trade grew more profitable in the 1840s, most madams made enough from the sex trade that they could absorb a $5–$25 fine without much difficulty. If not, they could usually count on their wealthy, real estate–owning landlords to bail them out. When Mary Ann Hill pled guilty to keeping a disorderly house in 1840, she was fined $50, a high sum considering that her Canal Street brothel was not especially affluent. Her landlord, Sarah Goldsmith, who owned numerous brothels throughout the city, secured her fine and court fees so that Hill could avoid jail time while she amassed the capital necessary to pay.[27] Meadow brothel keeper and landlord Elizabeth Osborne assisted six female brothel keepers, some of whom were her employees, in paying their fines and securities. In 1840 alone, Osborne secured $110 worth of fines and agreed to post $300 worth of securities to prevent Harriet Heaths, Elizabeth Merritt, Eliza Randolph, Leathy Ann Talbot, Nancy Thomas, and Emily Hinkety from going to jail.[28] Elizabeth Ann Miller, another Bath Street brothel keeper, posted securities or secured fines for Ann Wilson, Ann Thomas, and Ann Stubbins, all of whom pled guilty to bawdy-house charges. Once the fines were secured, most bawdy-house keepers simply returned to their trade until the court convened again.[29]

The City Court's system of fining and releasing those convicted of bawdy-house charges made it something of a revolving door for many brothel keepers, most of whom responded nonchalantly to charges against them. When longtime madam Mary Kelly was called to court in 1852 to offer testimony in a criminal case not directly related to her status as a madam, the state's attorney inquired about her occupation. Addressing the court, Kelly remarked wryly, "All of you gentlemen here know what kind of house I keep – I have been up here often enough."[30] Kelly's seeming nonchalance about her many trips to the City Court mirrored

---

[27] "Local Matters," *Sun*, Apr. 4, 1840; *Sun*, Mar. 30, 1840; "Local Matters," *Sun*, June 17, 1840; BCC, February Term, 1840, Case 312, Mary Ann Hill.

[28] BCC, February Term, 1840, Case 226, Harriet Heaths; Case 212, Elizabeth Merritt; Case 219, Eliza Randolph; Case 214, Leathy Ann Talbot; Case 220, Nancy Thomas; BCC, October Term, 1840, Case 105, Emily Hinkety.

[29] BCC, June Term, 1840, Case 260, Ann Wilson; Case 228, Ann Thomas; BCC, June Term, 1840, Case 289, Ann Stubbins.

[30] "Criminal Court," *Sun*, Nov. 20, 1852. Kelly had indeed been in court multiple times on bawdy-house charges. See, for example, BCC (Docket and Minutes), May Term, 1847, Case 394, Mary Kelly.

that of other brothel keepers, who began to treat their trips to court as an annual or semi-annual routine. Secure in the knowledge that they would not face jail terms if they were convicted, many brothel proprietors ceased to bother contesting the charges against them. In three sample years between 1839 and 1849, a total of 136 "keeping a bawdy house" cases progressed beyond the presentment or indictment stage. In 57 percent of those cases, the defendants avoided the cost and hassle of a trial by pleading guilty or nolo contendere to the offense and then paying their fines.[31]

The local press, for its part, was keenly aware that fines did little to dissuade brothel keepers from continuing in their trades, despite the justice theater that was the court's annual hauling in and sentencing of brothel keepers. The Baltimore *Sun*, the city's most popular penny paper, was a vocal critic of the justice system's handling of bawdy-house cases in the early 1840s. The *Sun's* staff writers railed against brothels and other assignation places, decrying them as "palaces of Satan" that destroyed communal morality, threatened the institution of marriage, and placed a blot on the reputation of the city. Several times, columnists expressed both frustration with the court's inability or unwillingness to stamp out havens of vice, as well as doubts about whether that was truly the court's goal. In 1843, the *Sun's* court reporter observed several bawdy-house cases. He wrote with some cynicism in his report that the court had been "engaged yesterday in … endeavoring to purify the morality of the community, so far as the imposition of fines upon the proprietors of licentious establishments is calculated [to] effect that object."[32]

Another writer, citing the frequency with which women returned to prostitution after their court dates, was more direct in his assertion that the fines levied on bawdy-house keepers were not intended as a suppressive measure against prostitution. He wrote, "Does anyone believe that the disease [of vice] can be removed in this way? No – not one. Neither the makers nor the ministers of the law believe any such thing."[33] The reporter suggested that the City Court's true motives were not to eliminate vice but to license it in a way that was covert enough that it did not draw public ire, that is, by disguising licensing fees as punitive fines for criminal offenses. "The periodical imposition of fines, for offenses that it is known, will be continued after payment," the reporter wrote, "amounts to neither more nor less than a license granted after some time spent in the

[31] BCC, sample years 1839, 1847, and 1849.
[32] "Local Matters," *Sun*, June 28, 1843, 2.   [33] "Licentiousness," *Sun*, June 19, 1841.

traffic, with an implied promise of renewal of it, to some future indefinite period."[34] The writer's contention that fines were the equivalent of regularized licensing fees was supported by the fact that Baltimore authorities had a tendency to release brothel keepers who were charged with keeping a bawdy house more than once per court term. When Mary Ann Hill was found guilty of keeping a bawdy house for the second time in the June Term of 1840, the court simply released her after it was "proved that a fine had already been imposed on her on an indictment found this term."[35]

In addition to shaping the contours of the sex trade by privileging sex workers and managers who kept prostitution indoors, the city's system of fining brothel keepers annually raised money for its court system and public health facilities. As more and more bawdy-house keepers opted to forgo trial in favor of pleading guilty, the city was spared from expending the time and money necessary to try them. Meanwhile, the fines and fees extracted from the women and men who profited most from brothel prostitution added modestly to the city's coffers. In 1840, the court extracted $1,810 worth of fines and an unspecified amount of court costs from bawdy and disorderly house keepers and their landlords. While the fines were not enough to contribute in any significant way to the municipal treasury, the court fees, which often ranged from $7 to $15 per trial, helped to compensate the sheriff for services and offset the operating costs of the City Court. By the 1840s, the city began to put the modest fines collected from bawdy-house keepers to public use. In a pragmatic arrangement that helped the city to avoid any allegations that it was lining its pockets with ill-gotten gains from prostitution, the City Court donated half of all the fines collected from bawdy-house keepers and liquor sellers to Baltimore's public dispensaries. Dispensaries, which were essentially free medical clinics open to anyone with a referral from a subscriber, provided medical care to thousands of indigent city residents each year. During a period in which Americans associated prostitution with disease, the arrangement functioned as a practical means of using the proceeds of prostitution to minimize its negative impact on the health of the city.[36]

---

[34] "Licentiousness," *Sun*, June 19, 1841.   [35] "City Court," *Sun*, June 20, 1840, 1.

[36] *Laws of the State of Maryland*, 1843, chapter 261, section 1; *Proceedings of the National Conference of Charities and Correction*, vol. 42, Baltimore (Chicago: Hildmann Printing Co., 1915), 426.

On the history of dispensaries, see Baltimore General Dispensary, *Rules and By-Laws of the Baltimore General Dispensary, with Other Matter, Relative to the Institution*

The City Court's willingness to tolerate and extract revenue from well-ordered brothels encouraged brothel keepers to maintain their establishments within certain standards of propriety while allowing local authorities to focus their energies on cracking down on houses that did not meet those standards. Local authorities tolerated brothels on the understanding that they were less disruptive than other forms of sex establishments and more compatible with an urban order based around quiet streets, defined racial hierarchies, and women contained within domestic spaces. If this proved not to be the case, the offending house keepers could expect swift and sometimes severe penalties for their failure to maintain their brothels in accordance with the informal standards that governed their trade.

Madams whose establishments were particularly loud or rowdy, for instance, could expect to be hauled into court on multiple bawdy-house charges annually instead of the usual one or two. Catharine Hill, a white brothel keeper who kept a house on Gough Street, found herself brought before the court as a result of the conduct of Charles Torrence, one of her clients. Torrence disturbed the peace and taunted the police by "springing [shaking] a watchman's rattle out of the window at night." The incident was only the most recent of a long string of bad behavior at Hill's brothel, where female residents of the house were "in the habit of donning the unmentionables and riding through the streets *en cavalier*."[37] Because the behavior of Hill's boarders was aurally and morally disruptive to her neighbors, the City Court issued her an unusually harsh punishment on her conviction for keeping a house of ill fame. Hill was not only fined the high sum of $50 plus court costs, but also ordered to pay a $100 security to ensure that she left the sex trade entirely.[38]

There were a variety of other offenses that made the courts especially apt to punish brothel keepers in ways that exceeded the standard fines. One of the most serious involved allegedly catering to respectable people, and particularly to respectable women. Dominant nineteenth-century sexual mores drew a sharp distinction between virtuous and "fallen" women; the former were to be placed on a pedestal as wives and mothers,

(Baltimore, 1803); Baltimore General Dispensary, *An Address to the Citizens of Baltimore and Its Vicinity: Containing a Concise Account of the Baltimore General Dispensary, Its By-Laws, and Other Matters Worthy of Notice* (Baltimore, 1812). For more on the history of dispensaries, see Charles E. Rosenberg, "Social Class and Medical Care in Nineteenth-Century America: The Rise and Fall of the Dispensary," *Journal of the History of Medicine and Allied Sciences* 29 (1974): 32–54.

[37] "City Court – June Term, 1839," *Sun*, June 14, 1839.
[38] "City Court – June Term, 1839," *Sun*, June 14, 1839.

and the latter were subjected to ridicule, ostracization, and violence on the basis of their sexual transgressions. Brothels were comparatively tolerated not just because they kept sexual commerce contained indoors and less visible, but also because they reinforced this distinction in a way that casual forms of prostitution did not. By creating what was essentially a professional class of prostitutes, brothels heightened the separation of sex workers from other women and made them legible as "fallen." They reinforced rather than challenged sexual hierarchies. However, brothel keepers who failed to enforce this separation by inviting non–sex workers to patronize their houses for assignations violated the unspoken contract and drew swift reprisals from the court.

Hannah Smithson, mentioned at the beginning of Chapter 3, drew particularly harsh reprisal from the court after she was accused in 1840 and 1841 failing to maintain the distinction between respectable and "fallen" women in renting rooms in her assignation house. Smithson's house was known for catering to sex workers, but it was alleged by unnamed witnesses that she also let rooms to "married ladies of respectability, passing as virtuous in society."[39] In the context of the early republic's gender hierarchies, the possibility that Smithson provided rooms to married women alarmed observers. Though it was common enough for married men to visit sex workers, the notion that women could exercise a similar sexual license by seeking the company of men who were not their husbands violated contemporary gender conventions. Prostitution was part and parcel of men's patriarchal privilege. When sex establishments challenged that privilege instead of reinforcing it, they became targets for policing.

The public reaction against Smithson and other assignation-house keepers suspected of catering to women who were not sex workers was swift. The Baltimore *Sun* published several tirades against assignation houses, which it deemed "high courts of Satan." The paper claimed that assignation houses that allowed married people to patronize their establishments in secret were "where is consummated that most utterly irretrievable of all the various species of destruction – the total annihilation of domestic happiness, by ruin of connubial virtue."[40] Ladies' presence in sex establishment represented a threat to the institution of marriage and

---

[39] "City Court – March 7, 1840," *Sun*, Mar. 9, 1840, 4; BCC (Criminal Docket), February Term, 1840, Case 199, Hannah Smithson. See also "Licentiousness," *Sun*, May 29, 1841; "Editorial Immorality," *Sun*, June 19, 1841; "The Fine," *Sun*, June 22, 1841.

[40] "Licentiousness," *Sun*, May 29, 1841.

an embarrassment to both respectable citizens and "the city itself."[41] As a reflection of the seriousness of the offense, the court fined Hannah Smithson the staggering sum of $500 following her conviction for keeping a bawdy house.[42] The court also went after Samuel H. Goldsmith, who at the time was Smithson's landlord. Goldsmith, who had testified at Smithson's trial that he was unaware of the type of house she kept, was charged with perjury and required to post a $500 bond for his appearance in court.[43] Although Smithson managed to get her fine reduced to $100, she continued to face scrutiny from the court even years after the initial charges were brought against her. In 1847, Smithson was again charged with keeping an assignation house after a wife stabbed her husband with a dirk knife after the husband had followed her to Smithson's house and confronted her about her infidelity. Following the stabbing, the court levied another $100 fine on Smithson.[44]

In keeping with the court's pattern of cracking down on sex establishments that challenged patriarchal authority, Baltimore's City Court also tended to utilize all resources at its disposal to punish madams who allowed the seduction of young women on their properties. While the age of consent was quite low in the nineteenth century, it was an unspoken rule of the sex trade that brothels should not board girls younger than sixteen, especially if they were virgins or otherwise had living parents who objected to their residence at a brothel. When locals discovered a sixteen-year-old who had been "seduced away from her father" hidden in the crawl space of Mary Ann Hill's house on Canal Street, they immediately called watchmen to arrest her. Hill was tried for keeping a bawdy house, fined the high sum of $100, and then, in a rare pattern of prosecution, charged with the same offense at least three other times in the same term of the City Court.[45] Ann Bartlett, who kept a house on Potter Street, had a similar experience after being caught with a young girl in her establishment. In 1840, Bartlett committed what

---

[41] "Assignation Houses," *Sun*, Mar. 2, 1840; "Assignation Houses," *Sun*, Mar. 3, 1840; "Licentiousness," *Sun*, June 19, 1841.

[42] "The City Court – March 7, 1840," *Sun*, Mar. 9, 1840, 4; BCC, February Term, 1840, Case 199, Hannah Smithson.

[43] BCC, February Term, 1840, Case 318, Samuel Goldsmith.

[44] "Local Matters," *Sun*, Aug. 5, 1847, 2; "City Court," *Sun*, July 1, 1841, 1; BCC, June Term, 1841, Case 221, Hannah Smithson; BCC, October Term, 1841, Case 280, Hannah Smithson.

[45] "Local Matters," *Sun*, Apr. 4, 1840; *Sun*, Mar. 30, 1840; "Local Matters," *Sun*, June 17, 1840.

newspapers described as the "very aggravated" offense of allowing a thirteen-year-old to be seduced in her establishment. The girl was from a respectable background, and Bartlett was so fearful of arrest after the girl was discovered on her property that she closed and locked her house. Presumably hoping that the sheriff would give up on serving the warrant against her if she absented herself for long enough, Bartlett left the brothel abandoned for months. However, the sheriff pursued and arrested Bartlett, assessed on her a prohibitively high bail set by the court, and jailed her to await trial.[46] Demand for young and even prepubescent prostitutes was high enough that the court had difficulty dissuading less scrupulous brothel keepers from engaging in what was ultimately a niche market. Still, the court's efforts in tracking Bartlett down and prosecuting her spoke to the perceived seriousness of her offense and the amount of public disdain that attached to it. Such was the public disgust over her conduct that Bartlett's house was mobbed and damaged by local men several times in the nearly three decades she kept a brothel, which suggests that extra-legal forms of policing occurred in instances when the court's forms of justice were insufficient to satisfy city residents.[47]

Not surprisingly, the court also saved some of its harshest treatment for men and women whose houses transgressed against the racial order of the city. Bawdy houses or rare, black-owned brothels that catered to a predominantly black clientele were almost always regarded as threatening, as they invited black Baltimoreans to convene together at night, to drink, and to do as they pleased with their bodies. In 1837, African American madam Harriet Carroll's brothel was raided at behest of her neighbors, who complained that her brothel catered to black men and women who "greatly harassed" people in the area with their "riotous and disorderly conduct."[48] During that raid, police arrested every black resident or visitor to the house, eleven men and women total, and took

---

[46] "Committal," *Sun*, Apr. 8, 1840, 2; "City Court – February Term," *Sun*, Feb. 2, 1841, 1; BCC, February Term, 1840, Case 251, Ann Bartlett; BCC, June 1840, Case 177, Ann Bartlett; BCC, June 1841, Case 239, Ann Bartlett; "Watch Returns," *Sun*, June 6, 1838, 2; "Destructiveness," *Sun*, Sep. 12, 1854, 1; "Destructiveness," *Sun*, Nov. 1, 1854.

[47] "Destructiveness," *Sun*, Sep. 12, 1854; "Destructiveness," *Sun*, Nov. 1, 1854.

[48] Disorderly Houses," *Sun*, Oct. 30, 1839. "Drunkards – Strollers," *Sun*, Aug. 1, 1841. Carroll appeared numerous times before the City Court and City Criminal Court during her tenure as a brothel keeper. She had several known aliases, including Anderson and Price. BCC, October Term, 1839, Cases 245 and 246, Harriet Price; BCC 1840, June Term, Case 293, Harriet Carroll, C184-7, MSA 16664; Baltimore City Court (Docket), 1841, February Term, Case 294, Harriet Carroll, C184-8, MSA 16665; Baltimore City Court (Docket), 1847, May Term, 292, Harriet Carroll, C185-10, MSA 16667.

Carroll herself into custody. The arrest of male brothel patrons was almost unheard of at the time and appears to have been practiced exclusively in black houses. As was often the case when black women were accused of crimes, Carroll's punishment came before she was ever convicted. She was ordered to post a bond of $50 for her appearance in court, an amount much higher than she could afford. She was incarcerated for over a month in the city jail before her trial and release by a magistrate.[49]

Bawdy-house keepers whose establishments catered to a mixed-race clientele were also subjected to special opprobrium, especially as abolition become a more visible social and reform movement in the North in the 1830s. Critics of abolition distributed propaganda that suggested that abolition and "amalgamation" were related and that interracial sex was the ultimate goal of the abolitionist movement. In light of this, any house that allowed black men and women to socialize outside the bounds of traditional propriety or fixed relationships of hierarchy to interact with one another sexually was regarded as threatening to the social order.[50] Houses that allowed black men to engage in sex with white women drew particular ire, but Baltimore's press and courts decried any disorderly house with mixed clientele. In October 1839, the City Court tried Patrick M'Nally, who resided in L Alley, for keeping a disorderly house. The *Sun* described the area of M'Nally's house as an "infected district" and complained that it was "a spot where amalgamation flourishes in a manner that would delight the heart of Garrison."[51] In coverage of another case originating in L Alley, that of a white disorderly house keeper named John Gibson, the paper wrote that Gibson catered to "the worst class of sable sporting men." The interracial prostitution, drinking, and gambling that took place in Gibson's establishment and in other businesses on that street were so strongly scorned that many Baltimoreans referred to the area as "Diabolic Alley."

Even sporting men who delighted in visiting Baltimore's vice establishments expressed their disgust at houses that allowed black and white sex

---

[49] "Central Watch – Saturday Morning," *Sun*, Aug. 29, 1837.
[50] Stephanie M. H. Camp, *Closer to Freedom: Enslaved Women and Everyday Resistance in the Plantation South* (Chapel Hill: University of North Carolina Press, 2004), 111–12; Leslie M. Harris, "From Abolitionist Amalgamators to 'Rulers of the Five Points'," in *Sex, Love, Race: Crossing Boundaries in North American History*, ed. Martha Hodes (New York: New York University Press, 1999), 191–212; Martha Hodes, *White Women, Black Men: Illicit Sex in the 19th-Century South* (New Haven, CT: Yale University Press, 1997); Long, *The Great Southern Babylon*, 10–59.
[51] "Disorderly Houses," *Sun*, Oct. 30, 1839.

workers and clients to mingle freely with one another. One commenter from the New York *Whip* noted that visitors could "enter some [brothels on Wilk Street] and view the Circassian and sable race beautifully blended together, and their arms intermingled so as to form a lovely contrast between the alabaster whiteness of the one, and the polished blackness of the other." Although the description itself was somewhat eroticized, the commenter went on to suggest that authorities should drive offending brothel residents out of the city:

I love amalgamation as the devil does holy water... if I was the mayor, I would with a posse of police officers very politely escort them to the Penitentiary, where they might enjoy the cool, refreshing breeze on the "margin of fair Jones's water" [i.e., on the banks of the Jones Falls, where the penitentiary was located], until they were perfectly satisfied with a rural retreat.[52]

Although authorities never resorted to the sending the keepers of bawdy establishments to the penitentiary, they did issue harsh punishments to those who allowed interracial sex and interaction. In 1839, tavern keeper George Savage was tried for "keeping a common, ill-governed, disorderly house" on the Causeway. Savage's house was described as "a place of resort for disorderly blacks, who were allowed to play cards therein, and were on several occasions protected by the inmates from arrest by the officers." In addition to being fined a typical $20 and costs, Savage also had his liquor license revoked.[53] Just months later, he was hauled into court again to answer charges of keeping a riotous and disorderly house. This time, he was fined $50 and costs. This was a particularly steep fine for a house on Wilk Street, and Savage, who had probably lost a great deal of business following the revocation of his liquor license, could not afford to pay it. He was jailed for a month in lieu of the fine. By the June Term of 1840, Savage was back in court on yet another disorderly house charge. Public sentiment against him was so strong that Savage had to ask for his case to be removed to Ann Arundel County on the basis that he could not get a fair trial in Baltimore City. The Court approved the request, but it forced Savage to testify against his landlord, William Shelley. Shelley, notably, became one of the first

[52] "Baltimore: Correspondent of the Whip," *The Whip*, July 2, 1842, in *The Flash Press*, 190–91.
[53] "Disorderly Houses," *Sun*, Oct. 30, 1839.

landlords on record to be charged in Baltimore City for renting a house for immoral purposes.[54]

The court's tendency to throw the book – or at least attempt to throw the book – at brothel keepers whose establishments transgressed against established social norms highlighted the degree to which "everyday" forms of brothel prostitution were taken for granted in antebellum Baltimore. Brothel prostitution was so well established as a trade by the 1840s that it had tacit standards and rules of conduct that governed its participants and their actions. The City Court enforced these standards whenever it singled out madams and landlords whose behavior transgressed against them. In doing so, the court took an active role not only in regulating prostitution, but also in defining the boundaries between acceptable and unacceptable forms of illicit sexuality. Toleration was the rule when it came to brothels, and harsh punishments were the exceptions that proved it.

As time went on, Baltimore authorities' toleration for brothels became more apparent in light of their increasingly strident policing of more public forms of prostitution. During the same period that local officials ceased to incarcerate bawdy-house keepers, watchmen and constables grew aggressive about arresting and jailing women found walking the streets at night. Some of these women were likely sex workers; others may simply have been violating curfews or prevailing social standards by moving about the city unescorted after dark. In 1840, the *Sun* noted that "Jane Jackson, black, was taking a sentimental stroll 'in the dead watches of the night, when e'en the stars did wink, as 'twere, with over watching'" when police in the Eastern District arrested her for streetwalking.[55] On April 2, 1839, Eastern District police arrested Emeline Shepphard, Jane Fountain, Sally Brown, Susan White, and Susan Norris after finding them arguing in the streets. The group was charged with fighting, rioting, and streetwalking.[56] At times, policing of public order offenses became so strenuous that the bulk of the prisoners in the Western District police station were "abandoned street walkers, and belated negroes [i.e., black people who had stayed out past curfew]."[57] Police magistrates and even

---

[54] "Disorderly Houses," *Sun*, Oct. 30, 1839; BCC, October Term, 1839, Case 238, George Savage; BCC, February Term, 1840, Case 166, George Savage; BCC, June Term, 1840, Case 257, George Savage.

[55] "Watch Returns," *Sun*, Feb. 14, 1840.   [56] "Watch Returns," *Sun*, Apr. 10, 1839.

[57] "Watch Returns," *Sun*, Apr. 7, 1838.

the Mayor of Baltimore ordered more than a few of these women to be institutionalized in the almshouse.[58]

By the 1850s, arrests for vagrancy and other public order crimes increased dramatically as the city developed a professionalized police force tasked with addressing the problems of "rowdyism" and controlling the city's black population during a period of heightened tensions over slavery. The police rounded up streetwalkers and all manner of the supposedly disorderly poor in large numbers. In 1853, constables reported that they had in the previous year arrested or otherwise took off the streets 47 "lewd" or "abandoned" women, and magistrates reported sending 267 people (230 white, 37 black) to the almshouse for vagrancy. By 1858 the number of vagrants sent to the almshouse had risen to more than 500 people.[59]

During the same period, prosecutions of bawdy-house keepers grew increasingly rare as Baltimore's City Court was dissolved and reconstituted as part of a statewide court system whose organization was designed to lower the costs of the judiciary. In 1851, Maryland ratified a new state constitution that eliminated older county and city courts in favor of placing the court system under the control of the state and dividing it into eight judicial circuits. Baltimore, which became an independent city under the new constitution, constituted its own circuit and was granted three courts: the Court of Common Pleas, the Superior Court, and the Baltimore City Criminal Court.[60] The latter took over the duties of City Court. Many Baltimoreans feared that the new constitution, which did not provide for a period of transition between the old courts and the new, would lead to prosecutorial chaos. The Baltimore *American* noted that "there were many men in Maryland, who, if they approved of every feature in the new constitution, save that which

[58] On the handling of vagrancy by local police courts and magistrates, see, for example, "The Honorable Delegates to the General Assembly of Maryland, from Baltimore City and County," Baltimore *Patriot & Mercantile Advertiser*, Jan. 15, 1823; "Before the Mayor," *Sun*, Nov. 17, 1858.

[59] Benjamin Herring, "Report of the High Constable," in *Ordinances and Resolutions of the Mayor and City Council of Baltimore, January Session, 1853* (Baltimore: Jos. Robinson, 1853), 134; Jeffrey Richardson Brackett, *The Negro in Maryland: A Study of the Institution of Slavery*, vol. 6 (Baltimore: N. Murray, 1889), 221–22.

[60] James Warner Harry, *Maryland Constitution of 1851* (Baltimore: Johns Hopkins Press, July–Aug. 1902), 79–81.

reorganized the judiciary, would vote against the constitution on account of that one insuperable object."[61]

Although their worst fears failed to come to fruition, the new City Criminal Court did appear to struggle under the weight of its cases. Almost immediately bawdy-house prosecutions declined precipitously. The decline was not a result of a lack of indictments and presentments, for the grand jury remained active in its investigations of sexual vice; indeed, the grand jury presented a record 187 bawdy-house cases to the court in 1859.[62] However, the elected State Attorney resolved to place a large number of bawdy-house cases on the court's stet docket. The stet docket, an oddity of Maryland law, allowed prosecutors to declare a criminal case inactive for a period of up to three years. During that time, the cases would remain on the books but not be prosecuted unless the defendant's conduct or other changes in circumstances motivated the prosecutors to revive the case. After three years, the cases were wiped from the docket entirely. The state's attorney employed the docket far more than his predecessors had. Throughout the 1840s, it had been common for the state's attorney to place between 8 and 15 percent of bawdy-house presentments on Maryland's stet docket. Under the Baltimore City Criminal Court, the number of stet cases rose sharply. In 1852, the state's attorney stetted nearly half of the 111 bawdy-house cases the grand jury presented. Some of these cases were "Non Est" cases, meaning that the sheriff had been unable to locate the defendant to serve the arrest warrant. Others, however, had no notations in the docket that indicated why the State's Attorney declined to prosecute. It is possible that the defendants posted bonds for their good conduct or otherwise agreed to forfeit certain sureties in return for avoiding a trial.[63] It is more likely that the new court, burdened by a growing number of arrests and criminal complaints during a decade when Baltimore saw unprecedented levels of

---

[61] *Baltimore American*, May 26, 1851, quoted in Harry, *Maryland Constitution of 1851*, 70.

[62] Based on an examination of Baltimore City Criminal Court (BCCC) (Docket), 1852, 1855, 1859, C-1849, MDSA 50334.

[63] Sometimes, cases were placed on the stet docket as a result of informal agreements between defendants and prosecutors. See Hugh Davey Evans, *Maryland Common Law Practice: A Treatise on the Course of Proceeding in the Common Law Courts of the State of Maryland* (Baltimore: Joseph Robinson, 1839), 95–96.

political rioting and violence, simply shifted its priorities away from policing commercial sex.[64]

Nevertheless, there were several signs even during the toleration period in the 1840s and early 1850s that the legal landscape was beginning to shift in ways that would disrupt the tentative toleration that had developed around brothel prostitution. One of these signs was the professionalization and growth of Baltimore's police force. In the decades that followed Baltimore's 1835 bank riot, the city began a slow process of expanding the authority of paid law enforcement officers. Although Baltimore did not officially adopt a uniformed police force until the city's Know Nothing mayor organized one in 1857, the old constable and watch system had already expanded its membership, authority, and discipline considerably by the late 1840s. This was in keeping with a pattern of professionalization common to many other US cities, one that historians such as Eric Monkkonen have argued was linked with a general expansion of municipal services in the mid-nineteenth century.[65]

Although the growth of organized policing was welcomed by many urban residents because it signaled the city's commitment to putting down rowdyism and racial disorder, it also disrupted long-standing traditions of diffuse policing authority. As historian Adam Malka has argued, Baltimore did not intend for uniformed police to detract from the authority that was vested in all white people, especially men, to enforce urban order in a slave city.[66] And yet, as the police assumed greater responsibility for reporting criminal offenses to the court, they gradually began to replace everyday civilians as complainants in most criminal cases, including bawdy-house cases. Constables, watchmen, and (later) police began to act as intermediaries between the citizens in their wards and the grand jury. By the 1850s, a majority of bawdy-house presentments issued by the grand jury had only one or two law enforcement officers as witnesses instead of the handful of citizens that had been common in earlier decades.[67]

---

[64] Matthew A. Crenson, *Baltimore: A Political History* (Baltimore: Johns Hopkins University Press, 2017), 204–17.

[65] Eric Monkkonen, *Police in Urban America, 1860–1920* (Cambridge: Cambridge University Press, 2004), 30–64.

[66] Malka, *The Men of Mobtown*, introduction.

[67] BCC Dockets and Baltimore City Criminal Court Dockets. On the history of the Baltimore City Police Department, see De Francais Folsom, *Our Police: A History of the Baltimore Force from the First Watchman to the Latest Appointee* (Baltimore: J. D. Ehlers & Co. and Guggenheimer, Weil & Co., 1888).

The formalization of policing practices put law enforcement officers in a position to control which brothels were reported to the court and which were not, which removed some of the grand jury's long-standing authority to investigate sexual vice in response to citizen complaints. Local influence on vice prosecutions diminished even further when the state, citing the partisanship of the Know Nothing–controlled police, passed legislation placing the Baltimore police under the control of a state-appointed Board of Police Commissioners.[68] One of the most immediate consequences of this expanded police power and the diminishing nature of local, civilian control over prosecutions was the growth of a system of corruption surrounding the bawdy trade. Even before the police played a major role in initiating bawdy-house cases, watchmen had attempted either to extort or to demand favors from madams in return for ignoring their activities. One Fells Point watchman, John Wesley Oldham, made a habit of threatening prostitutes with arrest or violence if they did not bribe him to keep quiet about their houses. At one point, Oldham even demanded sex in exchange for his silence, telling the women who worked in a brothel known as Three Gun Battery that he would take them to the watch house if they refused "connexion with him."[69] Oldham was disciplined, but such results were not typical; sex workers remained vulnerable to police exploitation. Once the task of providing lists of bawdy houses to the court fell to police officers rather than the citizenry as a whole, women's vulnerability only increased. Police could and did demand money or sexual services from women in exchange for their agreement not to report their houses to the court. One ward constable, Charles Hergersheimer, was actually prosecuted for demanding that Elizabeth Williams pay him $5 to ensure that bawdy-house charges against her were dropped.[70] Many more officers got away with demanding payouts that ultimately increased the cost of doing business for madams and sex workers and made their relationship to the state less certain and more dependent on the individual whims of police.

While new systems of bribery and corruption proved inconvenient for madams, more troubling still was a growing tendency of both local law enforcement and courts to reevaluate the meanings of property rights as

---

[68] Crenson, *Baltimore: A Political History*, 230.

[69] Mayor's Correspondence, R.G. 9, Series 2, 1833: 390, Baltimore City Archives.

[70] Historian Marilynn Wood Hill has suggested that widespread bribery and corruption were more characteristic of the late nineteenth century than the earlier period. Hill, *Their Sisters' Keepers*, 146; *Sun*, Mar. 13, 1858.

they pertained to brothels. Since their emergence, indoor sex establishments had occupied an ambiguous position when it came to the issue of property rights. On one hand, the common law had long conceived of bawdy houses as threats to city property in the sense that they were public nuisances that interfered with the rights of community members to enjoy their dwellings in peace. On the other hand, bawdy-house keepers were property owners (or the business partners of property owners) whose status as such gave them certain protections in a legal system that was deeply concerned with defending private property. Prior to the 1850s, the court had balanced community welfare and individual property rights by nominally punishing brothel keepers while also not interfering in fundamental ways with their establishments. Gradually, however, that balance shifted. Local courts came to understand brothel prostitution as a threat not just to communal morality or community rights to the enjoyment of property but also to the property rights of *individual landowners and homeowners* whose home values or enjoyment were threatened by the presence of brothels. A debate that had once pitted communal morality against individual property rights evolved into a debate about whose individual property rights mattered more. Commerce and property values replaced morality as the primary topic of concern in anti-prostitution legal battles. Both court and law enforcement officers came to see their legal responsibility as being to defend property rights of "legitimate" householders by calling into question the property rights of those involved in the sex trade.[71]

The earliest sign of the court's changing approach to property was its newfound willingness to prosecute brothel landlords for letting their properties as bawdy houses in the latter decades of the antebellum period. Prior to the 1840s, the court had limited itself to targeting the women and men who managed and labored within sex establishments rather than the landlords who owned the properties. Not only were madams and other brothel managers the more visible purveyors of commercial sex, but they could also be prosecuted without raising complicated questions concerning the rights of property owners. As the prostitution business became increasingly linked to the city's real estate networks, however, the grand jury and state's attorneys turned their attention to the men and women

---

[71] On brothels and property rights, see, among others, Timothy J. Gilfoyle, "Strumpets and Misogynists: Brothel 'Riots' and the Transformation of Prostitution in Antebellum New York City," in *The Making of Urban America*, ed. Raymond A. Mohl (New York: SR Books, 1997), 43.

whose leasing policies enabled commercial sex to prosper in the city. The court began to assert its power to penalize landlords for allowing their properties to become "public nuisances," and in doing so both challenged and reinforced long-standing notions in nineteenth-century jurisprudence that the right to use and enjoyment of private property was "sacred." By calling into question the right of landlords to dispose of properties as they wished, the court affirmed the importance of other citizens' ability to enjoy their properties free of interference from the sex trade.[72]

The prosecution of brothel landlords was a legal innovation derived from public outrage that resulted from news coverage of a number of high-profile bawdy- and assignation-house cases in 1840. Following Mary Ann Hill's arrest for keeping a sixteen-year-old in her house, prosecutor William Bond summoned Hill's landlord, Samuel H. Goldsmith, and demanded that Goldsmith answer for renting his property for disreputable purposes. Although Goldsmith denied that he was knew that Hill kept the house as a brothel, two men who lived in the neighborhood of the house testified that Goldsmith had told them he was aware of the character of the house. Given this testimony and the fact that Goldsmith had a history of paying Hill's court fines and fees for bawdy-house charges, State's Attorney Bond had him indicted for perjury. Sentiment against Goldsmith was hostile enough that he requested that his trial be removed to a court outside Baltimore to ensure the fairness of the proceedings. The court agreed. Goldsmith's case was removed to the Howard Municipal District of Anne Arundel County and later to Harford County Court, where he was eventually acquitted.[73] However, local prosecutors did not let their failure in the Goldsmith case dissuade them from their efforts to prosecute landlords who profited from their tenants'

---

[72] Legal historians have differed in their evaluations of nineteenth-century property law. In his study *The Guardian of Every Other Right: A Constitutional History of Property Rights* (Oxford: Oxford University Press, 2008), James W. Ely emphasized the "sacredness" of personal property rights in the history of early American courts. William Novak, whose book *The People's Welfare* sought to challenge the notion that liberal individualism was the dominant legal framework of the early nineteenth century, argued that the early state prized communal welfare over individual notions of rights. Novak also noted that there was a long history of the state impinging on property rights in the interest of community safety and comfort. Novak, *The People's Welfare*.

[73] Baltimore City Court (Docket and Minutes), February Term, 1848, 312, Mary Ann Hill, C184-7, MSA 16654; Baltimore City Court (Docket and Minutes), February Term, 1848, 318, Samuel H. Goldsmith, C184-7, MSA 16654; "City Court – Saturday, March 28, 1840," *Sun*, Mar., 30, 1840; "City Court – June Term, 1840," *Sun*, June 20, 1840.

illicit businesses. In the June Term of the 1840 session, the state's attorney charged John Walter, a grocer who lived on Pratt Street not far from the Causeway, and William Shelley, who owned a house whose keeper allowed black and white Baltimoreans to congregate, with "renting their house for immoral purposes." By 1845, Baltimore's grand jury was regularly issuing indictments for "renting a house for a bawdy house."[74]

Prosecutions of brothel landlords represented a new and controversial application of the common law, and it was not long before a landlord contested the charges against him. Martin Smith, an Irish-born grocer who owned a large lot at 52 Orleans Street, was convicted in 1845 of renting a house to Dorcas Smith (no apparent relation) for bawdy purposes. Smith escalated his case to the Maryland Court of Appeals, where his lawyer argued that his conviction should be overturned because the indictment against him "set ... forth no crime under the laws of this state." In delivering the appellate court's opinion, Justice J. MacGruder acknowledged that the charge of "Renting a House for Bawdy Purposes" was unprecedented. He remarked, "It may be that none of us can recollect any case like this, which was prosecuted with success in any court of Maryland."[75] However, MacGruder went on to argue in favor of the judiciary's right to intervene even when there was no exact precedent, stating that "it cannot be inferred, from the mere circumstance, that a particular offence has never been punished, that there is not law to authorize its punishment." The common law, the justices argued, allowed for the state's right to exercise police power to punish "crimes" even in the absence of statutes that defined them as such. Since keeping a bawdy house was decidedly an indictable offense at common law, the court found that a person who rented a house for bawdy purposes could legally be considered an "aider and abettor in the misdemeanor" and a violator of the "peace, government and dignity of the State." As such, he or she was subject to the judgment of the court.[76] The ruling had an immediate effect. In 1849, the year after the Court of Appeals issued its decision,

[74] BCC June Term, 1840, Cases 509, 522, 523, 524, and 525, William Shelley; BCC, June Term, 1840, Cases 507, 508, and 521, John Walters.

[75] *Smith* v. *State* (1848), *Reports of Cases Argued and Determined in the Court of Appeals of Maryland, 1852* (Baltimore: Geo. Johnston, 1852), 424–25. Prosecuting landlords of bawdy houses was not a well-established practice at the time, even outside Maryland. New York, for instance, did not add a statute specifying that landlords could be indicted for disorderly or bawdy houses until 1849. Hill, *Their Sisters' Keepers*, 133.

[76] *Smith* v. *State* (1848), *Reports of Cases*, 424–25.

Baltimore City heard twenty cases involving persons accused of renting bawdy houses or houses of ill fame.[77]

The practice of criminally charging landlords for renting properties as brothels was more significant in theory than it was in practice, at least initially. In most cases, the fines levied against landlords were not sufficient to dissuade them from continuing to let their houses to madams. After Samuel Goldsmith was acquitted of perjury in 1841, he and Sarah Goldsmith were tried numerous times for renting bawdy houses to women in the Meadow. Although the Goldsmiths had to post bonds as high as $1,500 and pay fines of $20 each in most cases, which represented a significant expense, the profits of the trade were such that they continued to be prolific brothel landlords more than twenty years after Samuel's first charges for renting.[78] Though the Goldsmiths were unusual in the scope of their operation, others charged with renting out bawdy houses were equally unfazed by their fines. Andrew Fitzpatrick, a grocer, was fined the relatively meager sum of $20 in 1849 for renting bawdy houses to eight different men and women, among them Mary Giles. In 1852, Fitzpatrick was still profiting from leasing his properties to purveyors of commercial sex. Not only did he continue to rent to Mary Giles, but he had also picked up four additional brothel keepers as tenants.[79] Despite its short-term failures to discourage landlords from renting to madams, the Criminal Court's move toward holding property owners accountable for their tenants' conduct represented a significant shift in its willingness to curtail individual property rights in cases involving sexual commerce.

By the late 1850s, a far more significant blow to the property rights of brothel owners and renters would come from an unexpected source: Baltimore's Circuit Court. In order to understand how the Circuit Court came to issue a ruling significant to the future of brothel prostitution, it is necessary to return to that July day when an enraged Margaret Hamilton

---

[77] Baltimore City Court (Docket and Minutes), 1849, C184-11, MSA 16668.

[78] BCC, Cases 946–51, 1001, and 1064, Samuel and Sarah Goldsmith, September Term, 1864. The 1860 Census listed Sarah Goldsmith as owning $75,000 of real property; 1860 US Census, Baltimore, Maryland, Ward 11, p. 190, dwelling 1184, family 1312, Sarah H. Goldsmith; digital image, Ancestry.com, accessed July 31, 2017.

[79] BCC, May Term, 1849, Cases 838–45, Andrew Fitzpatrick; BCC, January Term, 1855, Cases 222–27, Lewis and Sarah Goldsmith. City directories list Fitzpatrick as a grocer living at 151 Eastern Avenue in 1849: *Matchett's Baltimore Directory* (Baltimore: R. J. Matchett, 1849), 131. Earlier directories listed him as a stone mason living on Eastern Avenue near Caroline (*Matchett's Baltimore Directory*, 1842 [Baltimore: R. J. Matchett, 1842], 163).

stalked through the Centre Market carrying her whip. Hamilton was in search of Eliza Simpson, a fellow sex worker with whom she had a longtime feud. Whatever reason Hamilton and Simpson had for disliking one another is long lost to historians, but their conflict dated back to at least 1849, when Hamilton, then twenty-two and freshly ascended to the position of managing the Lovely Lane brothel in which she had once labored as a prostitute, assaulted Simpson. Simpson fought back, resulting in both of their arrests. While their mutual charges of assault went nowhere, Simpson was vigilant about the prospect of a future attack by Hamilton or another aggrieved party. When Hamilton finally found Simpson and threatened to whip her in the market, Simpson pulled out a pistol and shot Hamilton in the face.[80]

Remarkably, Hamilton survived. She recovered from her wound and, likely motivated by her near-death experience, decided to make a change that would prove fateful to Baltimore's legal history: she moved. Using the money that she had earned working as a sex worker and subsequently as a madam, she purchased a house of her own at 51 North Frederick Street in 1856. Unlike Lovely Lane, Frederick Street was a main thoroughfare. It had the benefit of being close to the theaters, the Baltimore Street commercial district, and (somewhat ironically) the Centre Market. Hamilton wisely judged that the neighborhood presented her with new opportunities to attract a more sizable and well-heeled client base, and she wasted no time preparing the house for her purposes. She hired contractors and painters and began to purchase furniture in preparation for opening her house of prostitution.[81]

However, just as Hamilton's luck seemed to be turning, a flaw emerged in her plans for upward mobility: she had not anticipated – or perhaps had not cared about – the reactions of her new neighbors. While the residents of Lovely Lane had tolerated the presence of a brothel on their block, the middle-class residents of Frederick Street and abutting Gay Street were less welcoming. Hamilton purchased a house on a lot that abutted that of John Whitridge, a local physician who owned his house and a rented another property at Frederick and Gay Streets to tenants.[82] Whitridge, like many members of Baltimore's nascent middle class,

---

[80] On the feud between Hamilton and Simpson, see "Local Matters," *Sun*, Jan. 23, 1849; "Doing Well," *Sun*, June 12, 1855.

[81] *Hamilton v. Whitridge, Maryland Reports: Containing Cases Argued and Adjudged in the Court of Appeals of Maryland* 11 (Baltimore, 1858), 128–47.

[82] *Woods' Baltimore Directory for 1856–57* (Baltimore: John Woods), 354.

desired to live in a genteel neighborhood whose residents were quiet, mannerly, and family-oriented.[83] Predictably, then, he was furious at Hamilton's presence in his neighborhood. In his view, Hamilton's house represented both a moral blight and a concrete threat to his property values. If Hamilton were allowed to move into Frederick Street and open her dwelling as a brothel, his tenants might be driven off and the value of both his properties lowered.[84]

Resin Haslup, a skilled coach smith who lived in the house immediately adjacent to Hamilton's on Frederick, shared Whitridge's concerns. He himself was fearful about the aural and moral impact a brothel would have on the neighborhood. A house like Hamilton's was likely to bring noisy foot traffic at all hours, and Haslup was not eager to have his teenage daughters residing near such an establishment.[85] Whitridge and Haslup both hoped to prevent Hamilton from opening 51 North Frederick as a brothel. They decided to pursue the matter legally.

Whitridge and Haslup – or more probably, their lawyers – were creative in their attempts to prevent Margaret Hamilton from occupying her property. They presumably understood that the City Criminal Court could provide them with only limited recourse against a brothel moving into their neighborhood. If they complained against Hamilton before local police or the grand jury, she would (at most) be fined and returned to her trade; possibly, she would not be prosecuted at all given the state's attorneys' tendency to stet bawdy-house cases. Therefore, Whitridge, Haslup, and two other property owners in the area of Frederick and Gay Streets tried another approach: they took their concerns about Hamilton before Baltimore's recently created Circuit Court. Their argument was novel and, in a sense, revolutionary: if Hamilton were allowed to run a brothel out of the house she had purchased, then their ability to enjoy and preserve the value of their properties would be compromised. On this basis, the case fell under the jurisdiction of the court of equity, which they argued had both the right and the duty to intervene and prevent Hamilton from inflicting concrete damages on the complainants.[86]

As basic as the men's argument seemed, it was radical in that it ran contrary to long-standing common-law understandings of equity. English common law traditionally upheld a distinction – blurry though it sometimes was – between public and private injuries, and, by extension,

---

[83] D'Emilio and Freedman, *Intimate Matters*, 142.   [84] *Hamilton v. Whitridge.*
[85] *Hamilton v. Whitridge.*   [86] *Hamilton v. Whitridge.*

between criminal offenses and equitable offenses. Criminal offenses were offenses against the broader public, which gave the state and the courts an interest in prosecuting them. Equity, in contrast, was supposed to address offenses against private individuals who suffered unique injuries (i.e., distinct from those of the broader public) for which there was no other legal remedy. Under these terms, offenses related to prostitution fell under the criminal rather than equitable jurisdiction, as prostitution had long been understood in the common law as both a public nuisance and an offense against the public peace and was criminalized on that basis. By long-standing common-law tradition, individuals offended by prostitution were excluded from seeking an equitable remedy, both because the criminal law already provided for such a remedy and because the injury done by prostitution was not understood to accrue to any one, private individual.[87]

In the *Hamilton* case, however, the Circuit Court made a decision that was as unprecedented as it would be damning for the long-term future of prostitution: it agreed to hear Whitridge et al.'s complaint. In doing so, it extended the principle of equity beyond its usual limits and collapsed the distinction between criminal and equitable remedies. Prostitution, long recognized as a threat to the public order, also became defined separately as an offense that injured private parties by jeopardizing their property rights. Not only did Hamilton's case make it onto the equity docket, but the court found for the plaintiff and issued an injunction barring Hamilton from living in her own property.[88]

Unsurprisingly, Hamilton immediately contested the decision. Her attorney, future Maryland Attorney General Charles J. M. Gwinn, argued before the Maryland Court of Appeals that the injunction should be thrown out on the basis that that any injury suffered by the plaintiffs as a result of Hamilton occupying her house as a brothel could not be considered an injury to their properties in the way that offenses against the "physical senses" – say, raw sewage or blocked sidewalks – might be. If anything, it would be an injury to their "moral senses," and therefore an injury to their persons. Gwinn, who was no doubt familiar with the fact that injuries to persons were not subjected to equitable remedies in

---

[87] Hennigan, "Property War," 123–98.

[88] *Hamilton* v. *Whitridge*, 140; Baltimore City Circuit Court (Equity Docket A, Miscellaneous), *John Whitridge et al.* v. *Margaret Hamilton*, 1/1/1856–3/8/1858, C185-2, MSA.

the same way that injuries to properties were, asserted that the court had no right to act as a moral censor by intervening against Hamilton.[89]

Unfortunately for Hamilton and her fellow brothel keepers, the appellate court dismissed Gwinn's logic. The justices denied that the case was about moral censorship, writing, "We need not inquire how far this jurisdiction can be defended on grounds of morality, and to preserve the decencies of life from gross violation. The case does not require this." Instead, the justices insisted that Hamilton's case fell under the principles of equity because she ran an illicit business that unfairly interfered with the property rights (and values) of her neighbors:

The ground on which [the court] interferes in this case, is not that this defendant, or those around her, or even her establishment, is offensive to the *moral senses* of the *complainants*, but that the *business* and *occupation which she intends to follow*, has been *condemned* by the courts as an *illegitimate employment*, and a *public nuisance*, and is punished as such, and that by establishing this nuisance alongside of *their property*, they *will be severally deprived* of the *comfortable enjoyment of it*, and *it will be greatly depreciated and lessened in value*. Nor is the action of this court directed against the defendant as an *immoral* or *vicious neighbor* simply, but as an individual *conducting* an *offensive business*, regarded by the law as a *nuisance*, and interfering with the enjoyment, and impairing the value of their property.[90]

On this basis, the court affirmed the injunction barring Hamilton from living in the house that she had purchased and furnished.

The court's reasoning in the *Hamilton* decision was both an odd acknowledgment of the degree that prostitution had become a business in the decades leading up the Civil War and a stunning reversal of long-standing policies of tolerating brothels. Previously, the fact that brothel keepers owned property, kept businesses, and/or commanded wealth had protected them somewhat from the harshest vagaries of the court, while the comparatively private nature of their establishments had granted them tacit toleration. The *Hamilton* decision functionally ended this form of toleration by establishing that even those brothels that were not severe enough violators of communal order to merit suppressive action by the Criminal Court could be suppressed by the Circuit Court if they were deemed to injure private individuals. Any complaint by an offended party

---

[89] *Hamilton* v. *Whitridge*, 139, 147. On the issue of injuries to persons vs. property, see Hennigan, "Property War," 132–38.

[90] *Maryland Reports*, 139–40. Emphasis in original.

could result in the issuance of an injunction that prevented a woman from opening a brothel or forced her to close an existing one.

By expanding the authority of the equity court, *Hamilton* gave police the ability to use the threat of injunction to pressure brothel keepers to close or relocate their establishments if they were deemed a threat to property values. It also opened the door for local authorities to intervene in the brothel trade without resorting to the Criminal Court. In practice, as Chapter 6 will argue, Baltimore authorities seldom used their power to suppress sex establishments in the decades after the ruling was handed down; instead, they used it primarily to expand the ongoing regulatory practice of spatially containing prostitution. That is, in addition to insisting that sex be contained within brothels, authorities used injunctions to insist that brothels be contained within particular neighborhoods where they would not threaten the material interests of wealthier citizens. In the long term, however, the *Hamilton* case set such a far-reaching precedent for police and courts to remake the sexual landscape of the city that William Novak described it as the legal innovation that "sealed the fate of many urban red-light districts in the Progressive Era."[91] In the decades that followed the decision, courts around the country would cite the appellant court's ruling to justify injunctions against bawdy houses, saloons, and even rail corporations whose practices they deemed disruptive to the rights of respectable property owners.

And yet the impact of the decision would not be felt immediately. Baltimore City's policing infrastructures were too underdeveloped in the late 1850s to allow the court's ruling to be enforced, and the city's middle class was only just beginning to organize in ways that would pressure the city to take advantage of the powers granted to it by *Hamilton*. Three years after the Circuit Court issued its original injunction against Margaret Hamilton and one year after the Maryland Court of Appeals upheld it, a New York printer published a *Directory to the Seraglios in New York, Philadelphia, Boston and All the Principal Cities in the Union*. Front and center in the section of the guide on Baltimore was a listing for "Maggy Hamilton" and her brothel at 51 North Frederick. The guide noted that Hamilton had "good wines constantly on hand," and proclaimed her house "one of the most magnificently furnished establishments in the Monumental City."[92] In the same year that the brothel guide was

---

[91] For a brief analysis of the long-term impact of *Hamilton* v. *Whitridge*, see Novak, *The People's Welfare*, 165–66.

[92] Loveyer, *Directory to the Seraglios*, 37.

published, the Baltimore City Circuit Court attempted to hold Hamilton in contempt for her refusal to comply with the terms of its ruling, but the charges were quashed for a reason that was not listed in the record.[93] Hamilton continued to operate her Frederick Street property as a bawdy house for another two decades, and it would be five years before the court would attempt to use the case as a precedent to justify further evictions of bawdy-house keepers.

As the next two chapters will suggest, the Civil War and its aftermath would change everything. As Baltimore's prostitution trade expanded to cater to the demands of occupying Union soldiers, authorities' attention would be drawn to commercial sex more pressingly than ever before. Changes in the nature and power of the state and the growth of the urban middle class in the decades following the conflict would give police and the courts the ability to enforce injunctions against brothel keepers on a larger scale. Although the injunctions were seldom used to suppress the sex trade entirely, they would be employed to force brothels into more marginal neighborhoods and control the geography of prostitution. The result would change the demographics of sex work and profoundly reorient its relationship to the urban economy, labor, and public order.

First, however, the war came.

---

[93] Baltimore City Circuit Court (Equity Docket), *Hamilton* v. *Whitridge*, Misc-A, MSA C185-4, pp. 316–17.

5

"Our Patriotic Friends"

Selling Sex in the Civil War Era

On April 19, 1861, Baltimore brothel keeper Ann Manley became one of the earliest heroes of the Union war effort. On that day, Baltimore was abuzz with the arrival of some of the first Northern troops in the city. The Sixth Massachusetts Regiment was passing through Baltimore on its way to Washington, DC, but the disconnected nature of the city's railroads meant that soldiers had to walk nearly a mile west across Pratt Street from the President Street Station in order to catch their train south. The sight of armed troops marching through the city was not a welcome one for many locals, who for a variety of reasons were apprehensive about the escalation of military tensions between the US government and the seceded Southern states. Although Maryland's strong economic ties to free labor economies of the North and West ultimately prevented its own defection to the Confederacy, Baltimore's cultural ties to the South and strong Democratic political base meant that many city residents were sympathetic to their Southern neighbors. Political tensions were high. As the soldiers began their march, those tensions tipped over into violence. Civilians pelted the soldiers with bricks and stones. The troops, many of whom were barely trained, answered by firing into the crowd. The melee that rapidly ensued left four soldiers and twelve civilians dead in the streets and dozens of others injured.[1]

[1] Brugger, *Maryland: A Middle Temperament*, 274–77. For a detailed popular account of the Pratt Street riot, see Harry A. Ezratty, *Baltimore in the Civil War: The Pratt Street Riot and a City Occupied* (Charleston, SC: History Press, 2010).

While the bloody confrontation between the militia and the citizens of Baltimore was playing out on Pratt Street, Ann Manley was at the center of another, less-famed skirmish taking place only a few blocks away. Due to a railroad delay, a regimental band dispatched from Philadelphia to march in front of the Sixth Massachusetts arrived too late to take their positions. By the time their train pulled into the station, the rioting was already at full swing. Rioters from Pratt Street broke off when they got word of the musicians' arrival and set upon the unarmed group. As locals pelted their train car with shot and rocks, the musicians could only scatter, fleeing the car and attempting to fend off the blows from the crowd waiting outside. Confusion reigned amid the tumult, until a figure appeared and began shepherding the soldiers away from the violence. The figure guided the soldiers into Ann Manley's Causeway bawdy house.

Manley, as it happened, was a devoted Unionist. Her husband and partner in business, James, had for years been the leader of a Know Nothing political gang, the Plug Uglies. When the Civil War broke out, he promptly enlisted in the Nineteenth Pennsylvania Infantry. Ann, who was sympathetic to the soldiers and their cause, dragged the wounded men who arrived at her doorstep into her dwelling and barricaded the door to ensure the rioters could not follow. Once she had ensured the musicians' safety, she tended to their wounds, fed them, and gave them civilian clothes that would allow them to pass unmolested through the streets. Later, she delivered their freshly laundered uniforms to the train station where they were waiting to depart.[2]

Baltimore newspapers, which were staffed by people familiar with Ann Manley's reputation, made little mention of the story. Outside the city, however, news of Manley's courageous deed spread quickly. Newspapers in Pennsylvania, where the soldiers returned after their harrowing time in Baltimore, deemed Ann Manley an "Amazon" and praised her "Samaritan kindness in the midst of most savage barbarity." One paper called her a saint. A book of wartime anecdotes published in 1866 proclaimed her the "Heroine in Baltimore" and praised her for doing what the police and local officials could or would not do by protecting the US soldiers and pronounced her "entitled to the grateful consideration of the country."

[2] Tracy Matthew Melton, *Hanging Henry Gambrill: The Violent Career of Baltimore's Plug Uglies, 1854–1860* (Baltimore: Maryland Historical Society, 2005); Tracy Matthew Melton, "The Lost Lives of George Konig Sr. & Jr., a Father–Son Tale of Old Fell's Point," *Maryland Historical Magazine* 101, no. 3 (2006): 332–61; "A Baltimore Saint," *Philadelphia Saturday Evening Courier*, reprinted in the *New Hampshire Farmer's Cabinet*, May 10, 1861.

So great was Manley's acclaim that even Elizabeth Cady Stanton and
Susan B. Anthony took notice of her actions. In their *History of Woman
Suffrage*, Stanton and Anthony compared the woman to Mary Magdalene, writing that she acted "with a pity as divine as that of the woman
who anointed the feet of our Lord and wiped them with the hair of her
head."[3]

The interaction between Ann Manley and the regimental band was
only the first and most dramatic of many to take place between Union
soldiers and sex workers in Civil War–era Baltimore. Prostitution would
boom during the war years as Union soldiers came to occupy dozens of
campsites and hospitals in and around the city, and war and occupation
would alter the city's sex trade in dramatic ways. Sex workers' interactions with Union soldiers, which ran the gamut from acts of patriotism
like Ann Manley's to acts of mutual self-interest and occasional outbursts
of animosity, gave the sex trade new social and political valences. Bawdy
houses were sites at which soldiers negotiated wartime masculinities and
bonded with one another, but they were also sites of tension, violence,
and disease transmission that posed a threat to military readiness and
order. As civil and military authorities contemplated how best to manage
the city's growing sex trade, Baltimore's sex workers took steps to secure
their businesses by negotiating, cooperating, and providing intelligence to
local officials. In doing so, they not only made their living and, in some
cases, their fortune selling sex, but also contributed in valuable ways to
the Union war effort. Nevertheless, the attention that the war brought to
the sex trade would not be quick to abate once the Confederacy surren-
dered. War would usher in a new regulatory regime in the city.

Following the Pratt Street Riot, state and city officials scrambled to
address the tensions in the Old Line State. In what they claimed was an
attempt to prevent further disorder, Maryland Governor Thomas Holliday Hicks and Baltimore Mayor George William Brown assented to
Police Marshal George P. Kane organizing a band of citizens to burn

---

[3] "A Baltimore Saint"; *Anecdotes, Poetry and Incidents of the War: North and South,
1860–1865*, ed. Frank Moore (New York, 1866), 36; *History of Woman Suffrage*, vol
2, ed. Elizabeth Cady Stanton, Susan B. Anthony, and Matilda Joslyn Gage (New York:
Charles Mann Printing Co., 1881), 13. Manley's actions during the rioting that day were
later referenced in *Records of the Proceedings of the Investigation before His Excellency
Thomas Swann, Governor of Maryland, in the Case of Samuel Hindes and Nicholas
L. Wood, Commissioners of the Board of the Police of the City of Baltimore, upon
Charges Preferred against Them for Official Misconduct* (Baltimore: William K. Boyle,
1866), 25.

the railroad bridges leading into Baltimore in order to prevent additional troops from passing through the city.[4] Given Maryland's position between the capital and the Northern states, however, the federal government could not abide by state officials' wishes to halt troop movements. The decision to destroy the rail lines prompted a swift response from the Lincoln administration. On April 27, Lincoln suspended the writ of habeas corpus in Maryland and deployed troops to secure rail lines running through the state.[5] Among the officers sent was Major General Benjamin Butler, who was ordered to guard the Relay House seven miles outside Baltimore. Butler, believing that the city had to be subdued if the Union had any hope of preserving transportation infrastructure in the long term, made an executive decision. On the night of May 13, 1861, he marched 1,200 troops through the streets of Baltimore and seized Federal Hill. From there, his troops could oversee the harbor and train their guns on the city proper. Just over a month after the start of the war, then, Baltimore became an occupied municipality.[6]

Initially, Union officials saw their duty as forcibly subduing the secessionist sympathizers in the city. Soldiers arrested Mayor Brown, Police Marshal Kane, and every civilian member of the state-appointed Police Board on suspicion of disloyalty. In the summer of 1861, the Baltimore police were disbanded, and law enforcement authority fell to federal troops, who took on the "not very pleasant work [of] . . . acting as police guard over the city."[7] Policing responsibilities would remain in their hands until March 1862, at which point military authorities deemed secessionist impulses suppressed enough to allow the state to reassume control over the Police Board.

The eventual triumph of Unionist sentiment in Baltimore prompted General Nathaniel Banks to recommend to his superiors in the summer of 1861 that they "could safely withdraw the best troops for service elsewhere, leaving the new levies in possession here."[8] Several areas in and

[4] Brugger, *Maryland: A Middle Temperament*, 248–305; Police Commissioners of Baltimore City, *Report of the Police Commissioners of Baltimore City, with Accompanying Documents* (Baltimore, 1861). Available from the University of Maryland at College Park Archive at http://archive.org/details/reportofpoliceco1861poli.

[5] Brugger, *Maryland: A Middle Temperament*, 248–305.

[6] Benjamin F. Butler, *Autobiography and Personal Reminiscences of Major-General Benjamin F. Butler*, Part 1 (Boston: A. M. Taylor's Book Publishers, 1892), 230–35.

[7] Henry M. Congdon to "Father," June 9, 1862, Henry M. Congdon Letters, 1861–73, NYHS.

[8] Nathaniel Banks to Simon Cameron, June 16, 1861, in *The War of the Rebellion: A Compilation of the Official Records of the Union and Confederate Armies*, Series I,

around Baltimore soon became camp and training grounds for newly mustered soldiers on their way to points south and hospital grounds for wounded troops. By the late summer of 1861, 4,633 troops occupied Fort Federal Hill, Fort McHenry, Mount Clare, and plots of agricultural ground a mile north of Baltimore. Patterson's Park, Potter's Race Course, and Isaac McKim's mansion became camps at the war progressed. At any given time during the conflict, thousands of troops surrounded the city. One young enlisted man who camped outside Baltimore over the summer of 1862 claimed that he had seen fifteen regiments pass around his camp in his short tenure in the city; similarly, another officer estimated in a letter home that there were more than 15,000 men encamped around Baltimore at the time of his writing.[9]

Baltimore's status as a waypoint and a training ground for new soldiers was a boon for the sex trade, as the introduction of thousands of recruits who were flush with enlistment bounties and subjected to lax duty requirements expanded the market for sexual services. Many soldiers who arrived in Baltimore were young men unaccustomed to military discipline and away from home for the first time. Especially as the war progressed and enthusiasm for enlisting waned in the face of the grim realities of the fighting, it was not unusual for them to arrive in the city with large enlistment bonuses. Private William Hall, for instance, arrived in Baltimore only eleven days after he received $500 for his three-year enlistment in the 2nd Massachusetts Cavalry.[10] Edward Hawkins, also of the 2nd Massachusetts, received $190.03 for a year's service thirteen days before he arrived at Baltimore,[11] and Private Henry R. Williams of the 1st Maine Volunteers received $400 for signing up for a year's duty just over a month before he was assigned to Fort Federal Hill.[12] When the men arrived in the city with their bonuses in hand, they found themselves faced with a relatively undemanding list of duties that mostly involved drilling and guarding the camp. For most soldiers, drill took up only a few hours

vol. 2, by the United States War Department (Washington, DC: Government Printing Office, 1881), 690.

[9] John A. Dix to G. W. Cullum, Aug. 17, 1861; George B. McClellan to Abraham Lincoln, Aug. 4, 1861, printed in *The War of the Rebellion: A Compilation of the Official Records of the Union and Confederate Armies*, Series I, vol. 5, by the United States War Department (Washington, DC: Government Printing Office, 1881), 7, 566; Michael Guigan to "My Dear Friend," MS 1860, Maryland Historical Society (MDHS).

[10] Records of the Judge Advocate General's Office (Army), Court Martials, RG 153, File OO522, National Archives.

[11] Court Martials, RG 153, File OO386.   [12] Court Martials, RG 153, File OO954.

per day by prescription and less in practice. Private James M. Bollar, of the 1st Indiana Artillery, wrote that his duties at Fort Marshall were minimal: "I seldom have to drill, the only duty we have is guard duty and that is once in 10 days." Even Sgt. George Mitchell, whose letters home indicated that his drill schedule was much more rigorous than average, noted that his evenings were free for "having a little fun."[13] Some men encamped around Baltimore had so much free time, in fact, that they referred to their assignment as a "summer vacation at Uncle Sam's expense."[14]

While many soldiers used their free time to write letters home, attend religious services, or engage in homosocial activities with men in their camps, others took advantage of the absence of family surveillance to do things that would have been unacceptable or inaccessible at home. Just as thousands of male migrants to Baltimore had done in the decades before the war, soldiers treated the city as a place of masculine ribaldry and sought out drink and female company. One chagrined Union officer blamed their behavior on the masculine culture of the camps and the mobility of military life, writing, "The influence of the armies has largely contributed to the state of things, as soldiers do not seem to feel the same restraints away from home, which at home regulated their intercourse with the gentler sex."[15] Sergeant Alfred Davenport of the 5th New York, the Zouave regiment responsible for constructing Fort Federal Hill, observed so much vice among his fellow troops that he claimed that Army life "ruined [soldiers] in morals and in health for they learn everything bad and nothing good."[16]

Soldiers in Baltimore who sought opportunities to partake in commercial sex usually did not find it in their camps. Although "camp followers" who provided services ranging from laundry to sex in exchange for compensation were common in many occupied areas during the Civil War, Union officers in Baltimore were careful to limit civilian access to military encampments. Following the arrests of the civilian police force

---

[13] James Bollar to Michael Hammons, Feb. 7, 1862, from the Catalog of the Historical Shop, Cary Delery, quoted in Lowry, *Sex in the Civil War*, 106.

[14] George Mitchell to his parents, Jan. 19, 1862, George A. Mitchell Letters, 1861–63, NYHS.

[15] Letter of June 6, 1863, quoted in Bell Wiley, *The Life of Johnny Reb: The Common Soldier of the Confederacy* (Baton Rouge: Louisiana State University Press, 2008), 55.

[16] Alfred Davenport to his Home Folk, December 1861, quoted in Wiley, *The Life of Billy Yank*, 247.

and a number of suspected secessionists in 1861, military authorities went so far as to erect barricades between their camps and the city proper and to prohibit civilians traveling at night without a pass as "a precaution taken against carrying information to the enemy of the number of United States troops in and about the city."[17] Even during the day, access was tightly controlled. One soldier stationed at Fort Federal Hill wrote home, "We don't see much of the people here, as but very few people are allowed in the fort."[18] Limited access made it difficult for sex workers to ply their trades in or near the camps or barracks, although the service economy that developed around Fort Federal Hill created some possibilities for sexual exchange. Black laundresses who took up residence in nearby Guilford Alley and made their living taking wash from soldiers were often accused of keeping their houses as bawdy houses, as were a smaller number of white women living in that area.[19]

Still, soldiers' ease of mobility ensured that they could take advantage of the thriving prostitution business that already existed in town. Leave policies in the camps around the city tended to be generous, not only because soldiers removed from the battlefield had light duty requirements, but because the logistics of supplying an army were complicated. If soldiers were encamped near urban centers that could provide them with food and supplies, it made little sense to insist that they rely on the military for such articles. Local commanders made it easy for soldiers to go into the city and buy what meals, basic services, and "luxuries" they desired. Some commanders handed out evening passes freely after long days of drill or granted passes to anyone who performed guard duty. Private Bollar wrote that in his camp, soldiers were allowed to visit Baltimore proper as often as every few days, and many soldiers took advantage of lax camp discipline to make even more frequent visits to the city.[20] One soldier noted that he was able to come and go as he pleased most of the time because his camp virtually ignored the pass system: "I don't ask for a pass [to take leave], I have taken it for granted

[17] Folsom, *Our Police*, 61.   [18] Lou to the Girls, June 22, 1863, MDHS.

[19] Bawdy-house prosecutions increased in the Southern District during the Civil War period. For examples of cases involving complainants from Guilford Alley, see BCCC, May Term, 1865, Case 3455, Jane Reed; BCCC, January Term (Holdover), Case 165, Mary McCaffrey. Guilford Alley remained an alleged haven for bawdy houses until 1870.

[20] James Bollar to Michael Hammons, Feb. 7, 1862.

that I don't need any, and as long as I am not asked for, I don't mean to get one."[21] A soldier from New York claimed that the men guarding his camp colluded with fellow soldiers who wished to be absent without proper leave: "The men slip out with the connivance of the sentries. I suppose there must be at least 30 or 40 go out and come in every night this way."[22] Even soldiers stationed far outside the city sometimes took advantage of their proximity to the railroads and boarded cars to Baltimore. Private Michael Graham of the 1st Michigan Volunteers was stationed nearly seventeen miles outside Baltimore in Annapolis Junction when he and a musician from his company decided to go on a "spree." Graham and the musician, Warren Smith, calculated that if they caught the 4 AM train, they could pass most of the night in Baltimore and still arrive back in time for roll call in the morning.[23]

Sneaking out of camp to seek sexual services became a popular pastime among soldiers. The three soldiers mentioned earlier as having arrived in Baltimore with large bounties, Privates Hall, Hawkins, and Williams, all left their camps to visit houses of ill fame within days of their arrival in the city. Hall, as he would later explain, "only wished a spree" with his bounty, and so he went to the city and "staid in a Drinking House and Brothel, 3 days."[24] Likewise, Private Hawkins, who left camp the same day he arrived with a group of other recruits and the assistance of the sentry on duty, quickly "got on a spree and got tight in a house of ill fame." He remained in the house for almost two days before he was arrested on suspicion of desertion.[25] While he was among only a handful of soldiers court-martialed for going absent without leave in order to patronize a sex establishment in Baltimore, it was not his initial behavior that earned him discipline so much as the fact that he exceeded his leave time. A soldier from 75th New York Infantry confirmed that leaving camp to partake in vice was anything but unusual. "Tonight," he wrote, "not 200 men are in the camp.... A hundred men are drunk, a hundred more at houses of ill fame."[26]

Soldiers who sought out pleasure in the city's houses of ill fame had an expanding sexual marketplace at their disposal. Even as their presence in the city drove demand for sexual services, the hardship and privation

[21] Lou to the Girls, June 22, 1863, MDHS.

[22] Quoted in Wiley, *The Life of Billy Yank*, 214.

[23] Court Martials, RG 153, File QQ2153.   [24] Court Martials, RG 153, File OO522.

[25] Court Martials, RG 153, File OO386.

[26] Bruce Catton, *Mr. Lincoln's Army* (Garden City, NY, 1956), 64–65, quoted in MacPherson, *Battle Cry of Freedom*, 329.

brought on by war prompted a growing number of women to sell sex in order to make ends meet. As what was initially supposed to be a short conflict dragged on for years and resulted in hundreds of thousands of casualties, life grew increasingly difficult for the wives, mothers, sisters, and daughters whom men left behind on the home front. The loss of a man's labor or wage could be devastating for familial enterprises, and enlisted men's pay, when it was issued at all, seldom matched what a man could earn in a semi-skilled position during peacetime. Deaths and disability permanently deprived thousands of families of male wages. Despite women's entrance into the labor force in larger numbers during the conflict, most women's work remained poorly paid, and selling sex to soldiers, travelers, and local civilians became a means of surviving.[27]

Unsurprisingly given the confluence of supply and demand factors, prostitution in Baltimore expanded rapidly between 1861 and 1864. Statistics on the expansion of streetwalking are difficult to come by, in large part because vagrancy was a capacious offense that was not usually prosecuted formally. However, court records reveal that prosecutions for brothel keeping more than doubled in the latter years of the conflict. The year before the war broke out, between 107 and 117 individuals appeared before the City Criminal court in 137 separate cases related to commercial sex: 126 charges of keeping bawdy houses, and 11 for renting properties for use as bawdy houses. In 1862, the number had risen modestly to 134 cases – 128 for keeping and 5 for renting bawdy houses – which involved between 116 and 122 individual defendants. By 1864, the Criminal Court was processing an unprecedented 378 cases – 339 for keeping and 39 for renting bawdy houses – involving between 274 and 283 individuals.[28] The court spent large parts of the January term as well as the entire month of December adjudicating bawdy-house presentments and indictments. There were so many that court clerks took to writing two names per space in the case docket book to avoid running out of room. Most of the expansion in the sex trade took place within the old vice districts in the Meadow, the Causeway, and Old Town. However, new bawdy houses and brothels also began to spring up in small streets and alleys in the southern part of the city, especially Guilford Alley.[29]

---

[27] See Giesberg, *Army at Home*, 57; Catherine Clinton, "Public Women," 14. On Northern women's experiences on the home front, see also Jeanie Attie, *Patriotic Toil: Northern Women and the American Civil War* (Ithaca, NY: Cornell University Press, 1998).

[28] BCCC, January, May, and September Terms, 1860; BCCC, January, May, and September Terms, 1862; BCCC, January, May, and September Terms, 1864.

[29] BCCC, January, May, and September Terms, 1864.

For madams and even some sex workers, military occupation and the expansion of the demand for sex work that came with it proved to be a financial boon, even with the increased competition that followed growth. While it is notoriously difficult to track the earnings of sex workers over time, federal income tax records from the war period provide some of the best evidence of the profitability of sex work during the war years. Several madams from the Meadow, where higher-end brothels and sex establishments catered to officers residing at the Eutaw House headquarters for the Union's Middle Department, appeared on federal income tax rolls. This was in and of itself impressive given that taxable income was defined during the war years as income exceeding $600 per annum, a sum substantial enough that around 90 percent of Union households were exempt from the tax.[30] Annette Travers, the madam whose house Hillard and Davies visited, reported a taxable income of $100 in May 1863, which indicates that her total income was $700. Travers and her neighbors also bought pianos, heavy silver serving platters, and liquor licenses for their establishments, as well as gold watches and other pricey trinkets for themselves. Emma Morton enjoyed even greater success: in 1863, Morton reported a whopping $1,594 in taxable income and paid additional luxury taxes on a forty-eight-ounce silver plate and what appeared to be a newly purchased, two-horse carriage valued at between $800 and $1,000. Her brothel, which was notorious for hosting Union Provost Marshal William Fish, among other officers, made her 3.5 times more affluent than the best-paid female wage earners in the United States (assuming she accurately reported her income). Lest there were any doubts that Morton's opulence was linked to a wartime boom in business, tax rolls covering 1861 and 1866 suggest far lower earnings. Morton paid no income tax in 1862 and reported a substantial decline in taxable income ($691) in 1866.[31]

[30] Steven Weisman, *The Great Tax Wars: Lincoln to Wilson – The Fierce Battles over Money and Power That Transformed the Nation* (New York: Simon & Schuster, 2002), 102.

[31] US IRS Tax Assessment Lists, 1862–1918, Roll Title: District 3; Annual Lists, 1862, Miss Emma Morton, 295; US IRS Tax Assessment Lists, 1862–1918, Roll Title: District 3; Annual Lists, 1863–64, 271; US IRS Tax Assessment Lists, 1862–1918, Roll Title: District 3; Annual Lists, 1865, 341; US IRS Tax Assessment Lists, 1862–1918, Roll Title: District 3; Annual Lists, 1866, 362. Miss Annie Travers, US IRS Tax Assessment Lists, 1862–1918, Roll Title: District 3; Annual Lists, 1863–64, 245; Mrs. Anne Traverse, US IRS Tax Assessment Lists, 1862–1918, Roll Title: District 3; Annual Lists, 1862.

The high demand for sex work during the war also created opportunities for enterprising women who sold sex to move up the chain and enter the managerial class. Elizabeth Brooks, a sex worker who lived in a brothel on Bath Street in the Meadow, met a young soldier named Thomas Dutcher during the war. Dutcher, who served in the 5th New York Volunteer Infantry stationed at Federal Hill, probably started as one of Brooks's clients. He and two other soldiers from his company boarded at Brooks's brothel for a short period. Eventually, Dutcher and Brooks became a couple and decided to settle down and open their own brothel. Brooks, aware that the Baltimore market was growing saturated and that points south may provide her with better opportunities to get out from under the heel of a madam, convinced Dutcher that they would be better off in Alexandria, Virginia. Alexandria, located just south of Washington, was experiencing a wartime boom in prostitution, and Dutcher went ahead to Virginia to scout potential brothel locations for Brooks. By 1865, he was running a retail liquor store and bawdy house on Henry and Cameron Streets, presumably with her assistance.[32]

Even women who labored in less affluent sectors of the sex trade made a good living for themselves during the war. Ann Manley, whose Causeway brothel attracted primarily enlisted men, continued to run 151 Eastern Avenue as a sex establishment throughout the war years. The Causeway had the advantage of being in close proximity to the President Street station where newly arrived soldiers disembarked from their trains.[33] Soldiers stationed at Snake Hill, the area at the far eastern end of Eastern Ave that later became Highlandtown, and at Federal Hill went to the Causeway for entertainment. Their business apparently benefited the Manley family. Over the course of the 1860s, Ann and James, who returned from war unscathed, added three children and several new boarders, male and female, to their household. They did well for themselves financially; by 1870, they claimed to own $3,000 of real property – double what they had reported in 1860 – and $600 of personal property. James, who was illiterate, took a job as a watchman at the Customs House. Ann managed the tavern and tended to the couples' eight boarders, five of whom were sex workers, with the help of a newly hired servant, a forty-year-old Bermudian woman named Ellen DeShield. Ann and James cared for James's eighty-year-old mother and made enough

[32] *Records of the Proceedings of the Investigation before His Excellency Thomas Swann*, 40.
[33] Court Martials, RG 153, File OO954.

money that they could allow their younger children to attend school on the weekdays and Sunday school at a nearby church on the weekend.[34]

Although the Civil War–era expansion of the sex trade undoubtedly benefited established sex workers (at least in the short term), its effects on soldiers who patronized sex businesses and on the local war effort were decidedly more mixed. Some soldiers who encountered sex workers, particularly early in the war, found sex workers' willingness to welcome soldiers comforting and in sharp contrast to the actions of Baltimoreans who spit at, jostled, and jeered them. Private James Bollar, who perceived women in Baltimore's bawdy trade as unusually obliging, assigned them motives similar to those of Ann Manley's – namely, love of Union. Bollar wrote to a friend, "Baltimore is full of 'patriotic young ladies' who devote their entire time to gratify the passions of the soldiers." He claimed that he and his fellow artillerymen frequently "ha[d] the pleasure to pay our patriotic friends a visit."[35] The perceived loyalty of sex workers could make a soldier feel bolstered in his cause as easily as contact with a seemingly hostile population could inspire pessimism.

Baltimore's bawdy houses also provided a degree of physical comfort to soldiers, particularly in the case of brothels that catered to officers and more well-off enlisted men. Correspondence from Baltimore soldiers reveals that conditions in Baltimore's forts and camps were often unpleasant. One soldier complained that his quarters at Fort Federal Hill were dirty and ramshackle, and that "the place is full of L[ice], B[ed].Bugs, and all other sorts of horrid things."[36] Another complained that there was no privacy because ninety-six men slept in a room that "is about 60 by 25, with 48 'bunks,' there is three tiers, arranged the same as the bearths on a steamboat ones above the other, two persons sleep in each bunk."[37] The food, while usually nutritionally complete, was "to[o] regular" and camp life was often dull and tedious. Many men missed home, excitement, and the company of women.

Baltimore's sex establishments were well positioned to ameliorate soldiers' yearning for the comforts of home, for entertainment, and for a good meal and a drink. High-end brothels, which were decorated to

---

[34] 1860 US Census, Baltimore, Maryland, Ward 2, Dwelling 1003, Family 1537, p. 170, Ann Manley; 1870 US Census, Baltimore, Maryland, Ward 2, Dwelling 1775, Family 2859, p. 327, Ann Manley.

[35] Bollar to Hammons, Feb. 7, 1862.

[36] Henry M. Congdon to his father, June 2, 1862, NYHS; Lou to the girls, June 22, 1863, MDHS.

[37] George A. Mitchell to his parents, Dec. 29, 1861, NYHS.

resemble middle-class homes and which provided soldiers with opportunities to socialize with women as well as engage in sex with them, were uniquely positioned to recreate domestic comforts. Meadow parlor houses like Nancy Thomas's, Annette Travers's, and Emma Morton's actively invited military clientele (especially officers) to make social calls at their house and to enjoy luxuries that were in short supply in military life. Some madams even hosted elaborate balls and parties for military men.[38] East Baltimore's bawdy houses were decidedly less fancy and less apt to provide domestic comforts than West Baltimore's, but they too provided soldiers with welcome opportunities for drink, meals, and sociability. Enlisted men often went to the Causeway and to Old Town's taverns in groups to drink and to participate in more ribald forms of masculinity than were regarded as acceptable in fancier houses. Bawdy houses in the area had a lewd, raucous character that invited soldiers to jeer at civilians, to brawl, and to participate in more public forms of sexual expression than were common in refined brothels.[39]

Significantly, brothels became sites at which common soldiers negotiated the complexities of wartime masculinity. Martial rhetoric of the Civil War period emphasized men's need to defend home and hearth, and enlisted men and officers alike embraced notions of personal honor that were heavily gendered and rooted in a shared sense of masculine duty. Even as military culture emphasized manliness, it also highlighted the instability of masculine identity. War removed men from the company of women and denied soldiers forms of heterosexual expression – that is, marriage, reproduction – that had historically been crucial to attainments of manhood and that were often thought to be important for the maintenance of men's sexual health. By granting men sexual access to women and by providing them with heterosocial leisure spaces, bawdy houses gave men space to articulate new forms of masculine expression that were suited to the dislocations of war. In doing so, they became sites in which men bonded with *each other* by establishing a shared sense of masculinity rooted in heterosexual expressions and sexual license.[40]

---

[38] William Fish Court Martial, NARG 153, MM1356. For more on brothels' genteel/domestic orientation during the antebellum period, see Cohen, *The Murder of Helen Jewett*; Hijar, "Sexuality, Print, and Popular Visual Culture in the United States, 1830–1870."

[39] This observation is based on newspaper research that is cited in subsequent footnotes.

[40] Judith Giesberg, *Sex and the Civil War: Soldiers, Pornography, and the Making of American Morality* (Chapel Hill: University of North Carolina Press, 2017), 36–37. On (white) masculinity and the Civil War period, see also Foote, *The Gentlemen and*

For all that soldiers found comfort and camaraderie in Baltimore's brothels, however, interactions between soldiers, sex workers, and other civilians were not always positive. Sex workers in the Causeway and Old Town were occasionally underhanded in their dealings with Union troops, who proved to be easy marks for theft because of their unfamiliarity with the city and their unwariness. When soldiers passed out drunk or fell asleep, sex workers sometimes took advantage of their incapacity to steal whatever money or trinkets they had on their persons. Josephine Oakley, who worked in Dorothy Giles's establishment on Eastern Avenue, stole $70 in treasury notes from Pvt. John Silver of the 10th New York Cavalry in 1862 and passed the money to a local laborer for safekeeping. It was not the first time Giles's house had been identified as a site of theft. Catharine Denny, a sex worker in the establishment who had a history of assaulting Union soldiers, had been arrested for stealing $60 in treasury notes from a man visiting from Washington only ten days before.[41] Henry Williams, the young soldier from the 1st Maine Volunteers mentioned earlier in this chapter, went to a house of ill fame only to be "robbed of about fifteen dollars and my overcoat, Blouse, Military Vest, and cap were stolen and in there [sic] place left an old hat, olde citizen coat, and vest."[42] Although Williams admitted that he was robbed after becoming intoxicated of his own accord, other soldiers who were robbed in brothels accused sex workers of drugging them in order to take their property them. Michael Graham testified before a court martial board that he was "drugged + otherwise stupified, so that I was unable to control my intellect" at a disreputable house on Potter Street. Graham claimed that the women of the house had robbed him of a "finger ring, a small sum of money, and 2 pocket watches" before dumping him on the corner of Low and Exeter Streets.[43]

While most sex workers who robbed soldiers were merely carrying on practices that had been making them extra money since long before the

the Roughs; Michael Kimmel, Manhood in America: A Cultural History, 3rd edition (Oxford: Oxford University Press, 2012), 56–60. On Civil War soldiers' perception of war and military service as a coming of age experience, see Reid Mitchell, "Soldiering, Manhood, and Coming of Age: A Northern Volunteer," in Divided Houses: Gender and the Civil War, ed. Catherine Clinton and Nina Silber (Oxford: Oxford University Press, 1992), 43–54.

[41] "A Charge of Theft," Sun, May 2, 1862; "Charged with Robbery," Sun, July 1, 1862; "Charged with Robbery," Sun, June 21, 1862.

[42] Court Martials, RG 153, File OO954.   [43] Court Martials, RG 153, QQ2153.

war started, some conflicts between Baltimore civilians and soldiers who visited houses of ill fame were explicitly political and rooted in anti-Union animus. Because Baltimore's sex trade had never shifted entirely to a camp follower trade, soldiers usually patronized the same sex establishments that Baltimore civilians did. Not all civilians were glad to encounter soldiers. Particularly in Democratic wards around Old Town and the Causeway vice district, the combination of civilian resentment of the Union occupation, abundant alcohol, and ready access to arms could create dangerous situations. Fights between soldiers and locals were commonplace. On September 17, 1862, for instance, a gunfight broke out between a group of local men and Union soldiers at the Arch, Susan Reese's establishment on Potter Street. The fight started when Jackson Hedrick, a butcher from Fells Point; Charles Norwood, the keeper of a tavern on nearby Chesnut Street; and a youth named George Gerbrich offered a toast to Jefferson Davis in earshot of a group of Union soldiers drinking nearby. The soldiers took offense to the insult and confronted the locals. During the ensuing argument, Charles Norwood drew a pistol and fired, missing the soldier he was attempting to shoot and hitting George H. White, a thirteen-year-old African American employee of the establishment, in the chest. White died of his wound.[44]

Incidents like the one at the Arch drew the attention of Union commanders, as they had the potential to damage public will toward the occupying soldiers. Granted, commanders could justify some outbursts as legitimate – if ultimately tragic – reactions to Baltimoreans' violent, secessionist impulses, but other violent altercations involving soldiers were difficult for military officials to defend. Only a few weeks after the incident in Reese's brothel, Potter Street became the site of yet another fatal gunfight. Several enlisted members of the 13th Pennsylvania were attending a dance at the house of "a female named Carroll" when a scuffle broke out in the early morning hours. City Marshal William A. Van Nostrand, the head of the Baltimore police force who had been chosen by the military Provost Marshal, attempted to quell the disturbance by arresting Jacob Kitcheman, a member of the cavalry. Kitcheman's fellow soldiers protested by pulling out their revolvers and firing at Van Nostrand and his guard, all of whom were unarmed save for weapons

---

[44] "Another Shooting Affray – Probably Fatal," *Sun*, Sep. 18, 1862. The men's occupations and residences were taken from *Wood's Baltimore City Directory* (Baltimore: John W. Woods, 1860).

they managed to wrest away from the brawling soldiers. A Union soldier named Duffy was shot in the head and killed during the ensuing fracas.[45]

In an even more embarrassing incident for the military, a group of intoxicated soldiers violently threatened James Manley, Ann Manley's husband, just months after his wife attracted public attention for her heroism. James drew the soldiers' ire after he amicably warned them that they were poised to miss their departing train. Although Manley, a staunch Unionist and a soldier himself, made an uncharacteristic show of restraint by retreating when the soldiers shoved a bottle against his chest and brandished a knife, he lost his patience when they yelled, "Kill the Baltimore son of a bitch!" He drew his pistol and fatally shot Edward W. Rayne. Manley was known as a violent man about town, but the behavior of the Union soldiers was so atrocious that even Manley's critics agreed that his victim had it coming. The state's attorney, conceding that Rayne was of poor character and stating that he believed Manley acted in self-defense, declined to mount a case against Manley even as he stood trial for manslaughter. The jury acquitted him.[46]

Incidents in which soldiers grew violent with locals or otherwise behaved boorishly exacerbated what at times was a tense relationship between the military, the public, and civilian authorities. The Baltimore police raised repeated objections to the conduct of soldiers who visited disreputable saloons and bawdy houses and the effects that this conduct had on the civilian population. Charles Howard, the president of the Baltimore Police Board in 1861, complained several times to military officials that soldiers were inciting civilian "excitement," behaving disrespectfully, and drawing weapons on civilians. After one incident in which intoxicated soldiers exchanged words and brandished revolvers at locals on Baltimore and Sharp Street, Howard penned a sharply worded letter to Major General Cadwalader of the Department of Annapolis: "You cannot be aware of the extent to which your wishes and your Orders are habitually thwarted and disobeyed by a number of those under your command." Howard expressed his own wish that Cadwalader's department would implement policies to address the "repeated complains made of [soldiers] strolling through the streets of the City, and behaving in an insulting and offensive manner."[47]

---

[45] "Fatal Affray," *Sun*, Oct. 8, 1862. The 13th Pennsylvania, or "The Irish Dragoons," as they were nicknamed, were stationed at the time at Fort Carroll, near Mount Clare.

[46] "Proceedings of the Courts," *Sun*, Sep. 20, 1861.

[47] Charles Howard, letter to Major General Cadwalader, May 25, 1861, Department of Maryland, Records of United States Army Continental Commands, 1821–1920, NARG 393.4, Entry 85, National Archives (Washington, DC), 216.

In addition to exacerbating existing tensions with locals, Union soldiers' tendency to resort to brothels for drink and sex impaired their ability to perform their duties, much to the consternation of their commanders. Not only did the revelry that took place at houses of ill fame leave many men drunk and insensible, it often led to more lasting impairments: venereal diseases. Although diseases like syphilis and gonorrhea were actually less common in the army during the Civil War period than they were before or after, rates of infection were nevertheless staggering by modern standards, especially in the early months of the war. Up to 14 troops per 1,000 sought treatment for syphilis or gonorrhea in any given month in late 1861 to mid-1862, and 82 out of every 1,000 white troops sought treatment for venereal ailments at some point throughout the conflict (statistics were less than half that for black soldiers, who had less access to brothels).[48] Infection rates were worse among troops stationed around cities, and surgeons whose regiments were encamped in Baltimore commented that venereal infection rates increased notably during their time there. Isaac F. Galloupe of the 17th Massachusetts reported in February 1863, "Syphilis and gonorrhea prevailed extensively in the regiment during its stay in Baltimore."[49]

The frequent occurrence of syphilis and gonorrhea among soldiers proved a significant burden to the army. The diseases themselves could take troops out of commission for days or weeks at a time, and treating them was costly and time consuming. The US Sanitary Commission recommended that all soldiers infected with gonorrhea be removed from quarters, put on bed rest, and subjected to hot baths and urethral injections applied frequently over the course of several days. Syphilitic patients faced an even more intense treatment regimen; they underwent risky and expensive cures involving regular mercury treatments over the course of weeks. While some surgeons gave these cures orally or as rubs, others favored more complex treatments; Surgeon Ezra Read of the 21st Indiana, for instance, wrote from Baltimore that he favored subjecting syphilitic troops to mercurial steam baths in airtight facilities to affect a cure.[50] Regardless of the method of treatment, soldiers undergoing mercury cures were often removed from duty and relocated to hospitals, as "the dangers

---

[48] US Army's Surgeon General's Office, *The Medical and Surgical History of the War of the Rebellion*, Part III, vol. 1 (3rd Medical volume) (Washington, DC: Government Printing Office, 1888), 890–91.

[49] *The Medical and Surgical History of the War of the Rebellion*, Part III, vol. 1, 892.

[50] *The Medical and Surgical History of the War of the Rebellion*, Part III, vol. 1, 892.

to be apprehended from exposure and hardship while pursuing a mercurial course, are too great to admit of this treatment being undertaken in camp."[51]

The high cost of venereal treatment – in terms of both the price of medicine and lost productivity – spurred military officials in many districts to attempt to check the "evils" of prostitution by interfering in the workings of the sex trade. In Union-occupied cities like Nashville and Memphis, military officials famously experimented with French-style medical regulation of the sex trade. Believing that prostitution could not be fully eliminated, authorities sought to mitigate the disorder and adverse health effects of prostitution by requiring women who sold sex in those cities to obtain a license and operate within brothels. Military and police surgeons examined the conditions of brothels on a frequent basis and performed physical examinations on the women who worked in them. Any woman who showed signs of infection with syphilis, gonorrhea, or chancre had her license revoked and was sent to treatment in order to preclude her from infecting soldiers.[52]

For a time, it seemed possible that Baltimore's expanded sex trade might be vulnerable to similar intervention. Military authorities could not implement their own regulatory system so long as Baltimore remained under civil authority, but civil officials expressed their concerns about prostitution and high rates of venereal infections during the war years. In the last months of the conflict, G. W. Wayson, a physician serving on the First Branch of Baltimore's City Council, introduced two resolutions concerning commercial sex and disease. First, Wayson proposed that the physicians of the almshouse should report the number of patients under their care suffering directly or indirectly from syphilis, with the goal of ascertaining the financial burden the disease placed on the institution. Second, Wayson requested that the city police provide a list of all houses of ill fame, their locations, and the number and identity of their inhabitants to the Council. The back-to-back nature of these resolutions was not coincidental, and, indeed, the almshouse physician's reply to the

---

[51] US Sanitary Commission, *Committee of the Associate Medical Members of the Sanitary Commission on the Subject of Venereal Diseases, with Special Reference to Practice in the Army and Navy* (New York: John F. Trow, Printer, 1862), 16.

[52] James Boyd Jones, "A Tale of Two Cities: The Hidden Battle against Venereal Disease in Civil War Nashville and Memphis," *Civil War History* 31, no. 3 (1985): 270–76; Jones, "Municipal Vice: The Management of Prostitution in Tennessee's Urban Experience. Part I: The Experience of Nashville and Memphis, 1854–1917," *Tennessee Historical Quarterly* 50, no. 1 (1991): 33–41.

query about syphilis focused extensively on prostitution.[53] Although Wayson did not explicitly cast it as such, his proposal that the city study the economic burdens that venereal disease placed on municipally governed almshouses was a likely attempt to lay the groundwork for the local state to intervene in intimate matters on the basis of definable interest. Indeed, as discussed in the following chapters, the years that followed witnessed a number of proposals from Baltimore physicians who argued that the state should create a medical regulatory system around sex work.

During the war itself, however, Baltimore brothel keepers managed to stave off excessive interference in their trade, largely by cooperating with Union military officials. In addition to reaching out and inviting prominent Union officers to attend parties and make social calls to their establishments, madams also opened their houses to members of the Provost Marshal's staff. Early on in the war, the Provost Marshal of the Middle District realized that many of the soldiers who deserted their posts or otherwise left their camps without permission were visiting local brothels and saloons. In order to round up errant soldiers, the Deputy Provost Marshal made regular sweeps of the city's commercial sex establishments. Brothel keepers cooperated with these sweeps, which rendered their establishments useful to military officials as easy collection points for wayward troops. Local military officials, perhaps realizing that tracking soldiers would be much more difficult if they were to shutter sex establishments and diffuse the trade, adopted a policy of toleration and collaboration rather than suppression.[54]

Sex workers in Baltimore also took advantage of their unique social positions in order to provide valuable intelligence to Union officers. In order to understand how brothels came to be centers of intelligence gathering, it is worth considering the case of Harry Davies and Otis K. Hillard. In 1861, when Maryland's position within the Union still seemed vulnerable, there were concerns among government officials that pro-Southern militia groups were forming in Baltimore and perhaps even

---

[53] Sadly, the results of this census do not appear to have survived. Baltimore City Council, *Journal of Proceedings of the First Branch City Council of Baltimore at the Session of 1864–1865* (Baltimore: James Young, 1865), 170; Samuel T. Knight to the Members of the First Branch of the City Council, March 13, 1865, in *Journal of Proceedings of the First Branch City Council of Baltimore at the Session of 1864–1865*, 320–38.

[54] 34th Congress, 2nd Session, House of Representatives, Report 79, *Alleged Hostile Organizations against the Government within the District of Columbia* (Washington, 1861), no. 25, Feb. 6, 1861, 144–55.

planning to carry out a plot against Lincoln's life. Harry Davies, a Pinkerton agent, was sent undercover to assess the threat that violent secessionist groups posed to local railroad infrastructure. Davis quickly befriended Otis K. Hillard, a suspected secessionist who had been sub-poenaed earlier in the month to give testimony before a Congressional Committee investigating pro-Southern militia organizations.[55] In his tes-timony, Hillard denied participating in militia activity himself, but he admitted that he knew several of the men who participated in the National Volunteers, a Democratic political organization that mobilized as a militia force following Lincoln's election. Davies believed that Hillard might be a valuable source of intelligence, and he set about gaining his trust by talking with him and bonding through their shared participation in the masculine world of urban leisure and entertainment. The pair dined together at Mann's Restaurant, played billiards at Hemling's, paid visits to Hillard's acquaintances at Barnum's Hotel, and patronized the theater and a local concert saloon. At Hillard's suggestion, he and Davies also made trips to Travers's brothel at 70 Davis Street, where Hillard "had a girl" named Anna Hughes.[56]

For Davies, the visits to Travers's house were crucial to building trust with Hillard. After Davies spent about an hour socializing in the brothel's parlor and watching Hillard kiss Hughes, the two proceeded back to their hotel. Hillard, apparently feeling bonded to Davies by their time at the brothel, finally confessed to him the full extent of his militia activities. Hillard not only relayed that he was a member of the National Volunteers and that he planned to drill with them, but also hinted that the group might be plotting to harm Lincoln as he passed through Baltimore on the way to his inauguration. Davies's reporting of this and similar inter-actions with Hillard would eventually help to convince Allan Pinkerton that Baltimoreans were plotting against Lincoln's life. At Pinkerton's urging, Lincoln ended up taking the controversial step of canceling his appearance in Baltimore without notice and passing through the city in secret.[57]

---

[55] Daniel Stashower, *The Hour of Peril: The Secret Plot to Murder Lincoln before the Civil War* (New York: St. Martin's, 2013), 126.

[56] Davies, Report from Feb. 12, 1861, in *Lincoln and the Baltimore Plot*, 28–29.

[57] Whether the Baltimore plot actually existed remains a matter of some debate among popular and academic historians. Prominent scholars of Maryland history, including Edward C. Papenfuse and Robert Brugger, have given the plot credence. Stashower's *The Hour of Peril* provides one of the most comprehensive arguments for the existence of the plot.

If brothels created bonds between men that sometimes loosened the lips of pro-secessionist conspirators, a subsequent episode that took place between Hillard and Davies revealed that the role of the brothel in facilitating the exchange of intelligence gathering was not always so indirect. The very same day Lincoln made his clandestine trip through Baltimore, Davies returned to Annette Travers's brothel. He sat drinking in the parlor as he listened to Hillard, Anna Hughes, and a local grocer named Smith (a friend of Hillard's who also "had a girl" at the house) talk about the events of the day. Not realizing that Lincoln had changed his travel plans at the eleventh hour, thousands of Baltimoreans had gathered at the Calvert Street Station to greet him at his appointed arrival time. Anna Hughes, who had witnessed many of the events at the station because of the brothel's proximity to it, related that the scene had been a violent one marked by clashes between Lincoln's supporters and opponents. Davies recounted that Smith laughed at news of the violence, saying with a wink that he expected nothing would have happened to Lincoln if he had passed through the city openly. Davies regarded what he witnessed in Travers's parlor as proof that he and his fellow agents had been correct that Lincoln would be in severe danger if he risked a public appearance in Baltimore.[58]

Davies's experience illustrates how brothel keepers and sex workers were able to establish themselves as a source of intelligence for the Union army during the war years. Because brothels and bawdy houses were social as well as sexual places, men tended to spend time drinking and talking in their parlors. Drunk men who were eager to seem important in front of their "women" and fellow clients were often careless about revealing information that they should not, including tidbits about military campaigns and troop movements. In the case of Middle District brothels in particular, the male clientele tended to be the types of men who had access to high-level intelligence information: local officers, visiting commanders, and political figures. Notably, not all of these men were Unionists; the proximity of the brothels to Barnum's Hotel, a hub of secessionist sympathizers, and the rail lines that carried out-of-towners into the city meant that brothels catered to men from a variety of political backgrounds. Many madams took information they gleaned from Confederate sympathizers and passed it along to Union officers.[59]

[58] Harry Davies, Report from Feb. 23, 1861, in *A Baltimore Plot*, 94–95.

[59] For more on secessionists in Barnum's Hotel, see Edward C. Papenfuse's work on Cipriano Ferrandini (1823–1910), Archives of Maryland (Biographical Series), MSA

The court-martial case of Colonel William S. Fish provides some of the best evidence that brothel keepers supplied valuable intelligence to the Union. Fish had assumed the role of Provost Marshal in Baltimore on January 1, 1863, and it was not long before he proved himself to be an unscrupulous and corrupt official. In December of that year, he was arrested and charged with one count each of undermining military discipline, committing fraud, violating the 39th article of war, and conducting himself in a way unbecoming an officer. The specifications relating to the last charge – that Fish had engaged in conduct unbecoming an officer and a gentleman – revolved exclusively around Fish's conduct with sex workers and madams in Baltimore's high-class North and Davis Street brothels. According to testimony from subordinate officers, Fish (like Hillard before him) paid frequent visits to Annette Travers's brothel. He also was alleged to have visited Emma Morton's bawdy house, which was perhaps the most glamorous establishment in all of Baltimore by that point, "as often as three times a week" for several months in early 1863. Allegedly, he visited Nancy Thomas's establishment at least once during that same period. The charges against Fish did not go so far as to state explicitly that Fish had paid for the services of women, but they implied as much.[60]

As part of his defense, Fish wrote and published a lengthy, point-by-point rebuttal of the charges against him, but he kept his response to the charges of conduct unbecoming brief. Fish denied having danced at a ball with a girl from Emma Morton's house and claimed that disloyal men had manufactured that allegation to discredit him.[61] However, Fish did admit readily that he made a habit of visiting brothels and "endeavor[ing] to make [himself] acquainted with them, and the inmates of the houses." He did so, he said, not for prurient reasons – although he noted that it was not a crime under the law to patronize sex workers – but rather because he saw the visits as an extension of his professional duties as Provost Marshal. Being on familiar terms with the women who worked in houses of ill fame allowed Fish "to get that information best obtained in such places, and which was of importance to the service ... The most

---

SC 3520-14473. Available at http://msa.maryland.gov/megafile/msa/speccol/sc3500/sc3520/014400/014473/html/14473bio.html (accessed on Sep. 30, 2013).

[60] BCCC, Case 267, May Term, 1864, Emma Morton; William Fish Court Martial, NARG, [RG153], MM1356; William S. Fish, *Defence of Col. Wm. S. Fish, U.S. Army* (Washington, DC, 1864), 48. Available at http://archive.org/details/defenceofcolwmsfoofish (accessed Sep. 29, 2013).

[61] Fish, *Defence of Col. Wm. S. Fish*, 48.

important information I ever obtained, was through such sources." Among other valuable pieces of information, sex workers had provided him with intelligence that led to the arrest of a noted Confederate officer. The officer, Lieutenant Col. Eugene Lamar of the 14th Louisiana Infantry, had been in Baltimore and Washington illicitly gathering information on US Army fortifications. He had been sought by the War Department for months before he was finally captured and imprisoned in Fort McHenry based on information gained from Baltimore madams.[62]

Although Colonel Fish certainly had reasons to exaggerate his professional interest in the brothels he was accused of visiting, Fish's commanding officer offered testimony that supported his assertions that houses of ill fame were of value to the Union war effort. The court-martial panel agreed. Although Fish was found guilty of conduct undermining military discipline and of defrauding the US government, he was acquitted of all specifications relating to conduct unbecoming an officer. In the case of the second specification – that Fish had attended an event at Emma Morton's brothel in uniform – the court found that the allegations were true, but that there was no criminality in the act because it appeared that it was done in accordance with Fish's duty.[63]

Brothel keepers had reasons for cooperating with the Union that ranged from patriotic to deeply self-interested, but the results of their intelligence-gathering efforts were the same: the Provost guard appears to have not just tolerated, but actually bestowed favor on particular establishments. That favor expressed itself in a variety of ways. In Annette Travers's case, the negotiated payoff for her cooperation appeared to have been that the Provost guard agreed to turn a blind eye to her dealings with Union soldiers. After Fish visited Travers, he ordered his Assistant Provost Marshal, Captain Edward J. Parker, "whose duty, as such ... was to enter houses of prostitution for the purpose of arresting officers and soldiers found there without passes, not to enter the [public] house of Annette Travers."[64] Travers may also have been granted a degree of leniency from the courts in return for her cooperation with local officers. In the January Term of 1862, she paid the outrageously high sum of $500

---

[62] Fish, *Defence of Col. Wm. S. Fish*, 49. Fish misidentified Lamar's unit as the 17th Louisiana Infantry. Scharf, *History of Baltimore City and County*, 146.

[63] William Fish Court Martial, NARG, [RG153], MM1356. Fish was ordered to forfeit his salary, pay a fine of $5,000, and to remain in the Albany Penitentiary for a minimum of one year until the fine was paid.

[64] William Fish Court Martial, NARG, [RG153], MM1356.

for pleading guilty to keeping a house of ill fame. Once Fish became Provost Marshal, however, her fines decreased to as low as $10 and costs. By the January Term of 1864, Travers's presentment for the same charge was simply placed on the stet docket and never pursued.[65]

While Baltimore's brothel keepers managed to stave off excessive intervention from authorities by offering their cooperation and intelligence, they would not be able to escape the broader consequences of the war. Military occupation increased the demand for sexual services to the point that brothel keepers and ordinary sex workers made a great deal of money catering to officers' and soldiers' demands for domestic comforts, sociability, and physical and emotional labor. However, the wartime boom in commercial sex also called attention to the negative effects of the sex trade on public health and order. The scrutiny that the war brought to prostitution and the debates it generated about the role the state should play in regulating, suppressing, or otherwise intervening in the sex trade would have legacies that extended years beyond the conflict itself. This was particularly the case given that the war brought with it profound changes to Americans' understanding of their relationship to the government and to their notions of the rights and freedoms that the state was required to protect. Annette Travers, Ann Manley, and other brothel keepers could not anticipate in 1863 the long-term effects that the Civil War and its greatest achievement, emancipation, would have on the sex trade in the coming decades. As Chapter 6 will note, however, the aftershocks of freedom and the rise of a reimagined liberal state ushered in a new era of regulation.

[65] BCCC, January Term, 1862, Case 519, Annette Travers; BCCC, May Term, 1862, Case 933, Annette Travers; BCCC, January Term, 1864, Case 586, Annette Travers.

6

Prostitution, Policing, and Property Rights
in the Gilded Age

Every man, for any injury done to him in his person or property, ought to
have remedy by the course of the Law of the land, and ought to have justice
and right, freely without sale, fully without any denial, and speedily without
delay, according to the Law of the land.

—Article 19, Declaration of Rights, Maryland Constitution of 1864

In March 1863, Baltimore Mayor John L. Chapman, the City Council,
and several prominent citizens took the unusual step of suing Sarah
Harper. Harper, who sometimes went by the aliases Sarah Fuller or Sarah
Sunderland, was a married woman who had kept bawdy houses in
Baltimore since at least 1849.[1] By 1860, she was living with her husband
and ten children in Towsontown, but she maintained ownership of a
brothel at 36 Saratoga Street, near Calvert Street.[2] While her business
was just one among hundreds of bawdy houses to operate during the Civil
War period, its location was particularly objectionable for city elites and
members of the middle class: her house adjoined a Baptist church and sat
directly across from Public School No. 9 in "one of the most respectable
neighborhoods in the city."[3] The presence of a house of prostitution so
close to a church and school and in the midst of a neighborhood with high
property values irritated owners of neighboring homes and shops. Harper
was indicted before the Baltimore City Criminal Court for keeping a

---

[1] BCCC, May Term, 1849, Case 664, Sarah Harper (alias Sunderland).
[2] 1860 US Census, Baltimore, Maryland, District 9, p. 140, dwelling 915, family 899, Sarah
Sunderland.
[3] "Circuit Court," *Sun*, Mar. 18, 1863.

bawdy house and held to the startlingly high bond of $2,000.[4] However, the criminal prosecution was deemed insufficient. Richard H. Atwell, a merchant and manufacturer; Hugh B. Jones, Secretary of the Baltimore Equitable Society; and John Merryland banded together with the support of city officials to seek an equitable remedy against the injury they believed Harper was inflicting on their businesses and properties. As Resin Haslup and John Whitridge had done six years before with Margaret Hamilton, they brought Harper before the Circuit Court to plead for an injunction that would prevent her from occupying her property as house of ill fame.[5]

Judge William George Krebs, the chief justice of the Circuit Court, agreed to issue the injunction against Harper. Krebs cited the precedent established in *Hamilton* v. *Whitridge* to justify his action, claiming:

The jurisdiction of a court of equity was fully established to prohibit the use of premises for such purposes upon the application of owners of property in close proximity thereto, stating that the nuisance to be created by such use would deprive them of the comfortable enjoyment of their property, and greatly depreciate and lessen its value.[6]

When Harper's defense council objected to the ruling on the basis that there was no precedent prior to *Hamilton* for the court to collapse the distinction between public and private injuries, Krebs replied that the absence of precedent did not in and of itself limit the court. "Courts are not to assume jurisdiction," Krebs wrote, "but may amplify remedies, and apply rules and general principles for the advancement of substantial justice" – that is, justice that met the standard of fairness even if it was not firmly rooted in the letter of the law. Krebs concluded, "It would be a great failure of public justice to deny relief merely because no decision can be found in which the jurisdiction had been evoked."[7]

Sarah Harper's case would mark a crucial moment in a new phase of legal regulation of the sex trade, one that would reach its full stride in the years following the Civil War. Wartime circumstances had brought the attention of the state to bear on the sex trade, its geographies, and its health implications more intensively than in previous years. Peace

---

[4] "Proceedings of the Court," *Sun*, May 4, 1863; BCCC, January Term, 1863, Case 88, Sally Harper.

[5] "Circuit Court," *Sun*, Mar. 18, 1863. Information on Atwell and Jones's occupations was derived from Baltimore City Directory records. *Wood's Baltimore City Directory, 1864* (Baltimore: John W. Woods, 1864), 27, 207.

[6] "Circuit Court," *Sun*, Mar. 18, 1863.   [7] "Circuit Court," *Sun*, Mar. 18, 1863.

brought with it public debates over what the newly empowered state's role should be in regulating and policing prostitution. The war and its greatest achievement, emancipation, had reoriented the relationship between ordinary people and the government, rendering the latter a more active guarantor of rights and liberties than it had been in the early republic.[8] By the 1870s, Baltimore's emerging generation of middle-class residents demanded that municipal and state governments secure their property rights (and values) through public interventions: expanded sanitation infrastructure, more organized policing, more neighborhood amenities, and more control over the city's disorderly populations.[9] These demands, combined with sweeping paranoia about vagrancy following the triumph of free labor, gave rise to more intensive policing of sex workers. As brothels became less economically significant to downtown real estate speculation with the rise of industry, sex workers were increasingly regarded as malingerers whose presence threatened private property and the liberal order rather than undergirded it.

Although the court's decision in *Hamilton* v. *Whitridge* had already granted the state expansive powers to regulate the geography of the sex trade in 1857, the state began to use these powers in earnest only in the years after the Civil War. When it did, it began to create new sexual geographies based on the need to protect children, property values, and commerce from the potential harm done to them by the presence of commercial sex establishments.[10] The courts had once treated prostitution as a general violation of the public order and of the peace of the community as a whole. This changed – albeit gradually and incompletely – in the 1860s and 1870s. Prostitution, which had for decades been a means by which middling entrepreneurs and wealthy investors alike profited from the labor of women, came to be understood as inflicting injury on the economic, social, and health interests of the urban middle class. The courts treated it accordingly and employed the language of defending

---

[8] On changing conceptions of the state and its role in securing rights for citizens during and after the war, see, among others, Chandra Manning, "Working for Citizenship in the Contraband Camps," *Journal of the Civil War Era* 4 (June 2014): 172–204.

[9] Joseph L. Arnold, "The Neighborhood and City Hall: The Origin of Neighborhood Associations in Baltimore, 1880–1911," *Journal of Urban History* 6 (Nov. 1979): 8. See also Dennis P. Halpin, "'The Struggle for Land and Liberty': Segregation, Violence, and African American Resistance in Baltimore, 1898–1918," *Journal of Urban History* 44 (July 2018): 691–712.

[10] Nicola Kay Beisel, *Imperiled Innocents: Anthony Comstock and Family Reproduction in Victorian America* (Princeton: Princeton University Press, 1997), especially 15 and 103.

property rights rather than morality to justify evicting women like Sarah Harper. That Harper's property rights were apparently not worth protecting said much about the limits of the new liberal order, whose guarantees of rights would exclude not just sex workers, but also newly enfranchised black city residents and other "undesirables."

New approaches to regulating Baltimore's sex trade in the 1860s and 1870s were rooted in a combination of antebellum legal innovations such as *Hamilton* v. *Whitridge*, wartime experiences, and the economic and social changes that occurred in Baltimore following emancipation. Preeminent among the latter were shifts in how Americans perceived the duties of the state. As William Novak and a number of other legal historians have argued, the state in the early nineteenth century was governed primarily by the principle of *salus populi suprema est lex*: the welfare of the people is the highest law.[11] Much of the state's energies and powers were directed at preserving the safety and order of communities, sometimes at the expense of individuals and their rights to use their properties as they pleased. The mid-nineteenth century witnessed a gradual shift from this relatively communitarian notion of public welfare to individualist discourses of rights and freedoms – a transformation that was accelerated by war and emancipation.[12] What were once conceived of as harms against the community came to be understood as harms against private citizens.

In Maryland as in other states, the need to define freedom for the roughly 87,000 enslaved people released from bondage by the 1864 Constitution heralded the rise of liberal discourses that positioned self-sufficiency and control of one's labor and property as core elements of what it meant to be free.[13] These discourses held that the state's role was to promote and defend this sort of freedom as far as it was possible to do so, by providing black and white citizens with basic education, using vagrancy laws and contracts to encourage (or force) labor, and protecting private property through law and policing. Although property ownership had always enjoyed a strong relationship with citizenship and rights

---

[11] Novak, *The People's Welfare*.

[12] Notably, Legal Scholar Herbert Hovencamp contested Novak's assertion that economic regulation was widespread in nineteenth-century America but ultimately agreed with Novak that morals policing tended to be communitarian. According to Hovencamp, "Individualism in economics and communitarianism in morals dominated orthodox American thought in the nineteenth century." Herbert Hovencamp, "Law and Morals in Classical Legal Thought," Fulton Lectures, Chicago, 1996, 17.

[13] Malka, *The Men of Mobtown*, 189–245.

discourses in America, the state's prescribed role in actively securing private property as a means of defending individual rights and freedoms expanded in the aftermath of the Civil War. This legal and political shift in understandings of the state would have profound consequences for Baltimore's sex trade.

And yet the prostitution business did not feel the effects of postwar transformations immediately. Despite the fact that the 1863 case against Harper was a watershed moment in expanding the state's authority, the state's pressing interest in regulating prostitution actually abated somewhat in the immediate aftermath of the war due to decline in the size of the sex trade. The exodus of US soldiers from Baltimore marked the end of the boom period for sexual commerce, and proprietors left prostitution in droves. Some property-owners who had rented their houses to madams or opened the doors of their businesses to sex workers and their clients during the military occupation simply dropped out of the trade, reverting their establishments back to the antebellum status quo. Others used the profits they had made from catering to soldiers to relocate their businesses to more lucrative markets. Annette Travers, the madam who had made a tidy sum catering to and exchanging intelligence with Union officers, vacated her brothel on Davis Street sometime after 1867 to take advantage of a new market in the South. Washington, DC, had expanded along with the federal government during the war, and Travers understood that the influxes of clerks, politicians, professionals, and military men into the city represented a potentially profitable new opportunity. She moved her operations to the capital, where she operated a small but successful house of ill fame on Capitol Hill. At the time of the 1870 census, Travers, who was thirty-two years old but claiming to be twenty-five, was living with a thirty-year-old, Maryland-born former sex worker named Hattie Clinton and two black domestic servants. She had accumulated a respectable $2,000 of personal property.[14]

Between the outmigration of wartime proprietors and the reversion of former "bawdy houses" to legitimate businesses or ordinary dwellings,

---

[14] On Lea, concert saloons, and law, see William Lawrence Slout, ed., *Broadway below the Sidewalk: Concert Saloons of Old New York* (San Bernadino, CA: Borgo Press, 1994), xii–xiv; Gillian M. Rodger, *Champagne Charlie and Pretty Jemima: Variety Theater in the Nineteenth Century* (Urbana: University of Illinois Press, 2002), 59–71, especially 65–66. Annette Travers's last appearance in the Baltimore City Criminal Court on bawdy-house charges appears to have been in 1867. BCCC, May Term, 1867, Case 489, Annette Travers; 1870 US Federal Census, Anna Travers, Washington Ward 2, Washington, District of Columbia; Roll: M593_123; Page: 355A; Image: 722.

most of the growth that had occurred in the sex trade during the war years was reversed. The years immediately following the conflict saw a sharp decline in the number of persons prosecuted for keeping bawdy houses and houses of ill fame. In 1864, the height of the wartime sex trade, the Baltimore City Criminal Court had heard 366 presentments and indictments for keeping a bawdy house. By 1866, the number of presentments and indictments had fallen to only 167, with many indictments never progressing to the trial stage. The sex trade was in such a state of flux with bawdy-house keepers abandoning or relocating their establishments that many of the alleged madams whose names were given to the grand jury could not be located after the court issued capias warrants for them. Local authorities, busy with the burdens and challenges that accompanied the early period of rebuilding after the conflict, did not devote much effort to tracking them down. The result was that approximately a fifth of all warrants in bawdy-house cases were never served. With so much in question in the aftermath of the war, the future of the sex trade and its regulation initially seemed uncertain as well.[15]

Within a few years, however, the sex trade began to bounce back from its temporary contraction. In the decade following the war, the number of individuals presented to the city's grand jury for keeping bawdy houses rose to well beyond even the highest antebellum levels. The average number of bawdy house cases presented annually to the City Criminal Court in sample years between 1866 and 1876 was 67 percent higher than the average number of cases prosecuted over four sample years between 1850 and 1860. After 1867, the number of bawdy-house keepers presented in any given year never dropped below 200 and sometimes exceeded it; in 1876, for instance, the grand jury issued 276 unique presentments or indictments for bawdy-house charges. While prosecution totals fluctuated annually according to everything from the efficacy of individual police officers to minor changes in the court system, the general upward trend was too sharp to be coincidental. By 1880, one Presbyterian pastor who lamented the condition of young men in cities would claim that the census recorded 300 bawdy houses in Baltimore, an estimate that roughly accorded with the number of bawdy-house prosecutions that year.[16]

---

[15] Data derived from BCCC, 1864; BCCC 1866. Numbers are adjusted to exclude cases that were carried from one term of the year to another.

[16] The ambiguity in the actual number of charges reflects the presence of especially common names in the criminal dockets (e.g., Mary Smith). In some cases, it was unclear whether a

As the sex trade rebounded, local officials and reformers turned their attention back to its policing and regulation. Concerns about sexual commerce, sex workers, and their position in society became more pronounced in the late 1860s and early 1870s than they had been before, due in large part to the economic and social transformations taking place in Reconstruction America. As historian Amy Dru Stanley argued, the end of slavery and the apparent triumph of free labor rendered the figure of the prostitute especially problematic in the late nineteenth century, in large part because prostitution and slavery had been rhetorically linked for much of the antebellum period as joint symbols of market capitalism's excesses and potential to render people property. Prior to emancipation, pro-slavery speakers and writers had pointed to prostitution as a symbol of the deficiencies of Northern economies and their reliance on free labor rather than "traditional" bonds of dependency and obligation. Even Southern writers like William Gilmore Simms, who acknowledged that prostitution was present in the South as well, claimed that Southern prostitution – mainly of enslaved women – was less objectionable on the basis that "it does not debase the civilized, as is the case with prostitution at the North."[17] Although Northern abolitionists in the antebellum period often hesitated to make direct comparisons between slavery and the prostitution trades that proliferated in their own cities, they too had conceived of prostitution and slavery as outcroppings of a common human frailty – namely, uncontrolled lust and immorality.[18] Among abolitionists, prostitution was a dominant metaphor for the

case represented a new charge against an individual who happened to have the same name of another woman or a continuation of an older charge against one woman. BCCC 1866, C1849–31-33; 1867, C1849–34-5; 1870, C1849–42-4; 1872, C1849–48-9, 51; 1873, C1849–52-3, 55; 1875, C1849–60-1, 63; 1876, C1849–65-6, 68.

The docket for the January Term of 1867 could not be located at the time that I requested it from the archives (July 2012). The January Term generally saw relatively few presentments for keeping a bawdy house (thirty-three in 1867, nine in 1870), and many of those were carried until the May/June Term. As a result, the effect of the missing January Term docket on the quality of the data is likely negligible. Clokey, *Dying at the Top*, 90.

[17] William Gilmore Simms, "On the Morality of Slavery," in *The Pro-Slavery Argument, as Maintained by the Most Distinguished Writers of the Southern States* (Philadelphia: Lippincott, Grambo, & Co., 1853), 230. See also William Harper, "Slavery in the Light of Social Ethics," in *Cotton Is King, and Pro-Slavery Arguments: Comprising the Writings of Hammond, Harper, Christy, Stringfellow, Hodge, Bledsoe, and Cartwright on This Important Subject*, ed. E. N. Elliott (New York: Negro Universities Press, 1969), 581–82.

[18] Ronald G. Walters, "The Erotic South: Civilization and Sexuality in American Abolitionism," *American Quarterly* 25 (May 1973): 171–201.

institution of slavery and the traffic in enslaved women.[19] As historian Lawrence B. Glickman argued, "Both slavery and prostitution involved being sold or selling oneself on the market and hence losing control of bodily activities related to production and reproduction which rightfully belong to the free individual."[20]

After the nation embraced – in theory, at least – the notion that unfree labor was immoral, prostitution was rendered at best an unwelcome remnant of an older order and a sign that the millenarian aspirations of abolitionists had gone unfulfilled even with the death of slavery. At worst, the proliferation of commercial sex as the Southern states were transitioning to free labor economies was a disturbing indication that "the triumph of free labor did not safeguard even the most intimate sexual bonds from the marketplace."[21] The prostitute, whose body was a site where sex and commerce collided, represented a disturbing anomaly in a society that embraced the idea of a gendered divide between the feminine world of the domestic and the masculine world of industry. Anxieties about the breakdown of moral values in a society that was increasingly characterized by rampant commercialism made Baltimoreans more aware of the sex trade as a commercial entity that symbolized commercialism run amok. In light of this, Americans from a variety of backgrounds and political persuasions began to grapple with the question of what should be done to address the "social evil" of sex work.[22]

The bureaucratic expansion of the government and the growing belief that the state had an important role to play in promoting the county's emerging liberal order ensured that many of the proposals about how to regulate the sex trade urged new kinds of state interventions.[23] One of earliest of these proposals came from American physicians whose wartime experiences had made them more aware than ever of the prevalence of venereal disease in the urban population. Physicians linked high rates of syphilis and gonorrhea with prostitution, and beginning in the 1870s, they began to lobby for cities around the country to implement medical regulatory systems for the sex trade to improve public health. They drew

[19] Stanley, *From Bondage to Contract*, especially 218–19.
[20] Lawrence G. Glickman, *A Living Wage: American Workers and the Making of Consumer Society* (Ithaca, NY: Cornell University Press, 1997), 36.
[21] Stanley, *From Bondage to Contract*, 219.
[22] Stanley, *From Bondage to Contract*, 218–63.
[23] Stephen Skowronek, *Building a New American State: The Expansion of National Administrative Capacities, 1877-1920* (Cambridge: Cambridge University Press, 1982); Manning, "Working for Citizenship in the Contraband Camps," 172–204.

their inspiration both from wartime experiments with medical inspection of sex workers in Tennessee and from French and British regulatory systems.[24] American physicians, who were eager to expand their own professional authority, launched campaigns for similar systems in cities like Baltimore. While physicians varied in their opinions on whether prostitution should be licensed (as in France) or not (as in Britain and its colonies), they all emphasized that prostitution was a permanent and ineradicable fixture of urban life and that the regular inspection of sex workers was necessary to prevent epidemic venereal disease and maintain the health of the urban population. Advocates of medical regulation lobbied authorities to require mandatory treatment for any women found to be suffering from disease.[25]

Several Baltimore medical men were active in the national movement for state regulation of the sex trade. Various city physicians, some of whom claimed to have the support of brothel keepers, made at least five attempts between 1874 and 1882 to convince the Baltimore grand jury and the state legislature to enact some variation on the French or British systems. John C. Morris, a physician who had treated Margaret Hamilton as she recovered from the gunshot wound inflicted on her by Eliza Simpson in 1856, became a national advocate for a revised system of medical inspection for prostitutes in the late 1870s and early 1880s.[26] In 1881, Morris served on the Special Committee of the American Public Health Association on the Prevention of Venereal Diseases, which drafted model legislation addressed to the Maryland State Legislature.

[24] For a general overview of European regulationism, see Peter Baldwin, *Contagion and the State in Europe, 1830–1930* (Cambridge: Cambridge University Press, 1999), 355–524. See also Alain Corbin, *Women for Hire: Prostitution and Sexuality in France after 1850* (Cambridge, MA: Harvard University Press, 1990). On the Contagious Diseases Acts, see Judith R. Walkowitz, *Prostitution and Victorian Society: Women, Class, and the State* (Cambridge: Cambridge University Press, 1980); Levine, *Prostitution, Race and Politics*; Howell, *Geographies of Regulation*.

[25] Anne M. Butler, *Daughters of Joy, Sisters of Misery: Prostitutes in the American West, 1865–90* (Urbana: University of Illinois Press, 1985), 74–95; Julia Bruggemann, "Prostitution, Sexuality, and Gender Roles in Imperial Germany: Hamburg, a Case Study," in *Genealogies of Identity: Interdisciplinary Readings on Sex and Sexuality*, ed. Margaret Sönser Breen and Fiona Peters (New York: Editions Rodopi BV, 2005), 34.

[26] Aaron Macy Powell, *State Regulation of Vice: Regulation Efforts in America. The Geneva Congress* (New York: Wood & Holbrook, 1878), 83–84. On Morris's previous experiences treating sex workers, see "Assignation Houses," *Sun*, Mar, 2, 1840; June 12, 1855; Report of the Trial of Michael Rock on an Indictment for a Rape on Elizabeth Black, MS. 174, Special Collections, Milton S. Eisenhower Library, Johns Hopkins University.

The proposed legislation criminalized both the willful spread of venereal diseases and the intentional harboring of infected persons. It also authorized the Baltimore City Board of Health to quarantine any afflicted persons, a measure that had the potential to stigmatize and dramatically restrict the movements of sex workers, their clients, and members of the urban poor in general.[27] Morris, in a minority report, urged strict oversight of houses of ill fame by the local state and proposed that keepers of establishments that allowed prostitution on their premises be required to report the names of all women frequenting their businesses. While Morris shied away from suggesting that the women be issued licenses or subjected to taxes, he specified that they should be subjected to bimonthly medical inspections conducted by one of four "regularly educated medical men" appointed by the Mayor of Baltimore and paid salary from revenue collected as part of the city's police tax.[28]

Morris's proposal and other similar plans circulated by physicians across the country were met with immediate and strong public opposition. Baltimore's antebellum toleration of vice was well known to anyone who paid attention, but it had the benefit of being tacit practice rather than official policy. The notion that the state would not only explicitly condone vice, but also devote resources to enabling it offended the sensibilities of groups that ranged from religious moralists to women's rights advocates. As early as 1865, Baltimore Health Officer Samuel T. Knight argued that state-sanctioned vice would represent nothing short of a "revolution" in American politics, and not one that was for the better.[29] In the years that followed, a number of Christian religious groups made similar arguments. Quaker philanthropists J. Carey Thomas and Francis King were responsible for halting two of the efforts to bring the issue of regulation before the Baltimore grand jury. They and other reformers viewed licensing vice as an abdication of government's responsibility to foster a moral society, as well as an assault on the virtue of Baltimore women. In an echo of Josephine Butler and the British repealers, opponents of medical regulation criticized physicians' proposals for what they saw as their blatant assertions of men's sex right at the expense of

[27] John C. Morris, "Minority Report of the Special Committee on the Prevention of Venereal Diseases," *Maryland Medical Journal* 8 (May 1, 1881): 440–43.

[28] Morris, "Minority Report of the Special Committee on the Prevention of Venereal Diseases," 440–43.

[29] First Branch, Baltimore City Council, *Journal of the Proceedings of the First Branch of the City Council at the Sessions of 1864 & 1865* (Baltimore: James Young, 1865), 332, 334; Powell, *State Regulation of Vice: Regulation Efforts in America*, 83–84.

women's bodily autonomy. They argued that it was an abomination to subject women to humiliating inspections for the sake of allowing men to satisfy their sexual lusts without consequence. Furthermore, they challenged physicians' understandings of human sexuality by arguing that men's sexual desires, far from being natural and ungovernable as advocates of medical regulation claimed, could and should be controlled. In their view, it was the state's duty not to encourage lust, but rather to help young men to keep it in check by, among other things, facilitating wholesome recreation and developing programs of gymnastic exercises for men that would help them to develop healthy habits and restraint.[30]

Opposition to medical regulation was so pronounced in the 1870s and 1880s that only one major US urban area – St. Louis – implemented a formal medical inspection system, which lasted for only four years before it was suspended due to its unpopularity.[31] The backlash against the very idea of state regulation of commercial sex proved far more enduring than that brief experiment. As Chapter 9 will discuss, the coalition of evangelical Christians, early feminists, and political reformers who were initially drawn together by opposition to medical regulation would eventually succeed in pressuring the state to end toleration of the sex trade. In the 1860s and 1870s, however, even reform-minded Baltimoreans were not yet ready to stage an organized push for the suppression. Instead, Baltimoreans turned to a different program of state regulation, one that combined antebellum techniques for suppressing public forms of sexual commerce with newer techniques for policing and containing sex work.

Newly intensified enforcement of vagrancy statutes and ordinances proved a particularly crucial part of the late nineteenth-century program of regulating and cracking down on prostitution. Maryland authorities, like those in other states to the North and South, grew increasingly

---

[30] First Branch, Baltimore City Council, *Journal of the Proceedings of the First Branch of the City Council at the Sessions of 1864 & 1865*, 332, 334; Powell, *State Regulation of Vice: Regulation Efforts in America*, 83–84. On Josephine Butler, see Walkowitz, *Prostitution and Victorian Society*; Jenny Daggers and Diana Neal, eds., *Sex Gender, and Religion: Josephine Butler Revisited* (New York: Peter Lang Publishing, 2006); Jane Jordan and Ingrid Sharp, eds., *Josephine Butler and the Prostitution Campaigns: Diseases of the Body Politic* (London: Routledge, 2003).

[31] On regulation campaigns in the United States, see John Parascandola, *Sex, Sin, and Science: A History of Syphilis in America* (Westport, CT: Praeger, 2008), 32–36; D'Emilio and Freedman, *Intimate Matters*, 147–50; Nichols, *Prostitution, Polygamy, and Power*, 83–135; Nayan Shah, *Contagious Divides: Epidemics and Race in San Francisco's Chinatown* (Berkeley: University of California Press, 2001), 110.

concerned with vagrancy in the aftermath of emancipation. Initially, at least, these concerns were more related to racial anxieties than to sexual ones. Between 1864 and 1867, Marylanders took steps to eliminate slavery and to ensure black residents basic rights under the law. They dismantled many of the state's more discriminatory statutes and affirmed via a new Constitution and several important court decisions that all people, regardless of race, had the right to legal protection and control over their own labor. Yet, even as they espoused the principles of free labor, many white Marylanders doubted that black men and women were capable of adjusting to or succeeding within the new economic and social paradigm.[32] Racialized fears that black people were by nature too idle, profligate, and servile to meet the demands of liberal citizenship and self-support were evident in the debates over abolition during the 1864 Maryland Constitutional Convention. Isaac D. Jones, a former US Congressman and lawyer from Somerset County, argued that ridding the state of slavery would only "plunge this unfortunate class [of emancipated slaves] into idleness, crime and degradation."[33] Richard Eleden, a slaveholder from Charles County, argued that an end to slavery would "turn upon the white population of the State and idle unthrifty, non-producing class to pray upon their substance." Eleden concluded, "Liberty to the slaves ... for many would be the liberty to starve."[34]

In light of concerns that freedpeople would fail to be productive and self-sustaining laborers, authorities turned to vagrancy laws to secure their vision for the new liberal order. Although Maryland did not join its fellow Northern or Southern states in passing harsher vagrancy statutes during Reconstruction, its authorities did enforce the existing laws with vigor. Police dockets from the late 1860s and early 1870s reveal that Baltimore police regularly arrested both men and women for violating city ordinances that functionally criminalized unemployment and poverty. As in the antebellum period, arrests for vagrancy usually resulted in the arrestees being institutionalized for a period of one to two months and forced to labor under the direction of the state.[35]

---

[32] Malka, *The Men of Mobtown*, 189–215.

[33] *The Debates of the Constitutional Convention of the State of Maryland, Assembled at the City of Annapolis, Wednesday, April 27, 1864*, vol. 1 (Annapolis: Richard P. Bayly, 1864), 600.

[34] *Debates of the Constitutional Convention of the State of Maryland*, 579. Adam Malka's work drew my attention to this quotation. Malka, *The Men of Mobtown*, 190.

[35] Information about vagrancy arrests was derived from examinations of Baltimore City Police Criminal Dockets housed at the Maryland State Archives. Baltimore City Police

The expansion of police power during Reconstruction led to waves of arrests that specifically targeted sex workers and other women whose economic independence or free use of public space marked them as disorderly. In 1871, the city's Board of Police Commissioners issued and publicized an order specifying that the night police should henceforth "arrest all that class of females known as street-walkers found on the street after dark."[36] Following the issuance of the order, police conducted sporadic sweeps of their districts' streets, sometimes arresting twenty or more streetwalking sex workers in a single district per night on vagrancy charges. Samplings of police dockets suggest that women, black and white, made up a majority of those arrested for vagrancy in the 1860s and 1870s.[37]

The risk to sex workers who solicited publicly was heightened by the fact that police magistrates had added financial incentive to label people as vagrants. In the period immediately following the war, magistrates received fees of $2.40 for every person they ordered incarcerated for vagrancy, a generous fee that some magistrates took advantage of by releasing and repeatedly incarcerating the same offenders to generate revenue. In 1868, a grand jury probe into vagrancy arrests found that "corruption, malpractice, and oppression are widely prevalent among many of the magistrates of the city, and also with the constables."[38] Suspicions of judicial malfeasance arising from greed prompted the Baltimore City Court to implement a regular review of vagrancy commitments by city magistrates, and city attorneys occasionally stepped in to file writs of habeas corpus in particularly controversial cases. Generally, however, high courts upheld the constitutionality of wide-ranging vagrancy statutes. Streetwalkers, a particularly unsympathetic group of defendants in the eyes of most Baltimoreans, often found themselves with little recourse when the full weight of those statutes befell them.[39]

(Criminal Docket, Eastern District), 1867–1868, C2111–4; Baltimore City Police (Criminal Docket, Southern District) 1867–1868, C2113–1.

[36] "Street-Walkers," *Sun*, Mar. 30, 1871.
[37] Data on vagrancy arrests derived from Baltimore City Police (Criminal Docket, Eastern District), 1867–1868, C2111–4; Baltimore City Police (Criminal Docket, Southern District) 1867–1868, C2113–1.
[38] "Report of the Grand Jury for May Term, 1868," *Sun*, Sep. 9, 1868.
[39] Stanley, *From Bondage to Contract*, 98–137. Kristin O'Brassill-Kulfan has noted that similar allegations that justices were abusing vagrancy laws to extract fees were common in Baltimore, Philadelphia, and other cities and towns. O'Brassill-Kulfan, "'Visible Means of Support': Conspicuous Poverty and Criminality in the Early American Republic," paper presented at SHEAR, Philadelphia, PA, July 2017.

At the same time that magistrates were increasing their enforcement of vagrancy statutes, Baltimore's changing institutional landscape was making it possible for alleged vagrants to be punished to the fullest extent of the law. Because vagrants were persons whom authorities deemed insufficiently inculcated into the liberal-capitalist ethos of self-regulation and work ethic, their successful reformation demanded a prolonged process that combined moral education, practical trade skills, and compulsive labor. Maryland law consistently prescribed incarceration for the offense; in the years immediately following the war, section 108, article 4 of the local law specified the penalty for vagrancy as thirty days in jail.[40] However, the city had struggled to house vagrants in its already crowded jail on the eve of the Civil War, and, for a time, it also lacked appropriate almshouse facilities. After Baltimore became an independent city in 1851, the original Baltimore City and County Almshouse at Calverton was ceded to Baltimore County, which forced the city to erect a new facility of its own. Enforcement of vagrancy statutes was thus difficult during the Civil War because there was a shortage of institutions capable of housing vagrants.[41]

After the war, however, the proliferation of new public, private, and semi-private institutions removed the institutional barrier to vagrancy prosecutions by expanding the number of sentencing facilities available to the court. In 1866, the city completed construction on its new almshouse complex, Bay View Asylum. Bay View, which was situated just outside the eastern boundary of the city, could house up to 800 impoverished, "insane," or ill men and women.[42] The institution quickly became the primary destination for those sentenced to incarceration for vagrancy. When Maria Bolton, a black woman, was arrested in the summer of 1867 and taken as a vagrant before a magistrate in the Eastern District, she was sentenced to two months in Bay View. Similar sentences became the standard for the offense among Baltimore magistrates.[43]

Cases involving women and girls whom the courts believed were redeemable on account of their youth or life circumstances sometimes resulted in sex workers being sent to private institutions run by moral or social reformers. Newly emerged charitable organizations, such as the

---

[40] Maryland, Public Local Law, Sec. 108, Art. 4.
[41] Weishampel, *The Stranger in Baltimore*, 114–15.
[42] Weishampel, *The Stranger in Baltimore*, 114–15.
[43] Baltimore City Police (Criminal Docket, Eastern District), July 29–30, 1867, Maria Bolton, 425, MSA-C2111-4, MSA.

Rosine Society, took in women at their facilities, as did other institutions, such as the Catholic-run House of the Good Shepherd, the Female House of Refuge, the Home for Fallen and Friendless Women, the Maryland Industrial School for Girls, and the Maryland Industrial Home for Colored Girls, among others. The Home for Fallen and Friendless women, which was founded by Baltimore Christians in 1871 for the purposes of ministering to sex workers and attempting to train "repentant" women in industry, took in more than 1,500 women into its facility in its first twenty-three years of existence. Though most women went to the Home for the Fallen and Friendless and other similar facilities voluntarily, that was not always the case. Local courts wasted little time in forging partnerships with these new religious reformatories and private (but city-supported) houses of industry. With the proliferation of privately run institutions that expanded the powers of the state, it became possible for the local courts in Baltimore to prosecute vagrancy to an extent not witnessed since the 1810s.[44]

While laws pertaining to vagrancy allowed authorities to suppress and punish streetwalkers and other allegedly disorderly persons, they proved unreliable at best when it came to cracking down on brothels and the women who operated within them. An 1875 case involving Baltimore madam Lizzie Johnson illustrated the complications of using vagrancy ordinances to punish indoor sex workers and women in managerial positions within the trade. Johnson, who had gotten her start as a madam during the Civil War, owned two houses of ill fame on Josephine Street and another on South Sharp Street. She first appeared before the Criminal Court on bawdy house charges in May 1865, and she continued to make appearances on and off for a decade. Usually, she pled guilty to the charges against her and paid fines of $20–$50 plus court costs.[45]

[44] Home for Fallen and Friendless Women, *Twenty-Fourth Annual Report of the Home* (Baltimore, 1893), 5; Baltimore City Council First Branch, *Journal of Proceedings of the First Branch City Council of Baltimore at the Sessions of 1879–80* (Baltimore: King Brothers, 1880), 562; Baltimore Yearly Meeting of the Religious Society of Friends, *Extracts from the Minutes of Proceedings of Baltimore Yearly Meeting of Men and Women Friends, Held in Their Meeting House on Lombard Street, in the City of Baltimore* (Baltimore: John W. Wood, Printer, 1883), 30–31; John Lee Chapman, "Mayor's Message," in *Ordinances and Resolutions of the Mayor and City Council of Baltimore Presented at the Session of 1862* (Baltimore: King Bro. & Armiger, City Printers, 1862), 8; George P. Bagby, *The Annotated Code of the Public Civil Laws of Maryland*, vol. 3 (Baltimore: King Bros., Printers and Publishers, 1914), 481–93.

[45] There were two Elizabeth Johnsons operating as madams in Baltimore in the 1860s and 1870s, and although the district codes for the officers testifying against them provide

In 1875, however, Judge Peters of the Baltimore City Criminal Court grew frustrated with seeing Johnson and other madams traverse before his court repeatedly only to be assigned fines insufficient to dissuade them from returning to sex work. When Johnson and her partner, Jesse Evans Porter, appeared before Peters on bawdy-house charges, the judge invoked section 2, article 43 of Baltimore's city code, which specified that "every person who leads a dissolute and disorderly course of life, and cannot give an account of the means by which he procures a livelihood" was legally a vagrant.[46] In light of Johnson's occupation, Justice Peters ordered her and her beau-cum-business partner incarcerated for vagrancy.

Johnson hired an attorney and was in the process of contesting the charges when Baltimore City Criminal Court Clerk William McKewen, who himself had been previously tried for renting a bawdy house, intervened. Writing with the authority of the court, McKewen ruled that Peters had no right to imprison Johnson and Porter. Not only could both parties afford to post securities to keep the peace, but Johnson also had an obvious livelihood. In a move that contradicted the letter of the local ordinance, McKewen asserted that Johnson, who was rumored to have accumulated $10,000 to $12,000 in savings from prostitution, "had visible means of support" and thus could not be considered a vagrant.[47] McKewen's intervention suggested that, while Lizzie Johnson's occupation may have been sufficient to qualify her by the letter of the law as a "dissolute" person, her status as a wealthy, white businesswoman who owned multiple properties exempted her, in practice, from vagrancy. Ultimately, Lizzie Johnson was not worth imprisoning, as the state had little to gain from rendering her a dependent when she was so obviously

some clues as to which court appearance belonged to which, it is impossible to tell definitively. However, both women first appeared in court records in the May Term of 1865. BCCC, May Term, 1865, Case 1319, Elizabeth Johnson; BCCC, May Term, 1865, Case 1748, Elizabeth Johnson.

[46] John Prentiss Poe, *The Maryland Code: Public Local Laws: Adopted by the General Assemble of Maryland, March 14, 1888*, vol. 1 (Baltimore: King Bros., Printers and Publishers, 1888), 565–68; "Commitments and Release from Jail – The Law Relating to Vagrants and Disorderly Persons," *Sun*, Aug. 25, 1875.

[47] "Commitments and Release from Jail," *Sun*, Aug. 25, 1875. McKewen had been tried for renting a bawdy house twelve years before. "Proceedings of the Courts," *Sun*, Dec. 5, 1863.

self-sufficient. Johnson and Porter were both released from jail by order of the Baltimore City Criminal Court within two days of their confinement.[48]

Although increasingly strident vagrancy statues were useless against madams, the precedent set by *Hamilton* v. *Whitridge* was not, and Baltimore authorities faced increased pressure to employ it against the city's sex establishments. The years following the war saw a dramatic increase in protests that were mainly, but not exclusively, staged by members of the middle class, against the presence of brothels in their neighborhoods and communities. These protests drew on moral language similar to that which had been used to condemn commercial sex establishments in the antebellum period: bawdy houses were dens of iniquity that degraded their communities and led to the moral downfall of young women and men. However, protestors combined this moral rhetoric with the kinds of economic and rights-based arguments that had already been so successful in the courts – that is, arguments that brothels were damaging to their property values and to their businesses. Middle-class people argued that having bawdy establishments on their blocks would render their neighborhoods undesirable for families and thus jeopardize their investments in their homes.

Growing demands that authorities act against brothels reflected changing expectations of what the municipal and state governments should seek to provide with regard to property protection and services. In Baltimore, taxes collected on real and personal property had risen noticeably in the 1850s and dramatically during the Civil War period as a result of growing state expenditures. The state and federal governments required revenue to pay for the war effort, and the city required money to pay for internal improvements and the expansion of municipal services that had taken place under the Know Nothing administrations on the eve of the war. In 1850, taxes collected in the city had totaled $380,240; by 1860, tax revenue nearly doubled to $750,206. By the end of the war, it had reached $1,320,326.[49] While some of this increase was rooted in the growth of the tax base, it was also the result of higher personal and real property taxes and the brief institution of income tax during the Civil War. As tax rates rose and the experiences of war crystallized many younger people's faith in the state and its power to improve society,

[48] "Commitments and Release from Jail," *Sun*, Aug. 25, 1875.
[49] Richard T. Ely, *Taxation in American States and Cities* (New York: T. Y. Crowell & Co., 1888), 428.

Baltimore experienced what historian Joseph Arnold described as a "middle-class revolution of rising expectations."[50] In the latter decades of the nineteenth century, well-to-do Baltimoreans came to expect in a way that the previous generation had not that the municipal government and the state's responsibility to protect property would extend beyond providing basic policing and guarantee of redress. They expected the city to guarantee the value of their properties by providing services that had previously been considered amenities: quality water, reliable transportation, good schools, professional fire and police services, and active removal of nuisances – including moral nuisances – from neighborhoods.[51]

Some of the earliest protests against the presence of brothels in middle-class neighborhoods took the form of campaigns to remove brothels from the areas around the city's new public schools. The Maryland Constitution of 1864 was most notable for its abolishment of slavery, but the Constitution also established a property tax to fund public education as part and parcel of the new birth of freedom it was intended to bring about. As revenues came in from the taxes, dozens of new educational institutions opened in Baltimore. A decade prior to the Civil War, the city had only twenty-four public schools, eleven for boys and thirteen for girls. By 1870, the number of public schools had increased more than fourfold to include 101 institutions devoted to educating students at high school level and below.[52] The simultaneous expansions in the public school system and the urban sex trade meant that the sites designed to inculcate children into liberal values overlapped with sexual spaces that represented – in the minds of middle-class city residents, at least – the failure or rejection of those values. The close proximity of brothels to schools bred fears that children would be exposed to sights and ways of life that would tempt them away from virtue. The 1870s and 1880s were, after all, a period in which many Americans were beginning to "discover" childhood as a distinct and especially vulnerable phase of life.[53] The sense

---

[50] Arnold, "The Neighborhood and City Hall," 8.
[51] Arnold, "The Neighborhood and City Hall," 8.
[52] Brugger, *Maryland: A Middle Temperament*, 307.
[53] Historians generally agree that the 1880s were a moment of transition in the history of childhood, as both Britain and many US states moved to pass new child welfare laws and to raise the age of consent. Harry Hendrick, *Children, Childhood and English Society, 1880–1990* (Cambridge: Cambridge University Press, 1997); Judith R. Walkowitz, *City of Dreadful Delight: Narratives of Sexual Danger in Late-Victorian London* (Chicago: University of Chicago Press, 1992), 81–120.

that young people were particularly impressionable and at risk of falling under bad influences prompted parents to worry about their children's exposure to the day-to-day happenings of the sex trade.

The decade following the war witnessed sporadic moral panics about school children's exposure to commercial sex. In one notable instance, the Baltimore *American* generated public controversy when it alleged that brothels on Orleans and Mullikin Streets were the sites of seductions of female students from the Eastern Female High School. The *American*'s allegations were so scandalous that they resulted in an urgent investigation by the city's grand jury. Although the jurors denied that the *American*'s charges of seduction had any validity, they issued statements to the local press that all bawdy houses deemed to be located too close to the high school would be immediately removed. Although they did not say so specifically, the grand jurors were announcing the intention of the police to use the power granted to them by *Hamilton* v. *Whitridge* to force the closure or relocation of sex establishments. The courts issued no injunctions against the houses of Mullikin and Orleans Streets; rather, they sent local police to notify madams that they had to move their houses or face raids, arrest, and injunctions. The threat of harsh action was sufficient to secure madams' compliance.[54] Seven years later, the Maryland House of Delegates reinforced the right of the police to remove houses of ill fame from neighborhoods where they might have a corrupting influence by passing a bill making it illegal for houses of ill fame to be located within four blocks of female academies or asylums.[55]

In the years that followed, Baltimoreans began to demand that sex establishments be removed not just from the areas around schools and asylums but also from entire neighborhoods and communities. In 1888, religious leaders who were inspired by the example of Anthony Comstock and his New York Society for the Suppression of Vice founded a Baltimore chapter of the organization (the BSSV).[56] As one of its first actions, the BSSV helped to organize a meeting of more than 1,500 men, black and white, to stage a public protest against the presence of disreputable establishments in the neighborhood around St. Vincent's Catholic Church on Front Street. Women were notably excluded from the event, both

---

[54] "Purification and Protection," *Sun*, Apr. 17, 1873.
[55] *Journal of the Proceedings of the Senate of the State of Maryland, January Session, 1880* (Annapolis: Wm. T. Iglehart & Co., 1880), 229.
[56] "The Ministerial Union: Upholding Strict Observance of the Sabbath and Other Matters," *Sun*, Mar. 30, 1886, 5; "Indecent Showbills," *Sun*, Feb. 23, 1886.

because its topic was seen as inappropriate for respectable ladies and because women did not enjoy the same standing to claim that brothels jeopardized their property rights or their control over members of their households. Speakers at the protest, mostly members of the clergy, highlighted both the alleged moral dangers of brothels and their threats to property. Rev. Edmund Didier, a Catholic priest who spearheaded the protest, argued that brothels "cause property to decrease in value" and that city officials who tolerated their presence "for the benefit of a few abandoned men" who owned them were acting unfairly.[57] Protestors complained that in St. Vincent's parish alone, there were eighty-three "low" saloons, forty-six gambling and gaming houses, seventy-eight houses of ill repute, and fourteen dance houses and low theaters. Men at the meeting signed a petition requesting that the mayor restore the moral character of the area by revoking the liquor licenses of disreputable establishments and force the closure of all-night music and dance halls in the neighborhood. The petition was among the first of many similar efforts.[58]

Not all complaints and petitions for the closure of sex establishments were successful, but the police and local authorities used the power granted to them by the *Hamilton* decision more frequently by the 1870s. When property owners or religious officials complained about bawdy houses and disreputable taverns, authorities began to take a more active role in suppressing or relocating (alleged) vice. In 1870, for instance, police purged Guilford Alley of many of its black residents after allegations arose that they were keeping bawdy houses. Guilford Alley had been home to groups of black laundresses since the Civil War years, and there had long been rumors – likely brought on by racial stereotypes of black women as licentious – that the area was a vice district. When the street "bec[a]me the residence of a great many respectable people" who pressured authorities to "break up" the houses, the Baltimore police and sheriff acted quickly. Seven black women from the area were hauled into court, convicted of bawdy-house keeping, fined $20 to $25, and committed to jail.[59]

[57] "To Suppress Vice: A Big Meeting to Protest against the Places on East Baltimore Street," *Sun*, May 28, 1888, 4.

[58] "To Suppress Vice," *Sun*, May 28, 1888.

[59] "Proceedings of the Courts," *Sun*, Dec. 6, 1870; BCCC, September Term, 1870, Case 1009, Louisa Schull; Case 1011, Hester Maddox; Case 1012, Emily Jackson; Case 1013, Hester Collins; Case 1026, Sophia Taylor; Case 1027, Mrs. Banks; Case 1031, Elizabeth Curtis.

White proprietors received greater courtesy from police, who refrained from immediate suppressive action in favor of serving them with notices to vacate their properties within a set time frame or face incarceration or injunction. Baltimore madam Laura Hobson, who eventually gained fame in the city as the result of her 1880 marriage to Alexander D. Brown of the Alex. Brown & Sons investment firm, was among the women who was forced to move in this manner. Hobson, who had purchased the use of improved two lots on Aisquith Street for $6,750 in 1871, promised Sheriff George Kane to vacate the property in 1873 in favor of relocating to a less desirable area in Bond Street.[60] Hobson, like many Baltimore madams, moved to avoid being shut down. "It is usually the case," Baltimore Police Commissioner William Fusselbaugh wrote with some satisfaction, "that a simple notice from the authorities to the keeper of the house, that she must find some other spot in which to ply her trade, is complied with quietly and promptly."[61]

The police's new authority to shape the geography of the sex trade by forcing the exile of sex workers from certain neighborhoods represented a significant departure from older traditions concerning the brothel trade. For one thing, it reduced the authority of the local court that had for decades played the primary role in policing and regulating sex establishments. The Baltimore City Criminal Court did not cease to prosecute bawdy-house keepers, nor did it radically change its long-standing practice of using fines as the primary punishment on conviction. However, the day-to-day practices of monitoring and controlling the trade increasingly fell not to the legal system, but rather to Baltimore's professional police force. As the police expanded their roles, opportunities for bribery and graft expanded too. Additionally, and perhaps more significantly, the power granted to the police heralded the end of a period in which Baltimoreans tolerated bawdy houses simply because they kept illicit sex and sexuality contained within the walls of a building. Now, illicit sex had to be contained within particular areas of the city, areas that were far from the residential neighborhoods occupied by the maturing urban middle class.

---

[60] "A Marriage to Make Talk," *Sun* (New York), Aug. 15, 1880; "Sales of Real Estate," *Sun*, June 6, 1871; "Exit Hobson," *Sun*, Oct. 30, 1873.

[61] William H. B. Fusselbaugh to Eugene Higgins, Secretary of the Senate of Maryland, Feb. 25, 1880, in *Journal of the Proceedings of the Senate of the State of Maryland, January Session, 1880* (Annapolis: Wm. T. Iglehart & Co., 1880), 318–20.

Part of the reason that brothels ceased to enjoy the comparative toleration that they once did was the fact that that postbellum brothel districts were no longer the revenue generators that they had been for real estate investors and landlords in the antebellum period. During the early decades of Baltimore's urban development, brothels had represented an economic boon for men and women who owned land or properties on the outskirts of the city or in less improved areas like the Meadow. Parlor houses could be constructed fairly cheaply, and they generated high rents as landlords waited for urban expansion and development to encompass their landholdings. However, as Baltimore's boundaries expanded in the decades following the Civil War and the city grew increasingly industrialized, many of the old red-light districts lost their economic luster for investors. Areas like the Meadow, which sat directly outside the Calvert Street Rail Depot, were desirable land for merchants and industrialists who depended on the railroads to move their products. Because their land could be put to more profitable industrial uses, some investors lost interest in renting their property to madams.[62] As a result, authorities' crackdowns on brothels did not distress landlords as much as they once might have; instead, they paved the way for landholders or householders to sell or rent their spaces as warehouses, factories, or shops. When the Sanborn Fire Insurance Company created its 1890s map of Baltimore, the blocks that had formerly composed the Meadow vice district were populated by oyster packing plants; carpentry and machine shops; warehouses for tools, dressed meat, and vinegar and cider; and a few hotels to cater to visitors who came into the city via the railroad. There were still several places of "female boarding" – the Sanborn euphemism for brothels – in the neighborhood, as well as a number of dives and liquor stores, but the area was clearly in transition. By 1902, the "female boarding" places had been replaced entirely by industrial buildings and warehouses.[63]

Some commercial property owners with an interest in development began to lobby city officials to close down older red-light districts in order to pave the way for new industrial development and transportation infrastructures. As Baltimore became home to a thriving garment and canning trade as well as a diverse array of other manufacturing and

---

[62] Keire, *For Business and Pleasure*, 9–10.

[63] Baltimore, Maryland [map], 1890, Sanborn Fire Insurance Maps, 1890 – Maryland, vol. 2, Image 53, ProQuest Sanborn Collection; Baltimore, Maryland [map], 1901–2, "Sanborn Fire Insurance Maps, 1901–1902 – Maryland, vol. 3, Image 262," ProQuest Sanborn Collection.

processing facilities, small-scale manufactories gave way to more centralized forms of production. Among the central concerns of capitalists,
merchants, and warehouse owners was the ease with which they could
transport their products and goods. In the 1870s, groups of merchants
and city residents began to express frustration with the persistence of
short, narrow, and enclosed alleys downtown. Small streets with names
like names such as "Dark Lane," "Jew Alley," "Broomstick Row," and
"Painters' Court" were remnants of early modern forms of city development that interrupted Baltimore's more rationalized, grid-based layout.
While these alleys were popular with the owners of sex establishments,
who were attracted to the inexpensive housing stock and relative privacy
that they provided, merchants and warehouse owners disliked that their
existence precluded the cutting through of major roads. In 1873, a group
of property owners and citizens petitioned the City Council to open a
section of Hanover running between Baltimore and Liberty Streets, a
move that would eliminate a square on North Sharp Street where several
brothel keepers resided. The developers' main motives were economic: the
triangle of land between Hanover to the east and Sharp Street to the west
was located at virtually the dead center of the city, and it had the potential
to be exceedingly valuable property if it was cut through with a road.
Opening the area to traffic would also relieve congestion on Light,
Charles, and Lombard Streets and make travel between the commercial
thoroughfares of Baltimore and Pratt Streets easier.[64]

Economic and moral arguments coalesced in the petition that the
proponents of the plan submitted to the City Council. Advocates of
condemning and opening the square argued that the city had a duty to
cut through Hanover Street as a means of "supplying the necessary
thoroughfares for the transaction of our increasing business."[65] Petition-
ers also claimed that the move was a necessary purification measure for
the area. Citing the proliferation of brothels around the proposed development and in nearby New Church Street, advocates of clearance characterized the square as "an eyesore as well as a dangerous nuisance" that
had to be eliminated. In a statement that evinced a liberal faith in the
power of infrastructure to shape the behavior of urban subjects, they
claimed that cutting through Hanover Street would create an

---

[64] "Hanover Street," *Sun*, Apr. 28, 1873.
[65] "Hanover Street," *Sun*, Apr. 28, 1873; City of Baltimore, *Ordinances and Resolutions of
the Mayor and City Council of Baltimore, Passed at the Annual Session of 1874*
(Baltimore: John Cox, 1874), 90–91.

environment of openness and light that would inevitably cleanse the city of a center of "pestilence, conflagration, and filth."[66] Notably, Francis T. King, who advocated condemning the square and who also provided some of the more spirited opposition to medical men's calls to license and medically regulate brothels in the 1870s, had a clear financial motive for lobbying for the vice district's demolition: if the resolution to extend Hanover passed, the extension would go directly to the corner of King's warehouse on the north side of Baltimore Street.

Ultimately, opponents of the resolution succeeding in preventing the expansion of Hanover Street by claiming that it was irresponsible to spend "five hundred thousand to one million of dollars merely to suppress a few houses of ill fame, for the closing of which the law already provides without any great expense."[67] Nevertheless, development in the area gradually eliminated older alleys like Watch Alley and Painters' Court, and sustained commercial pressures, protests from neighbors, and police actions continued to force many of the city's brothel keepers out of their old neighborhoods. As Police Commissioner Fusselbaugh explained to the state Senate in 1880:

If a house of assignation, or a bawdy house, should become notorious, and disturb the peace or the decency of the neighborhood where it is situated; if the mistress or keeper of any such house should break bounds and invade a quiet and respectable neighborhood; if, in fact, the evil appears upon the surface anywhere, or any-way, to the detriment or discomfort of society, repressive measures are at once resorted to.[68]

Even as Commissioner Fusselbaugh and his supporters asserted that the police strategy of maintaining order in "respectable neighborhood[s]" through selective repression of sex establishments was successful, they readily admitted that they did not expect that it was possible for the state to eliminate sex establishments entirely. After all, there was no law explicitly prohibiting the exchange of sex for money. Even if there were, most Americans in the late nineteenth century believed that enforcing it would be impractical given the nature of human sexuality. The best that authorities or city residents could hope for was to maintain order through regulation. As Commissioner Fusselbaugh put it, "The police exercise a careful and thorough surveillance over all houses of ill fame, of whatever

---

[66] "Hanover Street," *Sun*, Apr. 28, 1873.
[67] "Proceedings of the City Council-First Branch," *Sun*, June 3, 1874.
[68] Fusselbaugh to Higgins, 320.

description, for the purposes of order and decency and control ... rather than suppression."[69]

Because the goal of the new policing strategies was less to eliminate sex work so much as to render it more palatable for the city's residents, the result of police intervention was more often than not the creation of new red-light districts that sat outside respectable neighborhoods. Baltimoreans understood this as early as the 1870s. In the aftermath of the Eastern Female High School controversy, grand jurors noted with some regret that while they and the police had done what they could to purify the area around the school, they felt confident that they had only shifted the problem to another area of the city. "While a neighborhood may succeed in purifying itself," the jurors wrote, "the pollution will only have moved its abiding place."[70] As the jurors were well aware, that new abiding place was likely to be an area in which the residents lacked the political or social capital to protest the encroachment of commercial sex into their streets. "The dreadful stain of impurity," they wrote, "will, from the inadequacy of the laws, be only changed to another locality, probably nearer where poorer people live."[71]

As Chapter 7 will detail, the grand jury was right. In the 1860s and 1870s, economic opportunities for women remained barely more expansive than they had been prior to the Civil War. There was still a steady stream of women whose limited prospects for waged labor and need to make a living for themselves pushed them into sex work. There was also still a marked demand for sexual services among local men and visitors to the city alike. As middle-class, white Baltimoreans exerted pressure on city officials, police, and the courts to protect their property values by evicting madams and their tenants, they did not so much reduce the size of the sex trade as they did change its geography. With vagrancy laws posing a constant threat to sex workers who labored in public spaces, many women who sold sex relocated to indoor venues in neighborhoods where the local residents were less empowered to complain about their presence. As the grand jury noted, these neighborhoods were apt to be poor neighborhoods where residents would be hard-pressed to support claims that their respectability or property rights were being infringed on.

What the grand jury did not state outright was that not all poor neighborhoods were created equal. Some poor neighborhoods were far more likely to receive the groups of dispossessed brothel keepers and sex

[69] Fusselbaugh to Higgins, 319.   [70] Fusselbaugh to Higgins, 319.
[71] "The Grand Jury Reports," *Sun*, Sep. 8, 1873.

workers in search of refuge than others. Baltimore in the latter decades of the nineteenth century was home to an increasingly large black population that was limited in its political power and economic resources. As middle-class, white, city residents insisted that authorities remove brothels from their neighborhoods, madams and sex workers were pushed into more isolated and marginalized communities. As Chapter 7 will argue, many of these communities were the same ones that black Baltimoreans found themselves occupying, often as a result of a similar logic of defending white property values from forms of disorder that might threaten them. The process of segregating deviant sexuality and the process of segregating black Baltimoreans became intertwined, with dramatic results for the demographics of the sex trade and the fate of Baltimore's black community.

PART III

CHANGE AND DECLINE IN THE BROTHEL TRADE

7

Black Baltimoreans and the Bawdy Trade

Henrietta Brashears was forty years old the first time she appeared before the Baltimore City Criminal Court to face a charge of keeping a bawdy house. Brashears, a black woman and lifelong Maryland resident, had been free even before the Civil War brought emancipation to the slave states. So had her husband, William, although the couple's surname suggested that William's progenitors had been slaves to the French Huguenot "Brasseur" family at some point. William worked as a barber, an occupation that bestowed him with a special status and a unique degree of independence in Baltimore's black community. In the 1860s, he was able to support Henrietta on his salary while renting a house at 35 Clay Street, near the center of the city. Around 1870, the Brashearses relocated their residence further west to Josephine Street, perhaps as a result of a gradual pushing-out of black families from central Baltimore that had begun in the antebellum period and intensified after emancipation.[1] William moved his business to the newly expanding black neighborhood around Druid Hill Avenue, where he did well for himself. Henrietta supplemented William's income by doing occasional work as a seller at nearby Lexington Market.[2]

---

[1] In his history of Baltimore's free black community, Christopher Phillips found that black households were being pushed out of central Baltimore as early as 1810. Historians of other slave cities, including Atlanta, have found that 1870 marked the beginning of a period in which de facto residential segregation began to take hold. Phillips, *Freedom's Port*, 104; Tera Hunter, *To 'Joy My Freedom: Southern Black Women's Lives and Labors after the Civil War* (Cambridge, MA: Harvard University Press, 1997), 45–46.

[2] BCCC, September Term, 1873, Case 1056, Henrietta Brashears; 1860 US Census, Baltimore, Maryland, Ward 13, p. 458, dwelling 2768, family 3551, Henrietta Brashears and

The court, however, was interested only in what it alleged was Henrietta's participation in a less licit form of commerce: keeping a house of prostitution. By the time the Brashearses relocated to Josephine Street, their block was already becoming a haven for sex establishments. William and Henrietta, who had limited options for social and economic mobility because of the racial discrimination they faced, took up residence there anyway. Eventually, they sought to profit from the area's burgeoning sex trade by leasing parts of their multiroom dwelling to boarders. They rented rooms to three or four black laborers, waiters, and musicians – the latter of whom may have worked as entertainers in the house – and they appeared to let the other rooms on a more occasional basis for assignations.[3] Like so many white brothel keepers before them, they did not attempt to hide what they did. When Henrietta appeared in court in 1873, she pleaded guilty to keeping a bawdy house, paid her $20 fine and court costs, and returned home. She and William continued to reside in Josephine Street and keep their house as a bawdy establishment into the 1880s.[4]

Henrietta Brashears's entrance into the sex trade marked a new era of sexual commerce in Baltimore, one that emerged out of the tumult, rapid state expansion, and alterations to the social and racial order of the post–Civil War period. During the antebellum period, black women like Henrietta Brashears had been underrepresented among those arrested for the offense of keeping a bawdy house and among the ranks of indoor sex workers more generally. Low rates of black property ownership meant that few black women had the opportunity to become madams in the decades before the war.[5] Meanwhile, brothel keepers who catered to the new class of urban professionals excluded black women from working as sex workers in their establishments and relegated them instead to the roles of servants, washers, and dressers whose willingness to perform the "dirty work" propped up the gentility of white sex workers.

William Brashears; 1870 US Census, Baltimore, Maryland, Ward 13, p. 69, dwelling 395, family 444, Henrietta Brashears and William Brashears; 1880 US Census, Baltimore, Maryland, Enumeration District 113, p. 26, dwelling 184, family 281, Henretta Brashears; *Woods' Baltimore City Directory* (1860) (Baltimore: John W. Woods, 1860), 430; *Woods' Baltimore City Directory* (1870), 681; *Woods' Baltimore City Directory* (1871), 676.

[3] 1880 US Census, Baltimore, Maryland, Enumeration District 113, p. 26, dwelling 184, family 281, Henrietta Brashears.

[4] BCCC, September Term, 1873, Case 1056, Henrietta Brashears. Brashears was charged with keeping a bawdy house again in 1875, 1876, and 1880.

[5] On rates of black property ownership in the antebellum years, see Phillips, *Freedom's Port,* 98, 153–55.

Following the war and emancipation, however, black women (and some men) made inroads into the bawdy house business and became proprietors of sex establishments in much larger numbers. Although they were never more than a minority of Baltimore's madams, black women's entrance into the brothel sex business provides an important lens through which to examine how interrelated changes in the economy and in the nature of the state following the war created a new urban order via the regulation of sex work.

Freedwomen and others who entered the prostitution following emancipation did so for personal reasons not entirely dissimilar to those of previous generations of lower-tier sex workers, although racial discrimination ensured that their situations were often more precarious and desperate than those of white women. For them, selling sex was part of an economy of makeshifts, a reflection of their entrepreneurship, and an opportunity for stability and perhaps even advancement that was difficult for black women and families to achieve otherwise. Black sex workers survived and profited by fulfilling new demands for intimate labor that evolved out of emancipation and a postwar culture of nostalgia for the antebellum racial system.[6]

And yet, as this chapter argues, black women's ability to enter brothel prostitution was intimately tied to new and often distressing interventions by the state into the geography and workings of the sex trade. Black women's exclusion from brothels prior to the Civil War had been (at least in part) a result of racial ideologies and discriminatory practices that prevented black women from claiming the mantle of gentility or accessing property. In the aftermath of emancipation, these same ideologies would pave the way for black women's entrance into indoor prostitution. As Baltimore authorities set about creating – albeit in a piecemeal fashion – an urban order that secured the privileges of the white bourgeois in the 1870s and 1880s, they pushed sex workers and black residents of the city into the same marginal spaces, creating pockets of perceived racial and sexual disorder. A combination of proximity to brothels and narrowing economic opportunities prompted black women to enter the sex trade in larger numbers than before. While this arrangement undoubtedly created opportunities for black entrepreneurs where none had existed previously,

---

[6] Landau, *Spectacular Wickedness*. On Storyville, see also Long, *The Great Southern Babylon*, 148–224.

it ultimately reinforced white Baltimorean's conceptions that black city residents were licentious and inherently disorderly. By the 1910s, the logic of segregation that undergirded the city's sexual politics ultimately had devastating consequences for black communities as city officials and local white interest groups extended the logic to the segregation of race.

Understanding the processes by which black women like Henrietta Brashears came to enter the sex trade in larger numbers in the 1870s and 1880s requires understanding the effects of authorities' increased use of injunction following the war. As Baltimore's police and courts forced the removal of brothels from "respectable" white neighborhoods, the grand jury's assertion that sex establishments would simply relocate to poorer areas was quickly borne out. Two streets in particular became destinations for newly homeless sex workers. One of these was Raborg, a small West Baltimore street that consisted of several blocks bounded on the western side by North Carrollton Avenue and on the eastern side by Greene Street (see Figure 7.1). The other was Henrietta Brashears's future home, Josephine Street. Josephine was a short street bounded by Myrtle Avenue to the west and Arch Street to the east, not far from Lexington Market. Both Raborg and Josephine Streets had been developed in the 1850s, after land at the outskirts of the city's built environments was marketed to "speculators" who quickly improved it by constructing inexpensive two- and three-story brick row houses that would earn them ground rents.[7] By the eve of the Civil War, both streets housed large populations of skilled and unskilled laborers and their families.[8] Initially, at least, they were modest but largely respectable neighborhoods.

However, as authorities and commercial pressures began to force brothels out of their old neighborhoods in the late 1860s, Josephine and Raborg Streets became attractive destinations for madams and sex workers. The affordable nature of properties in the area made them accessible to women in the sex trade, and the neighborhoods themselves had few schools and churches whose proximity to sex establishments might bring negative attention from authorities – or, at least, they had few schools and churches that authorities cared to protect. Josephine Street was home to the Institute for the Colored Deaf and Blind, but disabled black Baltimoreans apparently did not register as important

---

[7] See, for example, "Executor's Sale," *Sun*, May 11, 1854; "Property on Raborg Street," *Sun*, June 23, 1853.

[8] Information about the residential makeup of Josephine and Raborg Streets was derived from an examination of city directories from the 1850s and 1860s.

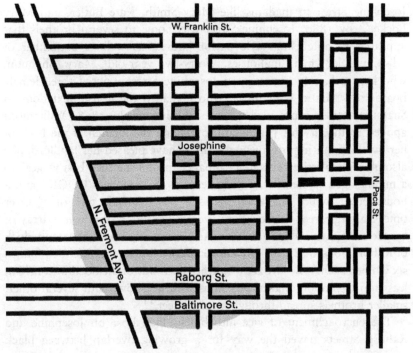

FIGURE 7.1 The western red-light district, encompassing Josephine and Raborg Streets.
Map by Kari Cadenhead, based on Charles Bruegel, *Rippey's Index Map of* Baltimore (1888)

enough to merit defending in the way that white children and asylum dwellers did. Local police tacitly approved of the clustering of bawdy houses in the neighborhood. The houses' proximity to the recently constructed Western District Police Station, which sat at the corner of Josephine and Pine Streets, made it easy for officers to monitor the goings-on in the vice district.[9] Sex workers in the area even came to enjoy close working relationships with some of the neighborhood's patrol officers.

The initial influx of brothels into Raborg and Josephine Streets was abetted by property holders, who attempted to reap the profits that came from renting their dwellings as sex establishments. Within a single year in the late 1860s, unknown property owners leased blocks of houses on

[9] The Western District Police station was constructed in 1871. The Baltimore *American* described it as a "stone's throw" from the row of brothels on Josephine. Baltimore *American*, Nov. 30, 1871.

Josephine Street to madams like Mary Smith, Kate Butler, and Mary Locke.[10] By 1880, Josephine Street was home to several brothels that appeared to antebellum-style parlor houses, as well as a number of "disreputable" boardinghouses. Forty-two-year-old Mary Shannon, who kept a bawdy house at 15 Josephine Street, housed three female boarders.[11] Mattie Williamson, who managed the house next door to Shannon, ran a more well-to-do establishment. In 1868, Williamson applied to the city for permission to expand the kitchen at the back of her dwelling, an improvement that must have pleased her landlord. She also placed advertisements in local papers promising the "best wages" to a middle-aged woman who could serve as "a first-class COOK" and a housekeeper, which suggested that she was relatively well off.[12] Over time, Raborg Street developed an even larger and more diverse array of brothels. As early as 1880, what would eventually become the 700 block of Raborg housed at least half a dozen parlor houses that boarded four to six women each.[13] By 1902, the northeastern side of the 600 block held at least fourteen additional bawdy houses all in a row, with several other, smaller brothels spread throughout the street.[14]

The encroachment of vice into blocks like those on Josephine and Raborg Streets paved the way for a growing overlap between black communities and sexual commerce and, in turn, for black women like Henrietta Brashears to enter the world of indoor sex work. As brothel keepers moved into the neighborhood to avoid police harassment, "respectable" white renters and property owners fled the area. Black Baltimoreans, who faced housing shortages in the decades after the war, quickly moved in to fill the void. The northeastern portion of Josephine Street – that is, odd-numbered houses 1–27 before the 1886 renumbering and even-numbered houses 630–656 after the renumbering – provides an example of this phenomenon. Immediately following the Civil War, all of

[10] BCCC, May Term, 1867, Case 646, Mary Smith; BCCC, September Term, 1880, Case 1742, Kate Butler; BCCC, January Term, 1864, Case 34, Mary Locke.

[11] 1880 US Census, Baltimore, Maryland, Enumeration District 113, p. 26, dwelling 190, family 288, Mary Shannon; digital image, Ancestry.com, accessed Sep. 20, 2017. Brashears pled guilty to keeping a bawdy house multiple times throughout the 1870s and 1880s.

[12] *Sun*, Apr. 13, 1868; "Wanted," *Sun*, June 25, 1868. See also "Wanted," *Sun*, June 24, 1870.

[13] Baltimore City renumbered all of its houses in 1886.

[14] 1880 US Census, Baltimore, Maryland, Enumeration District 125, 4–10, South Side of Raborg Street, digital images; "Sanborn Fire Insurance Maps, 1901–1902 – Maryland, Vol. 3," images 19–21, Proquest Sanborn Maps Collection.

the block's residents were listed in city directories as white laborers, artisans, or low-level professionals. In 1870, four women – Mary Shannon, Hester Wehn, Isabella Williamson, and Mary Kiningham — moved into houses 7, 9, 11, and 13, respectively. Mattie Williamson already occupied house 17. All of the newcomers except Kiningham kept a "boardinghouse" known to double as a bawdy house. The same year that the women moved in, two groups of black laboring men moved into houses 21 and 23. In short order, many of the block's white residents began to leave, likely out of fear of the effects that sexual commerce in their neighborhood would have on their property values. Black laborers began to replace them. By 1871, black laborers had moved into houses 5 and 15. Soon most of the street consisted of black households, usually with multiple families or large extended families occupying a single property, and brothels. The same process played out on the south side of Raborg Street. By 1880, madams and prostitutes were virtually the only white householders left in what had once been a biracial residential street, and black residents, like the Brashears family, had begun to dabble in the area's sexual economy.[15]

The influxes of black Baltimoreans into emerging red-light districts had much to do with the conditions of life in the city following emancipation. Shortly after Maryland abolished slavery in 1864, a local freedmen's relief organization wrote, "The faces of the newly freed population are naturally turned toward the City of Baltimore."[16] In the months and years that followed, emancipated people from the state's tobacco regions flocked to the city in search of work, opportunity, and freedom from the oppression that had characterized their lives in the countryside. Many arrived with little besides the clothes on their backs, which prompted associations like the Friends' Association in Aid of Freedmen to report of the influxes of freedpeople into Baltimore, "Thousands of women and children (many of the women who are soldiers wives) have been thrown out of homes and are now very destitute."[17] Black men and women flocked to the city in

---

[15] All data are based on an examination of City Directory records from houses numbered 1–27 on Josephine Street between 1867 and 1874 and additional research into Census enumerations for the area. *Woods' Baltimore City Directory* (Baltimore: John Wood).

[16] "The Freedmen of Maryland," *Sacramento Daily Union*, Dec. 12, 1864. Richard Paul Fuke's book on post-emancipation Maryland alerted me to the existence of this quote. Richard Paul Fuke, *Imperfect Equality: African Americans and the Confines of White Racial Attitudes in Post-Emancipation Maryland* (New York: Fordham University Press, 1999), 112.

[17] Fuke, *Imperfect Equality*, 115.

such large numbers that local authorities lamented the migration as a "nuisance" that Baltimore's public facilities and employment market was ill-equipped to accommodate.[18] Between 1880 and 1900, Baltimore's already sizable black population grew by almost 47 percent, and black Baltimoreans from rural Maryland made up a third of all migrants to the city.[19]

Unfortunately, neither the employment market nor the housing stock kept pace with the city's demographic growth. Natural increase and immigration from Europe swelled Baltimore's population, causing it to more than double between 1860 and 1890. Immigrants, poor native-born laborers, and largely unskilled black city residents competed for work and housing amid shortages and overcrowding. Many landlords and real estate investors did not wish to rent or sell to black tenants, as they assumed that the presence of black families – like the presence of sex workers – would naturally lower property values. As time wore on, white city residents began to employ restrictive covenants, street violence, and cooperative resistance to prevent black incursion into predominantly white residential areas.[20] By the latter decades of the nineteenth century, these street-level practices would succeed in segregating much of the city. Even before their effects took hold fully, black Baltimoreans could not afford to be as selective in their housing choices as whites could be. The presence of a brothel (or several) in the neighborhood was not sufficient to justify avoiding a particular property.

The overlap between red-light districts and black neighborhoods was reinforced by profit-seeking landlords who recognized opportunities for blockbusting. In some cases, especially in West Baltimore, real estate investors appear to have introduced commercial sex establishments into particular neighborhoods as a tool for clearing the area of its existing residents. By purchasing houses in middling neighborhoods composed of laboring families and renting them to madams who were eager to avoid

---

[18] Bayes et al. to Ross, in Major General Lew Wallace, "Communication on Freedmen's Bureau," House Journal and Documents 1865, J Government Publications and Reports, MSA, quoted in Malka, *The Men of Mobtown*, 226.

[19] Stephen Grant Meyer, *As Long as They Don't Move Next Door: Segregation and Racial Conflict in American Neighborhoods* (Lanham, MD: Rowman & Littlefield, 2000), 16–17; Fuke, *Imperfect Equality*, 113–17.

[20] Fuke, *Imperfect Equality*, 121–26; Halpin, "'The Struggle for Land and Liberty'," 691–712.

   Garrett Power, "Apartheid Baltimore Style: The Residential Segregation Ordinances of 1910–1913," *Maryland Law Review* 42 (1983): 289–98.

police interference, investors could make particular blocks undesirable for their inhabitants and prompt them to sell their properties at lower than market rates.[21] Then, they could either kick out the madams and transfer the properties back to residential use or continue to lease the properties while seeking new tenants or buyers for neighboring houses. While many property owners wished to avoid renting or selling to black families, brothel landlords realized that accepting black tenants would secure brothel holdings from excessive interventions by the police, who demonstrated little interest in protecting black property or defending the morality of black neighborhoods. Moreover, it allowed them to profit from black desperation, as landlords could maximize their profits by dividing single-family homes into multiple tenements and charging above-market rates for rent. The confluence of black enclaves and sex districts was thus a joint product of police interventions and economic scheming by landholders.[22]

As the overlap between areas of sexual commerce and black neighborhoods became a more established pattern, white keepers of sex establishments and disreputable saloons began to relocate in larger numbers to established black communities in the late nineteenth and early twentieth centuries. Such was the case in Northwest Baltimore. In 1901, Johns Hopkins University announced plans to relocate its campus from its original location at Howard and Center Street to Homewood.[23] The move created a housing surplus in Druid Hill as students, faculty, and staff moved out of the neighborhood. White property holders, desperate to recoup some of their investment in housing stock that was rapidly depreciating in value, began to sell to their properties to black Baltimoreans. Black city residents moved to the area in droves, fleeing the poor housing to which they had been relegated in other parts of the city. Druid Hill neighborhood quickly developed a reputation as one of the nation's leading black middle-class enclaves. However, it was not long before white madams and saloonkeepers also began moving to the area to take advantage of the open property and comparative protection from

[21] Smoking gun evidence of blockbusting practices by Baltimore brothel landlords is rare. However, the practice was common in many cities. Richard Tansey, "Prostitution and Politics in Antebellum New Orleans," in *History of Women in the United States*, vol. 9, ed. Nancy Cott (Munich: K. G. Saur, 1993), 48.

[22] Rhonda Y. Williams, *The Politics of Public Housing: Black Women's Struggles against Urban Inequality* (Oxford: Oxford University Press, 2004), 23.

[23] Antero Pietila, *Not in My Neighborhood: How Bigotry Shaped a Great American City* (Chicago: Ivan R. Dee, 2010), 12–13.

interference that black neighborhoods offered. In lower Druid Hill, the migration of sex workers and liquor dealers followed on the heels of black migration. By the early twentieth century, an area of lower Druid Hill seven blocks long and two blocks wide was home to forty-two saloons and numerous gambling dens that served as places of assignation.[24] Several smaller streets were lined with brothels and "side door saloons" that allowed customers to rent rooms for sexual transactions. Unlike their counterparts in the lower part of the city, many of these brothels and assignation houses were racially integrated and served both black and white clientele.[25]

The relocation of vice enclaves to black residential streets and neighborhoods intensified a trend that, by all appearances, was already underway during the Civil War period: the entrance of black women into the indoor sex trade. As soon as the Union confiscation policies began to grant legal freedom to enslaved people located near the Union lines, black women began to appear in the dockets of the Baltimore City Criminal Court on charges that they kept bawdy houses in much larger numbers than they had during the antebellum period. Between 1861 and 1865, fifty-two black Baltimoreans – forty-two women and ten men – faced charges of keeping or renting bawdy houses, a number that represented a significant increase from anything seen prior to the war. Of sixty-one total cases for keeping or renting bawdy houses, forty-six were prosecuted during the fall term of 1864 or in 1865, a period that coincided with the start of legal emancipation in Maryland. The increase in prosecutions continued through Reconstruction. In seven sample years of court dockets from between 1866 and 1879, the City Criminal Court heard seventy-four cases involving women (and a few men) of color facing bawdy-house charges.[26]

---

[24] Booker T. Washington, *The Story of the Negro: The Rise of the Race from Slavery*, vol. 2 (New York City: Association Press, 1909), 358; Power, "Apartheid Baltimore Style," 289–328; Karen Olson, "Old West Baltimore: Segregation, African-American Culture, and the Struggle for Equality," in *Baltimore Book: New Views of Local History*, ed. Elizabeth Fee, Linda Shopes, and Linda Zeidman (Philadelphia: Temple University Press, 1991), 57–80.

[25] Power, "Apartheid Baltimore Style," 289–98; James H. N. Waring, *Work of the Colored Law and Order League: Baltimore, MD* (Philadelphia: Press of the E. A. Wright Bank Note Company for the Committee of Twelve for the Advancement of the Interests of the Negro Race, 1908), 9–12.

[26] One case involved renting a bawdy house. BCCC 1864, 1865, 1866, 1867, 1870, 1872, 1873, 1875, 1876, 1879. The docket for the May Term of 1879 is missing from the archive, so the statistics reflect only the winter and fall terms.

Historians must be cautious in assuming that the growing number of bawdy-house charges levied against black women corresponded with an actual increase in black women's participation in the sex trade. Bawdy-house charges, like all criminal charges, were political, and they could be used to police women's sexuality and presence in public space even when the women in question were not actually sex workers. Black women were especially vulnerable to this type of policing. In the wake of slavery's demise, white authorities attempted to use the criminal justice system as a means of reasserting control over black bodies, and police in Baltimore disproportionately arrested and jailed black citizens for property crimes as well as nebulous offenses related to disruptions of public order.[27] Black women were likely targets of criminal charges related to sexual misconduct, as long-standing stereotypes that they were sexually unrestrained jezebels who were incapable of sexual restraint and virtue circulated widely among white city residents. Even as the years following emancipation saw both black and white reformers contesting the notion of black licentiousness and asserting black men and women's worthiness of liberal citizenship through their embrace of marriage and the nuclear family, the situation improved only slightly.[28] Discourses of rights rooted in heterosexual household relationships did little to remove suspicion from women who headed their own households or embraced living arrangements outside the nuclear family paradigm. Similarly, the sexual violations that black women as a group had suffered under slavery continued to mark them as sexually compromised and deviant in the eyes of white city residents.[29]

Out of a combination of economic necessity and the long tradition of non-blood-based kinship networks in black communities, many black women in Baltimore lived in dwellings with multiple families or unrelated

---

[27] Numerous historians have argued that the criminal justice system was used to reinstitute slavery by another name or to reassert control over black labor – including women's labor – in the aftermath of the Civil War and emancipation. See, among others, Malka, *The Men of Mobtown*, especially 217–46; Talitha L. LeFlouria, *Chained in Silence: Black Women and Convict Labor in the New South* (Chapel Hill: University of North Carolina Press, 2016); Douglas A. Blackmon, *Slavery by Another Name: The Re-enslavement of Black Americans from the Civil War to World War II* (New York: Doubleday, 2012).

[28] Laura F. Edwards, *Gendered Strife and Confusion: The Political Culture of Reconstruction* (Urbana: University of Illinois Press, 1997), 24–65, especially 37.

[29] On the Jezebel stereotype of black women, see White, *Ar'n't I a Woman?*. See also Cheryl D. Hicks, *Talk with You Like a Woman: African American Women, Justice, and Reform in New York, 1890–1935* (Chapel Hill: University of North Carolina Press, 2010), 8.

individuals of both sexes under the same roof, living arrangements that could easily cause them to fall under the suspicion of white authorities. Matilda Snell, for instance, lived in a house in the Southern District with her sister, Lizzie, as well as two (apparently unrelated) laborers, Nathan Johnson and James Spriddle. Also living in Snell's dwelling, though perhaps not in the same apartment, were a married couple named John and Louisa Ensor and two women in their thirties named Harriet Hudson and Mary Smith. The latter gave their occupations only as "keeping house."[30] Arrangements like Snell's that involved women cohabitating with men and that housed unemployed young women often drew negative attention from neighbors or police. Snell was brought before the court for keeping a bawdy house in 1870.[31]

Was Snell actually keeping a brothel or assignation house? Did the grand jury have solid evidence to that effect, or were they convinced that the Snell house was disorderly because Matilda and her sister lived with men to whom they were not married and boarded with women with no obvious source of income? Snell herself pled not guilty to the offense, as did almost all black women who were charged with keeping a bawdy or disorderly house during that same term of court. Was this plea a product of innocence or merely of her knowledge that the justice system was unlikely to grant her leniency if she admitted her guilt? The judge in Snell's case found that there was sufficient evidence to convict her, but it is impossible to know whether his verdict had any basis in Snell's actions or whether it was simply another case of the justice system using capacious public order charges to ensnare black women in the city's carceral complexes. Snell was sentenced to $20 and costs and committed to jail as a result of her inability to pay.[32]

Although court records need to be read with a cautious and critical eye, there are nevertheless strong indications that the growing number of bawdy-house charges brought against black women *did* reflect actual growth in the number of black brothel and assignation-house keepers following the war. By the mid-1870s, the number of black women pleading guilty to bawdy-house charges had already begun to rise, and several women who appeared in the dockets were more easily established as

---

[30] 1870 US Census, Baltimore, Maryland, Ward 15, p. 69, dwelling 1187, family 1516, Matilda Snell; digital image, Ancestry.com, accessed Sep. 20, 2017.

[31] BCCC, September Term, 1870, Case 499, Matilda Snell.

[32] BCCC, September Term, 1870, Case 499, Matilda Snell. On black kinship in the postwar South, see, for instance, Hunter, *To 'Joy My Freedom*, especially 36–38, 62.

brothel or assignation-house keepers by subsequent censuses or alternative sources. Henrietta Brashears was among these. So was Sidonia Young, who first appeared before the court on bawdy-house charges in 1880. Young, who ran a bawdy house for nearly three decades, would gain some minor notoriety in the summer of 1908 after respected Johns Hopkins University psychologist James Mark Baldwin was arrested in a raid at her Tyson Alley brothel (Baldwin, who claimed that he had only visited Young's bawdy house out of curiosity, was subsequently fired from his faculty post).[33] By the turn of the twentieth century, black anti-vice reformers readily acknowledged that the state's toleration of vice in black neighborhoods had drawn many young, black women into houses of prostitution.[34]

Black women who found their neighborhoods overrun with white-owned sex establishments were drawn into sex work by economic necessity and limited opportunities presented to them by "legitimate" employments. As numerous historians have acknowledged, most women in the nineteenth century struggled to support themselves and their families on the low wages paid to them for their work. However, black women's race and history of enslavement disadvantaged them further in the labor market. Many black migrants to Baltimore came with limited education and few skills that would serve them well as waged workers in an urban environment. As a result, their employment options were limited. The most privileged women, particularly those who had been free before the war, took up jobs teaching in Baltimore's segregated public schools. The more fortunate among the classes of unskilled laborers found work in industry, including tobacco and dressmaking manufactories. Too often, however, black women were shut out of many of the new types of professional employment that emerged for women in the city's industrializing economy. Most were relegated to domestic labor. As late as 1910, 84 percent of black women were still employed in washing or domestic service work.[35]

Domestic work and washing were as poorly compensated for black women as they historically had been for white women, but both forms of

---

[33] BCCC, September Term, 1880, Case 1796, Sidonia Young. On Young and the Baldwin incident, see Robert H. Wozniak and Jorge A. Santiago-Blay, "Trouble at Tyson Alley: James Mark Baldwin's Arrest in a Baltimore Bordello," *History of Psychology* 16, no. 4 (2013): 227–48.

[34] Waring, *Work of the Colored Law and Order League.*

[35] Hayward Farrar, *The Baltimore Afro-American, 1892–1950* (Westport, CT: Greenwood Press, 1998), 87.

labor had additional downsides for women with histories of enslavement. Domestic work put black women under the direct supervision of white householders. That arrangement was frustrating for domestics of all races, but it was particularly difficult for black women because it mimicked the conditions under which many of them had lived during slavery. Freedom, from the perspective of black women, often hinged on their ability to labor and live free from white control and surveillance.[36] Household labor, with all its entailing intimacies, did not provide that. To make matters worse, the arrival of new waves of immigrants from Europe increased competition for domestic work and decreased wages, driving black Baltimoreans out of service jobs and other employment in which they had traditionally been well represented. The only form of labor on which black women maintained a virtual monopoly was washing, an independent but ultimately back-breaking type of work.

Bawdy-house keeping and prostitution were no less physically risky or arduous than washing or domestic work, but they had the benefit of paying much better and often demanding fewer hours. Sex work was also easy to incorporate into the economy of makeshifts that characterized many black women's lives. Because prostitution was inherently a nighttime business, it allowed women to make money while also maintaining a legitimate source – or several legitimate sources – of income. Harriet Collins provides an example. Much of Collins's personal history remains mysterious; she may well have been a freedwoman who arrived in Baltimore from rural Maryland. From the late 1860s through the 1870s, she kept a small house sandwiched between several commercial buildings at 23 Sharp Street. In that house were seven children whom Collins was supporting without the assistance of a live-in male wage earner.[37] Six of these children were hers. The seventh was a boy, poignantly named Ulysses S. Grant, who had been born in 1865 and whose relationship to Collins was unclear. Perhaps his parents had died during the war, or perhaps Collins simply took him in as a foundling. Most of the children

---

[36] On black women's efforts to negotiate domestic service and gain increased autonomy for themselves after emancipation, see Thavolia Glymph, *Out of the House of Bondage: The Transformation of the Plantation Household* (Cambridge: Cambridge University Press, 2008).

[37] Women who had children by men to whom they were not married faced notoriously difficult economic prospects. Prior to 1888, Maryland law only allowed white women to seek financial support from men in bastardy cases. Dennis P. Halpin, "Reforming Charm City: Grassroots Activism and the Making of Modern Baltimore, 1877–1920," PhD dissertation., Rutgers University 2012, 118.

were too young to work, and Collins's daytime job as a washerwoman was not sufficient to support such a large household.[38]

In order to make ends meet, Collins took on five black female boarders, all of whom were between the ages of nineteen and twenty-seven. Allegedly, she kept her household afloat not just by collecting rents from her tenants, but also by opening the dwelling as a place of prostitution. Collins was indicted multiple times in the 1870s for keeping a bawdy house. None of the indictments against her ever progressed to the trial stage, which makes it difficult to know whether or not she would have conceded that the police were correct to label her house a bawdy house. Nonetheless, there is evidence to suggest that they were: Collins rented her house from prominent Baltimore merchant, silversmith, mill-owner, and real estate investor Hugh Gelston. Gelston, whose name still graces a street near where his estate once stood in West Baltimore, owned much of Collins's block of Sharp Street and had a history of renting the houses in that area out as brothels. In 1865, he had rented 23 Sharp Street to John Morgan, who was charged that year with keeping a bawdy house, and 21 Sharp Street to known madam Mary Hetter. Gelston himself was charged with four counts of renting a house for a bawdy house in 1865, and he continued to be prosecuted for the offense for leasing houses on both Sharp and Raborg Streets through 1870.[39] For Gelston, brothels were an investment; for Collins, dabbling in the world of prostitution probably provided a crucial means of support for herself and her children, one that would have been impossible to attain otherwise.

As Collins's example suggests, black women in post–Civil War Baltimore found ways to adapt the brothel model of sex work to their needs. In the antebellum period, discrimination no doubt played a significant role in keeping black sex workers out of brothels, but so did the restrictions that brothels and their managers placed on the women who boarded within them. Brothel keepers, white or black, were generally hostile to the presence of children and insistent on exerting control over their workers' labor schedules. These qualities probably made brothel prostitution unappealing to black women, many of whom were tasked with raising

---

[38] 1870 US census, Baltimore, Maryland, population schedule, Ward 10, p. 67, dwelling 318, family 401, Harriet Collins et. al.

[39] BCCC, January Term, 1870, Case 662, Harriet Collins. On Gelston, see, for example, BCCC (Criminal Docket), September Term, 1870, Cases 538 and 539, Hugh Gelsten [*sic*]. Gelston was also charged for renting to Lucy Sheldon and Charlotte Williams, who, like Collins, kept brothels in the Western District. Later cases had the correct spelling of his last name.

children on their own or with the limited assistance of fathers who were absent part of the year due to enslavement or seasonal labor. Women with personal histories of bondage may have especially resented the notion that a madam might live off of the proceeds of their sexual labor while dictating and controlling their behavior.[40]

After the war, however, black women founded bawdy houses that diverged from earlier parlor houses. Many of black-owned or black-managed bawdy houses featured a number of women living together with their children. Black-owned houses also adopted fee structures for sex workers different from those that were common in white brothels. In 1915, a report from the Maryland Vice Commission noted that madams in Baltimore almost universally took a 50 percent cut of every commercial sex transaction that occurred in their houses. "The exception," the report noted, "is the colored house where the madam charges a fixed sum for board and allows the girls to have all they make over that."[41] The system of charging a fixed fee almost certainly allowed women to keep a greater percentage of their earnings, and it also eliminated any financial stake the madam might have in forcing women to engage in intercourse with large numbers of clients. It allowed black sex workers a greater degree of autonomy and control over their own labor.

Black women's participation in prostitution was undeniably rooted in profound social and economic inequalities and reinforced by discriminatory policing strategies that pushed vice into black neighborhoods. Nevertheless, stories like that of Harriet Collins highlight the ways in which black women made the most of an unfortunate situation. Like their white counterparts in the bawdy trade, black proprietors like Collins and Henrietta Brashears managed to use the proceeds gained from sex work to carve better and more stable lives for themselves. Despite the fact that she certainly earned less than white sex workers at a comparable level, Collins managed to secure upward mobility for both herself and her children. She was able to arrange for her eldest daughter, Mary, to train as a dressmaker, a coveted trade for black women because of the independence and upward mobility it offered. Collins sent her eldest son, Willard, to school rather than making him start work at a young age. By the time he was seventeen, Willard had a job as a private waiter, a low-paying occupation, but one that was so common for young African

---

[40] Observers from the 1860s noted that black migrants to Baltimore were disproportionately women, including older women, and children. Fuke, *Imperfect Equality*, 121.

[41] MVC, vol. 1, 73.

American men that it was practically a rite of passage. Collins's younger girls, Georgiana, Augusta, Jennie, and Annie, all attended school as soon as they were old enough. Collins managed to extricate herself from the prostitution trade after less than a decade in the business. By 1876, she had moved to Washington, DC, where she continued to labor at "washing & c." Notably, her house had no additional boarders.[42]

The proliferation of black-owned sex establishments also had the benefit of lending protection to black sex workers during a period when such protection was very much needed. As Chapter 6 noted, enforcement of vagrancy statutes intensified during the years after the war, when the triumph of free labor gave rise to fears that freedpeople would refuse to work in the absence of white supervision and control. While there were undoubtedly many sex workers – black and white – who suffered as a result of newly stringent enforcement of vagrancy laws, black women's entrance into the bawdy-house trade had the effect of taking them off the streets and allowing them to work indoors, where they were less likely to be subjected to arrest. Revealingly, the period in which black madams began to gain control of brothels was the same period in which arrests of black women as vagrants declined in many of Baltimore's police districts – a surprising statistic given the degree to which Southern states used vagrancy laws as a means of controlling the black population in the absence of a slave system. By the late 1860s, black Baltimoreans were arrested for vagrancy at rates roughly proportional to their representation in the urban population. In 1867, for instance, 14 percent of those arrested as vagrants were black women during a period in which African Americans accounted for roughly 14 percent of Baltimore's population.[43]

Despite these minor benefits, however, the introduction of sex establishments into black communities had a number of stark, negative consequences. For one thing, it drew an increasingly large number of black

---

[42] On the relationship between black women's access to employment and the growth of black prostitution in the late nineteenth and early twentieth centuries, see Blair, *I've Got to Make My Livin'*; Hunter, *To 'Joy My Freedom*; Mumford, *Interzones*, 94–97; Landau, *Spectacular Wickedness*; 1880 US census, Washington, District of Columbia, population schedule, Enumeration District 72, p. 1, house 314, Dwelling 2, Family 2, Harriet Collins et. al.

[43] BCCC, 1866, 1867, 1870, 1872, 1873, 1875, and 1876. Baltimore City Police (Criminal Docket, Eastern District), 1867–1868; Baltimore City Police (Criminal Docket, Southern District) 1867–1868.

women into the criminal justice system on bawdy-house charges. Although bawdy-house charges were less severe than vagrancy charges in terms of their penalties, black women were often subjected to harsher punishments for the offense than those reserved for their white counterparts. Some black madams managed to escape bawdy-house charges with fines not dissimilar to those levied on white women, but others found themselves incarcerated for weeks or months at a time as a result of their indictments or convictions for prostitution-related offenses. Harriet Collins's neighbor Mary (alias Jane) Bull was among the latter. Bull, like Collins, was a tenant of Hugh Gelston's. Also like Collins, she ran her house as a multiuse commercial space rather than a more traditional parlor house. In addition to managing what was alleged to be a prostitution business, Bull labored as a seamstress and made a side business of taking in other people's children, most likely for wet nursing. At the time of the 1870 census, Bull had three women and four unrelated children living with her: two young black children named George Washington and James Logan, and two one-month-old babies, including one who was white. In the fall of that year, Bull was presented to the City Criminal Court on charges of keeping a bawdy house. Despite her cooperation in testifying against Gelston, she was found guilty and fined the substantial sum of $25 plus $11.98 in court costs. The penalty was steep and, in a departure from the antebellum practice of fining women according to their earnings, far more than Bull could afford. Bull was committed to jail in default of payment. She remained there for six months and a day before she was finally released.[44]

Numerous other black women (and a few men) who ran brothels shared similar fates, some before their trials even took place. In almost every case involving bawdy house charges, the sheriff required the accused to post bond for their appearance in court. If the defendant could not do so, they would be incarcerated to await trial. Black Baltimoreans, who enjoyed far more limited access to financial resources than their white counterparts, made up the majority of the bawdy-house defendants who were jailed for inability to post security. In the early 1870s, fourteen out of the twenty-three bawdy-house keepers who were held in jail to await trial were black. Many of these men and women spent days

---

[44] BCCC, September Term, 1870, Case 534, Jane Bull, September Term, 1870; BCJ, 1870–1872, Oct. 6, 1870, Mary Bull (Jane Bull was sometimes listed in records as Mary); 1870 US census, Baltimore, Maryland, population schedule, Ward 10, pp. 67–68, dwelling 319, family 402, Jane Bull et al.

incarcerated while their family members or allies in the sex trade attempted to scrape together bail.[45]

Black defendants were also more likely than their white counterparts to face jail sentences following conviction. Sample court dockets from the 1870s reveal that all eight of the persons listed in Criminal Court dockets as having received jail sentences for keeping a bawdy house were black. Between 1870 and 1874, sixteen other black men and women were sentenced only to fines but were subsequently jailed because they could not afford to pay them. Most of these were incarcerated for the full six months allowable under the law. Black defendants also accounted for 76 percent of bawdy-house cases in which the accused were incarcerated for reasons that are unclear from jail and criminal dockets – that is, cases in which no sentence appeared to have been handed down formally.[46]

The disproportionate punishment of black women for prostitution continued as the nineteenth century wore on and became more acute in the early 1900s. By the 1910s, the number of people appearing in court on bawdy-house charges had dropped precipitously as the police expanded their role in managing the trade to the point that most bawdy houses were never reported to the courts. White madams worked with the police to ensure the orderliness of their establishments and paid bribes and protection fees to exempt their establishments from raids and forced closures. Black proprietors of sex establishments were probably equally exploited economically by local authorities, but they were not afforded the same protections or exemptions from trial. Instead, they were arrested on bawdy-house charges in disproportionate numbers. In sample years 1910 and 1913, only 23 people were indicted on bawdy-house charges. Ten of them, or 43 percent, were black (at that time, black people made up only 16 percent of Baltimore's population). Virtually every black defendant accused of the offense was incarcerated prior to trial. It was not unusual for black women to spend two weeks or more in jail as they waited to see the inside of a courtroom, and many of them returned to jail again on conviction. Some women received sentences as short as a few days, while others spent months incarcerated.[47]

---

[45] These claims are derived from data taken from numerous Baltimore City Criminal Court and Baltimore City Jail dockets from the 1860s, 1870s, and 1880s.

[46] BCJ, 1870–1872, C2057–18; 1872–1874, C2057–19. It was common practice in the penitentiary, jails, and almshouses not to release inmates in the winter months when they were unlikely to find legitimate employment.

[47] Baltimore City Criminal Court (Criminal Docket), 1910, MSA C1489–119; BCCC, 1913.

In addition to introducing more women into the criminal justice system on sex charges, the growing black prostitution trade also created a crisis for Baltimore's black communities at the turn of the twentieth century. For decades at that point, Baltimore's police and courts had treated black neighborhoods as appropriate dumping grounds for bawdy houses, disreputable saloons, and all manner of other disorderly establishments that were unwelcome in the city's white, middle-class communities. However, Baltimore had a growing black middle class consisting of professional men and clergy who aspired to live in stable communities and to be recognized as respectable by the white municipal establishment. They had no more desire than their white counterparts to be surrounded by "immoral" establishments that introduced rowdiness into their otherwise quiet neighborhoods, and they grew frustrated as commercialized vice made incursions into even the most respectable black-majority areas of the city.[48] Members of the black middle class saw the incursion of prostitution as being associated with depreciating housing values and declining public health. This was especially the case in Lower Druid Hill, which became a wretchedly unsanitary place as the population rose, sanitation infrastructures lagged behind development due to municipal neglect, and predatory forms of commerce entered the neighborhood. Tuberculosis and other contagious diseases that were linked to poor sanitation and overcrowding ran rampant; one block of Biddle Street even came to be known as the "lung block" because its infection rates were so high.[49]

Members of the black middle class understood both the incursion of vice and the broader deterioration of their neighborhoods as part and parcel of the same strategies of municipal neglect. Both reflected city officials' understanding that black neighborhoods were unworthy of the same property protections afforded to white ones. As one city official put it, black people had no right to complain about their property values being depreciated by vice because "colored people always lowered the value of property" with their mere presence in particular neighborhoods.[50] The new generation of black professionals found it necessary to contest this notion, to clean up their neighborhoods, and to protest the

---

[48] Booker T. Washington, "Law and Order and the Negro," *The Outlook*, Nov. 6, 1909, 547–48; Waring, *Work of the Colored Law and Order League*.

[49] Olson, "Old West Baltimore," 61.

[50] Washington, "Law and Order and the Negro," 550.

city's discriminatory policies regarding the placement of red-light districts.

For black Baltimoreans, the sense of crisis surrounding the presence of sex establishments in their neighborhoods was rooted in more than concerns over property and a desire for an orderly environment, although those concerns were certainly present and important. Middle-class reformers were also fearful of the effects of vice on black children and on the social and political standing of the black community within the city at large. They were keenly aware that the proliferation of sexual commerce in their communities was likely to be used as a political tool against them during a period when black civil and political rights were already in severe jeopardy. The late nineteenth century saw a wave of social scientific studies of urban areas conducted by academics, Progressive researchers, and the US government. Many of these, including an 1894 study by the Bureau of Labor that focused on Baltimore, examined slum districts and the preponderance of crime and vice that took place within them.[51] As historian Khalil Muhammad has argued, the data these studies generated led to the construction of new ideas about race as Progressive reformers began to interpret black people's overrepresentation among those arrested for criminal violations and presence in urban slums as a sign that criminality and blackness went hand in hand.[52] Not only did the notion of inherent black criminality support the overpolicing and ghettoization of black communities, it also destabilized black claims to respectability and, by extension, to civil and political rights. By the 1890s, Jim Crow laws were beginning to take root in Southern cities and to shape political discourse in Baltimore.[53]

Even as they contested the idea that criminality was related to blackness, black reformers began to see cleansing their neighborhoods of vice as necessary to secure their political and legal futures. Prostitution may have been only one type of crime among many that had the potential to reinforce racial prejudice and stereotyping, but it carried a special weight because of the role that sexuality had historically played in development of anti-black, racist ideology. A glance at local newspapers confirmed that allegations of rampant sexual vice were an especially potent weapon in

---

[51] US Bureau of Labor, *The Slums of Baltimore, Chicago, New York, and Philadelphia* (Washington, DC: Government Printing Office, 1895).

[52] Khalil Gibran Muhammad, *The Condemnation of Blackness: Race, Crime, and the Making of Modern Urban America* (Cambridge, MA: Harvard University Press, 2010).

[53] Carl H. Nightingale, *Segregation: A Global History of Divided Cities* (Chicago: University of Chicago Press, 2012), 1–2.

the hands of white supremacists, who cited black city residents' resort to disorderly establishments as justification for segregation and police crackdowns on black communities. One letter writer who identified himself as an ardent segregationist wrote to the *Sun* in 1904:

The "Jim Crow" and suffrage laws should have been supplemented with a good vagrancy law, so that the vicious, work-hating negroes who infest the dives and poolrooms in the northwestern section might be made to work in chain gangs and thus save our white women from the humiliation and insults on the streets and cars and the respectable colored people from a serious drawback to their progress.[54]

Such editorials used the black men's presence in "dive" and other disreputable establishments as a shorthand for black idleness and immorality, one that justified black men's confinement and forced labor. Such rhetoric prompted members of the black middle class to see proliferation of sex establishments in their neighborhoods and black women's expanded presence in sex work as a pressing threat to their broader mission of claiming political and civil rights.

By the early twentieth century, the crisis of "dives" had become more urgent on account of both local power struggles and incidents taking place in other Southern cities. Locally, black Baltimoreans became politically vulnerable as Maryland's Democrats scrambled to defend their long-standing dominance in state and local politics against mounting Republican challenges. Because most black voters could be counted on to support Republicans, state Democrats, with the support of Democratic boss Arthur Pue Gorman, made suppression of the black vote a central part of their plan to secure their political fortunes. Maryland Democrats aggressively race-baited during their campaigns. Touting statistics about the lawlessness and undereducation of the state's black population, they lobbied for the introduction of literacy tests for voters in an attempt to disenfranchise black Marylanders.[55] In 1904, they proposed the Poe Amendment, which included grandfather clauses to enable native-born white voters to escape the requirements. Although the amendment did not pass, it seemed to many black Marylanders to herald a new and increasingly ugly period of race relations.[56]

---

[54] "A Vagrancy Law Needed," *Sun*, July 20, 1904.
[55] Harold McDougall, *Black Baltimore: A New Theory of Community* (Philadelphia: Temple University Press, 1993), 36–37.
[56] Brugger, *Maryland: A Middle Temperament*, 421–23; Farrar, *The Baltimore Afro-American*, 59–60.

The perception that hostility to black urbanites was increasing in the early twentieth century was reinforced by the happenings in other cities across the South, especially the events that took place in Atlanta in 1906. That year, Georgia was locked in a heated gubernatorial race in which both candidates employed race-baiting tactics in an attempt to gather white support and delegitimize black political participation. Atlanta newspapers entered the fray by publishing sensationalized articles that portrayed black men as sexually rapacious and uncontrolled when it came to white women. Papers devoted specific attention to the disreputable "dive" saloons in black neighborhoods, which they claimed hung nude pictures of white women and encouraged the baser instincts of black men.[57] Allegations of black men's sexual misconduct ramped up long-standing racial tensions related to segregation, the growth of a black middle class, and employment competition between blacks and whites. On September 22, tensions spilled over into violence following local papers' coverage of four separate rape allegations levied against black men. A large white mob attacked and killed dozens of black Atlantans in the city's red-light district.[58]

The brutal riot, occurring as it did in a city with a large and successful black population and a reputation for representing the promise of the New South, sent shock waves through black communities around the nation. Black residents of cities like Baltimore became increasingly convinced that the presence of vice in their neighborhoods invited violence and placed their families in physical danger.[59] Following the Atlanta riots, a group of prominent black ministers, school officials, and professionals met to discuss the creation of a society that would focus on ridding black neighborhoods of the liquor establishments and disorderly houses that they believed endangered their communities and promoted public immorality. The meeting resulted in the formation of the Colored Law and Order League of Baltimore (CLOL).[60]

Unable to control the city's power structures or prevent politicians from race-baiting, CLOL reformers sought to reform their own neighborhoods in ways that they hoped would convince white residents of their respectability. They adopted a public rhetoric that placed responsibility for events like the Atlanta riots onto black communities, which CLOL

---

[57] "The Atlanta Massacre," *American Lawyer* 14 (Jan.–Dec. 1906): 434–35.

[58] David Fort Godshalk, *Veiled Visions: The 1906 Atlanta Race Riot and the Reshaping of American Race Relations* (Chapel Hill: University of North Carolina Press, 2005).

[59] Godshalk, *Veiled Visions*.   [60] Waring, *Work of the Colored Law and Order League*.

reformers claimed "saw in their own neighborhoods more or less of the causes which led to the unfortunate affair" – namely, the proliferation of saloons and disorderly houses.[61] In an attempt to signal to white Baltimoreans that black communities were as frustrated by vice as their white counterparts, they staged a self-funded campaign to investigate and counteract the presence of disreputable establishments in their neighborhood.[62]

In Baltimore as in cities like Chicago, black anti-vice reformers faced the difficult task of highlighting the problem of vice in their communities in ways that would make the issue seem pressing to city officials and white reformers without playing into stereotypes of black criminality and sexual depravity.[63] Black women were involved in sex work, and black men patronized sex establishments. There was little to be gained, however, from explicit and sustained acknowledgment of this fact. Whereas white reformers might generate public sympathy for white sex workers by pointing out that low wages or limited economic opportunities drove women into prostitution, black Baltimoreans were unable to employ similar arguments successfully. They had to toe a perilous line when it came to levying criticisms of city institutions and the economic struc- tures that kept black Americans earning lower wages, living in poorer conditions, and amassing less capital. Criticisms that were too strident had the potential to alienate the white allies on whom the success of their reform efforts would depend. The path to rendering their anti-vice campaign palatable and respectable in the eyes of white Baltimoreans seemed to lie in appearing to embrace the liberal order rather than criticizing it.

Thus, black reformers said little about black women's participation in sex work or its root causes and focused instead on white-owned sex establishments. In particular, reformers focused on the dangers that white establishments posed to their communities' children. While middle-class and working-class black residents were divided on a number of other issues, they shared a concern that black girls and young women were endangered by constant exposure to vice.[64] The focus on children united the community, removed attention from black women's more voluntary

---

[61] Waring, *Work of the Colored Law and Order League*, 3.
[62] Waring, *Work of the Colored Law and Order League*, 3.
[63] Blair, *I've Got to Make My Livin'*, 187–221.
[64] Waring, *Work of the Colored Law and Order League*, 7–8; Hicks, *Talk with You Like a Woman*, 182–84.

forms of participation in sex work, and gave the social uplift movement an effective emotional register. Members of CLOL focused their investigations on identifying vice establishments located near churches and black educational centers. They found that Public School No. 105, a black school located on Caroline Street between Bank and Eastern Avenue in the heart of the Old Causeway, was surrounded by more than sixty disorderly houses and a dozen saloons. Forty-seven of the disorderly houses were within a block's radius of the school. The area around Public School No. 116 on Rogers Avenue near Orchard Street was not quite so saturated with sex establishments, but there were several houses of prostitution in the area that advertised their proprietors' names on their doors for all passerby to see.[65]

CLOL reformers complained that the presence of disreputable establishments so close to schools lured black children from their educations and into dens of vice and crime. According to a 1908 report penned by CLOL member James Waring, "It was most difficult to keep girls in this school [i.e., Public School No. 105] after they became thirteen or fourteen years of age. So powerful were the influences of this neighborhood upon them that at thirteen some of them passed from the school to the houses of prostitution and to lives of shame."[66] Investigators noted even worse conditions in Lower Druid Hill, especially the area near Biddle Street. There were hordes of saloons, schools, gambling dens, "numerous dance houses, clubs and billiard halls, which were in actual practice only assignation places for girls and young women, and to which many of them owed their downfall." Waring, perhaps anticipating that white reformers might seize on such statements as evidence of the failure of black families to protect their children, was careful to portray the offending establishments as products of white greed rather than black moral turpitude. According to Waring, a major part of the problem came from "saloons kept principally by white men of the lowest type," who were happy to profit from the suffering of black communities with the consent of the city's white police force.[67]

CLOL members hoped that drawing attention to the ways in which white entrepreneurs and police contributed to the depreciation of black neighborhoods would not only deflect criticisms of the communities, but

[65] Waring, *Work of the Colored Law and Order League,* 4–8.
[66] Waring, *Work of the Colored Law and Order League,* 7–8.
[67] Waring, *Work of the Colored Law and Order League,* 3.

also convince white reformers to intervene on their behalf. In the hope of gaining powerful allies who might help them to petition the Liquor Board to decrease the number of bawdy saloons in black neighborhoods, the members of CLOL reached out to prominent white businessmen, university officials, and religious leaders. These included Charity Organization Society founder and Johns Hopkins University President Daniel Coit Gilman, local philanthropist Eugene Levering, US Attorney and Baltimore Society for the Suppression of Vice member John C. Rose, and Bishop William Paret. While these reformers were sympathetic to the organization's goals, the Colored Law and Order League struggled to gain enough support to enact its agenda. The city police, who profited from bribery and payouts from disorderly saloons and bawdy houses, insisted that there was no problem with the saloons and assignation houses in black neighborhoods and that any depreciation of property values was simply a natural outcome of black homeownership in the area. At least one policeman commented that the saloons were "less troublesome than the colored churches in the neighborhood."[68]

In the absence of support and resources, CLOL had to settle for dropping its objections to bawdy houses around public schools on Caroline Street and Rogers Avenue in favor of focusing on closing saloons in Lower Druid Hill. The Colored Law and Order League lobbied the city Liquor Board – over the objections of the police – to rescind the licenses of several disreputable establishments in the area. They succeeded in securing the closure of only thirteen establishments, as well as a promise from the Liquor Board to deny licenses to applicants whose establishments had no door to the main roads.[69] The victory was modest at best. Ultimately, white Baltimoreans refused to abandon the logic that black neighborhoods were the appropriate locations for bawdy establishments that might prove damaging to the property values in white ones.

In a tragic irony, CLOL's strategy of highlighting the role that white vice proprietors played in fostering disorder and immorality in black communities not only failed to secure meaningful interventions into the vice problems in their neighborhoods, but also inadvertently leant support to intensifying segregationist rhetoric. Since the 1890s, white Baltimoreans had cooperated to prevent black incursion into

[68] Waring, *Work of the Colored Law and Order League*, 3.
[69] Waring, *Work of the Colored Law and Order League*, 12–15.

predominantly white residential areas. By the first decade of the twentieth century, some city residents began to demand that residential segregation be formally enshrined into law. Just two years after the publication of the Colored Law and Order League's report, CLOL member W. Ashbie Hawkins purchased a house on an all-white block of McCullough Street and leased it to fellow black lawyer George W. McMechen. Shortly after, three other black families moved in, prompting panic and anger among white residents who believed that black families should be contained west of Druid Hill Avenue. In response, the city passed the West Segregation Ordinance, the first residential segregation ordinance of its kind in the country. The ordinance, which enjoyed enthusiastic support of local neighborhood associations and became a template for other cities around the United States, barred black and white residents from moving into blocks predominantly occupied by members of the other race.[70]

Hawkins, an experienced civil rights campaigner, immediately led a charge to fight the new policy. However, the ordinance's supporters defended it by cynically co-opting the kind of rhetoric CLOL had employed in 1908 to suggest that segregation was good for black communities as well as white ones. Segregation, they claimed, was necessary not only to protect property values, but also to prevent the worst elements in each race from corrupting the other.[71] Barry Mahool, Baltimore's progressive mayor, defended the ordinance in an interview with the *New York Times* by claiming that the ordinance would help to maintain order in black communities by preventing white incursions:

It must be observed that this ordinance operates as well upon the white man as upon the negro. No white man may move into a block wherein the negroes predominate and wherein he would doubtless be as unwelcome as a negro among the whites. Experience has taught us in Baltimore that whether the negro goes to the white man or the white man to the negro, the result is equally disastrous and destructive to peace, good order, and good morals.[72]

---

[70] Gretchen Boger, "The Meaning of Neighborhood in the Modern City: Baltimore's Residential Segregation Ordinances, 1910–1913," *Journal of Urban History* 35 (Jan. 2009): 236–58; Power, "Apartheid Baltimore Style"; Farrar, *The Baltimore Afro-American*, 101–3; Jennifer Fronc, "The Horns of the Dilemma: Race Mixing and the Enforcement of Jim Crow in New York City," *Journal of Urban History* 33, no. 1 (2006): 3–25.

[71] Power, "Apartheid Baltimore Style"; Pietila, *Not in My Neighborhood*; McDougall, *Black Baltimore*, 46–61.

[72] "Baltimore Tries Drastic Plan of Race Segregation," *New York Times*, Dec. 25, 1910.

Mahool, whose rhetoric sounded much like that which CLOL had put forth with different intentions, went so far as to claim that the ordinance would secure peace between black and white city residents, who "cannot live in the same block in peace and with due regard to property security." CLOL's strategy of focusing on white disorder in order to avoid besmirching the morality of black men and women ultimately backfired as white Baltimoreans seized on its segregationist implications to legitimize their creation of all-white racial enclaves where white property values were protected above all else. Baltimore authorities' insistence that the West Ordinance was "not passed in a spirit of racial antagonism" so much as a desire to defend black *and* white communities became a crucial element of their public justification of segregation.[73]

For black Baltimoreans, then, the proliferation of brothel prostitution in their neighborhoods was simultaneously a source of opportunity for individual women and a reflection and reaffirmation of their marginalization within the city. In the decades after the Civil War, successful pressure from white middle-class activists to remove brothels from their communities and discrimination-fueled housing shortages among black city residents combined to create a special overlap between people perceived as sexually and racially deviant. Sex work provided some opportunities for black women, including freedwomen, to scrape by, to support families, and to alter the brothel model of prostitution to suit their needs and life circumstances. Unfortunately, it also intensified black women's vulnerability to interventions by police and the carceral state during a period in which the criminal justice system served as a means of reasserting the racial control that had been lost with emancipation.

Middle-class black Baltimoreans who sought to reform their neighborhoods and purge them of vice eventually attempted to harness the state's policing power on behalf of their communities, in much the same way that white neighborhood organizers had done in the decades before. Reformers had to approach the subject carefully, but they ultimately spoke a familiar language of property values, of protecting children, and of moral uplift. However, their pleas were largely ignored except insofar as their findings could be used as evidence that black and white city residents could not be allowed to coexist alongside one another if the fundamental rights to property and public order were to be preserved.

[73] "Baltimore Tries Drastic Plan of Race Segregation."

Commercial sex and its geographies served as a powerful means by which local authorities enforced and legitimized the city's racial hierarchies and inequalities.

Meanwhile, the gains that black women made from their entrance into indoor sex work were gradually being negated. As Chapter 8 will note, the same moment that black women were beginning to enter brothel prostitution in larger numbers was the moment that the brothel model of commercial sex was losing ground among Baltimore's native-born white and immigrant women.

8

Rise of Urban Leisure and the Decline of Brothels

I like the exciting life and the good time I have. All the girls I know have a good time.
                    —Unnamed sex worker, 1913[1]

I never had any pleasure[.] I heard the girls talk about what they made with the fellows, so I made up my mind I would get the money too.
                    —Unnamed sex worker, 1913[2]

On May 10, 1913, a young woman named Louise loitered outside one of Baltimore's new motion picture theaters. It was an unseasonably brisk Saturday afternoon, and Louise occupied herself by chatting with a friend who was working as a cashier at the ticket counter. Eventually, she looked up and noticed a man watching her. Recognizing his interest, she smiled at him, made an idle comment about the weather, and asked him if he would like to take in the show. He agreed and bought her a ticket. As the two settled into the theater, she told him that she was twenty-three and still living at home with her family. She liked to go out occasionally and meet men in much same way she met him, although she had to be careful because her parents certainly would not approve of such behavior.[3]

---

[1] MVCR, vol. 1, 278.
[2] The original quote had the typo "gettthe," which I corrected. MVCR, vol. 1, 283.
[3] MVCR, vol. 1, 323.

After the show, while Louise and her would-be suitor sat at a drug store counter and sipped sodas, she explained that she had recently quit her job working the ribbon counter of a department store. Being cooped up for ten hours a day for an $8 a week salary had not suited her. "I couldn't stand it," she told him. She decided on a new means of making a living: selling sex. After about two hours of chatting, Louise invited the man to accompany her back to a room her friend rented in a nearby boardinghouse. She told him that so long as he agreed to pay $1 for the accommodations in addition to the $2 she charged for her company, neither her friend nor the landlady would object to his presence in the room. The man declined but promised to call again later if she provided him with her address. Louise hesitated to tell him where she lived, but she assured him the woman at the movie ticket counter would know how to reach her if he asked.[4]

Louise's encounter with her would-be beau, taking place as it did in spaces associated with urban youth culture and courting, had all the elements of what would become a quintessential form of commercial sexual exchange by the turn of the twentieth century. During that period, brothel prostitution, which had been a dominant form of sex work in the mid-nineteenth-century trade, declined as the sex trade underwent a recasualization of its labor practices. Recasualization occurred in urban sex trades along the Eastern Seaboard in the late nineteenth century, and it had roots in both national trends – changing land use patterns, an evolving legal landscape around liquor, and a developing leisure culture for working youth – and specific local circumstances.

In Baltimore, the process of casualization began as brothels were relocated to more marginal neighborhoods and new classes of proprietors entered the sex trade. Rather than passively adopting the labor practices and business arrangements that had characterized older parlor houses, new generations of bawdy-house proprietors, especially black and German Baltimoreans, resorted to business models that better reflected their needs and priorities. Frequently, these models involved more flexible residential and labor arrangements than those that had characterized older parlor houses. As black and immigrant women took up brothel prostitution in greater numbers, brothels themselves entered a period of declining economic and cultural relevance, one that was reinforced as young white women who found themselves with expanded access to waged work and public space increasingly rejected the strictures of brothel life. Baltimore developed new spaces of entertainment and leisure to cater to young working people, and a growing number of sex workers like Louise opted to ply their trades in these spaces rather than in indoor sex establishments. The model of courting that brothels sought to replicate ceased to be fashionable as the city's emerging youth culture brought courting and courtship out of the realm of the domestic and into sites of leisure.

The decline of brothel prostitution and the growth of more public and casual forms of commercial sex altered long-standing foundations of Baltimore's sex trade. Not only did it change the labor arrangements of sex work, it also gave rise to new forms of sexual exchange that blurred the (often imagined) boundaries between courting and commerce, labor and leisure, and respectability and iniquity. In Baltimore, as in other cities, women who sold sex increasingly occupied the same spaces as "sitters," charity girls, and other women who bestowed their company and sexual favors on men who bought them drinks, meals, access to entertainment, or consumer goods. The rise of more casual and ambiguous forms of sexual exchange redefined the economic role that selling sex played in the lives of women like Louise, as well as the ways that Baltimoreans perceived the relationship between prostitution, sexual exchange, and mainstream youth culture.

The decline of brothels in Baltimore was a decades-long process that traced its origins to the 1870s, the period that saw downtown real estate speculators lose interest in parlor houses as a form of investment and middle-class property owners insist that brothels be moved from residential neighborhoods. As sex establishments were gradually forced into more marginal communities, new groups of nonwhite and immigrant proprietors altered decades-old labor arrangements to suit their own needs. Black women like Harriet Collins and Jane Bull found that parlor houses requiring women to board in, perform sex work as their primary form of labor, and have no visible male partners or children did not suit their lives, nor those of the women who worked for them. Because black sex workers were raising children on their own and using sex work as part of an economy of makeshifts, black proprietors of sex establishments often rented rooms for assignations and allowed women to make rent as they saw fit rather than seeking to create the kind of cultivated atmosphere that had been common in parlor establishments.

German proprietors, whose number increased following the Civil War, also favored less formal labor arrangements because they often dabbled in prostitution in the context of running saloons or lager houses. Throughout the antebellum period, Baltimore had been a popular destination for skilled German workers who were fleeing war and political unrest. In 1867, German immigration to the city increased significantly as the Baltimore & Ohio Railroad entered an agreement with the North German Lloyd Steamship Line. Ships laden with tobacco, textiles, and other goods sent from the port at Baltimore arrived in Bremen and came back bearing migrants. Although 90 percent of the German passengers who arrived at Baltimore's Locust Point caught trains inland and settled in rural, Western areas, a significant minority of Catholics from South Germany and German Jews remained in the city and opened businesses.[5] Brewing was a popular pursuit among new immigrants, including those who came from Bavaria with knowledge of how to brew light lagers.

German-style light lager beer became exceedingly popular in America, and German beer gardens, lager houses, and taverns attracted Baltimoreans of all backgrounds. Unsurprisingly, some of these sites also gained reputations as places of solicitation and carousing for sex workers and their clients. As early as the 1860s, local residents had complained to the city council about "profligate and abandoned women" who met in a lager house at 55 Marsh Market and added "to the noisy entertainment given there."[6] The overlap between sexual commerce and lager houses, beer gardens, and German-owned drinking establishments only grew as the development of new, steam-powered brewing technologies in the 1870s and 1880s allowed for the expansion of the lager industry.[7]

Germans who ran their saloons and taverns as "bawdy houses" employed a variety of labor arrangements in their establishments, few of which aligned with the regimentation and strict control that characterized life in parlor houses. August "Gustav" Kroedel, a Prussian immigrant who kept a saloon at 97 German Street in the Tenth Ward, pleaded guilty to keeping a bawdy house in 1880. Census records enumerated around

[5] On German immigration to Baltimore, see Dean R. Esslinger, "Immigration through the Port of Baltimore," in *Forgotten Doors: The Other Ports of Entry to the United States*, ed. M. Mark Stolarik (Philadelphia: Balch Institute Press, 1988), 61–74; Ron Cassie, "How Baltimore Became the New York of the South: European Immigration between 1867–1914 and the Development of Ethnic Neighborhoods around the Port of Baltimore," Master's thesis, Georgetown University, 2016.

[6] Charles R. [Golmar?] et al., Petition to the Mayor of Baltimore, 1861, Mayor's Correspondence, RG9, Series 2, Box 30, Item 634 (Folder 103-119), BCA.

[7] On Baltimore's brewing industry, see "Industrial Designs, 1840–1917," in *The Architecture of Baltimore: An Illustrated History*, ed. Mary Ellen Hayward and Frank R. Shrivers Jr. (Baltimore: Johns Hopkins University Press, 2004), 178–79.

the time he was charged reveal that his saloon housed no one besides his wife, three children, and a servant. In all likelihood, Kroedel did not board sex workers, but rather depended on walk-in business from nearby entertainment venues and concert saloons to drive room rentals.[8] In East Baltimore, where brothel prostitution had never succeeded in divorcing sex work from tavern culture, several German saloon proprietors rented their upstairs rooms to women on a longer-term basis. In the late 1870s, German immigrant Jacob Groff purchased Ann and James Manley's old property at 151 Eastern Avenue. Ann, whose old nativist prejudices had either faded or been tempered by the promise of a sufficient return on her property investment, had sold her house in 1876 to the United German Real Estate and Fire Insurance Company for the respectable sum of $4,300. She and James moved several blocks north to a less expensive lot on Caroline Street. Like the Manleys, Groff kept the property as a saloon and boardinghouse. He, his wife, and a servant managed the property and boarded six sex workers, two of whom were from Jacob's home state of Hanover. Just blocks away, Herman Herring kept a lager saloon at the southeast corner of Bond and Shakespeare Streets in Fells Point. Herring lived at the property with his wife Johanna, their two adult daughters, and a barkeeper. The family rented out numerous rooms above the bar, most of them to young women. At the time of the 1880 census, the Herring saloon had five female tenants whose occupation was recorded as "prostitute."[9]

Although German women made up only a tiny minority of sex workers – 2 out of 191 surveyed in the 1910s – German-run establishments had no trouble attracting boarders.[10] They had a reputation for being well-ordered, family-run, and peaceable establishments that placed few demands on their boarders other than paying their rent and comporting themselves subtly in the bar area. For women who wished to strike a balance between their desire to be free from supervision and their wish to remain safe in the trade, German saloons provided a viable and appealing alternative to the strictures of brothel life.[11]

---

[8] BCCC, January Term, 1880, Case 428, Gustav Kroedel; 1880 US Census, Baltimore, Maryland, Enumeration District 89, p. 18, dwelling 104, family 133, Augus Kroedel.

[9] Herman Herring's first recorded appearance in sample years of court dockets was in the September term of 1864: BCCC, September Term 1864, Case 953, Herman Herring; "Circuit Court for Baltimore County," *Sun*, Oct. 15, 1874; "Nearly Suffocated by Gas," *Sun*, Jan. 3, 1876, 4; 1870 US Census, Baltimore, Maryland, Ward 2, p. 174, dwelling 977, family 1509, Herman Hering.

[10] MVCR, vol. 1, 90.   [11] Sanger, *The History of Prostitution*, 559–61.

The decline of brothel prostitution was accelerated by women's expanded presence in the licit wage labor economy. In the early republic and antebellum years, the expectation that women's place was in the home made it difficult for those women who depended on paid labor to find employment that provided reasonable wages. Domestic work, sewing, finishing work, or (in the case of black women especially) washing work were the primary occupations open to female laborers. In the late nineteenth century, however, that changed. Women entered nursing and teaching roles in greater numbers following the Civil War, and they also gradually expanded their employment in new factory and clerical jobs that opened to them as manufacturing industrialized. In Baltimore, female laborers performed piecework labor for garment manufacturers and hatters and took waged positions in factories, tobacco sorting plants, and canneries. Better-off laboring women worked as secretaries in office buildings or as sales girls in local department stores, including Stewart's, Hochschild, Kohn, Huztler's and the May Company. As a result of more diverse and better-compensated labor opportunities, more women entered the paid labor force than ever before. By 1910, women composed upward of 40 percent of the workers in certain urban industries, including tobacco processing and garment making.[12]

Women's expanded access to paid employment outside the home had several significant consequences for the evolution of the sex trade, most notably an apparent reduction in the number of women who participated in sex work full-time. The new class of women workers that emerged in the nineteenth century faced many of the same difficulties as those who had labored in Baltimore in earlier decades, including low pay and seasonal labor markets that made steady employment difficult to attain. Companies continued to set women's wages according to the assumption that it would supplement a family income rather than provide self-sufficiency. The average white Baltimore shop girl or factory worker made only $6 to $8 per week by the 1910s.[13] Although this was barely a living wage by the standards of the time, it provided a significant enough

---

[12] Brugger, *Maryland: A Middle Temperament*, 348–49; Pamela S. Haag, "'Commerce in Souls': Vice, Virtue, and Women's Wage Work in Baltimore, 1900–1915," *Maryland Historical Magazine* 68 (Fall 1991), especially 294–96; Michael J. Lisicky, *Hutzler's: Where Baltimore Shops* (Charleston, SC: History Press, 2009); US Department of Labor, Women's Bureau, *Women in Maryland Industries* (Washington, DC: Government Printing Office, 1922).

[13] On wages of working women in Baltimore, see MVCR, vol. 2, 3–52. On "women adrift in cities" and their struggles to make a living, see Joanne J. Meyerowitz, *Women Adrift:*

financial base that more women chose to sell sex on a part-time basis as a means of augmenting their income from legitimate employment rather than performing sex work full-time. The choice to avoid brothel prostitution in favor of embracing more casual and "clandestine" forms of sex work allowed women to avoid the social stigma of prostitution while also maintaining a greater degree of independence and ability to choose the terms of their work.

Waged work that removed women from the homes of their families or employers made moving between the world of licit and illicit employments easier than it had been decades before. It was not unusual for women to work ten-hour days in factories or department stores, live at home with their parents, and otherwise retain all the trappings of a "respectable" life even as they participated in occasional prostitution on weekends. Often, their parents' unfamiliarity with the pay structures and typical wages of jobs in emerging industries enabled young women to live secret side lives as sex workers. Some women who sold sex were able to explain away their earnings or their ability to afford expensive consumer goods by claiming that their day jobs paid more money than they actually did.[14]

In addition to rendering full-time sex work unnecessary for an increasing number of women, new types of waged work changed women's relationship to urban space in ways that hastened brothels' obsolescence. During the antebellum period, it was often assumed that any woman found making "peregrinations about town" unescorted at night was disorderly and sexually disreputable.[15] This assumption made it permissible for peace officers to arrest virtually any poor woman who was on the public streets at night, and it rendered public forms of prostitution especially dangerous. As women's presence in the world of waged work expanded, however, their access to public space did as well. Most women employed outside the home worked ten-hour days and depended on walking or public transportation to get to and from work. Their presence in city streets, on omnibuses and streetcars, and in other public accommodations at all hours thus ceased to be as unusual as it had been decades before. With so many young and respectable working women traversing

---

Independent Wage Earners in Chicago, 1880–1930 (Chicago: University of Chicago Press, 1991), especially chapter 1.

[14] MVCR, vol. 2, 3–52.

[15] This phrase was sometimes used to describe the actions of street sex workers in the antebellum period. See, for example, "The Watch Returns," *Sun*, Apr. 26, 1843.

the city to travel between their homes and their jobs, police could no longer automatically assume that a woman's free movement through public space was indicative of sexual license. Although the difficulties of distinguishing between respectable women and disreputable ones were a source of constant consternation for the city's anti-vice reformers, they also provided sex workers with a degree of protection from arrest and harassment. The fact that sex workers could more easily blend in and solicit in public spaces deprived brothels of one of their central points of appeal, namely that they provided safe spaces for women to engage with would-be clients.[16]

The same period that witnessed the expansion of women's presence in the labor force and in public space also saw the creation of new spaces of recreation and entertainment that gradually displaced brothels as the primary sites of solicitation for sex workers. The rise of the industrial economy, with its centralized sites of production, reinforced the separation between the realms of home and work while also giving rise to a new realm that was largely separate from both: the world of leisure. As the works of Kathy Peiss, Randy D. McBee, and Elizabeth Alice Clement have documented, young immigrants and native-born members of the urban working class endeavored in the late nineteenth century to create their own youth culture rooted in places of recreation and entertainment. Eager to escape their parents' control and to distance themselves from the at-times suffocating world of the home, young people sought out public or semi-public spaces where they could preserve elements of their existing homosocial culture while also creating new possibilities for heterosexual interactions.[17] Concert saloons, dance halls, amusement parks, and other

---

[16] Notably, although working-class women entered public space in larger numbers than before, many middle-class reformers in major cities commented at length about the dangers that urban public space continued to pose to women. See, for instance, Sarah Deutsch, *Women and the City: Gender, Space, and Power in Boston, 1870–1940* (Oxford: Oxford University Press, 2000), chapter 3.

[17] In her path-breaking book *Cheap Amusements*, Peiss argued that the culture of dance halls, amusement parks, and movie theaters was focused heavily on heterosociability and heterosexuality, and thus represented a departure from the older emphasis on homosocial relationships. Kathy Peiss, *Cheap Amusements: Working Women and Leisure in Turn-of-the-Century New York* (Philadelphia: Temple University Press, 1986). In his 2000 monograph, *Dance Hall Days*, Randy McBee argued that homosociability remained an important element of both men's and women's leisure culture, even as heterosociability became an increasingly central part of dance hall culture. McBee, *Dance Hall Days: Intimacy and Leisure among Working-Class Immigrants in the United States* (New York: New York University Press, 2000). Clement, *Love for Sale*.

"cheap amusements" geared toward working-class youth of both sexes sprung up in cities around the country by the 1890s.[18] Young people flocked to them in the evenings and on weekends to drink, dance, "make love" to – that is, flirt with – one another, and spend what income they had left after their rent payments or financial contributions to family.

The development of youth leisure culture had profound effects on the sex trade, not just because it gave rise to new sites of solicitation for sex workers, but also because it disrupted the cultural context in which brothel prostitution was rooted. Parlor houses had succeeded in the mid-nineteenth century because they traded on their ability to provide men whose access to heterosexual relationships was delayed or otherwise disputed by urbanization with a simulacrum of traditional, domestically based courtship. Even as they presented male patrons with a fun-house-mirror world in which the restrictiveness of bourgeois sexual codes was removed, parlor houses thrived on their ability to evoke the feeling of a middle-class home for men who were not yet settled enough to have their own. And yet, by the late nineteenth century, the feeling of home was exactly what many young people were seeking to avoid. As working-class youth embraced a version of courtship that was divorced from home and from parental supervision, parlor houses no longer satisfied the demands and desires of young men in the way that they once did. Instead, they appeared as remnants of an older generation's practices that had grown obsolete in the face of a new culture in which courtship and courting took place in public sites of leisure.[19] Sex workers, many of whom were young, working-class women themselves, understood that it was these leisure spaces and not brothels that provided them with the best opportunities to make their living. Access to new spaces of leisure was often uneven, with white sex workers having far more opportunities to patronize Baltimore's semi-segregated public amusements than black women did. Nevertheless, those sex workers who had the ability to access new leisure spaces often opted to relocate there rather than working in brothels or strolling the streets.

Among the most popular leisure spaces in Baltimore – with both sex workers and youth in general – was the concert saloon, a precursor to vaudeville theater that have been a haven of working-class culture in New York since the 1840s. Baltimore was slower to develop the concert saloon model than other, larger cities, but several establishments opened in the

[18] Peiss, *Cheap Amusements*.   [19] Peiss, *Cheap Amusements*; Clement, *Love for Sale*.

commercial strip along Baltimore Street in the years just before and during the Civil War. Among the more popular saloons were Leavitt's Gemote Palace (later called the Bijou), founded in 1864 at the corner of Baltimore and Light Streets; George Nachman and Thomas Turpin's French Froliques, founded circa 1877 at Baltimore and North Street; Joseph Bucholtz's Pacific Garden Theater near the corner of Baltimore and Charles; and the Haymarket Concert Saloon, opened in the Centre Market space. These saloons entertained their audiences with variety acts that ranged from minstrelsy to touring singers and orchestras to comedic performances. Unlike older theaters, many of which dispensed with their third tiers in the 1860s and 1870s as a result of pressures from anti-vice reformers, concert saloons seldom had the pretense of respectability or high-brow offerings. They catered to the working classes and – as their name implied – complemented their lively theatrical and musical offerings with alcohol service. Some of the more disreputable concert saloons, including the French Froliques, relied so heavily on liquor sales that they did not charge admission fees.[20] Instead, they merely invited their audiences to stay for as long they continued to purchase drinks. Women who sold sex, recognizing the opportunity presented by large crowds of inebriated men, patronized the saloons in order to circulate among their patrons, drink, and attempt to pick up clients.

As concert saloons provided good business opportunities for sex workers, they also actively fostered the development of new forms of commercialized sexuality that commoditized forms of courting and intimacy without necessarily crossing into the outright exchange of money for intercourse. Among the earliest and most common of these new forms of commercialized sexuality was "sitting," which was a Maryland-specific term for a practice that became more generally popular in concert saloons in the late nineteenth century.[21] Women who worked as sitters in concert saloons did not sell sex per se, nor did they receive any money directly from the men who patronized them. Instead, sitters asked men to buy

[20] May's Dramatic Encyclopedia of Baltimore, 1750–1904, MS 995, Reel 7, MdHS. On concert saloons, see Brooks McNamara, *The New York Concert Saloon: The Devil's Own Nights* (Cambridge: Cambridge University Press, 2002); Robert Clyde Allen, *Horrible Prettiness: Burlesque and American Culture* (Chapel Hill: University of North Carolina Press, 1991), 73–76, 123–27; Gilfoyle, *City of Eros*, 224–50; "Have You Been to the Gemote Palace," *Sun*, June 20, 1864; "The 'French Froliques,'" *Sun*, July 13, 1885; "A Woman Shot," *Sun*, Feb. 3, 1886.

[21] I have not seen the term "sitting" used outside Maryland sources, though the practice it described was and is common in dance and strip clubs.

them drinks or to purchase meals or cigars from the establishments in which they worked in exchange for the pleasure of their companionship. If a man agreed to buy a drink or a meal, then a sitter would remain at his table, flirting and conversing for as long as it took to finish the drink or food.

The practice of sitting may initially have begun simply as a form of exchange that women themselves pioneered in order to gain access to urban entertainments they otherwise may not have been able to afford on their meager salaries.[22] While sitting may have begun as an informal practice, however, concert saloon proprietors quickly integrated sitting into their business models. In order to maximize their profits and ensure that their establishments always had an array of attractive young women present to draw male patrons, concert saloon owners began to hire women to work as sitters. In some cases, these sitters were performers at the saloon who circulated through the audience after their sets; in other cases, they were simply women who came in off the streets. In either instance, saloon owners compensated female sitters for their role in soliciting men to make purchases by offering them a percentage of their total sales. Granting women a percentage rather than a flat commission encouraged them to request more expensive drinks; indeed, it was not unusual for women who knew they were being treated to start out trying to order a bottle of wine before backing down to cocktails if their patron grew irritated.[23] By incentivizing sitting, concert saloons ensured that they provided their clientele with opportunities for heterosexual sociability and exchange while also circumventing the provisions of an 1864 state law – passed as a result of concerns about young women's sexual morality – that barred concert saloon owners from employing women as waitresses.[24] Sitters who were willing to sell more than the pleasure of their company had the option of supplementing their earnings by retiring to a nearby room with a male patron, but doing so was hardly a requirement of the job.[25]

[22] Kathy Peiss introduced this framework for understanding other forms of treating. Peiss, *Cheap Amusements*, especially 51–54.

[23] "Resorts Wide Open; Two Raids Made," *Sun*, July 21, 1913.

[24] *The Maryland Code: Public General Laws*, Vol. 1, Art 4, Section 913–914 (Baltimore: King Bros, 1888), 575–76. Proprietors who violated the law were subject to fines of $100 to $1,000, one to six months in jail, or both, plus the revocation of their liquor licenses.

[25] California Penological Commission, *Penology: Report of the California State Penological Commission* (Sacramento: State Office, P. L. Schoaff, Supt. State Printing, 1887), 236;

Although sitting was distinct from outright prostitution, it operated on a similar enough spectrum of sexualized commercial behavior that many Baltimoreans took umbrage at concert saloon's willingness to expose young women to unfamiliar men and profit from their flirtations. Almost as soon as concert saloons appeared on the urban landscape, local and state authorities took steps to regulate the content of their shows and to restrict young people's access to them. When "free" concert saloons – that is, saloons that depended entirely on alcohol sales for profit – began to appear on Baltimore Street in 1877, one local citizen wrote to the Baltimore *Sun* complaining that "So-Called Concert Saloons" were in reality "a snare to the unwary, a stench in the nostrils of the decent portion of the community, [and] a school of vice in all its hideous and varied forms."[26] The commenter lamented that the saloons were likely to make Baltimore's main thoroughfare the equivalent of New York's Five Points. The following year, the Maryland General Assembly 1878 made it illegal for concert saloons, theaters, or any place of entertainment that allowed obscene or vulgar displays or served liquor to admit women under the age of sixteen or men under the age of fourteen.[27] While the law was only sporadically enforced, it occasionally resulted in severe penalties for proprietors. Shortly after the law was passed, French Froliques co-owner George Nachman was indicted for violating the code against allowing minors into his concert saloon. Six years later, Nachman and his partner, Turbin, were arrested for allowing "indecent performances" in their establishment. The performances were likely can-can dances, which generated controversy at the time for their revealing and sexually suggestive movements. Judge Phelps, who proclaimed that he intended to make an example of Nachman and Turbin, sentenced them each to pay $250 in fines and court costs and spend six months in jail.[28]

The Maryland Code: Public General Laws, Vol. 1, Chapter 171 (Baltimore: King Bros, 1888), 487–88.

[26] "So-Called Concert Saloons," *Sun*, Aug. 9, 1877, 4.

[27] William Lawrence Slout, ed., *Broadway below the Sidewalk*, xii–xiv; Rodger, *Champagne Charlie and Pretty Jemima*, 59–71, especially 65–66. US Bureau of Labor Statistics, *Bulletin of the United States Bureau of Labor Statistics*, Issue 54 (Sep. 1904): 1140–41; Woman's Christian Temperance Union, *Minutes of the National Woman's Christian Temperance Union at the Eighth Annual Meeting, Boston, Mass., November 13 to 18, 1891* (Chicago: Woman's Temperance Publishing Association, 1891), 193.

[28] "Court of Appeals Decisions Howand Cooper Refused Another Trial," *Sun*, June 24, 1885.

Within a decade, the General Assembly also moved to close the loop-
hole in its 1864 law against hiring waitresses by explicitly banning sitting.
Chapter 171 of the General Local Laws of Maryland declared it illegal for
concert saloons to admit any women who "are allowed in or about the
said premises who shall drink, smoke, or partake in any kind of eatables
or refreshments at the expense of others, or solicit others to purchase such
things ... upon which they shall receive or expect to receive" some form
of compensation.[29] The law attempted to regulate women's behavior by
drawing a line between legitimate forms of exchange between men and
women – for example, a man volunteering to pay for dinner – and
illegitimate forms of exchange in which women received direct financial
remuneration for their sexual and emotional labor. They did not succeed.
Young women continued to use sitting as a means of earning extra money
while dining out on someone else's dime, and concert saloon proprietors
made enough money from the practice that they continued to welcome
both sitters and sex workers. Sitting remained a common practice in
concert saloons and other venues well into the twentieth century.

In the 1890s, concert saloons, vaudeville theaters, and hotels around
the main commercial strips furthered the opportunities for both prostitution and more ambiguous forms of sexual exchange by adding dance halls
to their premises. Dance halls were a craze among urban youth, attracting
crowds of upward of 100 people per night. While some halls cultivated an
air of respectability by framing their offerings as dance classes for women,
others cultivated a raucous internal culture in which young men and
women were welcome to flirt, court, and dance together in closer physical
proximity than would have been acceptable a generation prior. Because
dance halls were often connected to saloons, it was not unusual for young
men and women to drink as they danced. The heady combination of
alcohol and flirtation created an atmosphere in which both prostitution
and forms of sexual exchange in which men "treated" women to drinks in
exchange for dances, company, or sex thrived.[30]

As sex workers and other young woman turned to public leisure spaces
to flirt and solicit male company, they also began to take advantage of the

---

[29] Maryland Bureau of Industrial Statistics and Information, *Second Biennial Report,
    1886–1887* (Annapolis: James Young, 1888), 160–61. Maryland's law against female
    sitters was still enforced into the 1980s before it was eventually declared to be in violation
    of the state's Equal Rights Amendment barring gender discrimination. See *Turner
    v. State*, 474 A.2d 1297 (Md. 1984).
[30] MVC, vol. 3, 148–51. On the history of dance halls, see McBee, *Dance Hall Days*; Peiss,
    Cheap Amusements, 88–114.

city's increasingly diverse lodging options to carry out sexual exchanges. In the antebellum period, many women who solicited in the city's theaters or other public spaces resorted to brothels or assignation houses to have sex with clients. By the late nineteenth century, however, new types of boarding, hotel, and living arrangements made it possible for women to operate as sex workers without entering spaces that were specifically devoted to commercial prostitution. Most urban leisure districts were surrounded by a variety of furnished room houses, hotels, and saloons with rooms to let. Young women who picked up men while at dance halls, theaters, or concert venues could take them back to these establishments for liaisons, often with minimal resistance or even active support from the persons in control of the properties.[31]

Furnished room houses, which emerged in Baltimore to house the thousands of young men and women who flocked to the city from the countryside in search of work, proved perhaps the most popular alternative to brothels. Furnished room establishments provided single laborers and even young married couples with ready-to-occupy rooms that could be rented by the week – or, in the case of less reputable houses, by the hour. During a period when approximately 16 percent of Baltimore women boarded out, they were a common form of lodging, and one that afforded women with a great deal of privacy and autonomy.[32] Unlike some older boardinghouses, many furnished room houses had no common areas and no pretension of replicating any kind of household environment in which the keeper of the house behaved in loco parentis. Women could come and go as they pleased, and many keepers of furnished room houses either did not concern themselves with their tenants' conduct or actively welcomed women who might want to bring men to their rooms on the understanding that such tenants would pay high rents in exchange for discretion.[33] In 1914, undercover vice detectives who surveyed 796 of the city's more than 1,600 furnished room houses claimed that the owners of 622 houses allowed some form of "immorality," with most (426) allowing multiple men to make calls to female tenants and some (196) insisting that women could have only one male caller whom they pretended was their husband.[34] Baltimore Street, which housed some of the city's largest concert saloons and clubs, and West Fayette Street, which sat between the Josephine and Raborg brothel districts, had some of the highest concentrations of "immoral" houses.

---

[31] MVCR, vol. 3.   [32] Meyerowitz, *Women Adrift*, 4.   [33] MVCR, vol. 3, 25–26.
[34] MVCR, vol. 3, 1.

Sex workers and other young women who participated in sexual exchange took advantage of the loose boarding arrangements in furnished room houses to ply their trades in ways that were less restrictive than what brothels might offer. Furnished room houses entailed no supervision of women's sexual labor and afforded women the right to choose their own clientele. Along with this increased autonomy came more control over the revenue from their labor. Most women who used furnished room houses could expect to be charged $1 per hour, $2 per night, or between $2.50 and $8 per week for their lodging, all of which were significantly less than the room and bed fees in brothels by the early twentieth century. What is more, many of them never paid those fees. By custom, women who sold sex out of the new class of furnished rooms asked men to cover the nightly charge for the room in addition to their fee for sexual services.[35] The arrangement allowed women to pocket all of their earnings while also enjoying a great deal of freedom in how and when they engaged in sex work.

In addition to renting furnished rooms, sex workers also resorted to hotels and lodging rooms in saloons to carry out their liaisons. While not as subtle as furnished rooms, saloons and hotels provided the convenience of allowing women to pick up clients and carry out liaisons in the same space. In 1890, the number of establishments willing to rent rooms to sex workers increased as Baltimore adopted Sunday liquor policies similar to those outlined in New York's Raines Law.[36] The new policies banned liquor sales on Sunday except in hotels that served meals, which prompted many drinking establishments to add back rooms for the sake of labeling themselves hotels. Sex workers and their clients quickly became a primary customer base for these slapdash "hotels."

Meanwhile, larger hotels, many of which had previously shunned the presence of sex workers in their establishments for fear of alienating their respectable guests, took advantage of a new technology to incorporate sex

---

[35] Maryland Vice Commission Reports contain several recountings of undercover agents' interactions with sex workers. In almost all cases, the women demanded that the men furnish payment for the rooms, just as Louise did with the undercover agent discussed at the beginning of the chapter. MVCR, vol. 1.

[36] Baltimore City Board of Police Commissioners, *Report of the Board of Police Commissioners: For the City of Baltimore to His Excellency the Governor of Maryland, for the Year of 1912* (Baltimore: Baltimore City Printing and Binding Company, 1913), 19–21; Baltimore City Board of Police Commissioners, *Report of the Board of Police Commissioners: For the City of Baltimore to His Excellency the Governor of Maryland, for the Year of 1913* (Baltimore: Baltimore City Printing and Binding Company, 1914), 14. On Raines Law Hotels, see Gilfoyle, *City of Eros*, chapter 11.

work into their business models: the telephone. Telephones allowed hotel employees to summon women for male guests while avoiding the scandal of having sex workers solicit in their common areas. A 1913 sting operation by the Maryland Vice Commission found that hotels' headwaiters kept lists of the names, addresses, and phone numbers of neighborhood sex workers, whom they telephoned whenever a guest at the hotel requested it. Some hotels also hired women who were willing to sell sex to work as maids and cleaners. If a guest requested company for the night, porters, bellboys, or concierges would simply summon the woman down in exchange for a tip.[37] Notably, this arrangement provided black women with some of the few opportunities they had in the late nineteenth century to participate in the sex trade's newly casualized labor arrangements without resorting to streetwalking. Many dance halls and concert saloons were segregated spaces that did not hire black women to work, but Baltimore's hotels employed largely black staffs to fulfill janitorial, bell-hop, elevator operator, and housekeeping duties. This was especially true during the summer months, when oppressive heat drove away many white workers who could afford to seek employment elsewhere. House-keeping jobs were an entry point for black women who wished to make extra money from sexual labor, and the presence of black men in janitor-ial and elevator positions ensured that black sex workers made their way into hotels' registers of call girls.[38]

The rise of furnished room and hotel prostitution that was linked to the city's vaudeville and dance hall culture also enabled another group of sex workers to make their living and engage in the world of urban leisure: men who sold sex to other men. As George Chauncey and a number of other historians have noted, the turn of the century witnessed the emer-gence of some of the first visible homosexual subcultures in American cities. In many cases, vaudeville theaters and venues that hosted drag balls became centers of gay culture. Men who had sex with other men – commercial or otherwise – circulated among the city's theater crowds and were well represented among performers. Baltimore was no excep-tion. Men who participated in the city's queer sex scene were so connected to local theaters that they assumed the names of famed vaudeville stars like Gracie La Rue and Lillian Russell or movie characters like Maggie Pepper as aliases in correspondence with each other. Men who sold sex

[37] MVCR, vol. 1, 30–34.   [38] MVCR, vol. 1, 30–34.

often picked up trade or tricks at the theater and customarily retired to hotels or furnished room houses, where they charged between $1 and $5 for "perversion" and $10 for a full night with their clients.[39]

The constellation of concert saloons, dance halls, furnished room houses, and hotels enabled sexual commerce to transcend the brothel and assignation house in ways that would have been difficult in decades previous. However, perhaps the biggest blow to brothels and the model of courting on which they were based came in the 1890s, with the rise of a class turn-of-the-century leisure site: the amusement park.

Baltimore's amusement parks owed their origins to the growth of trolleys and electric streetcars, which, in turn, owed their development to an 1888 land annexation that had expanded Baltimore's boundaries and increased city landholdings from ten square miles to thirty. With the new city boundaries in place, real estate investors and developers started to buy up land in annexed areas in hopes of turning it into new, semi-suburban housing for people who wanted live further from the bustle of the city center. Recognizing that their success was contingent on providing quick, reliable transportation, developers and related corporations sponsored the creation of numerous streetcar lines – first horse-drawn, then electric – that ferried residents between home and work.[40] Constructing and managing these lines, however, was expensive business. In order to maintain the profitability of the streetcars, companies had to attract riders not just on weekdays, but also on the weekends and in the height of summer, when ridership typically lagged. Hoping to attract passengers during otherwise slow periods, many companies planned their own entertainment attractions at the ends of their lines. They expanded their streetcar and trolley tracks to areas near the water or to rural patches of land to northwest of the city and set about developing exurban amusement parks. Early on, these parks were usually beer gardens or small retreats. By the 1890s, however, many developers began to up the ante, creating larger entertainment venues that included concert saloons, dance floors, rides, and a variety of other attractions intended to draw city residents. For as little as five cents, Baltimoreans could take a trip to

[39] MVCR, vol. 1, 423–24.

[40] On this history of streetcars in Baltimore, see Thomas J. Vicino, *Transforming Race and Class in Suburbia: Decline in Metropolitan Baltimore* (New York: Palgrave Macmillan, 2008), 37–43. See also Sam Bass Warner, *Streetcar Suburbs: The Process of Growth in Boston, 1870–1900* (Cambridge, MA: Harvard University Press, 1978).

these amusement parks in the summer and enjoy inexpensive food and free entertainment at in-house concert venues.[41]

Although many of Baltimore's amusement parks strove to create a respectable and family-friendly atmosphere, others quickly developed a reputation for blending licit and illicit entertainments.[42] Several parks were "wet" resorts that had a reputation for providing young people, workingmen and women, and sailors in port with opportunities to escape the city's Sunday liquor regulations and indulge themselves. One of the earliest of these "wet" parks was River View Amusement Park on Point Breeze. Point Breeze had been a longtime favorite resort for city residents even before it was a developed leisure site. In the mid-nineteenth century, it had been a popular destination for Causeway brothel keepers and sex workers looking to escape the tumult of city life and enjoy the area's cooler river air and rural charm. In 1868, the area was transformed into a beer garden whose location at the end of Eastern Avenue made it an easy trip for East Baltimoreans. In the 1890s, the site's proprietor added bathhouses, a vaudeville stage, a boardwalk, and a casino for performances, as well as rollercoasters and a moving picture theater.

Within a few years, Hollywood Park on Baltimore's Back River would offer a similar slate of activities and entertainments. Hollywood was founded by Baltimore City theater proprietor James L. Kernan in 1899 and quickly cemented its reputation as Baltimore's most raucous and disreputable amusement park when it was purchased by saloonkeeper and brewery park owner Joe Goeller in 1904.[43] Goeller constructed a hotel on site, added cutting-edge rides and new concession stands with cheap seafood, and outfitted the park with brilliant electric lights. A man with strong connections to the alcohol business, Goeller also made sure Hollywood did a brisk business in beer bottle service seven days a week. In the 1890s, Baltimore City had banned the sale of liquor on Sunday and introduced a high license law to ensure that businesses had financial incentive to follow the policy. Although numerous proprietors within the city disobeyed the Sunday regulations with near impunity, the policy boosted business for alcohol sellers whose establishments sat outside the city limits and thus were not subject to the law. Goeller, whose establishment was located in Baltimore County, had a staunch conviction

---

[41] John P. Coleman, *Historic Amusement Parks of Baltimore: An Illustrated History*, Kindle edition (Jefferson, NC: McFarland & Company, 2014), introduction, chapter 10.

[42] Coleman, *Historic Amusement Parks*, chapter 2.

[43] Coleman, *Historic Amusement Parks*, chapter 11.

that workingmen had the right to drink on Sunday, and his park attracted laborers who sought fresh air and cold brews. One commenter noted of visitors to the park, "Their attention is engaged from noon until midnite by the show in the casino, the soft crabs, the popcorn, the fried fish, and the beer – particularly the beer. Hollywood indeed has taken on its perfume. The whole place smells beery."[44] The parks' promise of good drinks and good times drew young working men and women, who took the streetcar on weekends or after long days of work to enjoy the entertainments and opportunities for mingling.

As with concert saloons before them, Baltimore's amusement parks quickly became popular with sex workers, who found in them an opportunity to operate safely and profitably outside the world of brothel prostitution. The alcohol service, bright lights, and entertainment in the form of concerts and dancing made the amusement parks an ideal and relatively safe place for solicitation. Sex workers could blend into the crowds and enjoy freedom from the oversight of the city police while also benefiting from an atmosphere that hinted at sexual possibility and license. As an added benefit, attending the parks was affordable even for women who scrimped by on meager salaries. Recognizing that part of the attraction of their establishments was the opportunities they presented for courtship and courting, the parks' proprietors set admission policies that ensured that working women would be able to access amusements. Many parks admitted women to the dance pavilions for free even as they charged men twenty-five cents.[45] Sex workers who worked out of saloons and furnished room houses in the nearby working-class enclave of Highlandtown flocked to the parks in the hope of picking up men that they could take back to their rooms.

Prostitution in parks like Hollywood blended with and blurred into other, more ambiguous forms of sexual exchange that were integrated in the business models of park saloons and beer gardens. Hollywood and other parks in the Back River hired attractive women as sitters to keep alcohol sales up and compensate for the lost revenue from women's waived admission fees. In some cases, they also expected this service from their performers when they were not on stage. When anti-vice agents investigated the amusement resorts and interviewed actresses, dancers, and entertainers in the summer of 1913, most of the women admitted to

---

[44] "At Hollywood on Sunday among the Plain People," *Sun*, June 16, 1907, 13. Originally quoted in Coleman, *Historic Amusement Parks*.

[45] Coleman, *Historic Amusement Parks*, 134.

undercover agents that they worked the men in the crowds when they were not singing or dancing.[46] Despite the stationary passivity implied by the name, parks expected their sitters to circulate "unceasingly" through the large crowds at the parks, using their good looks and flirtations to encourage men to buy drinks or to "pilot" men to secluded bar areas.[47]

Successful sitters made a good deal of money for the park while also earning handsome rewards for themselves. Talented sitters could earn nearly as much money per week working the large crowds at amusement parks as the average brothel sex worker could earn for herself in the same time frame, and with much less physical danger, risk, and sacrifice of independence. One chorus girl identified only as J.L.D. told vice commissioners that she had enough loyal regulars at Goeller's that her proceeds from drink sales often rivaled the $25 she received each week for singing. "I make as much on commissions for drinks as my salary," the women remarked, "[and] depend more on my friends."[48] Several sitters claimed that they depended on the money they made from the practice to allow them to support families, save some of their income, and stave off extreme hardship. Others, however, framed their participation in the practice less in terms of an economy of makeshifts model that emphasized survival and more in terms of wanting to enjoy luxuries beyond those which their usual salaries would afford them. A forty-year-old burlesque dancer named Daisy, for instance, explained to investigators that she had a long-standing theatrical engagement but resorted to sitting as a means of expanding her disposable income. Daisy claimed that the money she made from drinks allowed her to participate in the consumer culture of the period and "keep herself in trim," which included diamond earrings.[49]

Although sitting itself need only involve flirting and perhaps some kissing or petting in exchange for drinks, many amusement park sitters supplemented their earnings by transitioning between soliciting men for drinks and directly selling sexual services. Emma, a chorus girl from Brooklyn who worked at a Back River amusement park, used sitting as an entry point for prostitution. As she solicited drinks from men, she made it clear to them that intercourse or oral sex were also on the table if

[46] Coleman, *Historic Amusement Parks*, 134; "Kiernan's Hollywood Park," *Sun*, June 30, 1900; "Held for Grand Jury," *Sun*, June 20, 1902; "Hired Girls to Dance. It Is Charged," *Sun*, June 19, 1902.

[47] "Resorts Wide Open: Two Raids Made," *Sun*, July 21, 1913.

[48] MVCR, vol. 1, 209–10.   [49] MVCR, vol. 1, 217–18.

they wished to purchase them. Much of her clientele consisted of sailors who were visiting the city, and waiters at the park assisted her in her solicitations by calling her over to meet men who seemed "likely."[50] Anna, a twenty-eight-year-old New York native who worked in Hollywood Park's Oriental dance show, took up prostitution as a result of economic need. As her career waned due to opium use and the strain that dancing put on her body, Anna found that her weekly salary had been reduced to less than half of what it used to be. She started to offer sexual services to the men who bought her drinks in exchange for additional cash. After prostitution became a regular business, she moved to Highlandtown so that she could see men for intercourse without paying the park $1 per night for the privilege of using its hotel. She claimed to make up to $100 a week through sex work, or nearly four times what she made in her prime as a dancer and more than she could have earned for herself in a brothel. Another singer and burlesque performer from England alleged that prostitution netted her up to $300 on a good week.[51]

As sex workers and sitters operated in amusement parks, so too did members of a newly emerging sexual subculture that was born out of the late nineteenth-century proliferation of amusements: "charity girls." Charity girls were women who performed romantic or sexual favors for men who were willing to provide them the opportunity to enjoy "the association, a dance, moving pictures, ice cream, or a glass of beer."[52] In Baltimore, they came from both the working and the lower-middle classes, but they tended to be young, usually between fourteen and eighteen years of age. As historians Kathy Peiss and Elizabeth Alice Clement have argued, charity girls appeared in cities at the turn of the century as a result of a paradox in turn-of-the-century urban youth culture. On one hand, cities offered young women access to a far larger array of leisure sites, places of amusement, and consumer products than ever before, and young women felt entitled to take advantage of these spaces and to create social worlds for themselves outside their families and the domestic realm.[53] As one commenter who interviewed several young women in Baltimore explained, "They feel that, since they have worked all day and have earned their own money, they have a right in the evening to choose their own pleasure."[54] On the other hand, women's wages were usually insufficient to allow them to take advantage of that access. The dual practices of male treating and female charity represented

[50] MVCR, vol. 1, 208.   [51] MVCR, vol. 1, 207.   [52] MVCR, vol. 1, 193.
[53] Clement, *Love for Sale*; Peiss, *Cheap Amusements*, 110–12.   [54] MVCR, vol. 1, 319.

an attempt on the part of young men and women to negotiate this imbalance. Negotiating with young men to purchase beverages or consumer goods for them instead of directly accepting money made it possible for girls and young women to participate in urban youth culture without crossing over into formal prostitution or sacrificing their reputations or respectability.

Working women and girls who could afford the inexpensive streetcar fare to Baltimore's Back River parks typically approached men in the hopes that they would agree to treat them to rides or tickets to the parks' shows. One undercover investigator who went to Hollywood Park had to stand by the Japanese Rolling Ball Game for only a few minutes before two teenage girls came up to him. After introducing themselves in a way that made it clear that they had no cash – "Why don't you take a chance? If we had money, we certainly would" – one of the girls asked the investigator if he would treat them to a vaudeville show. "If you take us in here, honestly I'd do anything for you," the girl intimated, accenting her suggestion with a squeeze to the investigator's hand.[55] Another girl asked the investigator to take her on a carousel ride. When he obliged, she explained that she was living with her aunt and did not get to come out to the park much, although when she did, "I never want to go home." The girl begged him to call on her again so that they could have "a jolly good time."[56] Other young women the investigator observed sitting in one of the park's casinos went off with two forty-five-year-old men in an automobile after the men agreed to buy them hats.[57]

Charity and treating culture complicated the boundaries between intimacy and commerce as well as those between courtship and prostitution. Although many charity girls only kissed or bestowed casual affections on the men who bought them drinks or presents, other women who accepted drinks or gifts did so with an understanding that men expected sexual favors in return for financial investments. It was not unusual for charity girls to take men back to furnished room houses or other spaces to engage in sex. This exchange of sex for goods or services of monetary value seemed to some observers to veer dangerously close to a form of prostitution, or at the very least an entry point into the commercial sex trade.[58]

---

[55] MVCR, vol. 1, 327.   [56] MVCR, vol. 1, 328.   [57] MVCR, vol. 1, 328–29.
[58] MVCR, vol. 1, 193–203. On charity girls, see also Clement, *Love for Sale*; Peiss, *Cheap Amusements*, 110–13.

And yet, as their counterparts in other cities did, charity girls insisted that they were not prostitutes and that their practices were distinct from prostitution. In many cases, they highlighted the fact that they, unlike sex workers, did not accept cash for sex. Many young women interviewed by the Maryland Vice Commission expressed in forceful terms that they found the mere suggestion that they might receive money from men offensive. A young woman listed only as R.H.S., who made $8.50 per week at her day job and frequented Baltimore's amusement parks at night, denied that she ever asked for money for sex, although she was happy to receive presents.[59] Another young woman, R.M.S., balked at the commissioners' implication that she was a prostitute on the basis of her charity activities. "I never take money," she snapped. "I am no whore."[60] Still another young woman who traded sexual favors for drinks and dinners made it clear that she felt that what she did was distinct from prostitution, a pursuit she would never consider participating in because the stigma of explicit monetary exchange around sex was too great. "[I] would never go into a house [i.e., brothel] to live," she explained. "I could not pick up the nerve to ask for money, and then the fellows put you down as a whore." Charity work allowed her to enjoy the parks while still maintaining a separation between herself and the "whores" who were the subjects of male derision.[61]

Charity girls who insisted on a separation between themselves and sex workers often situated their activities firmly within the realm of fun, courting, and ordinary youth culture rather than commerce. Many young women who traded sex for gifts insisted that they did so because sex had become an expectation for young women who were willing to accept treats and other gifts from men. Women felt that they had to "put out" if they hoped to keep men's attention. O.R.Y., who made $9 per week doing piecework for a hatter's shop, explained to investigators that she did charity work because "I love to dance" but that she relaxed her sexual standards out of necessity: "There is no use going around prim, you would never get a partner."[62] Other charity girls agreed that men expected sex while insisting at the same time that they engaged in it to satisfy their own desire for fun companionship. One young woman named Mazie, who had regular dance dates at one of the shore parks,

---

[59] MVCR, vol. 1, 196.
[60] MVCR, vol. 1, 200. The MVC transcribed the woman's wording as "W——," but the nature of the censored word was obvious.
[61] MVCR, vol. 1, 200.   [62] MVCR, vol. 1, 200.

told investigators that she engaged in sex with men who treated her because she liked them. "Sometimes I meet a nice fellow and fall," she explained.[63] B.B.N., who also frequented the parks, remarked that she was a charity girl because she saw it as a path to finding a man to marry so that she could get away from home.[64] While the vice commissioners who interviewed these women claimed that they were naïve about their romantic prospects and destined for lives of prostitution, even they had to admit that such women often ended up in happy relationships. According to the commissioners, "Many [charity girls] never drift into prostitution, but fall in love with a man, stop their promiscuity, marry and lead respectable and satisfactory lives."[65] This admission, made with great reluctance, revealed the degree to which premarital sexuality had become integrated into mainstream urban youth cultures.

Even as charity girls attempted to distance themselves from sex workers by citing their lack of concern with money and preference for fun and romance, many sex workers began to employ virtually the same rhetoric to explain why they participated in prostitution. Historians often interpret women's willingness to sell sex as a product of their economic desperation and difficulties in keeping themselves afloat in an economy in which women's work was often seasonal and poorly compensated. Although this framework undoubtedly fits the situation of many women who sold sex in Baltimore, it does not take into account the degree to which some sex workers were motivated by more than a desire for subsistence. By the twentieth century, many women who sold sex – particularly white women in the laboring or middle classes – claimed that they chose to do so not because they were desperate to survive (per the economy of makeshifts model) but rather because they wanted the same things that charity girls did: access to entertainment, stylish clothes and accessories, and fun. In 1913, the Maryland Vice Commission interviewed 187 women who worked as streetwalkers in Baltimore about their reasons for entering sex work. A significant number of women cited domestic abuse, familial rape, spousal abandonment, or seduction as a contributing factor, but many other women framed their choices around a desire for a "good time."[66] One woman told investigators that she was a

---

[63] MVCR, vol. 1, 199.   [64] MVCR, vol. 1, 195.   [65] MVCR, vol. 1, 193.

[66] The Maryland Vice Commissioners recorded dozens of pages of responses from women explaining why they chose to go into charity work and prostitution. MVCR, vol. 1, 269–88.

sex worker because she was "fond of life and excitement."[67] Another agreed and claimed that for her, sex work was valuable primarily because it allowed her to access urban entertainments that would be inaccessible without men's assistance. "You can never see anything unless you give up to a fellow," the woman remarked. "Before I did, I never saw a thing. Now, well nothing passes me."[68]

Other women claimed that they sold sex because they wanted to "get good clothes" and take part in a consumer culture that was inaccessible to them on their wages. Some even framed this desire around courtship by pointing out that young men were more likely to be attracted to a woman who was put together in the latest fashions. "I like good clothes and a nice time," said one woman, who added, "Fellows like you better when you dress nice."[69] Although they acknowledged the opportunities their earnings opened to them, several women claimed – in an echo of charity girls' rhetoric – that "pleasure" and excitement were more important to them than financial gain. One woman even told investigators, "Sometimes if I like the fellow, I don't ask for money."[70]

The blurry boundaries between sex workers and women who exchanged sex and affection for food, drink, and favors spoke to how firmly the rise of urban amusements had embedded exchange in young people's cultures of leisure and courtship. Despite charity girls' efforts to distinguish what they did from prostitution, treating served similar purposes to casual forms of sex work and operated on many of the same logics. Moreover, treating normalized the confluence of financial exchange and intimacy to a degree that – arguably – even brothel prostitution had not. After all, despite the fact that they were highly commercialized spaces, brothels throughout the nineteenth century made efforts to conceal the cash nexus in deference to the fact that courting, while certainly influenced in some ways by money, was not supposed to be explicitly commercialized. Brothel workers understood that the appearance of genuine affection and attraction to the men who visited them was part of the appeal of brothel prostitution and that an explicit tit-for-tat exchange undermined that premise. Treating, however, was based on opposite assumptions. While men who treated charity girls undoubtedly entertained the idea that there was real attraction or affection in the relationship, they also participated in a sexual and romantic culture where men derived status *from their ability to pay* for women.

[67] MVCR, vol. 1, 272.   [68] MVCR, vol. 1, 275.   [69] MVCR, vol. 1, 273.
[70] MVCR, vol. 1, 273.

Masculinity in treating culture was rooted in part on the act of bestowing commercial favors on women, who were conceived of as passive recipients of male generosity and support. Though treating was not synonymous with prostitution, it inadvertently succeeded in normalizing sexual exchange and in binding commerce to intimacy more explicitly than many parlor houses did.[71]

And yet, even as women's attempts to gain access to urban leisure made the exchange of sex for resources more mainstream and normalized, it also served in a strange way to marginalize brothels and the women who worked as professional sex workers. Ambiguities in the boundaries between charity exchange and prostitution prompted public anxieties about the morality of youth and the impingement of the market on even the most intimate human relationships. As Elizabeth Clement argued, young women who attempted to navigate this ambiguity and maintain their respectability often resorted to drawing a clear – if often forced – distinction between the treating practices in which they engaged and prostitution. In many cases, this prompted them to adopt a rhetoric of disdain for the "whores" against whose conduct they defined their own courting culture. The result was that sex workers, who had long been relatively accepted figures in working-class culture and participants in broader networks of female aid and solidarity, increasingly became outcasts. Furthermore, as extramarital sex became more embedded and accepted in the realm of courtship, prostitution itself no longer occupied the position it once had in urban youth culture. Paying for sex ceased to be as common of an experience as an increasingly large number of young women, though still a minority, engaged in sex or sexually charged behaviors outside marriage without demanding payment.[72] Patronage of brothels or other spaces in which sex was exchanged for money came to be regarded not just as unfashionable among many working men, but also stigmatized.

That being said, brothels' process of decline was a prolonged one, and they did not disappear from the urban landscape immediately. As late as

---

[71] Clement, *Love for Sale*, lxiv.

[72] Clement, *Love for Sale*. D'Emilio and Freedman, *Intimate Matters*, 240, 256–57. Alfred Kinsey found that 80 percent of women born before 1900 had engaged in premarital petting by the time they were thirty-five. Ninety-one percent of those born after 1900 did. Susan E. Harari and Maris A. Vinovskis, "Adolescent Sexuality, Pregnancy, and Childbearing in the Past," in *The Politics of Pregnancy: Adolescent Sexuality and Public Policy*, ed. Annette Lawson and Deborah L. Rhode (New Haven, CT: Yale University Press, 1993), 20–45.

1910, anti-vice reformers complained that there were 300–350 brothels in the city, although given that there had been more than 280 prosecutions for keeping a bawdy house in 1880 and that Baltimore's population had increased by more than 220,000 people since then, the estimate actually indicated a decline in brothels per capita.[73] Many brothel keepers attempted to keep their establishments afloat by adapting them to new circumstances and attempting to make them sites of entertainment. Several brothels in Old Town, for instance, featured lower levels that were structured similarly to the city's more reputable dance halls. Eubie Blake, who got his start as a paid musician in the late 1890s playing in Aggie Shelton's bordello, described Shelton's establishment as a palatial property with a dance floor. As he recalled, it was not a board-in brothel in the traditional sense: "No girls lived in that house. They had to call the girls up."[74] Nevertheless, the entertainments and the rooms for rent upstairs made Shelton's house a haven for prostitution. Sex workers and would-be clients alike were drawn to the bordello by the sound of the piano drifting into the street and the heady mix of alcohol and dancing it promised. Blake later told an interviewer, "All the girls'd come into the piano room, see, and the men would sit there and drink. And they'd dance just like in a cabaret. Then they'd go upstairs." Shelton offered to pay Blake $3 per night to play ragtime music, which Blake claimed entertained patrons more than the tamer musical offerings that white pianists favored. Blake later recalled that he earned enough in tips from playing the 9 PM to morning shift that he cleared $100 a week and eventually bought his parents' rowhouse. Later, Blake worked at Annie Gilly's dollar house at 317 Rogers Avenue, which did board women, but which also relied on entertainments to attract patrons. The women sitting in the windows "with wrappers on" drew in customers.[75] Other houses that declined to hire musicians installed player pianos in the hopes of creating a lively environment for patrons.

Other brothel keepers attempted to stay afloat by embracing the fact that paid sex was no longer part of mainstream youth culture and offering

---

[73] MVCR, vol. 1, 1; BCCC, All Terms, 1880.

[74] Max Morath, "The 93 Years of Eubie Blake," *American Heritage*, October 1976, www .americanheritage.com/content/93-years-eubie-blake.

[75] Morath, "The 93 Years of Eubie Blake." Interestingly, although Blake claimed in later interviews that he never worked in black "shops" or bordellos, there was a black woman named Ann Gilley who appeared in court records for keeping a bawdy house as early as 1865. See Baltimore City Criminal Court (Criminal Docket), May Term, 1865, Case 113, Ann Gilley.

niche sexual services that were difficult for (some) men to access outside a commercial transaction. By the late nineteenth century, "French houses" that traded in oral sex were becoming increasingly common in Baltimore and other US cities. Oral sex was not a new phenomenon at the time – indeed, it may have been on offer in Baltimore brothels for far longer than limited source materials indicate – but improved hygiene standards boosted its popularity.[76] Houses that were willing to offer it could double the price for service, as oral sex was regarded by many Americans as a form of "perversion" practiced primarily by "disreputable women." Sex workers who were willing to allow oral sex to be performed on them could also charge double their usual rates; cunnilingus, once popular primarily with older male clients who struggled to maintain erections, became a favorite sexual pastime of brothel clients of all ages by the early twentieth century. Several West Baltimore madams told vice investigators that they received multiple requests every day for such services.[77]

Some of these same madams also catered to other kinds of fetishists. A few Baltimore brothels courted the business of sadomasochistic clientele by employing women who were willing to beat or whip male clients or undergo beatings or whippings for a price. Other houses indulged men with paraphilias. A German woman named Aggie Shelton who ran a $5 house in Old Town had one regular client who was a foot fetishist. Eubie Blake, the famed ragtime musician, played at Shelton's house often in the 1890s. He recalled:

Sometimes freak guys would come in. Fellow named "Wine jack" – fine gentleman. You'd never know he was the way he was. If he was going to come in tomorrow night, he'd send over a box of shoes. The women, they'd put on the shoes, and he'd sit and look at them putting on the shoes. The girl that the shoes fit, he'd pick.[78]

By indulging sexual desires that were outside the mainstream, brothels like Shelton's managed to recast prostitution as a sexual domain where men could satisfy needs that were inaccessible outside paid sex. In doing so, they carved a new place for themselves in the sexual marketplace and staved off obsolescence for another day.

And yet, even as brothels grew increasingly marginal, the women (and some men) who kept and labored within them would suffer as a result of

---

[76] Sharon Ullman observed that gay men who participated in oral sex described it as "the twentieth-century way." Ullman, *Sex Seen: The Emergence of Modern Sexuality in America* (Berkeley: University of California Press, 1997), especially 66.
[77] MVCR, vol. 1, 102–3.   [78] Morath, "The 93 Years of Eubie Blake."

their similarities to other forms of sexual exchange that predominated in the early twentieth century. Young people in Baltimore increasingly understood prostitution – and particularly the culture of prostitution that existed within brothels – as distinct from the treating and courtship culture that proliferated in the city's sites of entertainment and leisure. As Chapter 9 will detail, however, middle-class reformers and moralists often failed to make the same distinction. As they observed young men and women mingling in dance halls, concert saloons, and movie theaters, reformers grew anxious that sexual "immorality" was reaching dangerous proportions in the city. They understood charity girls, flirtatious women, and sitters as young women situated on a path that eventually led to prostitution, disease, and death. Anxious about public morals and about the role that concert saloon keepers, hotel and amusement park proprietors, theater owners, and others played in enabling prostitution and other forms of commercial sex for their own profit, reformers began to issue calls for state interventions into the prostitution business.

9

The End of an Era

In the fall of 1914, an unnamed woman went around town calling on Baltimore's leading "jewelers, shoe merchants, druggists, milliners, tailors, and heads of department stores." She told them all the same thing: "I am a madam, conducting a house with eight girls. I wish to buy all my goods from you, if I can make suitable arrangements."[1] The arrangements she proposed involved price inflation: she would deposit $1,000 in cash with the store in return for the storekeeper agreeing to overcharge the women who resided in her brothel by 20–30 percent. The storekeeper would then pass the surplus along to her or, if the women borrowed against her account, simply let her claim the excess debt. The caller noted that of nearly sixty men and women she queried, only seven outright rejected her offer. Most were eager to make arrangements for markups of at least 10 percent, and several confided that they already had similar deals in effect with other madams in the city. Even the people who expressed strident disapproval of prostitution reasoned that their willingness to collude with a madam was justified. If they did not take the money, someone else – possibly someone with fewer scruples – inevitably would.[2]

None of the storekeepers ever received their deposit, for the anonymous woman was not a madam. Instead, she was an undercover agent hired at the behest of the state by the Maryland Vice Commission (MVC). The MVC had been created the previous year by Maryland's Republican governor, Phillips Lee Goldsborough, and was part of a wave of more

---

[1] MVCR, vol. 1, 45.   [2] MVCR, vol. 1, 145–66.

than sixty similar commissions tasked with investigating commercialized vice in cities around the country during the early twentieth century. After three years of undercover operations, visits to known brothels and sites of labor and amusement about town, and interviews with hundreds of people involved with the sex trade, the MVC compiled a five-volume, 1,200-page report on vice and sexual immorality in Maryland. The first volume of the report was devoted to prostitution. In it, MVC members detailed the backgrounds, living conditions, and health of Baltimore's sex workers; the homes and working conditions that led them into prostitution; and the vast numbers of apparently legitimate citizens – storekeepers, merchants, landlords, liquor dealers, police, and politicians – who profited from their labor.[3] The undercover agents' and vice commissioners' observations about the working conditions in brothels convinced them that the brothel trade was an exploitative one that made young women victims of rapacious profiteers. By 1915, the commissioners recommended that the Baltimore police close the city's remaining red-light districts.

The MVC's recommendation that Baltimore's already ailing brothels be shut down for good represented a sharp departure from the city's decades-old practice of tolerating establishments that contained sexuality indoors and within easily regulated zones. And yet it was a departure that had been foreshadowed for years. Since the 1870s, Baltimore had been home to an active social purity crusade whose members demanded that the city cease its toleration and tacit sanctioning of brothel prostitution. These social purity crusaders, like their counterparts in cities around the country, came from a diverse coalition of evangelical Christians (and some Catholics), good governance advocates, women's rights supporters, public health lobbyists, and members of the local middle class who were concerned about property values. Although they enjoyed only modest successes in attacking prostitution and other forms of sexual "immorality" in the first decades of their movement's existence, social purity crusaders' longtime alliances with anti-machine Progressives granted them a significant public platform as reform Democrats and Republicans began to win state elections in the early twentieth century. Reformers seized on public anxieties about women's changing roles in the industrial economy and the disruptions it wrought on the existing economic and social relationships between men and women to foment

[3] MVCR, vols. 1–5.

opposition to the sex trade. Prostitution, which sat at the intersection of a number of issues concerning gender, sex inequality, and the exploitative nature of free market capitalism, became in the hands of a new generation of social purity crusaders the ultimate metaphor for women's vulnerability at the hands of greedy business owners and urban politicians.[4]

Although the Maryland Vice Commission was not composed of dedicated social purity crusaders, the types of questions they asked about vice in the course of their investigation were shaped by the efforts of the social purity movement. Understanding that movement and its critiques of the gender and labor dimensions of urban capitalism is vital to understanding how city and state officials came to reject red-light districts and turn against a trade that had long been part of the city's social and economic fabric.

Baltimore, like many American cities, developed the first stirrings of a social purity crusade in the years immediately following the Civil War, when proposals for the medical regulation of prostitution were common. As physicians sought to expand their authority by lobbying the state to license or create a system of medical inspection for sex workers, a coalition of evangelical Christians, Catholics, and early woman's rights crusaders rose up to oppose what they understood as the state sanctioning of vice. Opponents of medical regulation questioned why the state should have an interest in making the purchase of sex safe for men, and they challenged proposals that would require women to undergo invasive, humiliating exams while exempting their male clients from any similar inspection. In the aftermath of their success at stifling efforts at medical regulation, social purity campaigners expanded their discourses about rejecting state sanctioning of vice into broader critiques of the state's policies of tolerating brothels and other forms of sexual immorality.

In 1886, Baltimore's Ministerial Union, a group composed of socially active Protestant clergy, held the first of what would become a series of meetings at the local YMCA to discuss the creation of an organization that would oppose state-sanctioned vice and take an active role in

---

[4] Mark Thomas Connelly was among the first to argue that progressive anti-vice campaigns were a result of anxieties about the both the decline of "civilized morality" and women's changing roles in the industrial economy. Connelly, *The Response to Prostitution in the Progressive Era* (Chapel Hill: University of North Carolina Press, 1980). Mara Keire argued that white slavery scares in particular were rooted in anxieties about trusts and their exploitative tendencies. Mara L. Keire, "The Vice Trust: A Reinterpretation of the White Slavery Scare in the United States, 1907–1917," *Journal of Social History* 35, no. 1 (Autumn 2001): 5–41.

promoting social morality.[5] The group's primary concern was the effect
that increased urbanization and the rise of urban leisure culture was
having on young men and women who left their homes in search of work.
Hoping to find ways to protect urban youth from what they saw as a
growing number of temptations to sin, Ministerial Union members
looked to Anthony Comstock's New York Society for the Suppression
of Vice (NYSSV) as an inspiration. Comstock, who had helped to found
the NYSSV in 1873, made a career of targeting the vendors and carriers of
"obscene" materials and raiding brothels, pornography shops, and other
disreputable businesses in New York City. He had also been instrumental
in securing the passage of federal laws banning obscene materials, including information about birth control, from the mails.[6] Baltimore's minister
invited Comstock and NYSSV President Samuel Colgate to speak at their
meeting. Colgate urged Baltimoreans to take action against vice. "The
devil is at work to corrupt our children," he warned, "and it is our duty to
eradicate the evil influences he employs."[7]

Though the assembled crowd was apparently moved by the speeches, it
would be nearly two years before a Baltimore Society for the Suppression
of Vice (BSSV) formed. The society was finally organized in December
1887 and chartered the following year. The early BSSV had wide-ranging
policy aims, including eradicating prostitution and saloons and eliminating the sale of birth control and abortion services as means of discour-
aging sexual licentiousness. The organization claimed that its goals were
nothing short of the moral elevation of the city. In keeping with the
practices of its counterpart in New York, the BSSV used heavily religious
and moralistic arguments to justify attacks on obscenity in all its forms,
from distasteful newspaper advertisements to risqué literature, art, and
even neon signs. They tried to prevent theaters from showing certain
plays, and they policed new sites of entertainment by insisting that
amusement parks honor Sunday liquor laws and that movie houses
strictly enforce their policies against admitting boys under the age of
fourteen without an adult. The organization also went after a number
of local businesses that it deemed disreputable and contrary to public

[5] "Indecent Showbills," *Sun*, Feb. 23, 1886; "Suppression of Vice," *Sun*, Mar. 22, 1886;
"The Suppression of Vice," *Sun*, Mar. 23, 1886; "The Suppression of Vice. Address by
Mr. Anthony Comstock, of New York," *Sun*, Mar. 24, 1886; "Ministerial Union," *Sun*,
Nov. 1, 1887.
[6] On Comstock, see Beisel, *Imperiled Innocents*; Giesberg, *Sex and the Civil War*, 59–103.
[7] "Anthony Comstock in Baltimore," *The Sun*, Dec. 19, 1887, 4.

morals. Saloons, gambling halls, and any "disorderly" houses – including brothels – were favorite targets.[8]

While the BSSV had its roots in religion, it drew a larger pool of support from members of the urban middle class, particularly native-born, white, professional men and women who were anxious about their children's futures. Historian Nicola Biesel has argued that the NYSSV succeeded in part because it tapped into potent middle-class anxieties about reproduction and the continued prosperity and health of future generations. The period following the Civil War saw the rapid growth of the urban middle class, but that growth was accompanied by fears on the part of the new urban bourgeois that they would not be able to pass their accumulated economic and social capital on to their children. Between influxes of new immigrant groups that threatened native-born, white political dominance and the rise of leisure spaces that offered new kinds of temptations for youth, it seemed possible that class-based power might slip away.[9] Older generations of Baltimoreans who were alarmed by the new cultures of sexual license and loosely supervised courting found solace in the BSSV's promises to shutter the establishments and censor the materials that might lead their children astray. By promising to shield youth from immorality, reformers sought to ensure that children's reputations remained intact so that they could enjoy the same wealth, prestige, and status as their parents did.[10]

In addition to positioning itself as the protector of youth, the newly founded BSSV also touted itself as a cure for Maryland's political ills. Around the same time the society was gaining traction locally, Maryland politics were in the midst of a transition. Maryland had been a solidly Democratic state since the immediate aftermath of the Civil War, when formerly Unionist politicians like Thomas Swann converted to the Democratic Party in the hopes of stemming Radical Republican influence in Maryland. By the 1880s, Maryland politics were dominated by a political

---

[8] "To Suppress Vice: A Big Meeting to Protest against the Places on East Baltimore Street," *Sun*, May 28, 1888; "The Ministerial Union: Upholding Strict Observance of the Sabbath and Other Matters," *Sun*, Mar. 30, 1886.

[9] Beisel, *Imperiled Innocents*, 49. Notably, Baltimore was not as popular a destination for immigration as other urban areas; indeed, by 1910 it had the fewest foreign-born residents – around 16 percent – of any major US city (Bureau of Labor, *The Slums of Baltimore, Chicago, New York, and Philadelphia*, 40). Nevertheless, the presence of greater numbers of Eastern European and German Jewish immigrants did cause anxiety among some Baltimore reformers.

[10] Beisel, *Imperiled Innocents*, 49–75.

machine headed by Democrats Arthur Pue Gorman and Isaac Freeman Rasin. Gorman, a long-serving US Senator, and Rasin, the clerk of Baltimore's Court of Common Pleas, were a savvy political duo with strong support among both workingmen and elites. Their machine was weak in comparison to Tammany Hall and other notable machines because of Baltimore's relatively small immigrant population and limited patronage opportunities in the municipal government. However, Gorman and Rasin proved adept at consolidating a base in Baltimore City and other parts of the state, and they held a good deal of control over political appointments in Maryland from the mid-1870s until the mid-1890s.

Unsurprisingly, however, their dominance in state politics brought them a number of political enemies in the form of Republicans and reform Democrats who were dissatisfied with both the Gorman–Rasin ticket's financial management of Baltimore and its hold on local politics. Reformers protested that loyalty to party or machine was a poor qualification on which to judge applicants for public positions, and they demanded that governments put city interests (or what reformers perceived as such) over partisan ones. When the Baltimore Society for the Suppression of Vice formed, many proponents of "good governance" attached themselves to the BSSV as a means of attacking the Gorman–Rasin power base and gaining more influence for their movement.[11]

Political reformers understood anti-vice campaigns like the BSSV as part and parcel of a broader attack on urban machine politics, in large part because of the nature of the machine's revenue apparatuses. Gorman and Rasin funded their political ambitions by requiring kickbacks from officials ranging from teachers to police officers, as well as by skimming from state funds. Rasin's position as clerk of the court was particularly crucial to his power, as it gave him control over accounts containing the fines levied on criminals and license violators, including bawdy-house keepers. The interest accrued on those accounts went to fund machine activities, as did protection money that police extorted from local brothel keepers, saloon proprietors, and other disreputable business owners. Machines, in turn, used saloons as centers for dispensing patronage that solidified their political influence with the lower classes.[12]

Political reformers were well aware of the economic networks that supported the machines, and they used the existence of these networks

[11] Brugger, *Maryland: A Middle Temperament*, 388–406.
[12] Brugger, *Maryland: A Middle Temperament*, 397–98.

to discredit machine politics as hopelessly corrupt. Many Republicans and reform Democrats around the country decried the political machines for being dominated by the urban "residuum," that is, immoral, uneducated, and low-class persons. Charles J. Bonaparte, a mugwump and future progressive Republican who led campaigns against the Gorman–Rasin machine, gave public speeches in which he asked, "Who put our public officers in their places?" He answered by proclaiming that "the saloon and houses of vice are the nurseries of the so-called statesmen."[13] Howard A. Kelly, a Johns Hopkins gynecologist and devout Christian who would become head of the Society for the Suppression of Vice, wrote in his journal, "The brewers, the saloon men, the bawdy houses, the grafting politicians, the pimps all stick together. You touch one you stir up the whole world of evil to activity."[14] By lobbying for crackdowns on sexual vice and liquor sales, anti-machine reformers hoped to deprive the machines of their financial base and pave the way for "rational" and merit-based government to replace the loyalty system.[15]

Given the overlapping agendas of political and moral reform activists, it is perhaps unsurprising that many members of the BSSV were also members of the Baltimore Reform League, an organization founded in 1884 for the purpose of promoting good and rational governance locally. Bonaparte, who was both devoutly Catholic and adamantly opposed to machine governance, pioneered the Reform League and became the BSSV's Vice President. John C. Rose, an executive committee member of the Reform League, became the longtime secretary of the BSSV and one of its most vocal spokesmen. Prominent reform Republicans Daniel Ammidon and Morris A. Soper, both of whom would eventually play a central role in the dismantling of the red-light districts as part of the city's Police Board, also became officers in the BSSV.[16]

The BSSV's fortunes remained tied to the success of political reform movements through the 1890s and into the twentieth century. As anti-machine coalitions picked up steam in the early 1890s, the society grew more ambitious in its reform agenda. In its first three years of existence, the BSSV succeeded in campaigning for the removal of brothels from particular neighborhoods and in convincing the Liquor Board to reduce

[13] "Suppression of Vice," *Sun*, Jan. 21, 1898.
[14] Howard A. Kelly, diary, undated entry [likely May 14], May 1914–June 20, 1914, Folder 25/7, Kelly Collection.
[15] On the connections between anti-machine politics and anti-vice activism in other US cities, see Keire, *For Business and Pleasure*, especially 6–8.
[16] "The War against Evil," *Sun*, Jan. 14, 1891.

the number of licensed saloons in the city from 2,802 to 2,008. Embold-
ened by these victories, members set their sights on reforming the practices of the Criminal Court with regard to brothels.[17] In particular, BSSV
leadership was frustrated by what it perceived as the increased routinization with which the court treated bawdy-house cases. The criminal court
had for decades been lenient in the fines it issued to brothel keepers, but
by the 1880s it has ceased to require that they even make an appearance
for arraignment. Once madams were indicted, the sheriff was sent out
with a capias warrant that listed the amount the fine would be in case of a
guilty plea. Madams who wished to end the matter then and there could
pay the fine and fees to avoid making a trip to the courthouse. From the
city's point of view, the practice was far cheaper and more efficient for the
already overburdened court system. From the point of view of the BSSV,
however, the practice smacked of the state conspiring with madams to
lessen the consequences of vice and refusing to take seriously the enforcement of the law banning bawdy houses.[18]

In 1893, the BSSV petitioned the court to alter its long-standing
practice of salutary neglect toward "orderly" brothels and adopt a
harsher stance toward bawdy-house keepers. To support their plea, they
cited a recent change to the Maryland criminal code that had no doubt
been prompted in part by their activism. In 1892, Maryland lawmakers
had voted overwhelmingly to update the criminal code to make keeping a
bawdy house a misdemeanor punishable by a fine of up to $500, impris-
onment in jail or the house of corrections for up to a year, or both.[19]
While this new law was roughly in keeping with how the courts had been
punishing bawdy-house keepers for decades, it did make one notable
change to the existing practice: it eliminated provisions that stated that
half of all the fines levied on bawdy-house keepers be given to the public
dispensaries. In their petition to the Supreme Bench, the BSSV insisted
that the change in the law concerning fines eliminated any legal basis for
treating bawdy-house charges as a unique class of misdemeanor. With
nothing to separate bawdy-house keepers from any other criminals, the
BSSV insisted that the court cease its practice of routinized fining in favor
of handling bawdy houses cases as they did other misdemeanor offenses.
That meant not allowing madams to avoid court dates and not calling

---

[17] "City News in Brief," *Sun*, Apr. 26, 1890; "To Suppress Vice," *Sun*, Dec. 19, 1888.
[18] "The Offenders' Parade," *Sun*, July 1, 1893.
[19] *Laws of the State of Maryland*, Ch. 522, Sec. 16 (Baltimore: John Murphy & Co.,
   1892), 725.

madams to court one after the other in one term of the court instead of prosecuting them as their offenses came to the attention of local authorities. The State's Attorney acceded to the demands.[20]

The court's pledge to reform prosecutorial practice was a victory for the BSSV, but the society nevertheless faced several stumbling blocks to fulfilling its agenda. By far the biggest impediment to their goals was that Baltimore police seemed disinterested in assisting the organization in cracking down on brothels, saloons, and other disorderly establishments. Baltimore had lost municipal control of its police force in 1857 as a result of well-founded allegations that local control had led to the police becoming a partisan instrument. Maryland's governor was charged with appointing members to the city's Board of Police Commissioners (also called the Police Board), which, in turn, controlled appointments of local officers as well as the police marshal. The Police Board's members were partisan appointees who were understandably not eager to help their political opponents.

Additionally, beat cops in Baltimore sometimes augmented their salaries with bribes from neighborhood saloon owners, brewing companies, and houses of ill fame, all of whom paid officers to look the other way when they violated the law. The acceptance of bribes was common enough that officers felt little shame in it. Indeed, many of them came from the ranks of working men who regarded prostitution as either a benign bit of fun or, at worst, a necessary evil, and some were active patrons of bawdy houses.[21] Howard A. Kelly, who made a practice of visiting brothels in the Hook and other areas of East Baltimore in the 1910s, noted that the women in the area told him of sexual liaisons with the police. Alice Brown, a sex worker operating around Canton Avenue, told Kelly that she had stayed with an Officer German at least fifteen times and offered a description of unusual marks on the head of his penis as proof.[22] With many police officers apathetic or averse to cracking down

---

[20] "The Offenders' Parade," *Sun*, July 1, 1893; "The City Courts," *Sun*, Mar. 1, 1893, 8; "Maryland Criminal Law and Practice," *Sun*, May 11, 1893, 8. See also "Mr. Kerr's Answer," *Sun*, May 23, 1888, 1.

[21] Undercover MVC officers interviewed numerous police officers about their feelings on sexual vice. Most supported segregation, and many insisted that commercial sex was a natural outlet for male desires. MVCR, vol. 1, 346–58.

[22] Howard A. Kelly, diary, undated entry, May 1914–June 20, 1914, Folder 25/7, Kelly Collection. According to Kelly, Brown claimed that "Of. German has same mark blue on top penis." The words "Like a Jew blue glans" were crossed out but still legible in the journal.

on the prostitution trade, the BSSV chose to bypass law enforcement in favor of attacking the commercial side of vice operations by appealing to the Liquor Board to rescind the licenses of disorderly house keepers. The tactic enjoyed only mixed success.[23]

The BSSV would have much better luck after Republicans and anti-Machine Democrats finally succeeded in defeating the Gorman–Rasin ticket in 1895. Following the machine candidates' ouster, the Police Board fell under the control of reform Republicans and Democrats. Grateful for the BSSV's help in supporting their push for "rational" governance and discrediting their political opponents, members of the new reform administration threw their support behind the society. Within a year of the election, the BSSV succeeded in getting the Liquor Board to rescind the liquor licenses of numerous individuals whom its counsel claimed were disreputable.[24]

At the same time the BSSV was beginning to enjoy greater political influence, the urban economy was changing in ways that made Baltimoreans more receptive to the organization's anti-vice messages. Prostitution sat at the intersection of labor, commerce, and intimacy, which made the sex trade a potent site of anxieties about the market economy's reach and the potentially dehumanizing and exploitative nature of life under industrial capitalism. Such anxieties were rampant in a turn-of-the-century world characterized by the growth of factories, wealth inequality, and the dramatic consolidation of economic power. Baltimoreans in the early 1900s found themselves occupying an increasingly corporatized world of work, one that highlighted both the contingent nature of labor and the vulnerability of workers in the face of increasingly impersonal labor structures. The late 1800s witnessed a period of rapid economic change and industrialization that shook the foundations of both middle-class and laboring people's lives. Mechanization and the rise of factories altered the nature of labor for people who worked in industries like oyster canning, box making, tobacco processing, and clothing production.

Meanwhile, corporations began to exert increasing influence on the local economy. During the first half of the nineteenth century, it was typical for businesses to employ only a handful of people. By 1890,

---

[23] Crenson, *Baltimore: A Political History*, 230–32. On the use of liquor laws and commercial regulation to eliminate vice, see Keire, *For Business and Pleasure*, 9–10; "Ministers against Saloons," *Sun*, Apr. 7, 1897. On the perceived (but ambiguous) relationship between anti-prostitution and prohibition activism, see Connelly, *The Response to Prostitution in the Progressive Era*, 24–26.

[24] Crenson, *Baltimore: A Political History*, 317–18.

Baltimore was home to ninety-seven corporations, many of which employed large workforces. By 1905, over 17 percent of the city's 374 industries were incorporated, and over half of all working city residents were employed by incorporated businesses.[25] As more and more Baltimoreans found themselves working for corporate entities that controlled the means of production, the ideal of the independent artisan-producer that had formed such a crucial part of men's social and political identities in the early nineteenth century lost its purchase. Many laboring men found themselves working for larger employers who treated them as contingent, kept wages low, and suppressed labor protests (often with the support of the state and local police). Even middle-class men, who enjoyed a position of privilege relative to laborers, found themselves working in an increasingly impersonal and anonymous environment. While reform movements and social clubs that flourished at the turn of the century helped to remedy their feelings of disconnectedness, they nevertheless feared that the consolidation of power and wealth in the hands of corporate interests threatened their influence and political standing.[26]

Anxieties about the changing nature of work and consolidation of economic power with corporations were coupled with anxieties about women's roles in the new economic order. As noted in Chapter 8, women at the turn of the century were entering waged labor in larger numbers than in any decades previous. The changing nature of work gave women a degree of mobility and economic independence that was unprecedented, but it also brought new concerns about disruptions to their familial roles and about their vulnerability as they entered public spaces in larger numbers. Many city residents feared that women working under the supervision of male bosses who dictated the pace and terms of their labor would be vulnerable to sexual overtures or even coercion by their superiors, a fear that was understandable given that control over women's labor and sexual access to their bodies historically had been overlapping rights of men under household labor regimes. Fears that female laborers would be "ruined" by their superiors combined with fears that long hours

---

[25] Statistics taken from Haag, "'Commerce in Souls'," 293–95.

[26] Kimmel, *Manhood in America*, 87–104; John Kasson, *Houdini, Tarzan, and the Perfect Man: The White Male Body and the Challenge of Modernity in America* (New York: Hill & Wang, 2002), 157–218; Anthony Rotundo, *American Manhood: Transformations in Masculinity from the Revolutionary to the Modern Era* (New York: Basic Books, 1993), chapters 8 and 9.

and difficult labor conditions might further disrupt them from assuming their "natural" roles as mothers and wives. The ultimate anxiety was that employers, who had no bonds of affection with or obligation to their female employees, would usurp rights that naturally belonged to husbands – and with poor results. Lacking a sense of duty and affection toward dependents that might temper their baser instincts, corporations and their agents could easily exploit the vulnerable women whose livelihoods they sustained.[27]

Fears that women would be exploited by their employers mingled with fears that they would be taken advantage of sexually or otherwise lured from the path of propriety as they moved through mixed and sometimes disreputable urban spaces. The proliferation of dance halls, shops, and leisure venues that catered to young laboring women or to mixed-sex crowds of youth made the city a space of both sexual possibility and sexual danger for female youth.[28] Not only might such sites tempt women to abandon their normal propriety for the sake of accessing amusements, but they also removed women from the realm of family surveillance of courtship practices.[29] This was especially the case for the many young women and girls who had no family in the city to monitor their activities. Historian Pamela Haag estimated that 30 percent of Baltimore's female workforce in the early twentieth century consisted of women who had left homes in the countryside or in other towns to find employment.[30] Many of these women lived in boardinghouses or furnished room houses with little in the way of family supervision or guidance on how to navigate urban life. Their freedom and their vulnerability in the face of the decline of older household structures were sources of anxiety for many urban residents, particularly as youth cultures that involved some degree of sexual exchange began to develop and displace older models of commercial sexuality. Social purity crusaders, in particular, expressed distress at

[27] On reformers' anxieties about women's entrance into the waged labor economy, see, for instance, Howard A. Kelly, "Dr. Howard A. Kelly Points Out One of the Foremost Causes of Vice and Immorality," *Evening Sun*, Dec. 28, 1915.

[28] James H. Adams, *Urban Reform and Sexual Vice in Progressive-Era Philadelphia: The Faithful and the Fallen* (Lanham, MD: Lexington Books, 2015), 40.

[29] Many historians of the Progressive era have documented contemporary anxieties about women's entrance into the work force leading to sexual immorality. See, among many others, Mary E. Odem, *Delinquent Daughters: Protecting and Policing Adolescent Female Sexuality in the United States, 1885–1920* (Chapel Hill: University of North Carolina Press, 1995); Meyerowitz, *Women Adrift*, especially 43–68.

[30] Haag, "'Commerce in Souls,'" 295.

the perceived breakdown of "traditional" relations between men and women ushered in by urbanization, industrial capitalism, and the rise of new working-class leisure cultures.[31]

Anxieties about larger economic and social forces rendering women sexually vulnerable culminated in the "white slavery" panic that swept the United States in the second decade of the twentieth century. In the United States, the term "white slavery" had originally been used to describe the disadvantaged circumstances of waged workers in US cities. Around the turn of the century, it took on new, gendered meanings.[32] Anti-vice reformers began to use the term to refer to the forced prostitution of American or (sometimes) immigrant women, often at the hands of ethnic or racial minorities who were working for larger networks of procurers or vice-mongers. Rumors of white women being forced or otherwise into prostitution by black, Jewish, or Chinese men circulated widely in American cities by 1908, as did stories in which immigrant women were duped into brothels by native-born urban dwellers. In Baltimore, such narratives gained popularity around the same time that the city was turning to legalized forms of racial segregation, which was not coincidental. White slave narratives often cast black men as villain figures whose nefariousness contrasted with the virtue and innocence of white women. Historian Brian Donovan has argued that the concept of white slavery itself served to reinforce racial boundaries and justify racial prejudice. However, white slavery narratives as they emerged in the media also emphasized women's exploitation at the hands of corporatized "vice trusts." Movies, books, and magazines all featured melodramatic and sensational stories – both fictional and allegedly true – about white women being ensnared into sex work and prevented from leaving through intimidation or debts levied on them by their captors.[33] According to historian Mara Keire, the language of white slavery reflected anxieties about "political and economic disempowerment of ordinary citizens" under an increasingly corporatized economy.[34]

Whether or not white slavery was a "true" phenomenon in any sense of that term, white slavery narratives' emergence marked a turning point

---

[31] Meyerowitz, *Women Adrift.*
[32] Keire, "The Vice Trust," 5–41; Donovan, *White Slave Crusades*; Rosen, *The Lost Sisterhood*, 112–36.
[33] Donovan, *White Slave Crusades*, particularly chapter 1.
[34] Keire, "The Vice Trust," 7.

in the success of the urban anti-vice movements in Baltimore and in other cities. Baltimore social purity crusaders seized on and peddled white slavery narratives as a means of lending their anti-vice crusade a sense of urgency that it had lacked for much of the nineteenth century. It was not simply sensationalism that made allegations of white slavery such a potent weapon in the hands of moral reformers, although sensationalism undeniably helped to attract media attention and an audience for anti-vice efforts. Instead, it was white slavery narratives' ability to open up broader discussions about prostitution and its coerciveness. By shifting the conversation about commercial sex to focus on forms of sex work in which women had no agency, reformers began to chip away at the nineteenth-century notion that prostitutes were morally corrupted in ways that made them inherently different from other women. The white slave was a prostitute, but her path into sex work was not of her own making. Instead, her sexual vulnerability was the result of nefarious collusion by greedy profiteers who were willing to sacrifice her virtue for profit. The parallels between this vision of white slavery and anxieties about industrial and other employers' willingness to exploit women's labor were obvious. Not only did these parallels lend potency to anti-prostitution campaigns by rendering the prostitute the ultimate symbol of broader forms of sexual and labor exploitation, but they also generated public sympathy for sex workers who had previously been granted little. The supposed helplessness of sex workers made them pathetic figures in the eyes of Baltimoreans who might otherwise care little about them. More acutely still, it highlighted for members of vulnerable groups that their own children and family members might be at risk of being lured or kidnapped into sex work, even if their upbringings might discourage them from entering sex work voluntarily.[35]

White slavery narratives proved to be a powerful tool in the hands of Baltimore's social purity crusaders because they challenged in fundamental ways the segregationist logic that had governed local authorities' approaches to prostitution since the 1860s. Baltimore's courts, neighborhood associations, and police had begun to create red-light districts based on the belief that the best way to manage vice was to contain it in particular areas where it would not affect white property values or corrupt the children of respectable white families. Red-light districts

---

[35] Rosen, *The Lost Sisterhood*, 112–36; Connelly, *The Response to Prostitution in the Progressive Era*, 114–34; Doezema, *Sex Slaves and Discourse Masters*; Keire, "The Vice Trust."

maintained the boundaries between respectable and disreputable people and, according to their supporters, protected "good" women from becoming victims to men's sexual lusts by allowing men a designated sexual outlet with fallen ones.[36] And yet, as Peter C. Hennigan has argued, white slavery narratives gave the lie to the notion that prostitution could be successfully segregated.[37] The alleged presence of white slavery in cities suggested that the corruption that coalesced in red-light districts extended its tendrils to ensnare respectable women and that vice profiteers were more than willing to steal women from outside their districts. Brothels may have been contained within poorer, black areas of the city, but they ensnared vulnerable white women just the same. The tendency of white slavery narratives to highlight the failures of brothel segregation proved to be a crucial intellectual contribution to the anti-vice movement, and it paved the way for red-light abatement efforts.[38]

In the hands of particularly adept anti-vice reformers, fears of white slavery also became a means of expanding the conversation about the exploitative nature of sex work beyond kidnapping. Many moral reformers in Baltimore and other cities insisted that white slavery should not be so narrowly defined as to refer to kidnapping alone and that, indeed, white slavery encompassed all forms of prostitution. Howard A. Kelly, who participated in the BSSV and various medical and social hygiene societies, was among the most outspoken of these reformers. Kelly, who believed that white slavery was "the worst plague spot on the social body today," regularly spoke against it at both churches and medical society meetings.[39] In a speech given before the American Medical Association, Kelly decried white slavery's effects on the physical and moral health of American cities and blamed it for hundreds of infant deaths, the breakdown of law, and three billion dollars in costs to the state each year. Although Kelly evoked the more sensationalist definition of white slavery by insisting that a woman in the next trade was "nearly always coaxed, dragged or cajoled into her life of shame," he made it contextually clear that he used white slavery synonymously with prostitution as a whole. For Kelly, coercion was not limited to kidnapping or threats. Rather, it was the sum total of social forces that placed pressure on young women to

---

[36] Shumsky, "Tacit Acceptance," 665–79.   [37] Hennigan, "Property War," 126–27.
[38] Hennigan, "Property War," 126–27.
[39] Howard A. Kelly, "The Social Diseases and Their Effects on the Community," *Journal of the American Medical Association* 59, no. 14 (Oct. 6, 1912): 1312.

avoid devastating poverty by entering sex work.[40] Citing low wages, industrial greed, poor housing conditions, exploitative pimps, corrupt public officials who took bribes from vice lords, and broader apathy on the part of Christians and other citizens to sex workers, Kelly insisted that the most dangerous white slaver was not a shadowy villain who stalked alleys and opium dens. Instead, it was a society that shrugged its shoulders at prostitution even as many of its members filled their pockets with its proceeds. In a broadside he had printed on the causes of prostitution, Kelly listed the "crime inducing and fostering of all others" as "THE UTTER INDIFFERENCE OF THE WELL-TO-DO AND THE MORALLY EDUCATED DEVOTED SOLELY TO THEIR OWN SELFISH INTERESTS IN LIFE."[41] Any given sex worker, Kelly insisted, "is really the poor suffering victim of our civilization."[42]

Kelly and other reformers' expansive definition of white slavery, critiques of industrial wage structures, and tendency to decry systems that subjugated women to the whims of men proved tremendously successful at attracting diverse coalitions to the anti-vice movement. Although Kelly himself was ardently Christian and deeply conservative in a number of ways, the anti-vice movement under his direction won the support of a wide range of people: religious leaders, fellow physicians who were concerned with the role of sexual vice in spreading "social diseases" like syphilis and gonorrhea, labor advocates, woman suffrage activists, and the usual array of anti-machine politicos. Advocates for women's rights in particular saw in anti-vice activism a reflection of their own frustrations with the marginalized position of women in society, as well as a powerful rejection of the notion that women's needs – and indeed, their basic dignity – should be subordinated to the needs of men. Critiques like those the BSSV levied on white slavery helped to make the prostitute a paramount symbol of women's oppression. The need to overturn white slavery and dismantle the "vice trusts," in turn, became a focal point for arguments in favor of women's political enfranchisement. Woman suffrage advocates such as Dr. Florence Sabin of the Just Governance League used the looming threat of white slavery, broadly defined, as evidence of the necessity of woman suffrage. According to Sabin, women's enfranchisement was one means by which corrupt officeholders

---

[40] Kelly, "The Social Diseases and Their Effects on the Community," 1312.

[41] Howard A. Kelly, "Prostitution: Its Causes" (flyer), 1903 and n.d., Box 23, Folder 11, Kelly Collection.

[42] Kelly, "The Social Diseases and Their Effects on the Community," 1312.

could be swept out and the immorality of white slavery could be eradicated.[43]

The white slavery scare brought so much attention to prostitution that Baltimore soon witnessed an explosion of anti-vice organizations and activism. The Colored Law and Order League (founded 1908), Johns Hopkins physician Donald Hooker's Maryland Society for Social Hygiene (founded 1908), and the Baltimore Women's Civic League (founded 1911) all joined the BSSV in lobbying for the eradication of white slavery and tolerated vice in Baltimore. While the organizations differed in their approaches to the vice problem, most shared a general progressive concern with bettering urban living conditions. Eliminating tolerated prostitution as a means of ending white slavery came to be a core part of their broader project of clearing slums, improving public health and labor conditions, and overhauling the state and municipal governments.[44] In the 1910s, Kelly, Hooker, and their compatriot and fellow anti-vice crusader Rev. Kenneth G. Murray formed a coalition of local church leaders with a commitment to combatting indifference toward vice within their congregations. Kelly, who was a primary organizing force behind the group, consciously aimed his efforts at a diversity of denominations and groups around the city, including black ministers. Throughout 1912, he hosted a number of catered dinners for local clergy, community leaders, and prominent citizens where he encouraged them to sign pledges agreeing to protect Baltimore from vice by mobilizing their communities against it. He received hundreds of signatures.[45]

In addition to rallying new coalitions to the anti-vice movement, the white slavery panic helped to bring changes in the law and law enforcement that would allow for greater crackdowns on the brothel trade and on prostitution more generally. In 1910, Maryland passed a state-level white slave act to mirror the federal Mann Act. Within the year, local courts had tried twelve people for violating it.[46] Baltimore also got a dedicated white slave agent who was tasked with investigating its

---

[43] "White Slavery Here?," *Sun*, May 1, 1910, 16.

[44] Crenson, *Baltimore: A Political History*, 230–32; Donald R. Hooker, "Social Hygiene," *Journal of Social Hygiene* 5 (Oct. 1919), 576–79; Power, "Apartheid Baltimore Style," 292–93.

[45] Kelly's diaries contain several entries about dinners that he hosted and signatures collected from his attendees. See, for example, Howard A. Kelly, diary, June 20, 1912, Folder 25/1, Kelly Collection.

[46] Oliver Edward Janney, *The White Slave Traffic in America* (New York: National Vigilance Committee 1911), 131–32.

red-light districts. Stanley W. Finch, who had been appointed chief of
the Bureau of Investigation (BOI) by former BSSV-member-turned-US
Attorney General Charles J. Bonaparte, became the head of the BOI's
White Slavery Division. He set up office in Baltimore, where he quickly
instituted a mandatory census of all madams, prostitutes, and peripheral
employees in the vice districts to determine their personal histories.
Finch's goal was to uncover how many, if any, of the women in
Baltimore's brothels were there as a result of direct coercion.[47]

Anti-vice and anti–white slavery activism reached such a significant
pitch in Baltimore that attacking tolerated vice in the city soon became a
significant part of Maryland Progressives' campaign platforms. In 1908,
following the deaths of Freeman Rasin and Arthur Pue Gorman, Marylanders elected reform Democrat Austin Crothers to the Maryland gover-
norship on a platform of cleaning up government and eliminating the
kind of corruption that allowed vice to flourish. Crothers quickly made it
his mission to clean up what he saw as the cronyism and networks of
bribery and graft that kept Baltimore's police in the pocket of brothel and
liquor interests. A heavy-handed attempt on Crothers's part to oust
Baltimore's state-appointed Board of Police Commissioners without the
consent of the state assembly cost him most of his political support and,
ultimately, failed to accomplish his hoped-for reforms. However, his
successor, Phillips Lee Goldsborough, would prove to be more politically
adept.[48] Goldsborough, a Progressive Republican who emphasized the
need to raise women's wages as a means of combatting white slavery, had
strong connections to Baltimore's most prominent anti-vice reformers and
enjoyed a solid base of support among them.[49] When it came time for
Goldsborough to make his appointments to the Police Board, he carried
on the work of his predecessor by choosing men who had a reputation for
demanding strict enforcement of the existing laws relating to liquor sales,
brothels, and gaming houses. As his two Republican selections, he chose
Daniel Ammidon, a former member of the BSSV, and Morris A. Soper, a
former US assistant attorney and counsel for the BSSV. For his

---

[47] Jessica R. Pliley, *Policing Sexuality: The Mann Act and the Making of the FBI* (Cambridge, MA: Harvard University Press, 2014), 85–87.

[48] Frank F. White Jr., *The Governors of Maryland 1777–1970* (Annapolis: Hall of Records
Commission, 1992), 239–42.

[49] Howard A. Kelly donated to Goldsborough's campaign and met with him to discuss the
vice crusade. On at least one occasion, he hosted Goldsborough at dinner. Howard
A. Kelly, diary, undated entry, 1912, Folder 25/1, Kelly Collection; "Goldsborough
Makes Pledges," *Sun*, Nov. 5, 1911, 7; White, *The Governors of Maryland*, 245–48.

Democratic selection (boards were required to be bipartisan), Goldsborough put forth businessman Alfred S. Niles, who also took the "social problem" of vice seriously.[50] The legislature approved his choices.

Goldsborough, his new Police Board, and members of his administration faced significant public pressure from constituents who made it clear that they intended to hold them to their promises regarding attacking vice and corruption. Howard A. Kelly and his compatriots in the BSSV convinced dozens of prominent Baltimoreans to pledge that they would demand that authorities "yield to repeated efforts at reform" and begin to enforce the existing laws concerning brothels and liquor.[51] If authorities refused, reformers called for their ouster. Speaking before the BSSV in February of 1912, sitting US Attorney General Charles J. Bonaparte urged the impeachment of any judge on Baltimore's Supreme Bench who did not follow the letter of the law when it came to punishing the keepers of disorderly houses and suppressing the trade.[52] When the justices shifted blame to the Police Board by claiming that they could not enforce bans on disorderly houses so long as police refused to bring cases, reformers circulated petitions in churches and synagogues that demanded that the new Police Board take action to remove brothels in the vicinity of their religious buildings and to appoint reliable police officers.[53]

In the face of political pressure from social purity campaigners, the new Police Board took immediate steps to establish its anti-vice bona fides. Shortly after their appointment, members of the Board of Police Commissioners moved to issue sixty-day eviction notices to the keepers of bawdy houses on Rogers Avenue and Watson Street in Old Town.[54] The move effectively shut down two of the city's most sizable vice districts and made a clear statement that the process of red-light abatement was beginning in the city. Where the commissioners could not outright evict brothel keepers from neighborhoods, they settled for attacking sex establishments' commercial foundations. Since 1898, Baltimore's city charter had dictated that no person could apply for a liquor license unless he or

---

[50] "Shift in Local Slate," *Sun*, Feb. 14, 1912; "Riggs and M'Kim Are Rejected by Senate," *Sun*, Apr. 2, 1912. Goldsborough's original choice for the Democratic position was Lawrason Riggs, whom the legislature rejected as too partisan.

[51] Howard A. Kelly, diary, undated entry, 1912, Folder 25/1, Kelly Collection.

[52] Crenson, *Baltimore: A Political History*, 354; "Would Impeach Judges," *Sun*, Feb. 28, 1912, 9; "Not in Judges' Hands," *Sun*, Feb. 29, 1912.

[53] "Police Board Acts," *Sun*, Dec. 24, 1912; "Social Evil Crusade On," *Sun*, Oct. 11, 1912; "Sees in It Family Peril," *Sun*, Oct. 15, 1912.

[54] "Police Board Acts," *Sun*, Dec. 24, 1912.

she pledged "that he or she will not keep, or permit to be kept, a bawdy house in the said house or on the said premises, or the gathering together in or visitation to said house or premises of women for lewd or immoral purposes."[55] Although the provision technically prevented brothels from serving alcohol, bribery by madams and the willingness of the police to turn a blind eye to violations had ensured that it was virtually a dead letter. The new Police Board sought to revive the law by dictating that any officer who wished to keep his position had to enforce it with vigor. Alcohol sales had been an important source of brothel revenue since the antebellum years, and the Board hoped that depriving madams of the ability to mark up prices on beer, wine, champagne, and other liquors might sap their profits and force them to abandon their business.[56]

The commissioners, no doubt anticipating that a mere order to enforce the law would be insufficient to reverse long-standing practices of police toleration toward brothels, coupled their policy changes with personnel changes. In June 1913, the board ordered thirty-four captains, lieutenants, and round sergeants to be transferred from their existing districts and placed in new ones around the city. The Commissioners stated that they believed transferring the officers would "give them greater familiarity with the city-wide conditions, and will tend to increase their interest and activity in the discharge of their duty."[57] In reality, the move was an effort to break down the bribery networks that officers had formed with madams and saloonkeepers in their districts. Notably, officers who had formerly been installed in districts with large concentrations of brothels – the western and the eastern – were moved to the southern and southwestern districts, which had the smallest number of brothels per capita. Meanwhile, officers from districts without large number of brothels were put in supervisory positions in the red-light districts. Captain Charles Cole, formerly of the Southern District, was placed in charge of the red-light area in the Western District and assigned a command of subordinate officers who had previously worked in the Southwestern and Central Districts.[58] A year after they reorganized the districts, the Board of Police Commissioners also took the controversial steps of removing Police Marshal Thomas F. Farnan and his deputy from their positions and installing new leadership in the department. Farnan had been a Baltimore policeman for forty-eight years and marshal since 1901, and he was popular in

---

[55] *New Charter of Baltimore City*, Section 64 (Baltimore: J. W. Bond Co., 1898), 258.
[56] MVCR, vol. 1, 1.   [57] "Police Shake-Up Stirs the Force," *Sun*, June 24, 1913.
[58] "Police Shake-Up Stirs the Force," *Sun*, June 24, 1913.

town despite consistent allegations that he participated in corruption. His firing was intended to make a statement that no one who was perceived as a foot-dragger or relic of the old system of graft was safe under the new Police Board.[59]

With old neighborhood familiarities dissolved and new command structures in place that made officers hesitant to participate in graft or protection rackets, Baltimore's brothels fell under concerted attack from the police. Sales of alcohol did not dry up completely in sex establishments, even as police began enforcing the liquor laws with vigor; indeed, many madams compensated by having liquor sent for from neighboring establishments, selling beer disguised as sodas, and hiding liquor bottles on the upper floors of their houses. Nevertheless, madams could not carry on a liquor trade to the extent that they had previously, and the reduction of their revenue hit the already stagnating brothel business hard.[60]

To make matters worse, individual police commanders began to implement regulations designed to limit the labor force available to brothels and to restrict sex workers' movement. Local police commanders in the red-light districts barred brothel keepers from having telephones installed in their houses, a provision that kept madams from calling out for girls. They also began to require that any women found in a bawdy house had to be over the age of twenty-one, a policy that was intended to prevent madams from recruiting vulnerable young women into their trade. Although the rule was never well enforced because of the ease with which women could lie about their ages, it did make it risky for brothels to open their doors to women who might under normal circumstances have provided their most ready and profitable labor force. Arrests for pandering, harboring female minors, or enticement were not common by the 1910s, but the charges carried stiff penalties of two to three years in prison if they resulted in conviction.[61]

A more significant blow to brothel keepers and sex workers alike came in 1913, when police began enforcing a rule that no woman who currently resided in a brothel was allowed to seek employment in any other house. The rule, which originated with a single police commander but

[59] "Rumor Alarms Police," *Sun*, May 16, 1914; "Manning Out, Farnan to Go," *Sun*, May 26, 1914; "Police Efficiency Is Board's Aim," *Sun*, May 27, 1914.

[60] MVCR, vol. 1, 16–17.

[61] Baltimore Police Commissioners, *Report of the Board of Police Commissioners for the City of Baltimore to His Excellency the Governor of Maryland, 1912* (Baltimore: Baltimore City Printing and Binding Company, 1913), 23. On prosecutions, see, for example, BCCC, 1912, Cases 470 and 2302; BCCC, 1915, 2586.

spread throughout the city within a year, stated that if a sex worker departed her place of employment in the red-light district for any reason, she was required to leave prostitution, to relocate her residence to another part of the city, and to provide police with her new address.[62] The policy deprived many houses of much-needed labor, and numerous brothels shut down as the new restrictions made it impossible for their already struggling businesses to compete with other, more casual forms of prostitution.[63]

In the case of the brothels that remained open, however, the new police rules succeeded primarily in ensuring that the very forms of coercion and exploitation that red-light abatement was designed to prevent took hold in the sex trade. For much of the nineteenth and early twentieth centuries, brothel workers had exercised a high degree of mobility as part of their strategy to secure good working conditions. Women moved brothels every few months in order to seek out the best terms of employment, to access the most high-paying clients, and generally to negotiate the terms of their own labor. The knowledge that a girl was free to go to another house forced madams to offer competitive board and fee arrangements in order to attract and maintain workers. However, once Baltimore police adopted a policy forbidding prostitutes from leaving their houses to seek work in new ones, sex workers' negotiating power disappeared, with devastating consequences. While the police reasoned that the prohibition would drive women out of the sex trade, the reality was that many women could not leave because they could not support themselves, their partners, or their families without the revenue from sex work. More entrepreneurial or desperate madams, understanding that they were now the beneficiaries of an unfree market in labor, began to take advantage of their tenants. Even those madams who may not otherwise have been inclined toward exploitative labor practices embraced them out of a sense that their business was dying and that it was imperative that they extract as much profit as they could while brothels remained open.[64]

---

[62] Pliley, *Policing Sexuality*, 93.

[63] MVCR, vol. 1, 1; Baltimore Police Commissioners, *Report of the Board of Police Commissioners for the City of Baltimore to His Excellency the Governor of Maryland 1912* (Baltimore: Baltimore City Printing and Binding Company, 1912), 22–23.

[64] By the time the Maryland Vice Commission began investigating brothels, madams were taking 50 percent of their workers' earnings as well as charging them rent. Madams also overcharged prostitutes living in their houses for clothing and other goods. The vice commissioners found that few prostitutes managed to amass any savings. MVCR, vol. 1, 9–17, 44–46.

Under the new regulations, madams charged sex workers more for board and forced them to labor longer hours in order to make up for revenue lost as a result of declining labor pools and alcohol sales. For decades, alcohol had been the product that allowed madams to make money from the flirtatious and sociable aspects of sex work. Without it, they had to find alternative sources of profit. Many brothel keepers in the remaining red-light districts purchased player pianos and required male patrons to buy a song or two before they went upstairs with the girls, but the earnings from this paled in comparison to those that had come from selling alcohol.[65] In many houses, madams expected their boarders to make up for the loss by dispensing with sociability and performing sex work at a pace that resembled that of an assembly line. By 1914, it was not unusual for brothel workers to engage in intercourse with a dozen or more men each night, often without any break for cleaning, douching, or rest in between. Not only was this brutal and taxing on women's bodies, but it also rendered the sex trade even less hygienic by exposing multiple men to each other's still-fresh semen deposits.[66] Working conditions became so oppressive under the new policies that some sex workers actually turned to federal law enforcement officers for help. Several women wrote to John Grgurevich, Baltimore's white slave officer, complaining that labor practices in brothels had worsened under the new police policy and pleading for his intervention.[67]

Madams who saw their labor forces dwindle as a result on bans on poaching from other establishments or introducing new tenants began to resort to underhanded practices in order to secure female boarders for their brothels. Some madams took to overcharging sex workers for clothing, food, and other goods bought on their account in order to keep them in cycles of debt and prevent them from departing the trade, which, ironically, was exactly the kind of exploitation that white slave crusaders claimed would be prevented by striking out against brothels. Other madams turned to paying professional procurers, pimps, and traffickers between $10 and $50 to bring them girls under the table.[68] Others forged connections with recruiters in industries that employed women in order to attract and sometimes trick new women into the trade.[69] These practices expanded male involvement in prostitution and generally increased the degree of coerciveness, violence, and exploitation involved in sex work.

[65] MVCR, vol. 1, 17.   [66] MVCR, vol. 1, 72, 99–100.
[67] Pliley, *Policing Sexuality*, 93; MVCR, vol. 1, 79–80.   [68] MVCR, vol. 1, 17, 28–30.
[69] MVCR, vol. 1, 34–44.

Notably, they also undermined reformers' efforts to isolate and under-mine the sex trade commercially by creating new illicit commercial net-works based around supplying labor to brothels. The existence of these networks opened the door for an expansion of trafficking, rather than the end of "white slavery."

It was within the context of a beleaguered and increasingly exploitative sex trade that the Maryland Vice Commission formed. Created in January 1913 at the behest of the Governor Goldsborough, the MVC was one of dozens of similar investigatory commissions that emerged around the United States in the 1910s. Although Goldsborough no doubt intended it to be a gesture to his Progressive, anti-vice supporters, the commission had a complicated relationship to the social purity and anti–white slavery movements. From the start, the MVC distanced itself from the affective, sensationalist, and moralistic appeals of white slavery and social purity crusaders in favor of adopting "empirical" approaches to the study of vice. The commissioners expressed skepticism of allegations of kidnap-ping and forced prostitution and proclaimed their belief that "the highly sensational stories of the capture of young girls and the holding of them in bondage has been grossly exaggerated."[70] As evidence, they noted that one of the brothel workers they interviewed had told them that she had seen the popular white slave melodrama *The Traffic in Souls* (1913) and "considered it the most ridiculous show she has ever witnessed."[71] They declined to give credibility to any of the rumors they gathered about the practice.[72] Furthermore, the commissioners denied that they had any moral agenda in investigating vice and insisted that their purpose was to be dispassionate and scientific observers. They claimed that whatever recommendations they might make concerning the policing of prostitu-tion would be based in careful study rather than prejudice, in keeping with Progressive emphasis on rational, scientific policy.[73] Adding cred-ibility to their assertion was the fact that Goldsborough declined to name any members of the BSSV or outspoken advocates of brothel closure to the commission.

The MVC also did not share social purity crusaders' sense of urgency about what the latter perceived as a moral crisis in the city. Historians who have written about the MVC have treated the commission as a

---

[70] MVCR, vol. 1, 292–95.   [71] MVCR, vol. 1, 81.

[72] MVCR, vol. 1, 295–99. The commissioners did record various white slave rumors, but they crossed them out of the final draft of their report.

[73] Connelly, *The Response to Prostitution in the Progressive Era.*

virtual extension of the social purity movement and credited its report with ending tolerated red-light districts in Baltimore. In actuality, social purity crusaders in 1913 and 1914 perceived the MVC less as an ally in the crusade against red-light districts and more as a hindrance to existing anti-vice efforts by the Baltimore police. The MVC's insistence on conducting an empirical study of vice as it existed in Baltimore was at odds with police commanders' desire to suppress brothels or to force their relocation to more isolated alleys and side streets. Longtime anti-vice crusaders expressed concerns that the police might be prevented from taking action against red-light districts while the commission carried out its investigation. In 1914, for instance, Howard A. Kelly met with both the MVC and the Board of Police Commissioners to voice strenuous objections to the interference of "those who have professed no moral aim" in the policing of brothels. Kelly, who was concerned that the MVC might attempt to prevent the police from moving some brothels in East Baltimore and closing others, voiced his distaste for the commission's dispassionate approach and lack of urgency. "It is but a specious argument," Kelly wrote, "to ask to leave a gross moral disease & a plague alone when recognized, for an indefinite period that it may be studied 'scientifically.'" He continued, "I am responsible & so are the Commissioners for all the girls & boys who go to the bad in the interval."[74] It would not be until the fall of 1915, when MVC Chairman Dr. George Walker declared himself in favor of abolition, that Kelly came around to the commission.

Yet despite these obvious divergences from the agenda of social purity and white slavery crusaders, the MVC actually shared much in common with members of these movements. For one thing, most MVC members were of backgrounds and social classes similar to those of most Progressive anti-vice reformers. Four commissioners – including Lilian Welsh, one of only two women on the commission – were physicians. Five were members of other professional groups. Three were members of local, religiously affiliated charitable organizations, and one, Anna Herkner, was social worker who did statistical work for the state. Several of the vice commissioners had personal connections to prominent social purity crusaders and hobnobbed with them socially.[75] Only the minority

---

[74] Howard A. Kelly, diary, undated entry, May 1914–June 20, 1914, Folder 25/7, Kelly Collection.

[75] Both Anna Herkner and Lilian Welsh attended Howard A. Kelly's dinners with reformers. Kelly, diary, June 20, 1912, Folder 25/1, Kelly Collection.

member of the commission, Frederick Gottlieb, had a profile that did not match that of a Progressive reformer. Gottlieb, a wealthy retired brewer, was probably chosen to reinforce the supposed neutrality of the commission.[76] All of the commissioners were white, which would presage their investigation's general lack of concern with vice in black neighborhoods or engagement with the any racial issues at the center of the city's prostitution trade.

In addition to sharing class backgrounds and social circles with anti-vice crusaders, MVC members betrayed concerns and assumptions about the sex trade that were remarkably similar to those that animated social purity advocates, particularly when it came to issues of exploitation. Even as they dismissed white slavery as sensational rumor and cleaved to supposed objectivity, MVC members ultimately shared white slavery crusaders' fear that vulnerable white women were falling victim to the exploitation of larger vice trusts in the context of a corporatized, industrialized economy.[77] Many MVC members believed that prostitution was a commercialized traffic that involved vast networks of co-conspirators, including entrepreneurs who profited from the trade, madams who kept women "under her control by coercion, threats, and networks of debt,"[78] and politicians who protected it (the MVC members alleged that several brothels in the more fashionable western vice district had signed and personalized photographs of a city official on display).[79] This sense that prostitution was not so much a type of labor that women performed as an industry governed and enabled by nefarious interests would inform the commission's study in profound ways. The avenues that vice commissioners explored and the types of questions they asked were shaped by their assumptions that prostitution was governed by a trust.

Vice commissioners spent the bulk of their investigative energies doing as the anonymous investigator did when she called local merchants asking to make a deal: trying to determine who participated in vice's economic networks and how they created conditions under which young women suffered.[80] In addition to querying department stores, vice commissioners

---

[76] Information about Vice Commissioner's Occupations derived from examinations of city directories and newspaper records. Winthrop D. Lane, "Under Cover of Respectability: Some Disclosures of Immorality among Unsuspected Men and Women," *The Survey* 35 (Mar. 25, 1916): 747; Jayme Rae Hill, "From the Brothel to the Block: Politics and Prostitution in Baltimore during the Progressive Era," MA thesis, University of Maryland, Baltimore County, 2008.

[77] Keire, "The Vice Trust."   [78] MVCR, vol. 1, 11.   [79] MVCR, vol. 1, 7.

[80] MVCR, vol. 1, 45–66.

visited employment agencies pretending to be madams in search of girls for employment in brothels. They checked into local hotels to see if the janitors or bellmen would offer to send girls in exchange for tips. They surveyed local amusement parks, dance halls, and theaters for evidence that they catered to "public" women. They inquired into the ownership of brothels, watched vice districts for any evidence of pimps or other brokers who sold girls into prostitution, and asked madams about how much they paid for their clothes and furniture and how much they took from their boarders' earnings. The vice commissioners even staged investigations of factories, department stores, and professional offices around town to explore whether any of them had social or working conditions that fostered sexual immorality among female workers. The volumes of reports they generated on various types of sexual immorality had little to unite them besides their overriding theme that Marylanders were willing to promote immorality for the sake of profit.[81]

In the course of their investigations into Baltimore's red-light districts, the commissioners found what they believed was ample evidence that there were large networks of people who profited from professional prostitution and the degradation of young women. Although the old brothel areas were already depleted by the casualization of the trade and crackdowns by police, East Baltimore still had several old, two-story brothels on Eastern Avenue, Spring Street, Fleet Street, and Dukers Alley, and West Baltimore maintained its more affluent vice districts. Three blocks of Raborg Street and one block of Josephine Street still held semi-genteel houses, while St. James Street and King Street featured the most and least affluent brothels in the area, respectively.[82] The vice commissioners noted that many houses in these districts were owned by people other than the madams who ran them. Several property owners possessed multiple houses; one owned more than a dozen.[83] All of the landlords rented houses to women for double the rent of neighboring dwellings that were not brothels, despite the fact that many of the houses were in poor repair and lacked bathing or indoor bathroom facilities. The commissioners also noted that merchants – including purveyors of clothing, furniture, and electric pianos – systematically overcharged madams for goods and that madams seemed beholden to procurers who charged them for bringing girls for their houses. Furnished room house keepers, proprietors of employment agencies, department store

[81] MVCR, vol. 3.   [82] MVCR, vol. 1, 32–38.   [83] MVCR, vol. 1, 9.

employees, and amusement park employees were all, according to the vice commissioners, involved in – and compensated for – recruitment for brothels. Local bartenders and taxi drivers also received money from madams in return for recommending their establishments to prospective clients.[84]

While MVC members observed exploitation everywhere, they reserved some of their harshest criticisms for madams, whom they understood to be at the heart of the system that profited from the misery of women. "This is the woman who turns the wheel of prostitution," the vice commissioners wrote of the brothel keepers. "There are many safe and respectable persons and institutions who ... more or less directly contribute to the existence of the system[,] but it is she who converts the wretchedest of all bargains between men and women into an organized industry; sets herself richly to make it pay." The commissioners claimed that madams duped young women into "sinister subjection" by recruiting from their hometowns or paying for them to be brought to brothels, sometimes under false pretenses of promises of the wealth they would receive from sex work.[85] Madams then required the women to participate in a virtual assembly line of intercourse that was brutal on their bodies and, according to the Vice Commission, far more profitable for the madams than it was for the prostitutes themselves. Madams charged excessive rents, kept half of women's receipts, and overcharged them for clothing and food with the cooperation of local merchants – doing whatever they could to extract money from their tenants. In a statement that betrayed concern over both women's vulnerability in the changing market economy and the potentially dehumanizing effects of capitalism, MVC members claimed that madams treated women "with no more feeling than a marketman evidences in the handling of vegetables and poultry for profit."[86]

Notably, many of the conditions that the vice commissioners observed were either decades-old practices – that is, landlords renting multiple properties for inflated rents – or a direct result of recent police interference in the trade. Nevertheless, MVC members took them as evidence that the trade had grown more commercialized as a result of state toleration. Much of their report seemed to confirm the worst fears of those like Howard Kelly, who believed that all prostitution was functionally a form

[84] MVCR, vol. I, 74.   [85] MVCR, vol. I, 10.   [86] MVCR, vol. I, 11.

of white slavery in which women were sold to satisfy men's lust for sex and business people's lust for profit.

The Vice Commission's report also reinforced a critique that social purity crusaders had made for some time, namely that prostitution represented a grave threat to public health. In addition to interviewing sex workers and touring brothels, the MVC carried out thousands of medical examinations of brothel denizens and men and women who were incarcerated in various institutions around the city for "immorality." By the time the MVC staged its investigation, physicians had access to a medical test – the Wasserman reaction – that made it possible to present more definitive data on syphilitic infection rates. The test, which was invented in 1906, required only a blood sample in order to determine with a reasonable level of accuracy whether a person had antibodies to treponemal diseases like syphilis. Because the test relied on antibodies rather than the observation of physical symptoms, it could be used to make a diagnosis even in asymptomatic subjects.[87] With the help of nearly a dozen local physicians and the (sometimes coerced) cooperation of their subjects, MVC members conducted nearly 3,000 Wasserman tests and oversaw physical examinations of brothel workers, penitentiary and jail inmates, students at the state training school, and inmates of Spring Grove Hospital. The commission reported that 63.27 percent of the 287 brothel sex workers it subjected to vaginal examination and blood work were infected with syphilis, with the percentage rising sharply in accordance with the number of years a woman had spent in the trade. Though tests for gonorrhea were less reliable, the MVC estimated that a staggering 92.1 percent of the sex workers its physicians examined showed signs of past or current infection. Many also had pelvic inflammatory disease, and nearly a third were infected with both syphilis and gonorrhea.[88] In the eyes of the commissioners, the sex trade, like other industries that were the subjects of contemporary muckraking, chewed up and spit out its laborers.[89]

Vice commissioners, like many of Baltimore's more active social purity crusaders, understood the exploitative nature of the sex trade as being related to the exploitative nature of women's work more generally. That is, they saw the sex trade as being fed and sustained by the conditions that

---

[87] Lois N. Magner, *A History of Medicine* (New York: Marcel Dekker, 1992), 181–82. Notably, the Wasserman test result would also be positive if the patient suffered from tuberculosis or other constitutional illnesses.

[88] MVCR, vol. 1, 105–13.   [89] MVCR, vol. 1, 113–14.

women faced when they entered the wage labor market, including poor pay and difficult working conditions. The commissioners found ample evidence for this understanding in their interviews with sex workers, both in brothels and in more casual sectors of the trade. Many women told the commissioners that they had gone into sex work because wages in the factories or department stores were too low to allow them to support themselves or to participate in the leisure and consumer economy to the degree that they liked.[90] One sex worker remarked, "How can a girl get along on $1. a week paying 60¢ for car fare? I go out to get some spending money and clothes."[91] Another responded to the MVC's queries by saying, "Poverty drove me into this life. My mother died 4 years ago, and $8. would not support me and my little brother."[92] Several women noted that the poor compensation they received from legitimate labor made sex work the more rational economic choice for them: while they could make $6 to $8 per week working ten-hour days at factories or department stores, they could make many times more than that selling sex for a few hours a night in assignation houses or brothels (up to $25 a week in brothels and more in $1 houses).[93] Sex work had the added benefit of being year-round, which was important for women who suffered during seasons when their employment was slow. One woman, a dressmaker by trade, told commissioners that she worked in prostitution seasonally because of the contractions in demand for clothing. "[I] do pretty well in Fall, Winter, and Spring, but not in the Summer," she remarked.[94]

MVC members were so committed to a narrative that cast the sex trade as a reflection and a product of the exploitation that took place in other industries that they chose to ignore alternative narratives from sex workers. While a number of women did state that poverty and desperation drove them into sex work, many women interviewed by the commission contested the notion that their entrance into prostitution was coerced, either directly or indirectly. Some noted that the people who "lured" them into the life were not procurers, but fellow working girls who shared their strategy for making extra money. One woman remarked to investigators that she had entered the sex trade because "I got going around with a married woman. She taught me the ropes and told me how foolish I was working steady and have no pleasure." Apparently satisfied with her decision to enter sex work, she continued, "I took her advice and

90 MVCR, vol. 1, 269–88.   91 MVCR, vol. 1, 278.   92 MVCR, vol. 1, 278.
93 MVCR, vol. 1, 70–74.   94 MVCR, vol. 1, 270.

no more Sunday-School for mine."[95] Another sex worker told vice commissioners that she and a "girl friend from the same factory started out
together" in the trade.[96]

Several women relayed that, contrary to perceiving sex work as
exploitative, they preferred it to "the dull routine and suppressed life of
the domestic, or the monotonous grind of the factory."[97] Prostitution,
after all, provided "money for luxuries, fine clothes and so on."[98] It also
provided "excitement." A number of women told investigators that they
preferred being prostitutes in the city to the dullness of country life, and
several remarked that they found going with men as casual prostitutes
fun.[99] At one point, vice commissioners were forced to note with some
chagrin, "Many of these girls, in fact most of them, seem satisfied and
believe that their lives as prostitutes are more desirable than what they
had before." However, the commissioners largely dismissed these women
as being of "low mentality and imperfect vision."[100]

Because they understood women's entrance into paid labor as the root
of prostitution, vice commissioners spent months investigating women's
working conditions in a number of shops, factories, and office buildings
around Baltimore. They found that while some businesses profited
enough from women's labor that they were able to pay enormous divi-
dends to their shareholders, they paid women consistently low wages with
virtually no possibility for raises. In most cases, women who labored full-
time barely made enough to cover room and board, and certainly not
enough to afford the consumer goods that many of them were exposed to
every day in their work as shop girls. MVC members believed that the
combination of laboring women's poor economic circumstances and
desire to participate in the emerging consumer culture made them vulnerable to "becoming immoral."[101] While the commissioners did not explicitly state that poor pay motivated women to enter sex work, one
commissioner used scathing language to highlight the hypocrisy of a
society that demanded that women conform to a strict standard of sexual
morality while also denying them a living wage. "We say to them [prosti-
tutes]: 'Reform, be good, be decent,'" the commissioner wrote, "when all
that society has to offer is $6 a week, a tiny hall bed-room, poor food,

---

[95] MVCR, vol. 1, 277.   [96] MVCR, vol. 1, 269–88, p. 277.   [97] MVCR, vol. 1, 76.
[98] MVCR, vol. 1, 76.
[99] MVCR, vol. 1, 269–88. One woman told investigators that she was "tired of slow life in
    Rossville, Md." (274). Another remarked, "Life in the country is so tiresome" (273).
[100] MVCR, vol. 1, 76.   [101] MVCR, vol. 2, 2–4.

meagre clothing and sparse amusements. Would you, my Christian man or woman, accept the change and be good at such a cost? I sincerely doubt it."[102]

In addition to suggesting that low wages played a role in women's decisions to enter sex work, the commissioners claimed that social conditions in department stores, factories, and office buildings encouraged women to engage in distasteful and sexually charged conduct. They noted that young workingwomen from good families mixed promiscuously with other female employees, some of whom were "very immoral," at their places of employment. Some women, the commissioners believed, were "seduced" into vice by the evil influences of their coworkers. Additionally, male workers and bosses frequently "made love" to – that is, flirted with, in the parlance of the 1910s – their female coworkers. In some cases, men presented women with gifts in exchange for intimacy, an arrangement that the vice commissioners viewed as suspect and commercial in nature (in reality, this may simply have been dating). In other cases, married men in positions of power over women solicited sex in return for promises to retain women as employees during slow seasons, pay them more, or do other professional favors for them. The MVC believed there was a direct connection between these workplace overtures and women's entrance into prostitution, casual or otherwise. According to the vice commissioners, some working girls ended up as mistresses to married men who supported them and bought them gifts. Others abandoned their legitimate employment in favor of taking up professional prostitution, while far more – ten times more, by the estimates of the commissioners – entered into arrangements that vice commissioners tentatively classed as "clandestine prostitution."[103]

Given the MVC's concerns about the rise of more casual forms of sex work and the conditions of employment in Baltimore, it initially seems odd that the only formal recommendations that the commissioners issued concerned the fate of the city's already shrinking brothel trade. Ultimately, however, the radical potential of the MVC's critiques of industrial capitalism were stymied by the fundamental conservatism of the bulk of the commissioners. The trait that the majority-male MVC members

---

[102] MVCR, vol. 1, 173. The editor of the report, perhaps unwilling to concede that prostitution was something anyone might choose given the right economic circumstances, struck the latter two sentences out after the draft was typed.

[103] MVCR, vol. 1, 173. The entire second volume of the MVC's report was devoted to exposing immoral working conditions for women (MVCR, vol. 2).

shared most in common with evangelical social purity campaigners was their belief that women were inherently too fragile to enter the world of waged work and therefore best suited to being relegated to the care and support of a husband or father. Instead of sustaining their critiques of business and industry throughout their report, the commissioners devoted space in their second volume to scolding families who sent their adolescent daughters to work even if they were not so impoverished that they absolutely required their daughters' incomes. According the commissioners, "This produces an overcrowding of girls demanding positions and consequent lowering of salaries."[104] The commissioners also dialed back their earlier suggestion that low wages contributed to the ruin of women by proclaiming that they were convinced that the issue of wages came into play only *after* women had already fallen from virtue from other causes, including the bad influence of coworkers or friends. "We did not find any direct evidence to show that girls had begun immoral conduct on account of a low wage," the commissioners wrote, "but we have much data indicating that *after a girl had become immoral* [emphasis mine] the low wage was in part responsible for her efforts to add more to her income by illicit relations with men."[105]

When MVC members critiqued industrial conditions and low wages, then, they were not suggesting that those conditions and wages be improved so much as they were suggesting that women needed to return to the home and the protections it provided. Or, at least, some of the commissioners were suggesting this; Lilian Welsh and Anna Herkner, who were themselves professional women devoted to helping laboring women secure medical care, safe recreation, and enfranchisement, likely disagreed.[106] Perhaps they were overruled, or perhaps their desires to see brothels closed in order to protect women's health and defend them from exploitation trumped their concerns about the gendered conservatism of the committee. Either way, as Pamela Haag argued, the final MVC report ultimately "reaffirmed marriage and motherhood as appropriate, 'safe' arenas for women's labors."[107] The commission could not prevent women's entrance into the workforce or reinstitute an older paradigm of separate spheres that they naïvely believed would provide women with the best protection against falling into "immorality." It could, however,

---

[104] MVCR, vol. 2, 5.   [105] MVCR, vol. 2, 2.
[106] Lilian Welsh, *Reminiscences of Thirty Years in Baltimore* (Baltimore: Norman Remington, 1925).
[107] Haag, "The Commerce in Souls," 305.

recommend the closing of brothels that social purity crusaders had for years cast as a symbol for women's broader exploitation in the labor market.

On March 16, 1915, the MVC did exactly that. The commission sent a letter to the Police Board recommending that the police department continue its existing regulations of brothels and add new ones intended to ensure that all brothels and houses of assignation in Baltimore be closed within the year. Only the minority commission member, Frederick Gottlieb, dissented from his fellow MVC members' recommendation by urging the police to continue the policy of segregating bawdy houses into red-light districts. His recommendation fell on deaf ears. At the behest of the Police Board, the Baltimore police began to shutter the city's red-light districts.[108]

In a sign of both how embedded prostitution was in Baltimore's urban culture and how resentful Baltimoreans were at state interference in the affairs of the city, efforts to close the red-light districts met with significant public resistance. When police had begun to intensify the restrictions that they placed on brothels in 1913, a Baltimore grand jury composed of elite citizens had excoriated both the BSSV and the MVC for attempting to pressure the police to adopt a policy of suppression toward red-light districts. Proclaiming that "Baltimore is too large a city to be run like a country village," the grand jurors insisted that the segregation of brothels on side streets and in concentrated districts remained the best way of limiting the ill effects of the bawdy trade.[109] H. L. Mencken, Baltimore's iconoclastic bard and a columnist for the *Evening Sun*, concurred. Between 1912 and 1915, Mencken devoted much of his "Free Lance" column to pillorying social purity crusaders and insisting that their fixation on suppressing commercial sex was "unsound, pernicious and nonsensical."[110] Mencken claimed, "Whatever progress is ever made in reducing the evils of prostitution will be made by men who have intellectual courage enough to admit openly that the facts of life are such and so, and who do not waste their time figuring out how much nicer the world would be if human beings were not as they are."[111] When the MVC

[108] "Gottlieb to Disagree," *Sun*, Mar. 21, 1915; "Halted on Vice Report," *Sun*, Dec. 28, 1915.
[109] "Segregation Urged; Crusaders Scored," *Sun*, Sep. 6, 1913.
[110] H. L. Mencken, "Free Lance," *Evening Sun*, Nov. 7, 1912.
[111] Mencken, "Free Lance."

released its recommendation for suppression, he decried the commission as "crippled by Charlatans and moral crusaders."[112]

By the MVC's own account, Baltimoreans ranging from professionals to police officers agreed with Mencken. In the course of writings its report, the MVC surveyed more than 200 city doctors, physicians, and "leading men" (mostly in business) about their favored approach to prostitution. The results of the surveys suggested that segregation and supervision remained a much more popular approach than closing the vice districts. Of 141 doctors queried, 102 said they wanted prostitution segregated within certain areas, while only 33 advocated for suppression. Thirteen out of sixteen lawyers and fifty-two out of seventy-five prominent men also favored segregation over suppression.[113] Meanwhile, the commission found that many of the police officers who participated in crackdowns on red-light districts at the behest of the Police Board did not actually believe in their efficacy. They did what they did only to keep their jobs, and they resented it.[114] Several officers who unknowingly spoke to an undercover MVC agent criticized the new Police Board and expressed their belief that "they should segregate all the whores and when a fellow wants one he will know where to find them."[115] Many also expressed their hope that the policy of toleration and segregation would return again once the political tide changed. "May be [sic] it will be better when the new administration gets in," one officer remarked.[116] Interestingly, the officer's optimism mirrored that of one of the city's madams, who dismissed the notion that toleration would ever cease to be the reigning paradigm in Baltimore: "These vice reformers are a nine-days' wonder, their craze soon blows over."[117]

In the end, however, the controversies over anti-vice crusaders' activities and the MVC's recommendations proved insufficient to overcome the intensity of anti-prostitution sentiment that suffused Progressive-era cities. Prostitution sat squarely at the intersection of Americans' various anxieties about urbanization, industrialization, and women's changing role in society. The complicated issues of consent that had always been at play in the sex trade became too difficult to ignore amid broader fears about diminished autonomy and nefarious corporate trusts. Progressives believed that it was the duty of the state to take an active role in addressing social inequalities and the excesses of capitalism, and their belief in

[112] "The Report of the Vice Commission," *Evening Sun*, Dec. 28, 1915.
[113] MVCR, vol. 1, 362–72.   [114] MVCR, vol. 1   [115] MVCR, vol. 1
[116] MVCR, vol. 1, 350.
[117] Raymond V. Phelan, "Publish the Names," *The Survey* 36 (July 8, 1916): 396.

intervention profoundly altered the political landscape in Baltimore. Long-standing practices of toleration for vice took on new and often sinister significance as reformers came to the see de facto licensing of brothels and toleration of other forms of prostitution less as a pragmatic compromise and more as the state abandoning its citizens to the whims of trusts. Police and court practices of fining and releasing brothel keepers, once seen as a valid means of generating revenue, came irrevocably to be seen as a form of graft and an abdication of officials' responsibility to enforce the law. The people in political power understood shutting down brothels as a crucial step in ensuring clean governance, rescuing women from the clutches of craven capitalists, and securing the moral and physical health of the city. Even in the face of resistance from city residents, state power structures that deprived Baltimore of both local control of its police force and proportional representation in state government ensured that red-light district closures would happen regardless of local sentiment.

The Baltimore police, who had begun the process of depriving brothels of their labor and financial bases even before the MVC released its recommendation, set about shutting down red-light districts in earnest after they received it. One madam who was forced out of her house had been in the trade for forty years. Scores of other women – more than 226, by police estimates – found themselves ejected from their homes. Local authorities, working with the Volunteers of America and Major Hattie Hopkins of Philadelphia's Chinatown Volunteer Rescue Home, designated a hotel to house former sex workers as they looked for legitimate employment. Marked by a stigma that had only been deepened by the police insistence on segregating prostitution into brothels and red-light districts in "slum" areas of the city, the women entered an uncertain economic world. Some of them had come to Baltimore from other cities because they felt that was safer for them. One sex worker had commented to a vice commissioner during the investigation, "You know, this is not New York. In New York, you get raided all the time. It isn't so here. Nobody will bother you."[118] Others had resorted to prostitution to supplement meager wages. In the aftermath of the evictions, women found themselves without their means of support and struggling to get by in a society that had rid itself of tolerated sex establishments but failed to challenge the economic inequalities that had led to their creation.

By September 1915, the last tolerated brothel in Baltimore had closed.

---

[118] MVCR, vol. 1, 313.

Conclusion

In December 1921, a twenty-nine-year-old black woman named Adelaine (sometimes spelled Adeline) Payne appeared before the Baltimore City Criminal Court on charges related to prostitution. At the time of her trial, Payne was living on North Dallas Street, a narrow road running up from Fells Point. She rented a house between the Washington Hill and Dunbar neighborhoods, not far from the old Orleans Street vice district. Payne was a divorced, single mother to her four-year-old daughter, Iona. Though she may have been fortunate enough to enjoy some family support, Payne almost certainly struggled with the burdens of raising a young child on only her own earnings. As a black woman living in a city that was increasingly segregated and rife with anti-black racism, she had limited options for well-compensated work, and at the time of the 1920 census she had no legitimate employment. Prostitution, if indeed she participated in it, probably helped her to pay her bills.[1]

Payne was just one of many women whose arrests for prostitution in the years after 1915 highlighted the false optimism of Baltimore reformers who hoped that closing brothels would stamp out commercial sex in the city. When the police first began closing bawdy houses in 1914, the Baltimore Society for the Suppression of Vice reported with some satisfaction that the predicted negative consequences of brothel closures –

---

[1] "Court Calendar," *Sun*, Dec. 1, 1921; 1920 US Census, Baltimore, Maryland, Ward 6, p. 15A, dwelling 185, family 283, Adeline Payne. Payne lived next door to a woman named Chastity Payne, who lived with her two sons. Both Adelaine and Chastity had been born in Virginia to parents also born in Virginia, which leads me to suspect that they were siblings.

namely, the diffusion of vice – had not materialized. Streetwalking, they claimed, had not become any more common; in fact, public prostitution had been declining along with indoor forms of sex work. What vice remained was mostly attributable to the survival of a few scattered assignation houses and disreputable cafes and saloons, which the BSSV identified as a "cause of the increased demand and supply of prostitution."[2] In a statement that evinced their faith in the ability to control the prostitution trade merely by shutting down certain types of commercial spaces, the BSSV expressed its confidence that the Liquor Board would move to deny licenses to such businesses and thus "reduce this phase of the evil to a minimum."[3]

Yet the actual effects of bawdy-house closures were far more mixed than vice reformers had hoped or anticipated. Some of the women who participated in sex work on a casual basis in order to supplement their incomes from legitimate work may indeed have left the trade when authorities began cracking down on brothels and assignation houses, departing the sex business – as most were wont to do anyway after a few years – or moving to other cities. However, there were still many women for whom sex work was not a means of earning a little extra money, but rather a necessity. For these women, a disproportionate number of whom were black, leaving either the sex trade or the Baltimore area was not a viable option. The closure of brothels and places of assignation did not end their stints as sex workers. Instead, it forced them to adjust to new policing practices, just as women in the sex trade had been doing since the state began to intervene in earnest in the sex trade during the early republic years. Some sex workers plied their trade out of taxis and dance halls; others took to the streets where work was more dangerous, the risk of arrest was higher, and the dependency on pimps who could provide protection and bail money was more pronounced.[4]

Even the bawdy-house closures that reformers had hailed as a sea change for Baltimore did not last. For over a year after police evicted

---

[2] Society for the Suppression of Vice of Baltimore, *Annual Report of the Society for the Suppression of Vice of Baltimore for the Year Ending December 31, 1914* (Baltimore), https://catalog.hathitrust.org/Record/100226992.

[3] *Annual Report of the Society for the Suppression of Vice of Baltimore for the Year Ending December 31, 1914*, 12.

[4] Reviews of newspaper records reveal that most of the women listed as being arrested for prostitution were women of color. White women and men of both races appeared occasionally as well. On the dangers of street prostitution and the effects of brothel closures on black women, see Blair, *I've Got to Make My Livin'*.

the last madams and tenants from brothels, the number of arrests for bawdy houses remained at zero. However, as the United States mobilized for entrance into World War I and Maryland became host to thousands of American soldiers, the indoor sex trade rebounded as cheap hotels and other spaces that allowed assignations reemerged. In 1917, police arrested twenty men and women for keeping bawdy houses and nine for pandering, and the Criminal Court heard forty-four total presentments for bawdy-house cases.[5] Bawdy-house arrests would increase to twenty-five the following year before dropping down to eight in 1919, but the number of arrests would not hit zero again.[6] US military officials perceived the sex trade to be a significant enough threat to troop health and readiness that Secretary of War Newton D. Baker personally requested that Baltimore Mayor James H. Preston assist the military in suppressing prostitution within a five-mile radius of its bases.[7]

The gradual reemergence of commercial sex did not go unnoted at the time, and it raised questions among Baltimoreans about the broader social and moral roots of prostitution. In 1917, a local resident who attended a public forum asked Dr. Howard A. Kelly about the persistence of commercial sex in Baltimore. "Why after the closing up of the segregated districts of prostitution in this city," he inquired, "do we still have so much of it on the streets of the city and in rooming houses?" Kelly's answer was that brothel closures were only a first step. Ending prostitution, he claimed, would require a combination of Christian faith and ministry and excellence in public service. Legal change was not enough; moral change, good policing, and the embrace of Christian values were ultimately the key to defeating vice.[8]

Kelly's assertion that good morals could solve the problem of prostitution echoed comments made by numerous public officials whom the Maryland Vice Commission had surveyed in the course of their investigation. The MVC had asked 313 mayors in US and Canadian cities what could be done to combat prostitution, and it received replies back from 124 of them. Although several mayors contested the idea that prostitution

[5] Board of Police Commissioners, *Report of the Board of Police Commissioners for the City of Baltimore to His Excellency the Governor of Maryland for the Year 1917* (Baltimore: George W. King Printing Company, 1918), 29, 39–40.

[6] Board of Police Commissioners, *Report of the Board of Police Commissioners for the City of Baltimore to His Excellency the Governor of Maryland for the Year 1919* (Baltimore: George W. King Printing Company, 1920), 30.

[7] "War Secretary Asks Mayor to Help Fight Vice Near Camp," *Sun*, Aug. 14, 1917.

[8] Howard A. Kelly, "To the Editor of the Sun," *Sun*, Feb. 12, 1918.

could be combatted, many of those who expressed optimism for reform highlighted the need for police suppression coupled with training that instilled strong morals in young people. The mayor of Joliet, Illinois, insisted that cities needed to "train your mothers; extend the powers of juvenile Courts; this is a home proposition ... immorality comes from lax home discipline or failure to tell the boys and girls what they should know."[9] The mayor of Akron, Ohio, suggested that prostitution could be lessened "through the education of the people, especially the young, so that they will know the moral and physical dangers."[10] While some mayors acknowledged that prostitution likely had a relationship to low wages and working conditions, others still clung to the idea – popular since the early nineteenth century – that prostitution was primarily a moral issue.[11]

One mayor, however, placed blame for prostitution squarely on the American economic system. Lewis Duncan, the Socialist mayor of Butte, Montana, did not equivocate as the Maryland Vice Commissioners did on the issue of whether low wages and financial strain played a role in women's entrance into sex work. Instead, he responded to the MVC's query by suggesting that prostitution was a product of capitalism and the inequality it bred. Women sold sex not because of some innate desire for intercourse or because of poor moral and sexual education, but rather because their nonsexual labor was so systematically undervalued under capitalism that they could not make a living any other way. Like Socialist leader and presidential candidate Eugene Debs, who criticized "the senseless methods employed by many cities in fighting prostitution, never seeking to root out the causes for prostitution,"[12] Duncan argued that only systemic change could rid cities of commercial sex. To the MVC's query regarding how vice might be combatted, Duncan replied, "Convert people to Socialism; abolish the profit system; overthrow the rule of capitalists; inaugurate industrial democracy where every person shall have free opportunity to work and be assured of the full value of his labor; this will abolish poverty and thus bring about an end to prostitution."[13]

---

[9] MVCR, vol. 1, 381.   [10] MVCR, vol. 1, 382.

[11] On the persistent tendency among Progressives to understand prostitution as a moral issue even as they also explored its social and economic roots, see, for instance, Rosen, *The Lost Sisterhood*, especially 12–13.

[12] "Debs to Fight for Presidency," *Sun*, Mar, 17, 1920.   [13] MVCR, vol. 1, 382.

Duncan's belief that socialism would eliminate commercial sex was probably naïve, especially given that economic change alone could not undo the combined structures of patriarchy, state toleration and graft, and white supremacy that helped to sustain prostitution in Progressive-era Baltimore.[14] Nevertheless, Duncan was fundamentally correct in his observation that prostitution as it existed in American cities was primarily a product of the development of market and industrial capitalism over the course of the long nineteenth century. The growth of prostitution in early Baltimore was inextricably linked to the expansion of the market economy and to the familial and intimate dislocations that accompanied it.[15] Commercial sex expanded into a sizable and highly profitable business in the city – and, indeed, in cities around the country – during a period in which increased trade, the rise of wage labor, and new patterns of work were creating significant social and economic changes. Urbanization and commercialization drove the sex trade's initial growth and continued to shape it for the remainder of the century. Although nineteenth-century Americans embraced the notion that the private world of intimacy was separate from the world of commerce, the rapid expansion of sex work in their cities gave the lie to that idea. As urbanization and mobility disrupted marriage and courtship, men turned increasingly toward the market to satisfy their demands for intimate and sexual labor.

Fundamentally, prostitution's existence was rooted in the gendered divisions – and gendered definitions – of labor that emerged with early industrialization and the rise of urban capitalism. Prostitution was an outgrowth of inequalities that allowed men to accumulate most of the benefits of economic growth even as women were denied those benefits and forced to attach themselves sexually to men in order to get by. Getting by did not merely mean survival; as I have endeavored to show here, women entered sex work for diverse reasons that extended beyond the makeshift economy. Some sex workers did turn to prostitution in order to subsist and support families, for sex work was better compensated than virtually any other form of female labor available to women. Others embraced sex work because they preferred it to marriage, because they

---

[14] Scholar Christine Overall characterized prostitution as the "inherently unequal practice defied by the intersection of capitalism and patriarchy." Christine Overall, "What's Wrong with Prostitution? Evaluating Sex Work," *Signs* 17 (Summer 1992): 724.

[15] Virtually every book written on prostitution in the nineteenth century has acknowledged the relationship between rapid urban growth, industrialization, and prostitution. For an overview, see Gilfoyle, "Prostitutes in History," 117–41.

enjoyed the independence it gave them, or because they relished the fact that it provided them with the money and resources needed to participate in urban consumer culture. By the early twentieth century, many casual sex workers and charity girls alike were using sex to supplement their earnings from day jobs so that they could purchase clothing, jewelry and accessories, and entertainments that would not be available to them otherwise. Regardless of why women went into sex work, however, the basic fact remained that the consumers of sexual labor were virtually always men, and the performers of sexual labor were most likely to be women. Related systems of gender and economic subjugation ensured this that this was the case.

Far from merely reflecting the effects of the so-called market and industrial revolutions, however, prostitution played an important role in Baltimore's commercial development throughout the long nineteenth century. In addition to keeping young women afloat in the turbulent world of the city, women's sexual labor made significant contributions to the urban economy. Culturally and socially speaking, women's willingness to provide sexual services in exchange for money smoothed over social tensions that might otherwise have resulted from early republic Baltimore's demographic imbalances and labor dislocations. Women who sold sex kept men's wages circulating locally and pumped money into the city's consumer economy with their purchase of furniture, clothing, alcohol, venereal remedies, and entertainment. Madams and sex workers transformed undesirable properties into profitable businesses, which in turn lined the pockets of the city's real estate investors and enabled them to move up in the economic hierarchy. Brothels provided revenue to the state through the system of legal regulation that had developed by the 1830s and helped to fund public dispensaries that maintained the health of the city's laboring population. Prostitution even helped, albeit indirectly, to make the streetcar lines that were so crucial to Baltimore's geographic expansion financially viable.

In attempting to wipe prostitution from the urban landscape, Progressive and moral reformers believed that they were ushering in a more civilized and humane urban order. However, they were also participating in a kind of historical amnesia common to maturing capitalist societies. In the past two decades, historians of capitalism, state building, and political economy have gradually grown more attentive to the ways in which informal, illicit, and even illegal economies shaped American development. They have found that smugglers, confidence men, food resellers, counterfeiters of money and products, "quacks," and other people who operated at the alleged "margins" of society actually played important roles in local economies and in an emerging culture of entrepreneurship. In fact, these figures were often not marginal at all in their time. It was only later when a stable middle class formed that state tolerance for illicit economies declined. Whig narratives of growth that emphasized orderly commerce, rational markets, and productive forms of state intervention obscured the role that illicit economic pursuits played in urban economic development.[16]

The trajectory of prostitution and its regulation in Baltimore and other cities conformed to the basic pattern of toleration and regulation followed by crackdown and criminalization when the city had reached a point of economic maturity. In nineteenth-century boomtowns ranging from Baltimore to the mining towns of the American West, both the state and members of the community tolerated prostitution during the early phases of settlement and development. People reaped the benefits of sex workers' contributions to the local economy and to the stability of the local labor force, and the state extracted money from women in the trade. Then, when a middle class emerged and the urban population became more entrenched, campaigns against prostitution began to coalesce. Although the language of morality was always a part of anti-vice discourses, the language of property rights and protection soon joined it. A trade that had once lined the pockets of real estate speculators began to be cast as a threat to property values once changing land use patterns and the declining cultural relevance of brothels made them less sound as an investment strategy.

As the nineteenth century progressed, critics of prostitution became increasingly strident in insisting on the spatial marginalization and, finally, the criminalization and suppression of the sex trade. While many historians have focused on the Progressive era as the crucial moment in

---

[16] Gautham Rao, "Review of *Smuggler Nation: How Illicit Trade Made America*," *Journal of Interdisciplinary History* 44 (Winter 2014): 7. On the pivotal role of illicit, informal, and sometimes illegal economies in American capitalist development, see, for instance, Brian Luskey and Wendy Woloson, eds., *Capitalism by Gaslight: Illuminating the Economy of Nineteenth-Century America* (Philadelphia: University of Pennsylvania Press, 2015); Peter Andreas, *Smuggler Nation: How Illicit Trade Made America* (Oxford: Oxford University Press, 2013); Stephen Mihm, *A Nation of Counterfeiters: Capitalists, Con Men, and the Making of the United States* (Cambridge, MA: Harvard University Press, 2009); Robert J. Gamble, "The Promiscuous Economy: Cultural and Commercial Geographies of Secondhand in the Antebellum City," in *Capitalism by Gaslight*, ed. Brian J. Luskey and Wendy A. Woloson (Philadelphia: University of Pennsylvania Press, 2015), 31–52.

which reformers began to alter the geographies of the brothel business, the developments of that period were actually part of a long-standing continuum of state efforts to manage the shape of the sex trade. Even in the early republic, Baltimore's police, courts, and citizens had attempted to contain and regulate prostitution as a means of rationalizing the organization of the city and minimizing disturbances to both public order and private property rights. Initially, they attempted to corral prostitution into brothels, where it would be both out of sight and easily monitored. However, in 1857, Baltimore's Circuit Court laid the groundwork for the creation of more organized red-light districts that were intended to protect the property rights and morals of white citizens.

As the Civil War and Reconstruction brought renewed attention to the prostitution trade and expanded the responsibilities of the state, local courts and the police moved in earnest to create new vice districts. By the 1870s, the sex workers and freedpeople whose labor had proven crucial in the early years of urban development but who were no longer regarded as useful or desirable residents of the city were gradually crowded into the same neighborhoods. By early twentieth century, debates about prostitution would overlap chronologically with debates about racial segregation of public facilities and housing. This was not coincidence, but rather a reflection of the way that the dominant classes naturalized their political and economic power through a denial of marginalized people's contributions to societal wealth and development.[17]

For all their understanding that prostitution bore some relationship to industrialization, urbanization, and the nature of women's work, Baltimore's most vocal anti-vice reformers ultimately failed to challenge either the gendered order of their society or the market relations it helped to structure. The majority of evangelical reformers and MVC members ultimately believed – as many nineteenth-century Americans had – that women were inherently unsuited to the harsh world of commerce. Their belief in women's natural vulnerability prompted them to seek out solutions to the prostitution "problem" that were conservative in their emphasis on women's roles within the household and family economies rather than as workers with rights to living wages. Even those reformers

---

[17] Historians of the American West in particular have noted that prostitution was tolerated in early boomtowns only to be treated as a moral and health hazard once white women began to arrive in larger numbers and a respectable middle class formed. For an overview, see Julia Ann Laite, "Historical Perspectives on Industrial Development, Mining, and Prostitution," *Historical Journal* 52, no. 3 (2009): 739–61.

who did attempt to improve women's working conditions and compensation were more likely to blame prostitution on corporate monopolies or the foibles of specific employers rather than market relations as a whole. At the core of their ideology was the idea that state intervention could make industrial capitalism more moral by breaking up coercive monopolies and trusts and enforcing protections for female workers like those that the Supreme Court approved in *Muller* v. *Oregon* (1908). Problems like prostitution were, in these reformers' view, the result of capitalistic excesses whose influences could be curbed with the right policies.[18]

Moral and political reformers' inability or unwillingness to engage in a broader, structural critique of market and industrial capitalism hampered their efforts to abolish Baltimore's sex trade. By opting to suppress prostitution without addressing the fundamental issues of inequality and exploitation that drove women into the trade in the first place, reformers succeeded only in making life worse for sex workers, whose voices they seldom listened to as they sought to implement new, more suppressive policies. Police and BSSV members who tried to cripple the sex trade by undermining its commercial foundations – banning the sale of alcohol, forbidding the installation of phones, and preventing madams from attracting new labor – ensured that brothels became more exploitative and coercive. The intervention into the sex trade created many of the oppressive conditions that reformers subsequently used to justify closing brothels, leading to vicious cycles of suppression.

Progressives' failure to secure a better existence for sex workers despite their (sometimes) best intentions serves as a cautionary tale for the architects of modern prostitution policy. Contemporary debates over sex work and sex trafficking share much in common with the debates that took place in Baltimore and other American cities in the Progressive era, especially with regard to white slavery rhetoric. Like participants in the white slavery scare, modern anti-trafficking activists often employ data of questionable veracity to outline the scope of the problem; tap into fears about immigration; insist that anyone not supportive of efforts to abolish prostitution must profit in some way from commercial sex; deny the agency of all sex workers; and embrace state intervention into the sex trade. The latter stances are especially problematic. As this book and numerous others studies of prostitution and sex work have demonstrated, state interference with the sex trade often involved – and involves – police

---

[18] MVCR, vol. 1; Haag, "Commerce in Souls," 292–308.

and courts extracting financial resources from sex workers while curtailing their liberties and placing them in greater poverty and danger.[19] The exploitative economic structures that support involuntary and coerced forms of sex work need to be addressed and sex workers need to be listened to if their situations are to be improved in any real way.

[19] See, for instance, Paul Amar, "Operation Princess in Rio de Janeiro: Policing 'Sex Trafficking,' Strengthening Worker Citizenship, and the Urban Geopolitics of Security in Brazil," *Security Dialogue* 40 (2009).

Bibliography

ARCHIVAL SOURCES

Alan Chesney Medical Archives, Baltimore, MD

Howard A. Kelly Collection

Baltimore City Archives, Baltimore, MD

Baltimore City Property Tax Records, RG 4, Series 2
City Council Records, RG 16, Series 2
Mayor's Correspondence, RG 9, Series 2

Enoch Pratt Free Library, Baltimore, MD

Maryland Vice Commission Report, Vols. 1–5

Library Company of Philadelphia, Philadelphia, PA

McCallister Collection of Civil War Ephemera
William H. Helfand Collection of Proprietary Medicine Pamphlets

Maryland State Archives, Annapolis, MD

Baltimore City Circuit Court (Equity Docket A, Miscellaneous), C185
Baltimore City and County Jail (Criminal Dockets), C2057
Baltimore City Court (Dockets and Minutes), C184
Baltimore City Criminal Court (Criminal Dockets), C1849
Baltimore City Justice of the Peace (Criminal Dockets), C211
Baltimore County Court of Oyer and Terminer and Gaol Delivery (Dockets and
  Minutes), C183

Baltimore County Register of Wills (Inventories), C340
Baltimore County Register of Wills (Orphan's Court Proceedings), C396
Baltimore Police Department (Criminal Dockets, Eastern District), C2111
Baltimore Police Department (Criminal Dockets, Middle District), C2109
Baltimore Police Department (Criminal Dockets, Southern District), C2113
Governor and Council (Pardon Papers), S1061
Maryland State Penitentiary (Prisoner Record), S257

Maryland Historical Society, Baltimore, MD

Alms-House Medical Records, 1833–1837, MS 2474
Baltimore City and County Poor Relief and Welfare Services, Alms-House
    Admissions Record, 1814–1826, MS 1866.1
Baltimore Country Trustees of the Poor
Almshouse Admissions Book, MS 1866.1
Minutes MS 1866
May's Dramatic Encyclopedia of Baltimore, 1750–1904, MS 995
Medical and Chirurgical Faculty of Maryland Manuscript Collection,
    MS 3000
Baltimore General Dispensary, Patient Records, Box 61
Francis Donaldson, Case Histories, Baltimore City & County Almhouses,
    1844–1845
Box 32, Folders 1–2
Francis Donaldson, Case Records, Marine Hospital, 1845–1848, Box 32,
    Folder 3

Milton S. Eisenhower Library Special Collections, Baltimore, MD

Anonymous. "A Manuscript Account of a Journey from Wilmington to
    Baltimore and Back," 1818, MS 523
Report of the Trial of Michael Rock on an Indictment for a Rape on Elizabeth
    Black, MS 174

National Archives, Washington, DC

US Army, Court Martial Records, RG 153

New-York Historical Society, New York, NY

Claudius W. Rider Diaries
George A. Mitchell Letters
Henry S. Congdon Letters
Henry Spencer Murray Letters
William Darlington Papers

NEWSPAPERS

Baltimore *Clipper*
Baltimore *Evening Suns*
Baltimore *Gazette & Daily Advertiser*
Baltimore *Patriot*
Baltimore *Sun*
Federal Gazette
Maryland Gazette
The Republican or, Anti-Democrat
Venus Miscellany (New York, NY)
Viper's Sting and Paul Pry (Baltimore, MD)

PUBLISHED PRIMARY SOURCES

34th Congress, 2nd Session, House of Representatives. Report 79, *Alleged Hostile Organizations against the Government within the District of Columbia.* Washington, 1861.

Acton, William. *Prostitution, Considered in Its Moral, Social & Sanitary Aspects, in London and Other Large Cities with Proposals for the Mitigation and Prevention of Its Attendant Evils.* London: John Churchill, 1863.

Annual Report of the Executive Committee of the American Society for the Promotion of Temperance, vol. 1.

Baltimore General Dispensary. *Rules and By-Laws of the Baltimore General Dispensary, with Other Matter, Relative to the Institution.* Baltimore: Bower and Cole, 1803.

Baltimore General Dispensary. *An Address to the Citizens of Baltimore and Its Vicinity: Containing a Concise Account of the Baltimore General Dispensary, Its By-Laws, and Other Matters Worthy of Notice.* Baltimore, 1812.

Butler, Benjamin F. *Autobiography and Personal Reminiscences of Major-General Benjamin F. Butler,* Part 1. Boston: A. M. Taylor's Book Publishers, 1892.

California Penological Commission. *Penology: Report of the California State Penological Commission.* Sacramento: State Office, P. L. Schoaff, Supt. State Printing, 1887.

Carey, Matthew. *Miscellaneous Essays.* Philadelphia: Carey and Hart, 1830.

Clokey, Joseph Waddell. *Dying at the Top: Or, the Moral and Spiritual Condition of the Young Men of America.* Chicago: W. W. Varnarsdale, 1890.

Colvin, John B. *The Magistrate's Guide, and Citizen's Counsellor: Adapted to the State of Maryland and Washington County, in the District of Columbia.* Washington, DC: Elijah Weems, 1819.

Davison, Gideon Minor. *The Traveller's Guide through the Middle & Northern States, & the Provinces of Canada.* Saratoga Springs: G. M. Davison, 1834.

Douglass, Frederick. *Narrative of the Life of Frederick Douglass, an American Slave. Written by Himself.* Chapel Hill: University of North Carolina Press, 1999.

Evans, Hugh Davey. *Maryland Common Law Practice: A Treatise on the Course of Proceeding in the Common Law Courts of the State of Maryland.* Baltimore: Joseph Robinson, 1839.

First Branch, Baltimore City Council. *Journal of the Proceedings of the First Branch of the City Council at the Sessions of 1864 & 1865.* Baltimore: James Young, 1865.

Free Loveyer. *Directory to the Seraglios in New York, Philadelphia, Boston and all the Principal Cities in the Union.* New York, 1859.

Fusselbaugh, William H. B., to Eugene Higgins, Secretary of the Senate of Maryland, Feb. 25, 1880. In *Journal of the Proceedings of the Senate of the State of Maryland, January Session, 1880.* Annapolis: Wm. T. Iglehart & Co, 1880.

The Gentlemen's Companion of New York City in 1870, reprinted in *New York Times*, 10. http://s3.amazonaws.com/nytdocs/docs/563/563.pdf.

Glenn, James. *The Venereal Disease; Its Primary Cause Explained.* New York, 1857.

Gross, Samuel D. *Syphilis in Its Relation to the National Health: Being the Address in Surgery, Delivered before the American Medical Association, at Its Meeting at Detroit, June 3, 1874.* Philadelphia: Collins, Printer, 1874.

Hall, Clayton Colman, ed. *Baltimore: Biography III.* New York: Lewis Historical Publishing Company, 1912.

Hamilton v. Whitridge. In *Maryland Reports: Containing Cases Argued and Adjudged in the Court of Appeals of Maryland* 11. Baltimore, 1858.

Harper, William. "Slavery in the Light of Social Ethics." In *Cotton Is King, and Pro-Slavery Arguments: Comprising the Writings of Hammond, Harper, Christy, Stringfellow, Hodge, Bledsoe, and Cartwright on This Important Subject*, edited by E. N. Elliott. New York: Negro Universities Press, 1969. Reprint.

Home for Fallen and Friendless Women. *Report of the Home for Fallen and Friendless Women.* Baltimore: J. F. Weishampel, Jr., 1870.

Hooker, Edith Houghton. *The Laws of Sex.* Boston: Gorham Press, 1921.

Janney, Oliver Edward. *The White Slave Traffic in America.* New York: National Vigilance Committee 1911.

Johnson, John. *Reports of Cases Decided in the High Court of Chancery of Maryland*, vol. 2. Annapolis: James Wingate, 1852.

Kelly, Howard A. "The Social Diseases and Their Effects on the Community." *Journal of the American Medical Association* 59, no. 14 (Oct. 6, 1912): 1312.

Lane, Winthrop D. "Under Cover of Respectability: Some Disclosures of Immorality Among Unsuspected Men and Women." *The Survey* 35 (Mar. 25, 1916).

Latrobe, John Hazlehurst Boneval. *Picture of Baltimore: Containing a Description of All Objects of Interest in the City.* Baltimore: Fielding and Lucas, 1832.

Maryland Bureau of Industrial Statistics and Information. *Second Biennial Report, 1886–1887.* Annapolis: James Young, 1888.

Maryland Governor (1865–1869: Swann). *Record of Proceedings of the Investigation before His Excellency Thomas Swann, Governor of Maryland, in the Case of Samuel Hindes and Nicholas L. Wood, Commissioners of the Board of Police of the City of Baltimore, Upon Charges Preferred against Them for Official Misconduct.* Baltimore: W. K. Boyle, printer, 1866.

Maryland Reports: Containing Cases Argued and Adjudged in the Court of Appeals of Maryland 11. Baltimore, 1858.

Mayer, Lewis. *Supplement to the Baltimore City Code; Comprising the Acts of the General Assembly of Maryland, Passed at the Sessions of 1870, 1872, and 1874, Relating to the City of Baltimore, and the Ordinances of the Mayor and City Council from June 1869, to June 1874, with Decisions of the Courts Construing the Acts and Ordinances. Also an Appendix of Ordinances, from June to Adjournment of Council, October 27, 1874.* Baltimore: John Cox, City Printer, 1874.

Mencken, H. L. *A Saturnalia of Bunk: Selections from the Free Lance, 1911–1915,* edited by S. T. Joshi. Athens: Ohio University Press, 2017.

Moore, Frank, ed. *Anecdotes, Poetry and Incidents of the War: North and South. 1860–1865.* New York, 1866.

Morath, Max. "The 93 Years of Eubie Blake," *American Heritage,* Oct. 1976, www.americanheritage.com/content/93-years-eubie-blake.

Morris, John C. "Minority Report of the Special Committee on the Prevention of Venereal Diseases." *Maryland Medical Journal* 8, no. 1 (May 1, 1881).

National Conference of Charities and Correction. *Proceedings of the National Conference of Charities and Correction,* vol. 42. Baltimore: Hildmann Printing Co, 1915.

Neal, John. *Randolph: A Novel in Two Volumes,* vol. 1. Philadelphia, 1823.

New York Magdalen Society. *Magdalen Report.* New York, 1831.

Parent-Duchâtelet, Alexandre-Jean-Baptiste. *Prostitution in Paris, Considered Morally, Politically, and Medically: Prepared for Philanthropists and Legislators, from Statistical Documents, Translated from the French, by an American Physician.* Boston: Charles H. Brainard, 1845.

Phelan, Raymond V. "Publish the Names." *The Survey* 36 (July 8, 1916).

Poe, John Prentiss. *The Maryland Code: Public General Laws.* Baltimore: King Bros., 1904.

Police Commissioners of Baltimore City. *Report of the Police Commissioners of Baltimore City, with Accompanying Documents.* Baltimore, 1861.

Report of the Board of Police Commissioners for the City of Baltimore to His Excellency the Governor of Maryland. Baltimore: Baltimore City Printing and Binding Company, 1912.

Report of the Board of Police Commissioners for the City of Baltimore to His Excellency the Governor of Maryland, 1912. Baltimore: Baltimore City Printing and Binding Company, 1913.

Report of the Board of Police Commissioners for the City of Baltimore to His Excellency the Governor of Maryland for the Year 1917. Baltimore: George W. King Printing Company, 1918.

Report of the Board of Police Commissioners for the City of Baltimore to His Excellency the Governor of Maryland for the Year 1919. Baltimore: George W. King Printing Company, 1920.

Powell, Aaron Macy. *State Regulation of Vice: Regulation Efforts in America. The Geneva Congress.* New York: Wood & Holbrook Publishers, 1878.

Reese, David Meredith. *A Plain and Practical Treatise on the Epidemic Cholera: As It Prevailed in the City of New York, in the Summer of 1832*. New York: Conner & Cooke, 1833.

Sanger, William. *The History of Prostitution*. New York: Harper & Brothers, 1858.

Simms, William Gilmore. "On the Morality of Slavery." In *The Pro-Slavery Argument, as Maintained by the Most Distinguished Writers of the Southern States*. Philadelphia: Lippincott, Grambo, & Co., 1853.

Smith v. State (1848). *Reports of Cases Argued and Determined in the Court of Appeals of Maryland, 1852*. London: Forgotten Books, 2013. Reprint.

Society for the Suppression of Vice of Baltimore. *Annual Report of the Society for the Suppression of Vice of Baltimore for the Year Ending December 31, 1914*. Baltimore, 1914.

The Stranger's Guide to Baltimore, Showing the Easiest and Best Mode of Seeing All the Public Buildings and Places of Note. Baltimore: Murphy & Co., 1852.

Swaim, William. *A Treatise on the Alternative and Curative Virtues of Swaim's Panacea, and for Its Application to the Different Diseases of the Human System: Interspersed with Remarks on Its Pharmaceutic Effects as a Remedial Agent*. Philadelphia: J. Bioren, 1833.

US Army's Surgeon General's Office. *The Medical and Surgical History of the War of the Rebellion*, Part I, vol. 1. Washington, DC: Government Printing Office, 1870.

The Medical and Surgical History of the War of the Rebellion, Part III, vol. 1. (3rd Medical volume). Washington, DC: Government Printing Office, 1888.

US Bureau of Labor Statistics. *Bulletin of the United States Bureau of Labor Statistics*, issue 54 (Sep. 1904).

US Department of Labor, Women's Bureau. *Women in Maryland Industries*. Washington, DC: Government Printing Office, 1922.

US Sanitary Commission. *Committee of the Associate Medical Members of the Sanitary Commission on the Subject of Venereal Diseases, with Special Reference to Practice in the Army and Navy*. New York: John F. Trow, Printer, 1862.

US War Department. *The War of the Rebellion: A Compilation of the Official Records of the Union and Confederate Armies*, Series I, vol. 5. Washington, DC: Government Printing Office, 1881.

Vansant, Joshua. *Mayor's Message to the First and Second Branches of the City Council of Baltimore*. Baltimore: John Cox, 1874.

Waring, James H. N. *Work of the Colored Law and Order League: Baltimore, MD*. Philadelphia: Press of the E. A. Wright Bank Note Company for the Committee of Twelve for the Advancement of the Interests of the Negro Race, 1908.

Washington, Booker T. *The Story of the Negro: The Rise of the Race from Slavery*, vol. 2. New York: Association Press, 1909.

Woman's Christian Temperance Union, *Minutes of the National Woman's Christian Temperance Union at the Eighth Annual Meeting, Boston, Mass., November 13 to 18, 1891*. Chicago: Woman's Temperance Publishing Association, 1891.

ONLINE DATABASES

America's Historical Newspapers, www.infoweb.newsbank.com
Ancestry.com Census and Tax Collections
Baltimore City Directories, University of Maryland, http://lib.guides.umd.edu/
content.php?pid=355337&sid=2905985
Historical Census Browser, University of Virginia, http://mapserver.lib.virginia
.edu/
JScholarship Map Collections, https://jscholarship.library.jhu.edu/handle/1774.2/
32585
ProQuest Sanborn Map Collection

SECONDARY SOURCES

Adams, James H. *Urban Reform and Sexual Vice in Progressive-Era Philadelphia:
The Faithful and the Fallen*. Lanham: Lexington Books, 2015.
Alexander, Robert L. "Baltimore Row Houses of the Early Nineteenth Century."
American Studies 16, no. 2 (Fall 1975): 65–76.
Allen, Robert Clyde. *Horrible Prettiness: Burlesque and American Culture*.
Chapel Hill: University of North Carolina Press, 1991.
Amar, Paul. "Operation Princess in Rio de Janeiro: Policing 'Sex Trafficking,'
Strengthening Worker Citizenship, and the Urban Geopolitics of Security in
Brazil." *Security Dialogue* 40 (2009): 513–41.
Anbinder, Tyler. *Five Points: The Nineteenth-Century New York City Neighbor-
hood*. New York: Free Press, 2001.
Andreas, Peter. *Smuggler Nation: How Illicit Trade Made America*. Oxford:
Oxford University Press, 2013.
Arceneaux, Pamela D. "Guidebooks to Sin: The Blue Books of Storyville."
Louisiana History: Journal of the Louisiana Historical Association 28
(Autumn 1987): 397–405.
Arnold, Joseph L. "The Neighborhood and City Hall: The Origin of Neighbor-
hood Associations in Baltimore, 1880–1911." *Journal of Urban History* 6
(Nov. 1979): 3–30.
Attie, Jeanie. *Patriotic Toil: Northern Women and the American Civil War*.
Ithaca, NY: Cornell University Press, 1998.
Ayers, Edward L. *Vengeance and Justice: Crime and Punishment in the Nineteenth-
Century American South*. Oxford: Oxford University Press, 1984.
Bagby, George P. *The Annotated Code of the Public Civil Laws of Maryland*,
vol. 3. Baltimore: King Bros., Printers and Publishers, 1914.
Baldwin, Peter. *Contagion and the State in Europe, 1830–1930*. Cambridge:
Cambridge University Press, 1999.
Baptist, Edward E. "'Cuffy,' 'Fancy Maids,' and 'One-Eyed Men': Rape, Com-
modification, and the Domestic Slave Trade in the United States." *American
Historical Review* 106 (Dec. 2001): 1619–50.
Barber, E. Susan. "Depraved and Abandoned Women: Prostitution in Richmond,
Virginia across the Civil War." In *Neither Lady Nor Slave: Working Women*

of the Old South, edited by Susan Delfino and Michele Gillespie, 155–73. Chapel Hill: University of North Carolina Press, 2002.

Beckert, Sven. *The Monied Metropolis: New York City and the Consolidation of the American Bourgeoisie, 1850–1896*. Cambridge: Cambridge University Press, 1993.

Beisel, Nicola Kay. *Imperiled Innocents: Anthony Comstock and Family Reproduction in Victorian America*. Princeton: Princeton University Press, 1997.

Beisel, Nicola Kay, and Tamara Kay. "Abortion, Race, and Gender in Nineteenth-Century America." *American Sociological Review* 69 (Aug. 2004): 498–518.

Best, Joel. *Controlling Vice: Regulating Brothel Prostitution in St. Paul, 1865–1883*. Columbus: Ohio University Press, 1998.

Blackmar, Elizabeth. *Manhattan for Rent, 1785–1850*. Ithaca, NY: Cornell University Press, 1989.

Blackmon, Douglas A. *Slavery by Another Name: The Re-enslavement of Black Americans from the Civil War to World War II*. New York: Doubleday, 2012.

Blair, Cynthia M. *I've Got to Make My Livin': Black Women's Sex Work in Turn-of-the-Century Chicago*. Chicago: University of Chicago Press, 2010.

Bledstein, Burton J. *The Culture of Professionalism: The Middle Class and the Development of Higher Education in America*. New York: W. W. Norton, 1976.

Block, Sharon. *Rape and Sexual Power in Early America*. Chapel Hill: University of North Carolina Press, 2006.

Blumin, Stuart M. *The Emergence of the Middle Class: Social Experience in the American City, 1760–1900*. Cambridge: Cambridge University Press, 1989.

Boger, Gretchen. "The Meaning of Neighborhood in the Modern City: Baltimore's Residential Segregation Ordinances, 1910–1913." *Journal of Urban History* 35 (Jan. 2009): 236–58.

Bolster, W. Jeffrey. *Black Jacks: African American Seamen in the Age of Sail*. Cambridge, MA: Harvard University Press, 1997.

Boydston, Jeanne. *Home and Work: Housework, Wages, and the Ideology of Labor in the Early Republic*. Oxford: Oxford University Press, 1994.

Brackett, Jeffrey Richardson. *The Negro in Maryland: A Study of the Institution of Slavery*, vol. 6. Baltimore: N. Murray, 1889.

Brandt, Allan M. *No Magic Bullet: A Social History of Venereal Disease in the United States since 1880*. Oxford: Oxford University Press, 1985.

Breen, T. H. *The Marketplace of Revolution: How Consumer Politics Shaped American Independence*. Oxford: Oxford University Press, 2004.

Brodie, Janet Farrell. *Contraception and Abortion in Nineteenth-Century America*. Ithaca, NY: Cornell University Press, 1994.

Brown, Kathleen. *Foul Bodies: Cleanliness in Early America*. New Haven, CT: Yale University Press, 2009.

Bruggemann, Julia. "Prostitution, Sexuality, and Gender Roles in Imperial Germany: Hamburg, a Case Study." In *Genealogies of Identity: Interdisciplinary Readings on Sex and Sexuality*, edited by Margaret Sönser Breen and Fiona Peters, 19–38. New York: Editions Rodopi BV, 2005.

Brugger, Robert. *Maryland: A Middle Temperament, 1634–1980.* Baltimore: Johns Hopkins University Press, 1996.

Bushman, Richard. *The Refinement of America: Persons, Houses, Cities.* New York: Vintage, 1993.

Butler, Anne M. *Daughters of Joy, Sisters of Misery: Prostitutes in the American West, 1865–90.* Urbana: University of Illinois Press, 1987.

Bynam, William F., and Roy Porter, eds. *Medical Fringe and Medical Orthodoxy, 1750–1850.* London: Croom Helm, 1987.

Bynum, Victoria. *Unruly Women: The Politics of Social and Sexual Control in the Old South.* Chapel Hill: University of North Carolina Press, 1992.

Cahif, Jacqueline. "'She Supposes Herself Cured': Almshouse Women and Venereal Disease in Late Eighteenth and Early Nineteenth Century Philadelphia." PhD thesis, University of Glasgow, 2010.

Camp, Stephanie M. H. *Closer to Freedom: Enslaved Women and Everyday Resistance in the Plantation South.* Chapel Hill: University of North Carolina Press, 2004.

Caplan, Jane. "'Educating the Eye': The Tattooed Prostitute." In *Cultural Sexology: Labeling Bodies and Desires, 1890–1940,* edited by Lucy Bland and Laura Doan, 100–15. Cambridge: Cambridge University Press, 1998.

Cassie, Ron. "How Baltimore Became the New York of the South: European Immigration between 1867–1914 and the Development of Ethnic Neighborhoods around the Port of Baltimore." Master's thesis, Georgetown University, 2016.

Chapelle, Suzanne Ellerly, Jean B. Russo, et al. *Maryland: A History.* Baltimore: Johns Hopkins University Press, 2008.

Chateauvert, Melinda. *Sex Workers Unite: A History of the Movement from Stonewall to SlutWalk.* Boston: Beacon Press, 2013.

Chauncey, George. *Gay New York: Gender, Urban Culture, and the Making of the Gay Male World, 1890–1940.* New York: Basic Books, 1994.

Clayton, Ralph. *Black Baltimore, 1820–1870.* Bowie, MD: Heritage Books, 1987.

Clement, Elizabeth Alice. *Love for Sale: Courting, Treating, and Prostitution in New York City, 1900–1945.* Chapel Hill: University of North Carolina Press, 2006.

Clement, Priscilla. "The Transformation of the Wandering Poor in Nineteenth-Century Philadelphia." In *Walking to Work: Tramps in America, 1790–1935,* edited by Eric H. Monkkonen, 54–84. Lincoln: University of Nebraska Press, 1984.

Click, Patricia. *The Spirit of the Times: Amusements in Nineteenth-Century Baltimore, Norfolk, and Richmond.* Charlottesville: University of Virginia Press, 1989.

Clinton, Catherine. *Public Women and the Confederacy.* Milwaukee: Marquette University Press, 1999.

Cohen, Patricia Cline. *The Murder of Helen Jewett.* New York: Vintage Books, 1999.

Cohen, Patricia Cline, Timothy J. Gilfoyle, and Helen Leftkowitz Horowitz. *The Flash Press: Sporting Male Weeklies in 1840s New York*. Chicago: University of Chicago Press, 2008.

Cole, Stephanie. "Keeping the Peace: Domestic Assault and Private Prosecution in Antebellum Baltimore." In *Over the Threshold: Intimate Violence in Early America*, edited by Christine Daniels and Michael V. Kennedy, 148–72. London: Routledge, 1999.

Coleman, John P. *Historic Amusement Parks of Baltimore: An Illustrated History*. Jefferson, NC: McFarland & Company, 2014.

Connelly, Mark Thomas. *The Response to Prostitution in the Progressive Era*. Chapel Hill: University of North Carolina Press, 2011.

Corbin, Alain. *Women for Hire: Prostitution and Sexuality in France after 1850*. Cambridge, MA: Harvard University Press, 1990.

Cordell, Eugene Fauntleroy. *The Medical Annals of Maryland, 1799–1899*. Baltimore: Williams & Wilkins, 1903.

Crenson, Matthew. *Baltimore: A Political History*. Baltimore: Johns Hopkins University Press, 2017.

"Baltimore, MD 1854–1877." In *Cities in American Political History*, edited by Richardson Dilworth, 243–49. Los Angeles: Sage Press, 2011.

Cuthbert, Norma. *Lincoln and the Baltimore Plot, 1861: From the Pinkerton Records and Related Papers*. San Marino, CA: Huntington Library, 1949.

Daggers, Jenny, and Diana Neal, eds. *Sex Gender, and Religion: Josephine Butler Revisited*. New York: Peter Lang Publishing, 2006.

Dantas, Mariana L. R. *Black Townsmen: Urban Slavery and Freedom in the Eighteenth-Century Americas*. New York: Palgrave Macmillan, 2008.

Davidson, Roger, and Leslie Hall, eds. *Sex, Sin and Suffering: Venereal Disease and European Society since 1870*. London: Routledge, 2001.

D'Emilio, John. "Capitalism and Gay Identity." In *Making Trouble: Essays on Gay History, Politics, and the University*, edited by John D'Emilio, 3–16. New York: Routledge,

D'Emilio, John, and Estelle B. Freedman. *Intimate Matters: A History of Sexuality in America*, 3rd edition. Chicago: University of Chicago Press, 2012.

Dennis, Donna. *Licentious Gotham: Erotic Publishing and Its Prosecution in Nineteenth-Century New York*. Cambridge, MA: Harvard University Press, 2009.

Deutsch, Sarah. *Women and the City: Gender, Space, and Power in Boston, 1870–1940*. Oxford: Oxford University Press, 2000.

Dilts, James D. *The Great Road: The Building of the Baltimore and Ohio, the Nation's First Railroad, 1828–1853*. Stanford, CA: Stanford University Press, 1993.

Doezema, Jo. *Sex Slaves and Discourse Masters: The Construction of Trafficking*. London: Zed Books, 2010.

Donovan, Brian. *White Slave Crusades: Race, Gender, and Anti-Vice Activism, 1887–1917*. Champaign: University of Illinois Press, 2006.

Dorsey, Bruce. *Reforming Men and Women: Gender in the Antebellum City*. Ithaca, NY: Cornell University Press, 2002.

Dorsey, Jennifer Hull. *Hirelings: African American Workers and Free Labor in Early Maryland.* Ithaca, NY: Cornell University Press, 2011.

Dubber, Markus Dirk. *The Police Power: Patriarchy and the Foundations of American Government.* New York: Columbia University Press, 2005.

Edwards, George John. *The Grand Jury: Considered from an Historical, Political and Legal Standpoint, and the Law and Practice Relating Thereto.* Philadelphia: George T. Bisel Co., 1906.

Edwards, Laura F. *The People and Their Peace: Legal Culture and the Transformation of Inequality in the Post-Revolutionary South.* Chapel Hill: University of North Carolina Press, 2009.

Scarlet Doesn't Live Here Anymore: Southern Women in the Civil War Era. Champaign: University of Illinois Press, 2000.

Ely, James. *The Guardian of Every Other Right: A Constitutional History of Property Rights.* Oxford: Oxford University Press, 2008.

Esslinger, Dean R. "Immigration through the Port of Baltimore." In *Forgotten Doors: The Other Ports of Entry to the United States,* edited by M. Mark Stolarik, 61–74. Cranbury, NJ: Associated University Presses, 1988.

Ezratty, Harry A. *Baltimore in the Civil War: The Pratt Street Riot and a City Occupied.* Charleston, SC: History Press, 2010.

Farrar, Hayward. *The Baltimore Afro-American, 1892–1950.* Westport, CT: Greenwood Press, 1998.

Fields, Barbara Jeanne. *Slavery and Freedom on the Middle Ground: Maryland during the Nineteenth Century.* New Haven, CT: Yale University Press, 1985.

Fitch, Catherine A., and Steven Ruggles. "Historical Trends in Marriage Formation: The United States 1850–1990." In *The Ties That Bind: Perspectives on Marriage and Cohabitation,* edited by Linda J. Waite et al., 59–90. New York: Aldine de Gruyer, 2000.

Flannery, Michael A. "The Early Botanical Medical Movement as a Reflection of Life, Liberty, and Literacy in Jacksonian America." *Journal of the Medical Library Association* 90, no. 4 (Oct. 2002): 442–54.

Folsom, De Francais. *Our Police: A History of the Baltimore Force from the First Watchman to the Latest Appointee.* Baltimore: J. D. Ehlers & Co. and Guggenheimer, Weil & Co., 1888.

Foote, Lorien. *The Gentlemen and the Roughs: Violence, Honor, and Manhood in the Union Army.* Baton Rouge: Louisiana State University Press, 2009.

Foucault, Michel. *Discipline and Punish: The Birth of the Prison.* New York: Vintage Books, 1995.

History of Sexuality: An Introduction, vol. 1. New York: Vintage Books, 1990.

Freedman, Estelle B. *Their Sisters' Keepers: Women's Prison Reform in America, 1830–1930.* Ann Arbor: University of Michigan Press, 1984.

Friedman, Lawrence. *Guarding Life's Dark Secrets: Legal and Social Controls over Reputation, Propriety, and Privacy.* Stanford, CA: Stanford University Press, 2007.

Fronc, Jennifer. "The Horns of the Dilemma: Race Mixing and the Enforcement of Jim Crow in New York City." *Journal of Urban History* 33, no. 1 (2006): 3–25.

New York Undercover: Private Surveillance in the Progressive Era. Chicago: University of Chicago Press, 2009.

Fuentes, Marisa J. *Dispossessed Lives: Enslaved Women, Violence, and the Archive*. Philadelphia: University of Pennsylvania Press, 2016.

Fuke, Richard Paul. *Imperfect Equality: African Americans and the Confines of White Racial Attitudes in Post-Emancipation Maryland*. New York: Fordham University Press, 1999.

Furguson, Ernest B. *Freedom Rising: Washington in the Civil War*. New York: Vintage, 2004.

Gallman, James Matthew. "Relative Ages of Colonial Marriages." *Journal of Interdisciplinary History* 14 (Winter, 1984): 609–17.

Gamber, Wendy. *The Boardinghouse in Nineteenth-Century America*. Baltimore: Johns Hopkins University Press, 2007.

Gamble, Robert J. "The Promiscuous Economy: Cultural and Commercial Geographies of Secondhand in the Antebellum City." In *Capitalism by Gaslight*, edited by Brian J. Luskey and Wendy A. Woloson, 31–52. Philadelphia: University of Pennsylvania Press, 2015.

Garnett, Nicole Stelle. *Ordering the City: Land Use, Policing, and the Restoration of Urban America*. New Haven, CT: Yale University Press, 2009.

Giesberg, Judith. *Army at Home: Women and the Civil War on the Northern Home Front*. Chapel Hill: University of North Carolina Press, 2009.

Sex and the Civil War: Soldiers, Pornography, and the Making of American Morality. Chapel Hill: University of North Carolina Press, 2017.

Gilfoyle, Timothy J. *City of Eros: New York City, Prostitution, and the Commercialization of Sex, 1790–1920*. New York: W. W. Norton, 1992.

"Prostitutes in History: From Parables of Pornography to Metaphors of Modernity." *The American Historical Review* 104 (Feb. 1999): 117–41.

"Strumpets and Misogynists: Brothel 'Riots' and the Transformation of Prostitution in Antebellum New York City." In *The Making of Urban America*, edited by Raymond A. Mohl, 37–52. New York: SR Books, 1997.

Gilje, Paul A. *Liberty on the Waterfront: American Maritime Culture in the Age of Revolution*. Philadelphia: University of Pennsylvania Press, 2007.

Godbeer, Richard. *Sexual Revolution in Early America*. Baltimore: Johns Hopkins University Press, 2002.

Goldman, Marion S. *Gold Diggers and Silver Miners: Prostitution and Social Life on the Comstock Lode*. Ann Arbor: University of Michigan, 1981.

Green, James N., Charles E. Rosenberg, and William H. Helfand. *Every Man His Own Doctor: Popular Medicine in Early America*. Philadelphia: Library Company of Philadelphia, 1998.

Greenberg, Amy S. *Cause for Alarm: The Volunteer Fire Department in the Nineteenth-Century City*. Princeton: Princeton University Press, 1998.

Manifest Manhood and the Antebellum American Empire. Cambridge: Cambridge University Press, 2005.

Grossberg, Michael. *Governing the Hearth: Law and the Family in Nineteenth-Century America*. Chapel Hill: University of North Carolina Press, 1985.

Haag, Pamela S. "'Commerce in Souls': Vice, Virtue, and Women's Wage Work in Baltimore, 1900–1915." *Maryland Historical Magazine* 68 (Fall 1991): 292–308.

Hall, Clayton Colman, ed. *Baltimore: Its History and Its People*, vol. 1. New York: Lewis Historical Publishing Company, 1912.

Halpin, Dennis P. "'The Struggle for Land and Liberty': Segregation, Violence, and African American Resistance in Baltimore, 1898–1918." *Journal of Urban History* 44 (July 2018): 691–712.

Halttunen, Karen. *Confidence Men and Painted Women: A Study of Middle-Class Culture in America, 1830–1870*. New Haven, CT: Yale University Press, 1982.

Murder Most Foul: The Killer and the American Gothic Imagination. Cambridge, MA: Harvard University Press, 1998.

Harari, Susan E., and Maris A. Vinovskis. "Adolescent Sexuality, Pregnancy, and Childbearing in the Past." In *The Politics of Pregnancy: Adolescent Sexuality and Public Policy*, edited by Annette Lawson and Deborah L. Rhode, 20–45. New Haven, CT: Yale University Press, 1993.

Harris, Leslie M. "From Abolitionist Amalgamators to 'Rulers of the Five Points'." In *Sex, Love, Race: Crossing Boundaries in North American History*, edited by Martha Hodes, 191–212. New York: New York University Press, 1999.

Harry, James Warner. *Maryland Constitution of 1851*. Baltimore: Johns Hopkins Press, 1902.

Hartigan-O'Connor, Ellen. "Gender's Value in the History of Capitalism." *Journal of the Early Republic* 36 (Winter 2016): 613–35.

Harvey, Karen. *Reading Sex in the Eighteenth Century: Bodies and Gender in English Erotic Culture*. Cambridge: Cambridge University Press, 2004.

Haynes, April R. *Riotous Flesh: Women, Physiology, and the Solitary Vice in Nineteenth-Century America*. Chicago: University of Chicago Press, 2015.

Hayward, Mary Ellen, and Frank R. Shivers, eds. *The Architecture of Baltimore: An Illustrated History*. Baltimore: Johns Hopkins University Press, 2004.

Hechtlinger, Adelaide. *The Great Patent Medicine Era; or, Without Benefit of Doctor*. New York: Galahad Books, 1974.

Heins, Marjorie. *Not in Front of the Children: "Indecency," Censorship, and the Innocence of Youth*. Piscataway, NJ: Rutgers University Press, 2007.

Hemphill, Katie M. "Selling Sex and Intimacy in the City: The Changing Business of Prostitution in Nineteenth-Century Baltimore." In *Capitalism by Gaslight: Illuminating the Economy of Nineteenth-Century America*, edited by Wendy Woloson and Brian Luskey, 168–89. Philadelphia: University of Pennsylvania Press, 2015.

Hendrick, Harry. *Children, Childhood and English Society, 1880–1990*. Cambridge: Cambridge University Press, 1997.

Hennigan, Peter C. "Property War: Prostitution, Red-Light Districts, and the Transformation of Public Nuisance Law in the Progressive Era." *Yale Journal of Law and the Humanities* 16, no. 1 (2004): 126–27.

Herndon, Ruth Wallis. "The Domestic Cost of Seafaring: Town Leaders and Seamen's Families in Eighteenth-Century Rhode Island." In *Iron Men, Wooden Women: Gender and Seafaring in the Atlantic World, 1700–1920*,

        edited by Margaret Creighton and Lisa Norling, 55–69. Baltimore: Johns
        Hopkins University Press, 1996.
"Poor Women and the Boston Almshouse in the Early Republic." *Journal of the
        Early Republic* 32 (Fall 2012): 349–81.
Hershatter, Gail. *Dangerous Pleasures: Prostitution and Modernity in Twentieth-
        Century Shanghai.* Berkeley: University of California Press, 2007.
Hessinger, Rodney. *Seduced, Abandoned, and Reborn: Visions of Youth in
        Middle-Class America, 1780–1850.* Philadelphia: University of Pennsylvania
        Press, 2005.
Hicks, Cheryl D. *Talk with You Like a Woman: African American Women,
        Justice, and Reform in New York, 1890–1935.* Chapel Hill: University of
        North Carolina Press, 2010.
Hijar, Katherine. "Brothels for Gentlemen: Nineteenth-Century American Brothel
        Guides, Gentility, and Moral Reform." *Common-Place* 18 (Winter 2018).
        http://common-place.org/book/vol-18-no-1-hijar/.
"Sexuality, Print, and Popular Visual Culture in the United States, 1830–1870."
        PhD dissertation, Johns Hopkins University, 2008.
Hill, Jayme Rae. "From the Brothel to the Block: Politics and Prostitution in
        Baltimore during the Progressive Era." MA thesis, University of Maryland,
        Baltimore County, 2008.
Hill, Marilyn Wood. *Their Sisters' Keepers: Prostitution in New York City:
        1830–1870.* Berkeley: University of California Press, 1993.
Hobbs, Catherine. "Introduction: Cultures and Practices of U.S. Women's
        Literacy." In *Nineteenth-Century Women Learn to Write,* edited by
        Catherine Hobbs, 1–36. Charlottesville: University of Virginia Press,
        1995.
Hobson, Barbara Meil. *Uneasy Virtue: The Politics of Prostitution and the
        American Reform Tradition.* New York: Basic Books, 1987.
Hodes, Martha. *White Women, Black Men: Illicit Sex in the Nineteenth-Century
        South.* New Haven, CT: Yale University Press, 1997.
Holland, Brenna O'Rourke. "Free Market Family: Stephen Girard and the Cul-
        ture of Capitalism in Philadelphia." PhD dissertation, Temple University,
        2014.
Horowitz, Helen Lefkowitz. *Rereading Sex: Battles over Sexual Knowledge and
        Suppression in Nineteenth-Century America.* New York: Knopf Doubleday
        Publishing, 2006.
    *Rewriting Sex: Sexual Knowledge in Antebellum America: A Brief History with
        Documents.* New York: Palgrave Macmillan, 2006.
Hounshell, David A. *From the American System to Mass Production, 1800–1932:
        The Development of Manufacturing Technology in the United States.* Balti-
        more: Johns Hopkins University Press, 1984.
Hovencamp, Herbert. *Law and Morals in Classical Legal Thought.* Chicago:
        Fulton Lectures, 1996.
Howell, Philip. *Cities and Sexualities.* New York: Routledge, 2011.
    "Foucault, Sexuality, Geography." In *Foucault and Geography: Space, Know-
        ledge, Power,* edited by J. Crampton and S. Elden, 291–315. Aldershot:
        Ashgate, 2007.

Geographies of Regulation: Policing Prostitution in Nineteenth-Century Britain and the Empire. Cambridge: Cambridge University Press, 2009.

"Sex and the City of Bachelors: Sporting Guidebooks and Urban Knowledge in Nineteenth-Century Britain and America." *Cultural Geographies* 8, no. 1 (2001): 20–50.

Hubbard, Phil. "Desire/Disgust: Mapping the Moral Contours of Heterosexuality." *Progress in Human Geography* 24, no. 2 (June 2000): 191–217.

Sex and the City: Geographies of Prostitution in the Urban West. Aldershot: Ashgate Publishing, 1999.

Hufton, Olwen. *The Poor of Eighteenth-Century France, 1750–1789.* Oxford: Oxford University Press, 1974.

Hunt, Alan. *Governing Morals: A Social History of Moral Regulation.* Cambridge: Cambridge University Press, 1999.

Hunter, Tera W. *To 'Joy My Freedom: Southern Black Women's Lives and Labors after the Civil War.* Cambridge, MA: Harvard University Press, 1997.

Irvin, Benjamin. "Of 'Manly' and 'Monstrous' Eloquence: The Henpecked Husband in Revolutionary Political Debate, 1774–1775." In *New Men: Manliness in Early America,* edited by Thomas A. Foster, 195–216. New York: New York University Press, 2011.

Jenner, Mark, and Patrick Wallis, eds. *Medicine and the Market in England and Its Colonies, c. 1450–c. 1850.* New York: Palgrave Macmillan, 2007.

Johnson, Claudia D. "That Guilty Third Tier: Prostitution in Nineteenth-Century American Theaters." *American Quarterly* 27, no. 5 (1975): 575–84.

Johnson, Susan Lee. *Roaring Camp: The Social World of the California Gold Rush.* New York: W. W. Norton, 1991.

Jones, James Boyd. "A Tale of Two Cities: The Hidden Battle against Venereal Disease in Civil War Nashville and Memphis." *Civil War History* 31, no. 3 (1985): 270–76.

"Municipal Vice: The Management of Prostitution in Tennessee's Urban Experience. Part I: The Experience of Nashville and Memphis, 1854–1917." *Tennessee Historical Quarterly* 50, no. 1 (1991): 33–41.

Jones, Jacqueline. *Labor of Love, Labor of Sorrow: Black Women, Work, and the Family, from Slavery to the Present.* New York: Basic Books, 2010.

Saving Savannah: The City in the Civil War. New York, 2008.

Jordan, Jane, and Ingrid Sharp, eds. *Josephine Butler and the Prostitution Campaigns: Diseases of the Body Politic.* London: Routledge, 2003.

Joyce, Patrick. *The Rule of Freedom: Liberalism and the Modern City.* London: Verso, 2003.

Kann, Mark. *Taming Passion for the Public Good: Policing Sex in the Early Republic.* New York: New York University Press, 2013.

Kasson, John. *Houdini, Tarzan, and the Perfect Man: The White Male Body and the Challenge of Modernity in America.* New York: Hill & Wang, 2002.

Katz, Sarah. "Rumors of Rebellion: Fear of a Slave Uprising in Post-Nat Turner Baltimore." *Maryland Historical Magazine* 89 (Fall 1994): 328–33.

Keire, Mara. *For Business and Pleasure: Red-Light Districts and the Regulation of Vice in the United States, 1890–1933.* Baltimore: Johns Hopkins University Press, 2010.

"The Vice Trust: A Reinterpretation of the White Slavery Scare in the United States, 1907–1917." *Journal of Social History* 35, no. 1 (Autumn 2001): 5–41.

Kelly, Catherine E. *Republic of Taste: Art, Politics, and Everyday Life in Early America.* Philadelphia: University of Pennsylvania Press, 2016.

Kent, Frank Richardson. *The Story of Maryland Politics.* Baltimore: Thomas and Evans Printing Co., 1911.

Kerber, Linda K. "Separate Spheres, Female Worlds, Woman's Place: The Rhetoric of Women's History." *Journal of American History* 75 (June 1988): 9–39.

Kessler-Harris, Alice. *Out to Work: A History of Wage-Earning Women in the United States.* Oxford: Oxford University Press, 1983.

Kimmel, Michael. *Manhood in America: A Cultural History,* 3rd edition. Oxford: Oxford University Press, 2016.

Klepp, Susan E. *Revolutionary Conceptions: Women, Fertility, and Family Limitation in America, 1760–1820.* Chapel Hill: University of North Carolina Press, 2009.

Knopp, Lawrence. "Sexuality and the Spatial Dynamics of Capitalism." *Environment and Planning D: Society and Space* 10, no. 6 (1992): 651–69.

Kunzel, Regina G. *Fallen Women, Problem Girls: Unmarried Mothers and the Professionalization of Social Work, 1890–1945.* New Haven, CT: Yale University Press, 1993.

Laite, Julia. *Common Prostitutes and Ordinary Citizens: Commercial Sex in London, 1885–1960.* New York: Palgrave Macmillan, 2012.

"Historical Perspectives on Industrial Development, Mining, and Prostitution." *Historical Journal* 52, no. 3 (2009): 739–61.

Landau, Emily Epstein. *Spectacular Wickedness: Sex, Race, and Memory in Storyville, New Orleans.* Baton Rouge: Louisiana State University Press, 2013.

Langley, Harold. *Social Reform in the United States Navy, 1798–1862.* Annapolis: Naval Institute Press, 1967.

Laqueur, Thomas W. *Making Sex: Body and Gender from the Greeks to Freud.* Cambridge, MA: Harvard University Press, 1992.

"Sexual Desire and the Market Economy during the Industrial Revolution." In *Discourses of Sexuality: From Aristotle to AIDS,* edited by Domna C. Stanton, 185–215. Ann Arbor: University of Michigan Press, 1992.

Solitary Sex: A Cultural History of Masturbation. New York: Zone Books, 2003.

Lee, Catherine. *Policing Prostitution, 1856–1886: Deviance, Surveillance, and Morality.* London: Routledge, 2013.

LeFlouria, Talitha L. *Chained in Silence: Black Women and Convict Labor in the New South.* Chapel Hill: University of North Carolina Press, 2016.

Levine, Philippa. *Prostitution, Race and Politics: Policing Venereal Disease in the British Empire.* New York: Routledge, 2003.

Liebel, Tom. *Industrial Baltimore.* Charleston, SC: Arcadia Publishing, 2006.

Lisicky, Michael J. *Hutzler's: Where Baltimore Shops.* Charleston, SC: History Press, 2009.

Long, Alecia P. *The Great Southern Babylon: Sex, Race, and Respectability in New Orleans, 1865–1920.* Baton Rouge: Louisiana State University Press, 2005.

"(Mis)remembering General Order No. 28: Benjamin Butler, the Woman Order, and Historical Memory." In *Occupied Women: Gender, Military Occupation in the American Civil War,* edited by LeeAnn Whites and Alecia P. Long, 17–32. Baton Rouge: Louisiana State University Press, 2009.

"The Woman Order (General Order 28)." In *Women in the American Civil War,* vol. 1, edited by Lisa Tendrich Frank, 593–94. Santa Barbara, CA: ABC-CLIO, 2008.

Lowry, Thomas. *Sexual Misbehavior in the Civil War.* Bloomington, IN: Xlibris, 2006.

The Stories the Soldiers Wouldn't Tell: Sex in the Civil War. Mechanicsburg, PA: Stackpole Books, 1994.

Lynch-Brennan, Margaret, *The Irish Bridget: Irish Immigrant Women in Domestic Service in America, 1840–1930.* Syracuse: Syracuse University Press, 2009.

Lyons, Clare A. "Discipline, Sex, and the Republican Self." In *The Oxford Handbook of the American Revolution,* edited by Edward G. Gray and Jane Kamensky, 560–77. Oxford: Oxford University Press, 2013.

Sex among the Rabble: An Intimate History of Gender and Power in the Age of Revolution, Philadelphia, 1730–1830. Chapel Hill: University of North Carolina Press, 2006.

Mackey, Thomas C. *Red Lights Out: A Legal History of Prostitution, Disorderly Houses, and Vice Districts, 1870–1917.* New York: Garland Publishing, 1987.

MacPherson, James. *Battle Cry of Freedom: The Civil War Era.* Oxford: Oxford University Press, 1998.

Magner, Lois N. *A History of Medicine.* New York: Marcel Dekker, 1992.

Mahood, Linda. *The Magdalenes: Prostitution in the Nineteenth Century.* London: Routledge, 2012.

Malka, Adam. *The Men of Mobtown: Policing Baltimore in the Age of Slavery and Emancipation.* Chapel Hill: University of North Carolina Press, 2018.

Maloney, Linda M. "Doxies at Dockside: Prostitution and American Maritime Society, 1800–1900." In *Ships, Seafaring, and Society: Essays in Maritime History,* edited by Timothy J. Runyan, 217–25. Detroit, MI: Wayne State University Press, 1987.

Manion, Jen. *Liberty's Prisoners: Carceral Culture in Early America.* Philadelphia: University of Pennsylvania Press, 2015.

Manning, Chandra. "Working for Citizenship in the Contraband Camps." *Journal of the Civil War Era* 4 (June 2014): 172–204.

Marcus, Steve. *The Other Victorians: A Study of Sexuality and Pornography in Mid-Nineteenth-Century England.* New York: Basic Books, 2009.

Martin, Ann Smart. *Buying into the World of Goods: Early Consumers in Backcountry Virginia.* Baltimore: Johns Hopkins University Press, 2008.

Martin, James Kirby. *Drinking in America: A History.* New York: Free Press, 1982.

Martin, Jonathan D. *Divided Mastery: Slave Hiring in the American South.* Cambridge, MA: Harvard University Press, 2004.

Maynard, Steven. "Rough Work and Rugged Men: The Social Construction of Masculinity in Working-Class History." *Journal of Canadian Labour Studies* 23 (Spring 1989): 159–69.

McBee, Randy. *Dance Hall Days: Intimacy and Leisure among Working-Class Immigrants in the United States.* New York: New York University Press, 2000.

McCracken, Jill. *Street Sex Workers' Discourse: Realizing Material Change through Agential Choice.* New York: Routledge, 2013.

McLaren, Angus. *Impotence: A Cultural History.* Chicago: University of Chicago Press, 2007.

McNamara, Brooks. *The New York Concert Saloon: The Devil's Own Nights.* Cambridge: Cambridge University Press, 2002.

Melton, Tracy Matthew. *Hanging Henry Gambrill: The Violent Career of Baltimore's Plug Uglies, 1854–1860.* Baltimore: Maryland Historical Society, 2005.

——— "The Lost Lives of George Konig Sr. & Jr., A Father-Son Tale of Old Fell's Point." *Maryland Historical Magazine* (Fall 2006): 332–61.

Meranze, Michael. *Laboratories of Virtue: Punishment, Revolution, and Authority in Philadelphia, 1760–1835.* Chapel Hill: University of North Carolina Press, 1996.

Merians, Linda E., ed. *The Secret Malady: Venereal Disease in Eighteenth-Century England and France.* Lexington: University Press of Kentucky, 1996.

Merish, Lori. *Archives of Labor: Working-Class Women and Literary Culture in the Antebellum United States.* Durham, NC: Duke University Press, 2017.

Meyer, Stephen Grant. *As Long as They Don't Move Next Door: Segregation and Racial Conflict in American Neighborhoods.* Lanham: Rowman & Littlefield, 2000.

Meyerowitz, Joanne J. *Women Adrift: Independent Wage Earners in Chicago, 1880–1930.* Chicago: University of Chicago Press, 1991.

Mihm, Stephen. *A Nation of Counterfeiters Capitalists, Con Men, and the Making of the United States.* Cambridge, MA: Harvard University Press, 2009.

Miller, Heather Lee. *From Moral Suasion to Moral Coercion: Persistence and Transformation in Prostitution Reform, Portland, Oregon, 1888–1916.* Portland: University of Oregon, 1996.

Mitchell, Charles W., ed. *Maryland Voices of the Civil War.* Baltimore: Johns Hopkins University Press, 2007.

Mitchell, Reid. "Soldiering, Manhood, and Coming of Age: A Northern Volunteer." In *Divided Houses: Gender and the Civil War,* edited by Catherine Clinton and Nina Silber, 43–54. Oxford: Oxford University Press, 1992.

Mohr, James C. *Abortion in America: The Origins and Evolution of National Policy* Oxford: Oxford University Press, 1978.

Mort, Frank. "The Sexual Geography of the City." In *A Companion to the City,* edited by Gary Bridge and Sophie Watson, 308–15. Oxford: Blackwell Publishing, 2003.

Mumford, Kevin J. *Interzones: Black/White Sex Districts in Chicago and New York in the Early Twentieth Century.* New York: Columbia University Press, 1997.

Nead. Lynda. *Victorian Babylon: People, Streets and Images in Nineteenth-Century London.* New Haven, CT: Yale University Press, 2000.

Nichols, Jeffrey D. *Prostitution, Polygamy, and Power: Salt Lake City, 1847–1918.* Champaign: University of Illinois Press, 2008.

Novak, William J. *The People's Welfare: Law and Regulation in Nineteenth-Century America.* Chapel Hill: University of North Carolina Press, 1996.

Odem, Mary E. *Delinquent Daughters: Protecting and Policing Adolescent Female Sexuality in the United States, 1885–1920.* Chapel Hill: University of North Carolina Press, 1995.

Olson, Karen. "Old West Baltimore: Segregation, African-American Culture, and the Struggle for Equality." In *Baltimore Book: New Views of Local History,* edited by Elizabeth Fee, Linda Shopes, and Linda Zeidman, 57–80. Philadelphia: Temple University Press, 1991.

Olson, Sherry H. *Baltimore, the Building of an American City.* Baltimore: Johns Hopkins University Press, 1980.

O'Prey, Maureen. *Brewing in Baltimore.* Charleston, SC: Arcadia Publishing, 2011.

Overall, Christine. "What's Wrong with Prostitution? Evaluating Sex Work?" *Signs* 17 (Summer 1992): 704–24.

Parascandola, John. *Sex, Sin, and Science: A History of Syphilis in America.* Westport, CT: Praeger, 2008.

Pateman, Carole. "What's Wrong with Prostitution?" *Women's Studies Quarterly* 27 (Spring–Summer 1999): 53–64.

Peiss, Kathy. *Cheap Amusements: Working Women and Leisure in Turn-of-the-Century New York.* Philadelphia: Temple University Press, 1986.

Peiss, Kathy, and Christina Simmons with Robert A. Padgug, eds. *Passion and Power: Sexuality in History.* Philadelphia: Temple University Press, 1989.

Phillips, Christopher. *Freedom's Port: The African-American Community of Baltimore, 1790–1860.* Urbana: University of Illinois Press, 2007.

Pietila, Antero. *Not in My Neighborhood: How Bigotry Shaped a Great American City.* Chicago: Ivan R. Dee, 2010.

Pivar, David J. *Purity Crusade: Sexual Morality and Social Control, 1868–1900.* Greenwood: Greenwood Press, 1973.

Pliley, Jessica R. *Policing Sexuality: The Mann Act and the Making of the FBI.* Cambridge, MA: Harvard University Press, 2014.

Porter, Roy, and Leslie Hall. *The Facts of Life: The Creation of Sexual Knowledge in Britain, 1650–1850.* New Haven, CT: Yale University Press, 1995.

Health for Sale: Quackery in England, 1660–1850. Manchester: Manchester University Press, 1989.

Power, Garrett. "Apartheid Baltimore Style: The Residential Segregation Ordinances of 1910–1913." *Maryland Law Review* 42 (1983): 289–98.

Rice, James D. "Laying Claim to Elizabeth Shoemaker." In *Over the Threshold: Intimate Violence in Early America,* edited by Christine Daniels and Michael V. Kennedy, 185–201. New York: Routledge, 1999.

Roberts, Mary Louise. "Gender, Consumption, and Commodity Culture." *American Historical Review* 103 (June 1998): 817–44.

Rockman, Seth. *Scraping By: Wage Labor, Slavery, and Survival in Early Baltimore.* Baltimore: Johns Hopkins University Press, 2009.

Rodger, Gillian M. *Champagne Charlie and Pretty Jemima: Variety Theater in the Nineteenth Century.* Urbana: University of Illinois Press, 2002.

Rolfs, David. *No Peace for the Wicked: Northern Protestant Soldiers and the American Civil War.* Knoxville: University of Tennessee Press, 2009.

Rosen, Ruth. *The Lost Sisterhood: Prostitution in America, 1900–1918.* Baltimore: Johns Hopkins University Press, 1982.

Rosenberg, Charles E. *The Care of Strangers: The Rise of America's Hospital System.* Baltimore: Johns Hopkins University Press, 1987.

———. "Social Class and Medical Care in Nineteenth-Century America: The Rise and Fall of the Dispensary." *Journal of the History of Medicine and Allied Sciences* 28, no. 1 (1974): 32–54.

Rothman, Ellen K. "Sex and Self-Control: Middle-Class Courtship in America, 1770–1870." *Journal of Social History* 15 (Spring 1982): 409–25.

Rothman, Joshua. *Notorious in the Neighborhood: Sex and Families across the Color Line in Virginia, 1787–1861.* Chapel Hill: University of North Carolina Press, 2003.

Rotundo, Anthony. *American Manhood: Transformations in Masculinity from the Revolutionary to the Modern Era.* New York: Basic Book, 1993.

Rubin, Gayle S. "Thinking Sex: Notes for a Radical Theory of the Politics of Sexuality." In *Deviations: A Gayle Rubin Reader*, 137–81. Durham, NC: Duke University Press, 2011.

Ruffner, Kevin Conley. *Maryland's Blue and Gray: A Border State's Union and Confederate Junior Officer Corps.* Baton Rouge: Louisiana State University Press, 1997.

Ryan, Mary. *Cradle of the Middle Class: The Family in Oneida County, New York, 1790–1865.* Cambridge: Cambridge University Press, 1981.

———. *Mysteries of Sex: Tracing Women and Men through American History.* Chapel Hill: University of North Carolina Press, 2009.

Sandoval-Strausz, A. K. *Hotel: An American History.* New Haven, CT: Yale University Press, 2007.

Sanghera, Jyoti. "Unpacking the Trafficking Discourse." In *Trafficking and Prostitution Reconsidered: New Perspectives on Migration, Sex Work, and Human Rights*, edited by Kamala Kempadoo with Jyoti Sanghera and Bandana Pattanaikv, 3–24. Boulder, CO: Paradigm Publishers, 2005.

Schafer, Judith Kelleher. *Brothels, Depravity, and Abandoned Women: Illegal Sex in Antebellum New Orleans.* Baton Rouge: Louisiana State University Press, 2009.

Scharf, J. Thomas. *The Chronicles of Baltimore: Being a Complete History of "Baltimore Town" and Baltimore City, from the Earliest Period to the Present Time.* Baltimore: Turnbull Brothers, 1874.

———. *The History of Baltimore City and County: From the Earliest Period to the Present Day.* Philadelphia: Louis H. Everts, 1881.

Schley, David. "A Natural History of the Early American Railroad." *Early American Studies* 13, no. 2 (2015): 443–66.

"Making the Capitalist City: The B&O Railroad and Urban Space in Baltimore, 1827–1877." PhD dissertation, Johns Hopkins University, 2013.

Schmidt, James D. *Free to Work: Labor Law, Emancipation, and Reconstruction, 1815–1880.* Athens: University of Georgia Press, 1998.

Schudson, Michael. *Discovering the News: A Social History of American Newspapers.* New York: Basic Books, 1978.

Scribner, Vaughn. *Inn Civility: Urban Taverns and Early American Civil Society.* New York: New York University Press, 2019.

Sedgwick, Eve Kosofsky. *Between Men: English Literature and Male Homosocial Desire.* New York: Columbia University Press, 1985.

Shah, Nayan. *Contagious Divides: Epidemics and Race in San Francisco's Chinatown.* Berkeley: University of California Press, 2001.

Shepherd, Henry H. "Drama, Theatres, and Music." In *Baltimore: Its History and Its People,* vol. 1, edited by Clayton Colman Hall, 651–77. New York: Lewis Historical Publishing Company, 1912.

Shugg, Wallace. *A Monument to Good Intentions: The Story of the Maryland Penitentiary.* Baltimore: Maryland Historical Society, 1999.

Shumsky, Neil Larry. "Tacit Acceptance: Respectable Americans and Segregated Prostitution, 1870–1910." *Journal of Social History* 19 (Summer 1986): 665–79.

Siena, Kevin. *Venereal Disease, Hospitals, and the Urban Poor: London's "Foul Wards," 1600–1800.* Rochester, NY: University of Rochester Press, 2010.

Silber, Nina. *Daughters of the Union: Northern Women Fight the Civil War.* Cambridge, MA: Harvard University Press, 2008.

"Northern Women during the Age of Emancipation." In *A Companion to the Civil War and Reconstruction,* edited by Lacy Ford. Malden, MA: Blackwell Publishing, 2005.

Sismondo, Christine. *America Walks into a Bar: A Spirited History of Taverns and Saloons, Speakeasies and Grog Shops.* Oxford: Oxford University Press, 2011.

Sklansky, Jeffrey. "Labor, Money, and the Financial Turn in the History of Capitalism." *Labor* 11, no. 1 (2014): 23–46.

Skowronek, Stephen. *Building a New American State: The Expansion of National Administrative Capacities, 1877–1920.* Cambridge: Cambridge University Press, 1982.

Slout, William Lawrence, ed. *Broadway below the Sidewalk: Concert Saloons of Old New York.* San Bernardino, CA: Borgo Press, 1994.

Smith, Daniel Scott, and Michael S. Hindus. "Premarital Pregnancy in America 1640–1971: An Overview and Interpretation." *Journal of Interdisciplinary History* 5 (Spring 1975): 537–70.

Smith, Lizzie. "Dehumanising Sex Workers: What's 'Prostitute' Got to Do with It?" *The Conversation,* July 29, 2013. https://theconversation.com/dehumanising-sex-workers-whats-prostitute-got-to-do-with-it-16444.

Smith, Michael Thomas. *The Enemy Within: Fears of Corruption in the Civil War North.* Charlottesville: University of Virginia Press, 2011.

Smith-Rosenberg, Carroll. *Disorderly Conduct: Visions of Gender in Victorian America*. Oxford: Oxford University Press, 1985.

Sommerville, Diane Miller. *Rape and Race in the Nineteenth-Century South*. Chapel Hill: University of North Carolina Press, 2004.

Spongberg, Mary. *Feminizing Venereal Disease: The Body of the Prostitute in Nineteenth-Century Medical Discourse*. New York: New York University Press, 1997.

Srebnick, Amy Gilman. *The Mysterious Death of Mary Rogers: Sex and Culture in Nineteenth-Century New York*. Oxford: Oxford University Press, 1995.

Stanley, Amy Dru. *From Bondage to Contract: Wage Labor, Marriage, and the Market in the Age of Slave Emancipation*. Cambridge: Cambridge University Press, 1998.

"Histories of Capitalism and Sex Difference." *Journal of the Early Republic* 36 (Summer 2016): 343–50.

Stansell, Christine. *City of Women: Sex and Class in New York, 1789–1860*. Urbana: University of Illinois Press, 1987.

Stanton, Elizabeth Cady, Susan B. Anthony, and Matilda Joslyn Gage, eds. *History of Woman Suffrage*, vol. 2. New York: Charles Mann Printing Co., 1881.

Steffen, Charles G. *The Mechanics of Baltimore: Workers and Politics in the Age of Revolution, 1763–1812*. Urbana: University of Illinois Press, 1984.

Stott, Richard. *Jolly Fellows: Male Milieus in Nineteenth-Century America*. Baltimore: Johns Hopkins University Press, 2009.

Stover, John F. *History of the Baltimore and Ohio Railroad*. West Lafayette, IN: Purdue University Press, 1987.

Sutton, William R. *Journeymen for Jesus: Evangelical Artisans Confront Capitalism in Jacksonian Baltimore*. University Park: Pennsylvania State University Press, 1998.

Tansey, Richard. "Prostitution and Politics in Antebellum New Orleans." In *History of Women in the United States*, vol. 9, edited by Nancy Cott, 45–75. Munich: K. G. Saur, 1993.

Tone, Andrea. *Devices and Desires: A History of Contraceptives in America*. New York: Hill and Wang, 2001.

Towers, Frank. *The Urban South and the Coming of the Civil War*. Charlottesville: University of Virginia Press, 2004.

Ullman, Sharon. *Sex Seen: The Emergence of Modern Sexuality in America*. Berkeley: University of California Press, 1997.

Vicino, Thomas J. *Transforming Race and Class in Suburbia: Decline in Metropolitan Baltimore*. New York: Palgrave Macmillan, 2008.

Vickers, James. *Young Men and the Sea: Yankee Seafarers in the Age of Sail*. New Haven, CT: Yale University Press, 2007.

Walkowitz, Judith R. *City of Dreadful Delight: Narratives of Sexual Danger in Late-Victorian London*. Chicago: University of Chicago Press, 1992.

"The Politics of Prostitution and Sexual Labour." *History Workshop Journal* 82, no. 1 (2016): 188–98.

Prostitution in Victorian Society: Women, Class, and the State. Cambridge: Cambridge University Press, 1980.

Walters, Ronald G. *American Reformers, 1815–1860*, revised edition. New York: Hill and Wang, 1997.

Warner, John Harley. *Against the Spirit of System: The French Impulse in Nineteenth-Century American Medicine.* Princeton: Princeton University Press, 1998.

Warner, Sam Bass. *Streetcar Suburbs: The Process of Growth in Boston, 1870–1900.* Cambridge, MA: Harvard University Press, 1978.

Weeks, Jeffrey. *Sex, Politics, and Society: The Regulation of Sexuality since 1800.* London: Longmans, 1989.

Weishampel, John F. 1888. *The Stranger in Baltimore: A New Hand Book.* Baltimore: John F. Weishampel.

Weisman, Steven. *The Great Tax Wars: Lincoln to Wilson – The Fierce Battles over Money and Power That Transformed the Nation.* New York: Simon & Shuster, 2002.

Welter, Barbara. "The Cult of True Womanhood: 1820–1860." *American Quarterly* 18, no. 1 (1966): 151–74.

White, Deborah Gray. *Ar'n't I a Woman? Female Slaves in the Plantation South.* New York: W. W. Norton, 1999.

White, Frank F., Jr. *The Governors of Maryland 1777–1970.* Annapolis, MD: Hall of Records Commission, 1992.

White, Luise. *The Comforts of Home: Prostitution in Colonial Nairobi.* Chicago: University of Chicago Press, 1990.

Whiteaker, Larry Howard. *Seduction, Prostitution, and Moral Reform in New York, 1830–1860.* New York: Garland Publishing, 1997.

Whitman, T. Stephen. *The Price of Freedom: Slavery and Manumission in Baltimore and Early National Maryland.* Lexington: University Press of Kentucky, 1997.

Wiley, Bell. *The Life of Billy Yank.* Baton Rouge: Louisiana State University Press, 2008.

The Life of Johnny Reb. Baton Rouge: Louisiana State University Press, 2008.

Williams, Rhonda Y. *The Politics of Public Housing: Black Women's Struggles against Urban Inequality.* Oxford: Oxford University Press, 2004.

Wolff, Justin. *Richard Caton Woodville: American Painter, Artful Dodger.* Princeton: Princeton University Press, 2002.

Woloson, Wendy A. *In Hock: Pawning in America from Independence through the Great Depression.* Chicago: University of Chicago Press, 2009.

Wood, Sharon E. *Freedom of the Streets: Work, Citizenship, and Sexuality in a Gilded Age.* Chapel Hill: University of North Carolina Press, 2005.

Wozniak, Robert H., and Jorge A. Santiago-Blay. "Trouble at Tyson Alley: James Mark Baldwin's Arrest in a Baltimore Bordello." *History of Psychology* 16, no. 4 (2013): 227–48.

Wulf, Karen A. *Not All Wives: Women of Colonial Philadelphia.* Ithaca, NY: Cornell University Press, 2000.

Yamin, Rebecca. "Wealthy, Free, and Female: Prostitution in Nineteenth-Century New York." *Historical Archaeology* 39, no. 1 (2005): 4–18.

Young, Linda. *Middle Class Culture in the Nineteenth Century: America, Australia and Britain.* New York: Palgrave- Macmillan, 2003.

Zagarri, Rosemarie. *Revolutionary Backlash: Women and Politics in the Early American Republic.* Philadelphia: University of Pennsylvania Press, 2007.

Index

Printed in the USA
CPSIA information can be obtained
at www.ICGtesting.com
LVHW021522200823
755747LV00003B/155